SECRET
PARIS

Thomas Jonglez

JONGLEZ PUBLISHING

Travel guides

Thomas Jonglez was born and grew up in Paris. At the age of 22 he set out to discover the world, and spent most of 1992 backpacking around South America. Next he bought a one-way ticket to Beijing, from where he decided to make his way back to Paris overland – a trip that took him seven months. On his return, he tirelessly trawled the streets of Paris for material to write his first guidebook, which was published in 1996. After several years with the steel industry, he launched his publishing company in 2003. The first edition of *Secret Paris* came out in 2007. Ever since, he has regularly strolled around the capital, constantly surprised to discover new secret places in a city he thought he knew so well.

We have taken great pleasure in drawing up *Secret Paris* and hope that through its guidance you will, like us, continue to discover unusual, hidden or little-known aspects of the city. This practical guide is the result of over five years' work: all the places mentioned are accessible and clearly indicated on the plans at the beginning of each arrondissement.

Descriptions of certain places are accompanied by thematic sections highlighting historical details or anecdotes as an aid to understanding the city in all its complexity.

Secret Paris also draws attention to the multitude of details found in places that we may pass every day without noticing. These are an invitation to look more closely at the urban landscape and, more generally, a means of seeing our own city with the curiosity and attention that we often display while travelling elsewhere ...

Comments on this guidebook and its contents, as well as information on places we may not have mentioned, are more than welcome and will enrich future editions.

Don't hesitate to contact us:
E-mail: info@jonglezpublishing.com

CLICHY
PORTE ST-OUEN
PORTE DE CLICHY
BESSIÈRE
BOULEVARD
AV. DE SAINT-OUEN
NEUILLY-SUR-SEINE
LEVALLOIS-PERRET
PORTE D'ASNIÈRES
BERTHIER
17e
Place de Clichy
BOULEVARD
PORTE DE CHAMPERRET
PEREIRE
BOULEVARD WAGRAM
BINEAU
GA ST-LA
AVENUE CHARLES DE GAULLE
AV. DES TERNES
AVENUE DE COUCELLES
BD DE COUCELLES
Parc Monceau
BOULEVARD
Op Ga
PORTE MAILLOT
HAUSSMANN
La Madelei
PORTE DAUPHINE
Arc de Triomphe
Place Charles-de-Gaulle
8e
BOULEVARD MALESHERBES
Palais de l'Elysée
Place de la Madeleine
AVENUE FOCH
AVENUE DES CHAMPS
AV. FRANKLIN ROOSEVELT
BD CAPU
RUE ROYALE
BOIS DE BOULOGNE
AVENUE
AV. KLÉBER
ELYSÉES
Grand Palais
Petit Palais
Place de la Concorde
BD LANNES
AV. GEORGE V
Jardin Tuiler
AV. HENRI MARTIN
Place du Trocadéro
Musée du Quai Branly
QUAI
D'ORSAY
Assemblée Nationale
PORTE DE LA MUETTE
Palais de Chaillot
Esplanade des Invalides
Musé d'Ors
SUCHET
Musée du Vin
AV. RAPP
St-Louis-des-Invalides
BD SAINT GERMAIN
Tour Eiffel
7e
AVENUE MOZART
Champ de Mars
BD RASPAIL
16e
La Seine
Ecole Militaire
AV. DE BRETEUIL
BOULEVARD
PORTE D'AUTEUIL
BD DE GRENELLE
BD GARIBALDI
RUE DE
DE VERSAILLES
AVENUE ÉMILE ZOLA
15e
VAUGIRARD
Parc des Princes
RUE DE LA
LECOURBE
GARE MONTPARNASSE
AVENUE
Parc André Citroën
DE
Cimetière Montparna
PORTE DE ST-CLOUD
RUE
CONVENTION
RUE DE VOUILLÉ
P De Roc
RUE
14
Palais des Sports
RUE D'ALÉSIA
ISSY-LES-MOULINEAUX
BOULEVARD LEFEBVRE
BOULEVARD BRUNE
PORTE DE VERSAILLES
Les Puces de Vanves
PORTE DE VANVES
BOULEVARD
VANVES
PORTE DE CHÂTILLON
MONTROUGE
PORTE D'ORLÉANS
CLAMART
0   1 km
Reproduction interdite
Jean-Baptiste Nény
Mars 2007

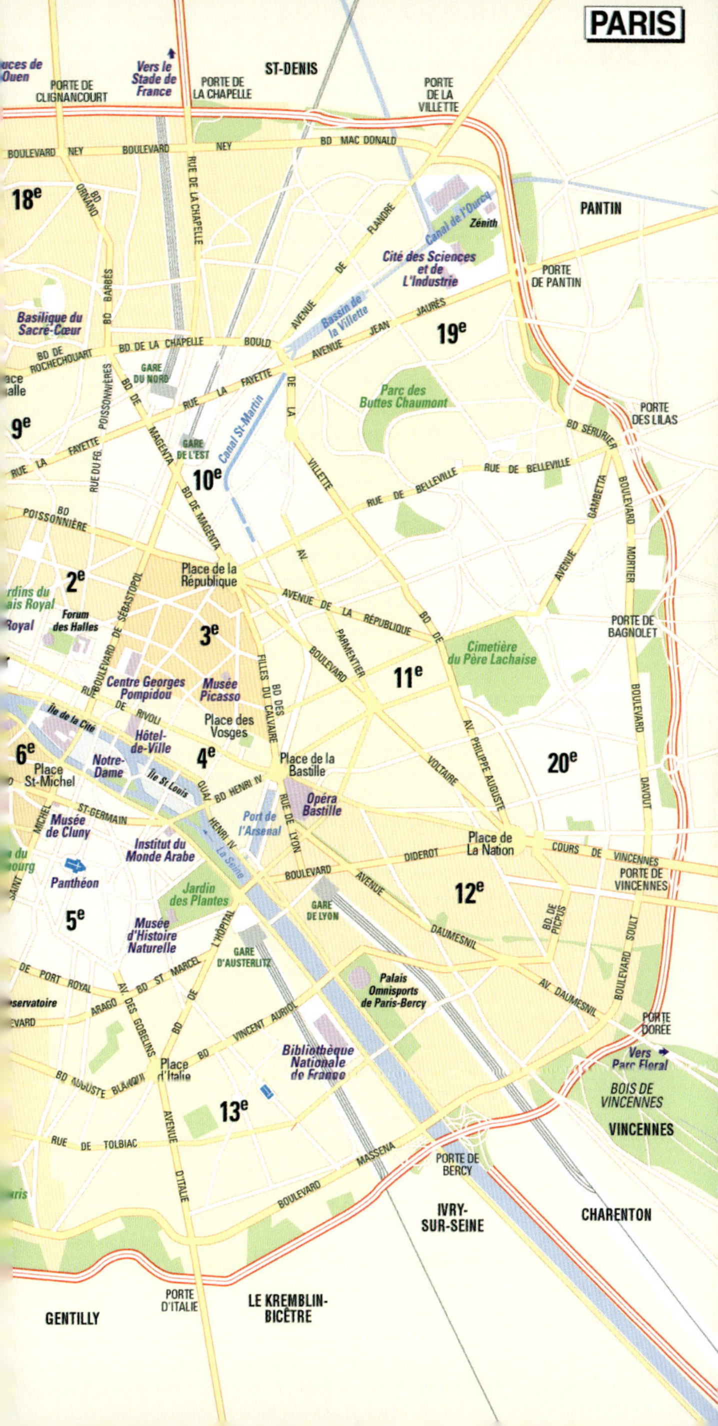

PARIS
St-Denis
uces de Ouen
PORTE DE CLIGNANCOURT
Vers le Stade de France
PORTE DE LA CHAPELLE
PORTE DE LA VILLETTE
PORTE DE PANTIN
PANTIN
18e
BOULEVARD NEY
BOULEVARD NEY
BD MAC DONALD
BD ORNANO
RUE DE LA CHAPELLE
Canal de l'Ourcq
Zénith
Cité des Sciences et de L'Industrie
BD BARBÈS
BD DE LA CHAPELLE
BOULD
Bassin de la Villette
AVENUE JEAN JAURÈS
19e
PORTE DES LILAS
Basilique du Sacré-Cœur
BD DE ROCHECHOUART
GARE DU NORD
RUE LA FAYETTE
AVENUE
BD SÉRURIER
ace alle
POISSONNIÈRES
RUE DE LA
Parc des Buttes Chaumont
9e
BD POISSONNIÈRE
RUE DU FG
RUE LA FAYETTE
BD DE MAGENTA
GARE DE L'EST
Canal St-Martin
VILLETTE
RUE DE BELLEVILLE
RUE DE BELLEVILLE
GAMBETTA
BOULEVARD MORTIER
10e
MAGENTA
AV.
PORTE DE BAGNOLET
rdins du ais Royal
2e
Place de la République
AVENUE DE LA RÉPUBLIQUE
BD DE
Cimetière du Père Lachaise
BOULEVARD DAVOUT
Royal
Forum des Halles
BOULEVARD DE SÉBASTOPOL
3e
PARMENTIER
BOULEVARD
FILLES DU CALVAIRE
11e
BD DES
Centre Georges Pompidou
Musée Picasso
20e
Île de la Cité
RUE DE RIVOLI
Place des Vosges
6e
Hôtel-de-Ville
4e
AV. PHILIPPE AUGUSTE
Place St-Michel
Notre-Dame
Île St Louis
Place de la Bastille
VOLTAIRE
Musée de Cluny
ST-GERMAIN
QUAI
BD HENRI IV
Opéra Bastille
Place de La Nation
COURS DE VINCENNES
MICHEL
Institut du Monde Arabe
HENRI IV
Port de l'Arsenal
RUE DE LYON
DIDEROT
PORTE DE VINCENNES
u du ourg
Panthéon
La Seine
Jardin des Plantes
BOULEVARD
AVENUE
12e
BD DE PICPUS
SAINT
5e
GARE DE LYON
DAUMESNIL
Musée d'Histoire Naturelle
L'HÔPITAL
AV. DAUMESNIL
BOULEVARD SOULT
DE PORT ROYAL
AV. BD ST-MARCEL
GARE D'AUSTERLITZ
servatoire
ARAGO
BD DES GOBELINS
BD DE
VINCENT AURIOL
Palais Omnisports de Paris-Bercy
PORTE DORÉE
evard
Place d'Italie
Bibliothèque Nationale de France
Vers Parc Floral
BD AUGUSTE BLANQUI
BOIS DE VINCENNES
aris
13e
VINCENNES
AVENUE
RUE DE TOLBIAC
MASSENA
PORTE DE BERCY
D'ITALIE
BOULEVARD
IVRY-SUR-SEINE
CHARENTON
PORTE D'ITALIE
GENTILLY
LE KREMBLIN-BICÊTRE

CONTENTS

1st arrondissement

2nd arrondissement

3rd arrondissement

4th arrondissement

CONTENTS

5th arrondissement

6th arrondissement

CONTENTS

7th arrondissement

8th arrondissement

9th arrondissement

CONTENTS

10th arrondissement

11th arrondissement

CONTENTS

14th arrondissement

15th arrondissement

16th arrondissement

17th arrondissement

CONTENTS

18th arrondissement

19th arrondissement

20th arrondissement

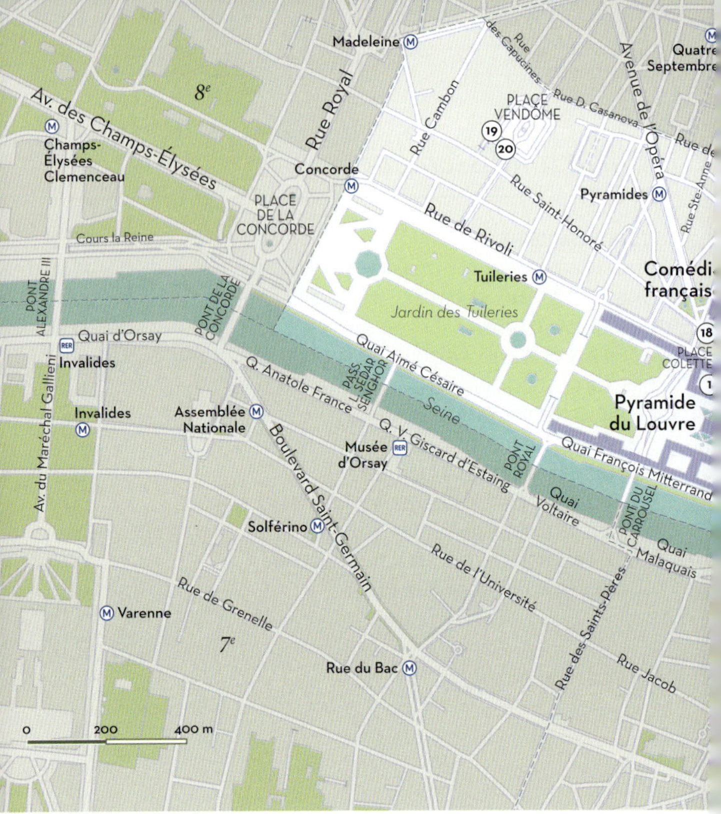

1st arrondissement

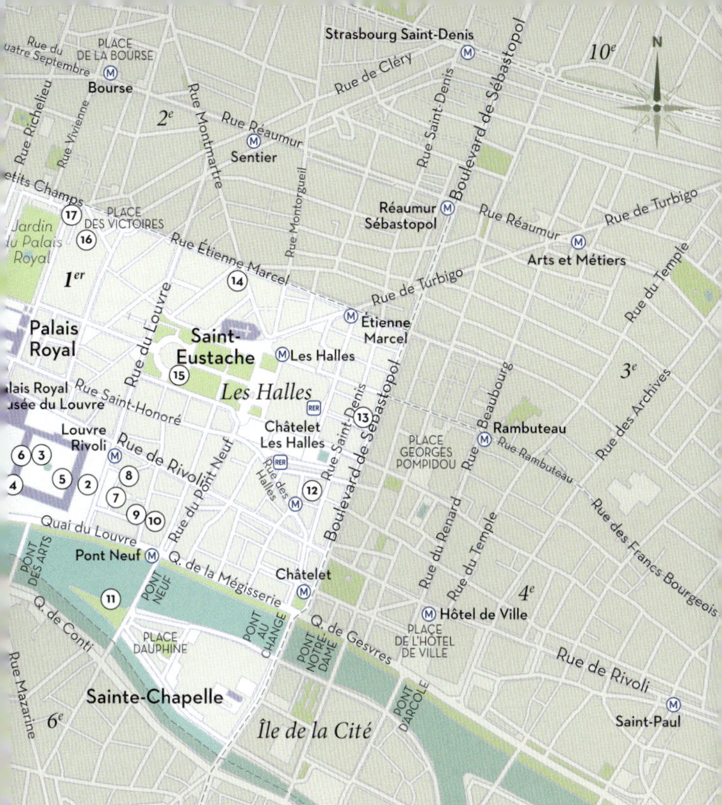

Rue du Quatre Septembre
PLACE DE LA BOURSE
Bourse
Rue Richelieu
Rue Vivienne
2e
Rue Montmartre
Rue Réaumur
Sentier
etits Champs
PLACE DES VICTOIRES
Jardin du Palais Royal
1er
Rue Étienne Marcel
Rue Montorgueil
Strasbourg Saint-Denis
Rue de Cléry
Rue Saint-Denis
Boulevard de Sébastopol
10e
N
Réaumur Sébastopol
Rue Réaumur
Rue de Turbigo
Arts et Métiers
Rue du Temple
Rue de Turbigo
3e
Rue des Archives
Palais Royal
Saint-Eustache
Les Halles
Les Halles
Étienne Marcel
lais Royal usée du Louvre
Rue du Louvre
Rue Saint-Honoré
Louvre Rivoli
Rue de Rivoli
Rue du Pont Neuf
Châtelet Les Halles
Rue des Halles
Rue Saint-Denis
Boulevard de Sébastopol
PLACE GEORGES POMPIDOU
Rue Beaubourg
Rue Rambuteau
Rambuteau
Rue des Francs-Bourgeois
Quai du Louvre
Pont Neuf
Q. de la Mégisserie
Châtelet
Rue du Renard
Rue du Temple
4e
Hôtel de Ville
PONT DES ARTS
Q. de Conti
PONT NEUF
PLACE DAUPHINE
PONT AU CHANGE
PONT NOTRE DAME
Q. de Gesvres
PLACE DE L'HÔTEL DE VILLE
Rue de Rivoli
Saint-Paul
Rue Mazarine
6e
Sainte-Chapelle
PONT D'ARCOLE
Île de la Cité

POUSSIN'S PAINTING
ET IN ARCADIA EGO

There is no esoteric revelation in Poussin's painting

Louvre Museum – Metro Palais-Royal – Musée du Louvre

Et in Arcadia ego is the title of two paintings by Nicolas Poussin (1594–1665) of which the most famous, titled *Les Bergers d'Arcadie*, exhibited at the Louvre, was probably painted around 1638. The painting shows three shepherds leaning on a tomb with the Latin inscription *Et in Arcadia ego*. One of them is bending over, pointing his finger at this phrase while, lower down, another reads it (note that the shadow of his arm is in the shape of a scythe, an allegory of death). A shepherdess, standing with her hand on the shoulder of the bending shepherd, watches the scene. They are dressed in classical Greek style. The background is mountainous with some scattered trees, the largest of them just behind the tomb.

A tomb bearing this inscription first appeared in the 3rd century BC in the Greek pastoral poetry *Idylls of Theocritus*, then in ancient Rome in Virgil's Eclogues (7 and 10), also called Bucolics. The idea was taken up between 1460 and 1470 by the Florentine Renaissance in the circle of Lorenzo de' Medici.

In 1504, Jacopo Sannazaro fixed the modern perception of a lost world of idyllic happiness in his painting *Arcadia*, and in 1618 Italian Baroque artist Guercino painted *The Arcadian Shepherds*, now at the Galleria Nazionale d'Arte Antica at Palazzo Barberini in Rome. Note that another lesser-known painting is kept at Musée Labenche at Brive in the south of France. *Paysage aux bergers d'Arcadie* (*Landscape with the Shepherds of Arcadia*, anonymous, late 18th century) also carries the famous formula. A marble bas-relief in the garden of the English stately home Shugborough Hall deals with the same subject.

Although *Et in Arcadia ego* is grammatically correct, a noun phrase without verb (omitting the verb is usual in Latin), some Latin grammar 'experts' concluded that the sentence was incomplete and lacked a verb.

They speculated that it was concealing an esoteric message, code-linked to the anagrams *Tego Arcana Dei* (I Keep God's Secrets) and *Arcam Dei Iesu Tango* (I Touch the Tomb of the God Jesus), suggesting the tomb contained the mortal remains of Jesus or another major biblical figure.

The claim was even made that the divine tomb on Poussin's canvas was to be found at Les Pontils estate near Rennes-le-Château in southern France. In 1978, researcher Franck Marie, like Pierre Jarnac in 1985, concluded this grave was actually quite normal and had been dug in 1903 by the owner of the land, Jean Galibert, who buried his mother and grandmother there. Their two bodies were exhumed and reburied elsewhere, doubtless the village cemetery, when the land was sold to Louis Lawrence, an American from Connecticut who emigrated to France. He in turn buried his mother and grandmother in the empty grave and built a tombstone with the inscription *Et in Arcadia ego*. Lawrence's son, Adrien Bourrel, testified before Franck Marie and Pierre Jarnac that he had seen the stone sepulchre in construction in 1933 when he was a young boy.

Despite this, a certain Pierre Plantard (see page 202) had time to elaborate on his 'Priory of Sion' mythology while in prison and claimed the Pontils tomb was a prototype for Poussin's painting. This tomb was finally demolished in 1988 by the landowner, with permission from the local authorities, to discourage those flocking there from all over the world vainly seeking esoteric revelations. So, far from possessing an esoteric message invented from scratch, Poussin's painting and the phrase Et in Arcadia ego simply mean that death awaits us all.

Arcadia: a taste of paradise

Arcadia is a region in the central and central-east Greek Peloponnese peninsula. In antiquity it was considered a primitive and idyllic place populated by shepherds living in harmony with nature. In this sense it symbolised a golden age echoed by many literary and artistic works such as Virgil's Eclogues or Ovid's *Fasti*, sometimes translated as *The Book of Days*. Rediscovered in the Renaissance and 17th century, notably through Poussin's painting *Les Bergers d'Arcadie*, Arcadia is geographically crossed by the river Alpheus, which was said to sink underground then resurface in Sicily to mingle with the waters of the fountain of Arethusa. As Alpheus was a sacred river-god, mythological son of Titans Oceanus and his sister, Tethys, whose underground waves symbolise the occult tradition of esoteric knowledge, some have mistakenly seen a link between Arcadia and esotericism. The name Arcadia comes from Arcas, which is in turn from the ancient Greek *arktos*, meaning 'bear'. Arcas, King of Arcadia, was in Greek mythology the son of Zeus and the nymph Callisto. Callisto is said to have offended Artemis, goddess of hunting, who changed her into a bear during a hunt. Raised to heaven by Zeus, Callisto was set among the stars as Ursa Major (the Great Bear), while her son Arcas was changed into the Little Bear constellation when he died.

A STRANGE IMAGE OF NAPOLEON

Napoleon disguised as Louis XIV!

Louvre Museum – Perrault Colonnade
Metro Palais-Royal – Musée du Louvre

The colonnade facing the place du Louvre, designed by Claude Perrault and begun under Louis XIV, bears a curious detail.

Although during his reign Napoleon had had his image sculpted near the centre of the colonnade, at the Restoration of the monarchy (1814/1815–1830), an attempt was made to disguise that awkward heritage by adding a wig to make the bust look more like Louis XIV.

Just below, the letter L stands for Louis XVIII (see opposite, monograms on Louvre façades), which in 1815 replaced the N of Napoleon I. But below the medallions carrying the letters can be seen some bees, one of the principal symbols of the First Empire: was it out of laziness or subversion that the sculptor neglected to obliterate them?

ROYAL MONOGRAMS HIDDEN IN THE LOUVRE COURTYARD

③

Secrets of the Cour Carrée

Cour Carrée, Louvre Museum
Metro Louvre – Rivoli

The Louvre in general, and the Cour Carrée in particular, conceal some fascinating details that will impress your partner, or new-found friend, in Paris! Here's how: sit down peacefully on the fountain in the courtyard, preferably in the evening when the twilight and the superb lighting make it one of the most magical places in the city.

On each wing of the courtyard are inscribed the ciphers of the sovereigns who had them built.

On the pyramid side, left of the Pavillon de l'Horloge: Henri II (H and H interwoven with a double C for Catherine de Médicis, which could quite easily be confused with a double D in homage to Diane de Poitiers, his mistress).

On the riverside to the right: K (signifying Karolus) for Charles IX, H for Henri III, HDB (Henri de Bourbon) for Henri IV and finally HG for Henri IV and Gabrielle d'Estrées, his mistress.

On the Pavillon de l'Horloge to the right: L and LA for Louis XIII and his wife Anne of Austria.

On the other wings, built by Louis XIV, you can read LMT (Louis and Marie-Thérèse, the queen) and LB (Louis de Bourbon).

Outside the courtyard, these monograms are found at regular intervals on the façades and have the same significance.

Evidence of the site of Charles V's donjon ④

Metro Louvre – Rivoli

In the Cour Carrée, gratings and a circle traced on the paving mark the outlines of the former donjon of Charles V.

Visit the Sully aisle to see the base of this donjon and the Salle des Maquettes, open only at weekends, which retraces the different stages in the construction of the Louvre.

Real human hearts in Louvre paintings?

An amazing story recounted in 1950 by Y. Ranc in an article published in *Paris Presse* was circulating at the beginning of the 20th century: Once, for certain artists, the human heart possessed an extraordinary quality that other animal hearts did not – it alone secreted an organic substance, known as 'mumie', which when mixed with oil made a unique glaze for paintings. Until the 18th century, it was difficult to get hold of this unusual raw material: corpses came from the Orient and the price of extracting and conserving the 'mumie' under satisfactory conditions was high. Since the 17th century in France it had become customary to deposit the hearts of members of the royal family, including that of Anne of Austria, in the chapel of Val-de-Grâce. With the Revolution, the sans-culottes dispersed the royal assets, among which were the embalmed hearts. They soon found buyers from the artists' fraternity. The painter Drolling, notably, found himself owner of the heart of Anne of Austria, that of Marie-Thérèse and even that of the duchess of Montpensier. His painting *Intérieur de Cuisine* in the Louvre thus still retains today traces of the ground-up royal organs on the canvas. Although this hypothesis makes an interesting anecdote, it has not been borne out by scientific analysis of the works, so in the end may only be a legend.

Why does the axis of the Louvre oratory pass through the centre of the Cour Carrée?

At the beginning of the 17th century, Louis XIII realised that the Louvre, then under construction, had no chapel. It occurred to him to use the church that Jacques Lemercier was building for the Oratorians. In the end, though, the church and the Louvre palace were never united. Under Napoleon the chapel became a Protestant temple, but its name (Temple de l'Oratoire) and orientation is a reminder of its historic links with the Louvre.

ROOSTER SCULPTURE

Hermetic bird at the Louvre

Cour Carrée, Louvre Museum
East Façade
Metro Louvre – Rivoli

On the east façade of the Cour Carrée (Square Courtyard) is a very surprising depiction of a rooster inside an ouroboros (a snake biting its own tail, see following double-page spread) projecting the Sun's rays. On either side, two winged figures, one male and one female, stand on clouds each holding a garland of leaves. On the other side of the courtyard, as if it were an extension of the ouroboros in front, another ouroboros is repeated within a shield surrounded by two female figures, one winged and the other wingless but holding a laurel wreath that she places before the shield. The rooster is the well-known symbol of pride, justified by its posture, and the emblem of France thanks to the double meaning of the Latin word gallus – 'rooster' and 'Gaulish'.

The bird appears next to Mercury in some Gallo-Roman representations, just like on this moulding where the rooster looks at the winged man, a representation of the god Mercury (Hermes for the Greeks), who here is not simply the God of commerce and travellers but, as the presence of the snake that bites its own tail (ouroboros) indicates, is the symbol of Hermetic wisdom. The winged woman is the goddess Aphrodite, the goddess of love, sailing on the clouds of imagination and creative spirit. The presence of Hermes and Aphrodite together produces the Hermaphrodite, the perfect being because it has achieved the union of opposites, which is hermetically signalled by the rooster, the universal emblem of the Sun.

The rooster is a solar bird, for its song announces the rising of the Sun, and at the same time it exorcises the darkness of the night. It corresponds to the personification of solar energy, to the manifestation of light itself. The rooster was also the symbol of emerging light for the Greeks, and therefore a particular attribute of Apollo, god of the Dawn. In Ancient Greece, the ritual sacrifice of a rooster to Asclepius (Esculape), son of Apollo and god of Medicine, was customary. Asclepius was a healing hero before becoming a god, and by analogy it was believed that the rooster cured diseases, because the Greek miracle worker healed the sick by resorting to the superior 'solar' knowledge of invoking the rooster, announcing spiritual or heavenly rebirth. We find here the adoption of the Egyptian myth of Aton, the dead and resurrected rooster god. This psychopomp role (conductor of souls, intermediary between life and death), returning to life and continuously returning to death, also explains why the rooster was associated with Hermes, the divine messenger who travelled through the three universal worlds: Heaven, Earth and Hell.

In this way the rooster became an emblem of Christ, alongside the eagle and lamb, with the emphasis on solar symbolism: light and resurrection. In the Bible (Book of Job 39:36 – 'which gave Jehovah's wisdom to the ibis and God's intelligence to the rooster'), the rooster is a symbol of God's intelligence. In Islam, the rooster enjoys veneration without equal compared with other animals and in the Qur'an, the prophet Muhammad himself forbids that the rooster be cursed because it invites morning prayer.

Placed judiciously on the east side of the courtyard (the Sun rises in the east), the rooster surrounded by the ouroboros, a symbol of divine illumination, is a reminder that France (the rooster), illuminated and blessed by the gods (the ouroboros), is indeed the eldest daughter of the Church, and it is she who brings and diffuses the light and perfection around her. Napoleon, whose figure is diametrically opposite to the rooster in Cour Carrée, looks upon this message benevolently …

The Ouroboros: a symbol of divine illumination

The figure of a coiled serpent biting its own tail is sometimes found in iconography and literature. This symbol is traditionally known as the Ouroboros, a Greek word derived from the Coptic and Hebrew languages – *ouro* is Coptic for 'king' and *ob* Hebrew for 'serpent' – meaning 'royal serpent'. Thus the reptile raising its head above its body is used as a symbol of mystical illumination: for Eastern peoples, it represents the divine fire they call Kundalini.

Kundalini is the origin of the association that Western medicine of the Middle Ages and Renaissance made between, on the one hand, the body heat that rises from the base of the spine to the top of the head and, on the other, the *venena bibas* ('ingested venom' mentioned by Saint Benedict of Nursia) of the snake whose bite can only be treated by an equally potent poison. Just as the Eastern techniques of spiritual awakening, Dzogchen and Mahamudra, show how a meditating person must learn to 'bite his tail like the serpent', the theme of the Ouroboros and ingested venom is a reminder that spiritual awareness can only result from a devout life: by elevating your consciousness onto a mental plane surpassing the ordinary, you search within to truly find yourself as an eternal being.

The Greeks popularised the word *ouroboros* in its literal sense of 'serpent biting its tail'. They acquired this image from the Phoenicians through contact with the Hebrews, who had themselves adopted it from Egypt where the Ouroboros featured on a stele dated as early as 1600 BC. There it represented the sun god Ra (Light), who resurrects life from the darkness of the night (synonymous with death), going back to the theme of eternal return, life, death, and the renewal of existence, as well as the reincarnation of souls in successive human bodies until they have reached their evolutionary peak, which will leave them perfect, both physically and spiritually – a theme dear to Eastern peoples. In this sense, the serpent swallowing itself can also be interpreted as an interruption of the cycle of human development (represented by the serpent), in order to enter the cycle of spiritual evolution (represented by the circle).

Pythagoras associated the serpent with the mathematical concept of infinity, coiled up as zero – the abstract number used to denote eternity, which becomes reality when the Ouroboros is depicted turning around on itself.

Gnostic Christians identified it with the Holy Spirit revealed through wisdom to be the Creator of all things visible and invisible, and whose ultimate expression on Earth is Christ. For this reason, the symbol is associated in Greek Gnostic literature with the phrase *hen to pan* ('The All is One'); it was commonly adopted in the 4th and 5th centuries as a protective amulet against evil spirits and venomous snakebites. This amulet was known as Abraxas, the name of a god in the original Gnostic pantheon that the Egyptians recognised as Serapis. It became one of the most famous magical talismans of the Middle Ages.

Greek alchemists very quickly espoused the figure of the Ouroboros (or Uroboros) and so it reached the Hermetic philosophers of Alexandria – among them, Arab thinkers who studied and disseminated this image in their schools of Hermeticism and alchemy. These schools were known and sought out by medieval Christians. There is even historical evidence that members of the Order of the Knights Templar, as well as other Christian mystics, travelled to Cairo, Syria and even Jerusalem to be initiated into the Hermetic sciences.

STATUES OF ISIS AND MANCO CÁPAC

Hidden symbolism of the Legislators' façade

Cour Carrée, Louvre Museum
Metro Louvre – Rivoli

In 1806, sculptor Jean-Guillaume Moitte was commissioned to decorate the first façade to the right of the Pavillon de l'Horloge (Clock Pavilion) in the Louvre Cour Carrée, on the theme of legislators. He did so following the Egyptian trend set by Napoleon Bonaparte after the invasion of Egypt (1798–1801). Thus, in a strange way he placed Moses, Numa Pompilius, Isis and Manco Cápac side by side, the last two clearly visible on each side of the window.

Like Napoleon, these four lawmakers had imperial powers in common. Numa Pompilius (754–653 BC) was the second King of Rome, and founded the Collegium Pontificum (College of Pontiffs) by grouping Vestal Virgins and Salii (Salian priests) into a single solar cult to the supreme god Janus. This god, identified with Jupiter, had the double-headed eagle as a symbol. The eagle is frequently associated with the Sun as it flies high and, thanks to its double eyelid, is the only creature able to look the sun in the face. Moses, for his part, established the Laws of the Pentateuch (the first five books of the Old Testament) among the Hebrew people and founded the worship of the one true God.

Isis, in turn, is the Goddess-Queen of Egypt who, after the death of her husband Osiris, had a dual prerogative. She had to ensure the permanence of the cult of the solar God (Osireth-Per-Amen-Ra), imbued with the greatest purity, and to strengthen the Imperial power of the pharaohs. All of them were to embody the divine qualities of the Son of the Goddess, to whom she bequeathed the throne. This son, Horus, is depicted in the form of a hawk or eagle with spread wings. Because of this last attribute, the name Isis or Iset literally means 'the throne', which explains why, according to classical iconography, Isis is originally represented as a woman with a throne-shaped headdress.

Manco Cápac was the first Inca emperor of Cuzco, Peru. He was the son of Huayna Capac, whom the Incas considered to be the incarnation of the Sun god Inti. It's said that Manco Cápac and his wife Mama Ocllo came to Earth from the underground city of Pacaritambo ('Place of the Dawn'), leading a golden-skinned people called the Tapac-Yauri. He founded the city of Cuzco and established the solar cult of Inti, represented by the condor, the eagle of the Andean highlands. He also established a code of law that included the prohibition of human sacrifice and marriage between brother and sister. Under the Manco Cápac Empire, the Inca civilisation reached its peak, characterised by peace and progress.

Napoleon does not feature in these sculptures, but his presence is implied in the angelic figure of the Republic on the cornice moulding. This sculpture, set above the others, expresses his claim to be a universal emperor, bringing together all the civilising prerogatives of his predecessors, the legislators. Napoleon Bonaparte would come to dominate and conquer Africa (Isis), the East (Moses), Europe (Numa) and America (Manco Cápac), and become a kind of king of the world.

> For more information on the links between Isis and Paris, see the following double-page spread.

Disputed origins of the name Paris

In the 3rd century BC, a Gallic tribe, the Parisii, settled on the future Île de la Cité and founded a first town, Lutèce, that was more of a stronghold which served as a place of worship and trade than a real city. Julius Caesar, the Roman general, was the first to name the place in his work on the Gallic Wars. Since then, several competing theories have attempted to explain the etymology of Lutèce and then Paris.

The Gallo-Roman toponym Lutetia binds together the themes *lut* (or *luth*) and ata, which translates as a 'place with walls' or a 'wall belt', which also prevented the city from falling under the yoke of the Huns, during the attack led by Attila in 451 AD. The Latins had a term of Iranian origin to denote this wall belt: *pari*, which is found in the word *pari-daiza*, meaning 'belt' (*pari*) and 'model' (*daiza*). *Pari-daiza* gave its origin to *paradhesa*, which is the archetypal expression of the European words that designate paradise. According to this theory, the Parisii were the inhabitants of Paradise: in a particularly interesting way, the earthly paradise of the first humans (the Garden of Eden) was strongly defended by a wall of fire erected by St Michael, the angel of God. This wall of fire became stone when mankind succumbed to the original sin of sexual desire and lust, and was expelled from Eden, as the sacred scriptures of the Jews, Christians and Muslims tell.

Gilles Corrozet (1510–68) claimed that the name Lutece instead came from a certain Lucus (or Luce), a descendant of Noah and King of the Celts, who founded a river city: Lutèce or Lucotèce. Lucus being the primordial god of the Celtic pantheon (also named Lug, from which is derived, for example, Lugdunum, the old name for Lyon), we find once again the particular and privileged aspect of the origins of the city, especially as Noah embodies a 'second Adam', with humanity having disappeared into the universal flood.

Settled on the banks of the Seine, the Gauls, who had adopted aspects of Egyptian culture and religion through the Greeks whose alphabet they used, as witnessed by Caesar, also ended up worshipping Isis, the primordial mother goddess, the incarnation of the waters of life. Thus, a temple was dedicated to Isis near what is now Saint-Marc-des-Carrières church, the oldest in Paris, and the local residents became known as 'Para-Isis', 'devotees of Isis'. After conversion to Christianity, they transferred this cult of the Mother Goddess to the pious form of Our Lady, in a kind of adaptation of the ancient cult of Isis. Father du Breul, abbot of Saint-Germain-des-Prés, took up this idea in 1612: 'Where King Childebert had the church of Saint-Vincent, now known as Saint-Germain, built and to which he gave his fief of Issy, there is a widespread opinion that it was the site of the Temple of Isis, which had given its name to the hamlet of Issy.' To highlight the cultural and spiritual importance of Paris, two very significant Greek legends (Greece being the historic homeland of European culture) were subsequently imported in which two demigods cease being Greek and Trojan and become Parisians. The first, in vogue at the beginning of the 15th century, recounts that Francis, son of Hector and grandson of King Priam, left Troy after the war of the same name to come to settle in this fertile place and found a city which he named Lutetia. He soon renamed it Paris and its residents Parisians in honour of Priam's son Paris. He was one of the argonauts on the ship Argo, which sailed on the western seas in search of the Golden Fleece that belonged to a white ram with golden horns and gave immortality to anyone who touched it.

Another myth relates that the demigod Hercules visited the region. In order to perform the 11th of the 12 works that King Eurystheus had ordered him to accomplish, Hercules went to the Iberian Peninsula to pick golden apples from the Garden of the Hesperides. On the way he stopped at an island to rest from his supernatural exploits: Île de la Cité. Resting in such an idyllic spot pleased him so much that he decided to stay longer, and for distraction built some houses there. Soon a city began to grow. He left it to his vassals known as Parasios ('Parisians'), so named because they were originally from Parasia Asiatica, a country that had turned its back on Greece.

Isis on the city of Paris coat of arms

In 1811 the commission led by Louis Petit-Radel approved the conclusions of Antoine Court de Gébelin, Freemason and Kabhalist. Famous for his studies of hermeneutics and symbolism, this ancestor of modern occultism claimed that the origin of Paris was derived from the sign of Isis (see opposite). On this date, the Egyptian goddess even occupied a place of honour on the new coat of arms of the city, as can be seen in the patent letter of 29 January 1811 granted by Napoleon I (drawing above): besides the appearance of a silver star above the nave (sailing ship), the goddess Isis can be seen appearing on the bow of the nave.

RAT BALL
OF SAINT-GERMAIN-L'AUXERROIS

An enigmatic ball

2, place du Louvre
+33 1 42 60 13 96 – saintgermainlauxerrois.fr
Metro Louvre – Rivoli

Directly opposite the Louvre, beneath the central gargoyle on the façade of Saint-Germain-l'Auxerrois facing the courtyard to the left of the church, there is a highly enigmatic rat ball. On this one, unlike the others found in France (see below), the rats, under the gaze of a demonic cat, seems to be emerging from the ball rather than rushing into it.

Even today, interpretations differ... Could this signify that the Church is the only remedy for the misery of the world, represented by the rats and the sphere?

The nine rat balls of France

There are said to be nine rat balls in France: in addition to the one in Paris, there is one at Saint-Siffrein Cathedral in Carpentras (see the guide *Secret Provence* from the same publisher), one at Le Mans Cathedral, one in the crypt of Saint-Sernin Church in Toulouse, one at Saint-Maurille Church in the town of Les Ponts-de-Cé in Maine-et-Loire, and four others in Île-de-France: in Saint-Jacques Church in Meulan-sur-Yvelines (Yvelines), on a stall of a mercy seat in the former collegiate church of Champeaux-en-Brie (Seine-et-Marne), on a mercy seat in Saint-Spire Church in Corbeil-Essonne (Essonne), and at Gassicourt Church in Mantes-la-Jolie (Yvelines).

TOWN HALL OF THE 1ST ARRONDISSEMENT

Town hall or church?

4, place du Louvre – +33 1 44 50 75 01
See opening hours on mairiepariscentre.paris.fr/pages/coordonnees-et-horaires-de-la-mairie-9749#horaires
Metro Hôtel de Ville

Leaving Saint-Germain-l'Auxerrois, visitors cannot fail to notice the town hall of the 1st arrondissement, which is perfectly symmetrical with the church. In order to extend the axis from the Louvre eastwards to the Hôtel de Ville, dilapidated old buildings surrounding it were demolished in the early 19th century; a vast open space had been cleared in front of the Louvre colonnade, and the church, situated on one side, disrupted the overall balance. Rather than demolish the historic church from which the signal for the St Bartholomew's Day massacre had been given (see opposite), Baron Haussmann, who was himself a Protestant,

commissioned the construction in 1858 of this magnificent Renaissance-style Hôtel de Ville by Jacques Ignace Hittorff (1792–1867), the architect of the Gare du Nord, in a style very similar to that of the church, in order to provide the architectural unity required by the imposing, uniform façade of the Perrault colonnade.

> The present-day avenue Victoria, which today stands out for its width compared to the surrounding streets, is a remnant of the plan to extend the axis of the Louvre eastwards to the Hôtel de Ville.

The bloody bells of Saint-Germain-l'Auxerrois

This church is also associated with a bloody episode in the history of France. Its bell, donated by François I in 1527, was rung to announce the beginning of the Massacre of Saint Bartholomew's Day (the massacre of Protestants by Roman Catholics in Paris on 24 August 1572).

THE REBUS ON RUE DE L'ARBRE-SEC

Slices of carp

Opposite 17, rue de l'Arbre-Sec
Metro Pont-Neuf

At the side of Saint-Germain-l'Auxerrois church, an unusual detail escape most passers-by.

Just above the pointed windows overlooking rue de l'Arbre-Sec, a frieze runs along the south and east façades of the chapel overhanging the street. It clearly shows a fish cut into several pieces, each slice separated by leaves.

The chapel was built in 1505 thanks to donations from a draper named Tronson, whose idea it was to have slices of carp engraved on the chapel wall by sculptor Jean Solas.

Why carp? Tronson might have had a family or personal connection with that fish, or perhaps it is because the word has a Greek homonym, *karpos*, which means fruit, harvest or profit, relating to the wealth that allowed him to finance the chapel.

NEARBY

Fleurs-de-lis on rue de l'Arbre-Sec

Metro Pont-Neuf

During the French Revolution the *sans-culottes* removed as many royal emblems as they could, including the decorative lilies around the city. At the corner of rue de Bailleul and rue de l'Arbre-Sec, two fleurs-de-lis escaped destruction. They are discreetly set just above the inscription 'S.G.' (for Saint-Germain-l'Auxerrois).

What is 'L'arbre sec' ('dry' tree)?

There are several different interpretations of the dry tree. One of them refers to a tree planted near Hebron in present-day Palestine, which was always green and leafy. It shed its leaves on the day Jesus died on the cross, but could revive on the day when a 'Prince of the West' again celebrates Mass there.

In other versions the tree is in Khirbet es-Sibte, 2 kilometres southwest of Mamre, near Hebron, but this oak has another meaning. As mentioned in the Bible (Genesis 12:6), it stood at the place where Abraham pitched his tent and spoke with three angels, when it was revealed that his wife Sarah would bear a son and he pleaded for the cities of Sodom and Gomorrah to be spared. Traditionally, this oak must die before the arrival of the Antichrist. Although in 1996 a botanist claimed the tree may have died, it has since produced several shoots and is still alive, supported by a concrete and steel structure.

Finally, there is another tradition that the dry tree stood alone in the north of Persia to mark the exact position of the great battle between Darius and Alexander, symbolising the boundary between East and West.

PLAQUE TO THE MARTYRDOM OF JACQUES DE MOLAY, GRAND MASTER OF THE TEMPLARS

A king of France who could no longer repay his debts

Wall at entrance to square du Vert-Galant
Metro Cité

Ile aux Juifs, later called Île des Templiers, lay on the Seine west of Île de la Cité. It was here that Jacques de Molay, 22nd and last Grand Master of the Order of the Templars, together with his companion Geoffroy de Charnay were burned alive on 18 March 1314. With the construction of what is now Place du Vert-Galant and the inclusion of two neighbouring islets, the island was then connected to Île de la Cité.

A plaque commemorating the martyrdom of Jacques de Molay was placed on the site of the execution by the Freemasons of the French National Grand Lodge (with the help of American Freemasons), with an inscription reading: 'At this place / Jacques de Molay / last Grand Master / of the Order of the Temple / was burned on 18 March 1314.'

The greed of King Philip IV the Fair (le Bel) led him to accuse the Order of the Templars of the worst heresies, never proven. But these accusations were enough to convince Pope Clement V, whom he had brought to the throne, of their veracity (denial, idolatry, sodomy, usury, etc.). It was the year 1307. In truth, the monarch was only interested in the wealth of the Temple, its furniture and buildings, because he had incurred debts with the Order and had no means of paying them. By 1297 the Templars had advanced him 2,500 livres. One year later he was given another 200,000 guilders, and in 1300 he received a new loan of 500,000 francs. Unable to repay the debt, in 1305 he requested honorary admission to the Order in the hope of manipulating things as an insider. He was categorically refused.

Philip the Fair then turned to intrigues and lies, using the Pope as a henchman to achieve his sinister ends. At dawn on Friday 13 October 1307, the Templars and their Grand Master, who were installed in Temple Villeneuve in Paris, were arrested without resistance. They believed that the Pope would intervene in their favour since they were an ecclesiastical military order whose supreme leader was indeed the Pope – what a mistake. The king was also disappointed, as the seat of the Temple was empty of all the riches he had imagined. The result was mass and arbitrary imprisonment of the Templars throughout France, torture, and deaths, and false confessions were extracted. The scandal spread throughout Europe. Everyone knew that Philip the Fair was cruel and ambitious, but nobody wanted war, and the trial took place despite everything. Pope Clement V first abolished the Order of the Temple on 22 March 1312, then its Grand Master was burned alive, as a martyr, on the morning of 14 March 1314. The King of France and the rest of the grieving court stayed by the entrance of the island, which was in fact already cursed: its soil was marked by the death of the outcasts, heretics and other offenders of the 'cursed race of Judas who killed the Lord' (the Jews, who had given their name to this end of the island) for centuries.

When a monk approached the master, crucifix in hand, to urge him to repent of his crimes, Jacques de Molay rebuked him with the serenity of the righteous: 'Monk, keep your prayers for the Pope, who is going to need them.' And, addressing the King of France, he prophesied 'in less than a year, he will have to appear before the supreme Judge of the living and the dead'. That's exactly what happened: the King died on 29 November 1314, the Pope died on 20 April 1314, the King's chief financier, Enguerrand de Marigny, was hanged on 30 April 1315, and Esquieu de Floyran, former Prior of Montfaucon and a renegade Templar, was stabbed to death.

> For more on the remains of the Order of the Temple in Paris and the reality of Baphomet, see page 90 and page 149.

LES HALLES le MATIN
devant l'EGLISE St EUSTACHE

NEARBY

Plaque of the Murder of Henri IV by Ravaillac 

11, rue de la Ferronnerie – Metro Les Halles

A plaque on the ground with a fleur-de-lys marks the spot where Henri IV was murdered in 1610 by Ravaillac.

The elephant at 3, rue de la Cossonnerie 

Metro Les Halles

The upper part of this façade is decorated with a beautiful elephant's head, probably inspired by Indian Muslim art (see page 179).

Ceramic tiles of the Cochon à l'Oreille *restaurant* 

15, rue Montmartre – +33 1 40 15 98 24
Daily 11.30am–3pm and 6pm–11pm (closed on Monday)
Traditional French cuisine
Metro Les Halles or Étienne Marcel

Superb decoration with ceramic tiles from 1914 on the theme of Les Halles (the former central market), which was a short distance away.

Origin of the semicircular niches on the Pont Neuf

Completed in 1604, the Pont Neuf is one of the oldest bridges in Paris. When it was built, it had three unique characteristics: it had footpaths (which did not come into general use until the 19th century), it was decorated with 384 mascarons (grotesque masks on the cornices), and it did not have houses built on the roadway, with the exception of the shops that were installed in the demi-lunes that still exist today.

COLONNE MÉDICIS

Predictions of the astrologer ...

Rue de Viarmes
Metro Louvre-Rivoli or Les Halles

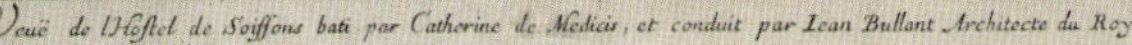
Veuë de l'Hostel de Soissons bati par Catherine de Médicis, et conduit par Iean Bullant Architecte du Roy.

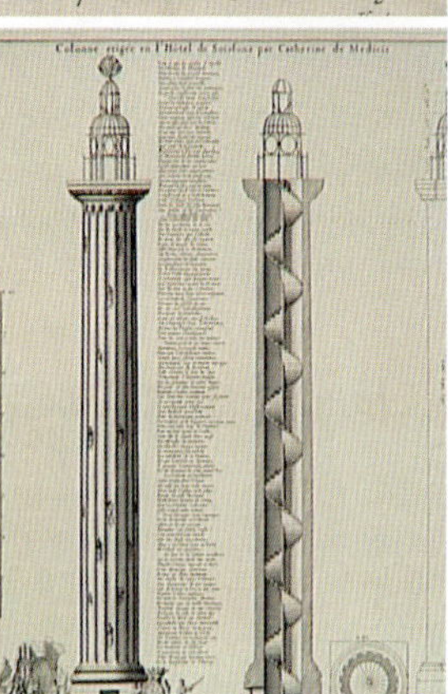

There is a mysterious column, not very noticeable although it is 28 metres high, not far from Les Halles, just in front of the *Bourse du Commerce* (Stock Exchange). Its history is intriguing: the Queen of France Catherine de Médicis, who was fascinated by astrology, had it built around 1575 by her architect, Jean Bullant, a few years after the construction of her magnificent residence, the Hôtel de la Reine.

The fluted tower, crowned by a platform reached by a spiral staircase with 147 steps, was once covered with a glass roof, but all that is left now is the iron frame. It was connected to the queen's apartments. This column, which is not mentioned in the plans for the construction of the mansion, some believe has a commemorative function: the intertwined ciphers of King Henri II and Catherine de Médicis (H and C) are believed to be a tribute to the king killed in circumstances predicted by Nostradamus.

Many feel that it is in fact a result of the queen's obsession with astrology. After Nostradamus had made his prophecies and left for Provence, Catherine de Médicis is reported to have ordered the column built to serve as an observatory and a place for the experiments of Cosimo Ruggieri, her astronomer, sorcerer and childhood friend. Nothing if not mysterious, Ruggieri was among other things the author of the famous prediction of the death of his benefactor. The four corners of the column's capital are oriented with the four points of the compass. The preservation of this column, after the palace was destroyed in 1748 and the construction of the current Bourse du Commerce, is almost a miracle.

Where and when was Molière really born?

The plaques at 31, rue du Pont-Neuf and 98, rue Saint-Honoré contradict each other. The first states that Molière was born there in 1620, and the second that he was in fact born on 15 January 1622 at the other address! Experts seem to support the second claim. The Molière Fountain, at 37, rue Richelieu, was the first statue in Paris to honour someone other than a king.

GALERIE DORÉE
OF THE BANQUE DE FRANCE

A rare example of Regency style

2, rue Radziwill
Pre-booked tours only on Saturday mornings at 10.30am
Individuals: visits organised by Centre des Monuments Nationaux
(around 5 a year)
Programme at banque-france.fr (Organisation/History/Gallery photos) or
monum.fr (News/Visiting conferences/Programme)
Direct registration one month in advance at the Centre, terms indicated
Groups: write to PHAR — 19-2205-Banque de France, 75049 Paris Cedex 01
Metro Bourse

The organised tour offers the rare privilege of admiring the magnificent gilded gallery of the Hôtel de Toulouse, headquarters of the Bank of France. The building as we see it today is the result of a number of improvements and the annexation of several houses adjoining the original main structure. Models displayed at the entrance to the Galerie Dorée give an accurate idea of the work carried out over the years. In 1635, Louis Phélipeaux, lord of La Vrillière, acquired a small plot left vacant by Richelieu. He decided to build, under the direction of François Mansart, a 'hôtel particulier' in which one of the rooms, the Grande Galerie, covered in white stucco and of imposing dimensions (40 metres long by 6.5 metres wide) would serve as an exhibition space

for his exceptional collection of Italian paintings. In 1713, the Count of Toulouse acquired the mansion, which was naturally renamed Hôtel de Toulouse. The new owner, none other than the illegitimate son of Louis XIV and Madame de Montespan, appealed to Robert de Cotte, the king's chief architect, to refurbish the building as a princely residence. In pure Regency style, gold dominated the Grande Galerie and its decoration was updated to illustrate the hunting and marine themes dear to the heart of the Count of Toulouse. In 1793, after the Revolution, this property was declared national heritage and the artworks were distributed among several museums (a Veronese and a Poussin can be seen at the Louvre). The Galerie Dorée was used at the time for paper storage for the Imprimerie Nationale, which had taken over the premises.

The Bank of France bought the mansion in 1808. In 1870, the gallery building required total restoration: the vault frescoes were thus copied and the Regency woodwork reintegrated into the design. Today the effect is perfect and the gallery, lit by its huge windows, is resplendent in its gilding.

'Tenir le haut du pavé'

The expression *Tenir le haut du pavé* (Keep to the highest point on the pavement: to consider oneself superior) dates from the time when pavements were still rare: in the middle of the street ran a stream of dirty water. High on the pavement, where the better-off walked, there was no sewage.

DOUBLE STAIRCASE AT 33, RUE RADZIWILL

Two sets of steps to avoid crossing paths ...

33, rue Radziwill and 48, rue de Valois
Accessible on weekdays during office hours, ring bell at media library (5th floor)
Metro Palais-Royal – Musée du Louvre

The building at 33, rue Radziwill, now an office block, has a unique feature. Apart from the eight floors which made this one of the city's highest buildings in 1781, when it was raised by one floor, its magnificent double staircase is remarkable. The two identical sets of steps are a few metres apart, so those heading up can avoid chance meetings with those coming down – a hugely practical detail when their activities were less than praiseworthy. The fact that the building (still) has another entrance at 48, rue de Valois obviously added to the discretion of places used by prostitutes and a vast casino with 19 rooms: seven on the ground-floor side of rue de Valois, eight still on the ground floor but on the opposite side, and four in the basement. The building is intersected by the Radziwill passage, named after the Polish Prince of Radziwiłł (1734–90) who had it built. The passage is now closed to the public.

For other remains of Parisian brothels, see page 78.

NEARBY

Comédie-Française Museum ⑱

1, place Colette
+33 1 44 58 13 16 / 13 17 – comedie-francaise.fr/fr/musee#
See opening hours on the website
Metro Palais-Royal – Louvre or Pyramides

Unknown to most Parisians, the Comédie-Française Museum is an excellent way to access private areas of this theatrical institution. The guided tour includes public areas accessible to audiences during performances (vestibule, main staircase, public foyer, galleries and hall) and private areas. Visitors will discover the committee room, the artists' foyer and La Grange foyer with their displays of some unexpected works of art.

The standard metre of 13, place Vendôme ⑲

Metro Tuileries or Opéra

Along with the standard metre on a plaque in the rue de Vaugirard, the standard metre in place Vendôme, to the left of the Ministry of Justice, allowed the French to familiarise themselves with the new unit of measurement adopted during the Revolution (see page 204). In contrast to that displayed in rue de Vaugirard, this standard metre is not in its original place: it was moved here in 1848.

Commemorative plaque of the Texas Embassy 

Metro Tuileries or Opéra

At the corner of rue de Castiglione and place Vendôme, an inscription marks the site of the embassy that Texas, yes Texas, opened in Paris in the 19th century. It is often forgotten that after gaining independence from Mexico in 1836, Texas was an independent republic until 1845, when it was annexed to the United States.

Balconies in place Vendôme in tribute to Louis XIV

On both sides of the column, the balconies of place Vendôme are a tribute to the glory of Louis XIV. They are decorated with an allegory of the sun surrounded by gilded leaves, which clearly make reference to the sovereign known as the Sun King. Earlier, this square was named place des Conquêtes or place Louis-le-Grand, also in honour of Louis XIV and had at its centre an equestrian statue of the king sculpted by Girardon. Inaugurated in 1699, it was demolished during the Revolution.

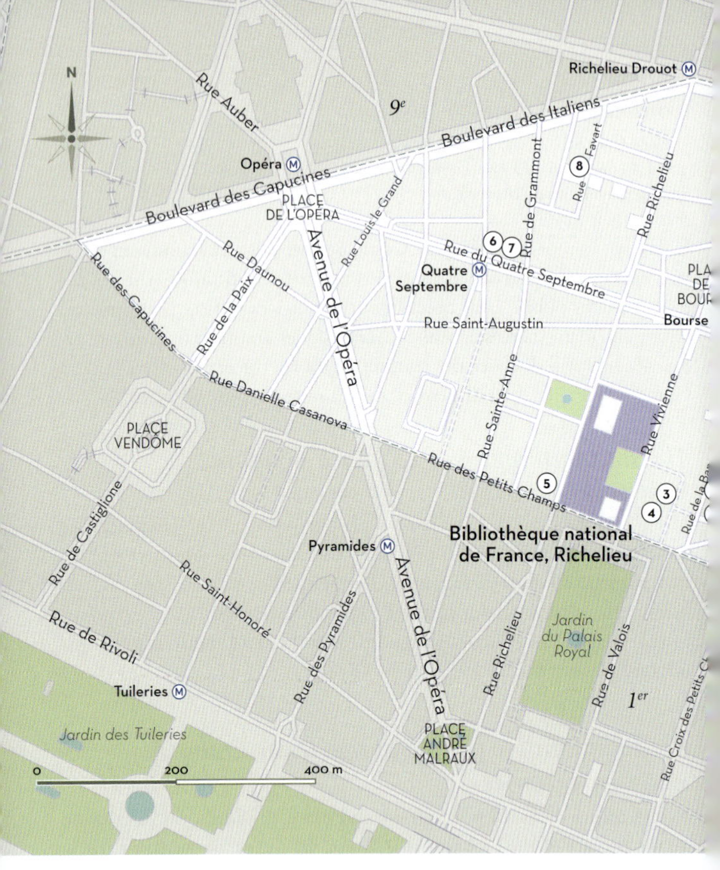

2nd arrondissement

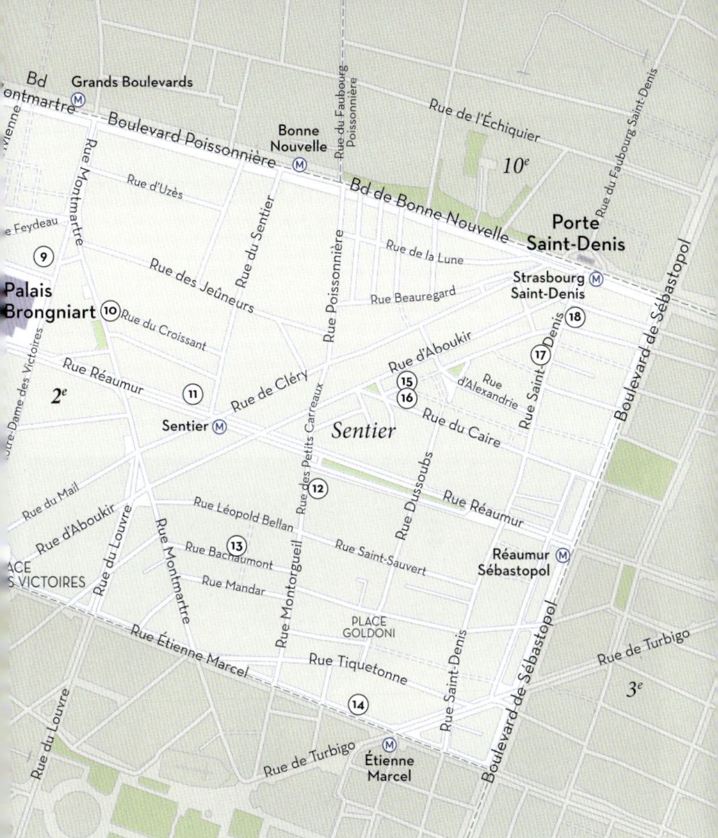

Bd Montmartre
vienne
Grands Boulevards
Rue Montmartre
Boulevard Poissonnière
Rue d'Uzès
Bonne Nouvelle
Rue du Faubourg Poissonnière
Rue de l'Échiquier
10e
Rue du Faubourg Saint-Denis
Bd de Bonne Nouvelle
e Feydeau
Rue du Sentier
Rue de la Lune
Porte Saint-Denis
9
Rue des Jeûneurs
Rue Poissonnière
Rue Beauregard
Strasbourg Saint-Denis
Palais Brongniart
Rue du Croissant
18
Boulevard de Sébastopol
re-Dame des Victoires
Rue Réaumur
Rue de Cléry
Rue d'Aboukir
17
Rue Saint-Denis
2e
11
Rue de Cléry
15
16
Rue d'Alexandrie
Rue du Caire
Sentier
Rue des Petits Carreaux
Sentier
Rue Dussoubs
Rue Réaumur
Rue du Mail
Rue Léopold Bellan
12
Rue d'Aboukir
Rue du Louvre
Rue Montmartre
Rue Bachaumont
13
Rue Saint-Sauvert
Réaumur Sébastopol
ACE
S VICTOIRES
Rue Mandar
Rue Montorgueil
PLACE GOLDONI
Boulevard de Sébastopol
Rue Étienne Marcel
Rue Tiquetonne
Rue de Turbigo
Rue du Louvre
14
Rue Saint-Denis
3e
Rue de Turbigo
Étienne Marcel
Boulevard de Sébastopol

EX-VOTOS OF
NOTRE-DAME-DES-VICTOIRES

Over 37,000 ex-votos cover the basilica walls and ceilings

Place des Petits-Pères
6, rue Notre-Dame-des-Victoires
+33 1 42 60 90 47
notredamedesvictoires.com
See opening hours on the website
Metro Bourse

Rather unexpectedly, the Notre-Dame-des-Victoires church has a unique collection of over 37,000 ex-votos fixed here, there and everywhere. The prevailing atmosphere of contemplation and the expressions of gratitude of these thousands of marble plaques cannot fail to impress and move visitors, even non-believers. So take the time to examine these testimonials, some of which are particularly poignant.

Founded in 1629 by Louis XIII at the request of the Augustin brotherhood known as the *Petits Pères* (Little Fathers), the basilica was named Notre-Dame-des-Victoires in thanksgiving for the royal troops' defeat of the Huguenots at La Rochelle. The king attributed this victory to prayer and the intervention of the Holy Virgin. As soon as the church was built a statue of the Virgin erected in the convent chapel evoked great devotion from worshippers.

In 1836, when the parish was becoming less popular with pilgrims, its priest, Abbé Desegenettes, twice heard the following command: 'Consecrate your parish to the Very Holy and Immaculate Heart of Mary.' He rapidly set up an association of prayers in honour of the Cœur Immaculé de la Très Sainte Vierge, which had the effect of greatly increasing the number of faithful and newly converted. Through his actions the abbot turned his church into an 'immense hymn of love' of which the ex-votos now in the basilica bear ardent witness.

NEARBY

Trompe-l'œil on a bank building ②
Place des Petits-Pères – Metro Bourse
Just beside Place des Petits-Pères, the street windows of the bank building are only trompe-l'œil.

THE HANDSHAKE MEDALLION

A Masonic gallery

Galerie Vivienne
6, rue Vivienne
Metro Bourse

The Vivienne gallery, built in 1823 by Marchoux, president of the Chambre des Notaires (Board of Notaries), is a superb covered passage that opened to the public in 1826 under the name Galerie Marchoux. The gallery, which was renamed Vivienne before long, was designed from the outset as a marketplace sheltered from the rain, as was fashionable in the 19th century.

Designed by the architect François Jean Delannoy and decorated with mosaics by Giandomenico Facchina, the gallery, in addition to its symbols relating to trade (a cornucopia and Mercury, god of commerce) also features many Masonic symbols. At the entrance to 6, rue Vivienne, for example, at the top right of the door, the handshake medallion is a typical symbol representing the brotherhood that unites the Freemasons (see facing page). In addition to this medallion, other Masonic symbols inside include the hive (representing love of labour and cogitation in the Lodge), and a spirit level (a symbol of equality) …

The masonic salute

The Freemasons greet each other by shaking hands in a special way: they apply small pressures with their thumb to indicate their rank. The apprentice touches slightly (from the tip of the thumb of the right hand) the first joint of the index finger of the other's right hand, three strokes: two fast and one spaced. The companion does the same thing, but touches with his right thumb the first joint of the other's middle finger, five strokes: two rapid, one spaced, two rapid. The Master does the same, seven times: four rapid and three spaced.

NEARBY

The monumental staircase at Galerie Vivienne   ④

Galerie Vivienne – 6, rue Vivienne – Metro Bourse

At No. 13 of the shopping arcade, a beautiful staircase leads to the house where François Vidocq (1775–1857) lived after his release. He was the conman and convict who founded and ran the world's first investigative police force, the Parisian Sûreté, from 1811 to 1827.

FP inscription   ⑤

Metro Quatre Septembre or Bourse

At the corner of rue des Petits-Champs and rue de Richelieu, the discreet inscription 'FP' on each side of the corner stone marks the boundary of the former Popin fiefdom, a set of properties with over a hundred houses owned by a lay lord (himself a vassal or tenant of the archdiocese) in the 18th century.

AIRCRAFT BOMB INSCRIPTION

Tactful memory of a painful period

Rue de Choiseul, almost at junction with rue du Quatre Septembre
Metro Quatre Septembre

© Poulpy

Y ou could pass by a hundred times and never spot it. And yet rue de Choiseul, almost at the junction with rue du Quatre Septembre, on the façade of the historic headquarters of the former Crédit Lyonnais, a discreet plaque is inscribed '*Bombe d'avion – 30 janvier 1918*' (Aerial bombing – 30 January 1918). The wall around the plaque is studded with shrapnel impacts preserved for posterity.

According to historian Pierre Miquel, these impacts were from a 300 kg bomb dropped by a Gotha G.V. bomber or a Zeppelin Staaken R VI. The bombing of civilian targets by *Gothas* flying over Paris began on 30 January 1918. The aircraft came by wagon-loads into Aisne Département and the great plains surrounding Clermont-les-Fermes (where the German strategic bombardment was based), Montigny-les-Fermes and La Ville-aux-Bois, in the north-east of the département.

Thirty aircraft each carrying 10 bombs of 10, 50 or 100 kg (a total of 18 tonnes of explosives) headed towards the capital on the night of Wednesday 30 to Thursday 31 January 1918. Eleven of them managed to avoid the air defence fire. From 11.30 pm, 91 bombs fell on Paris and 164 on the suburbs within 20 minutes, igniting among other targets the general stores of Aubervilliers. In Paris, rue Réaumur, rue Saint-Sauveur and avenue de la Grande Armée suffered the most damage. According to the *Écho de Paris* newspaper of 1 February 1918, these bombardments killed 22 people. Other sources claimed 61 people were killed and 198 were injured by the morning.

As *Le Matin* of 1 February 1918 announced, reports of the bombing were censored to avoid letting the Germans know the places affected.

NEARBY

Eiffel glass roof of the former Crédit Lyonnais 

18, rue du Quatre Septembre
Metro Quatre Septembre

The head office of the former Crédit Lyonnais, destroyed by fire in May 1996, was completely rebuilt. Only the Eiffel dome and the façades, which are listed as Historic Monuments, have been preserved.

Although the building is closed to the public, you can still admire the magnificent glass roof by Gustave Eiffel inside the hall of No. 18, rue du Quatre Septembre, which is freely accessible.

TORTOISE SHELLS
AT THE OPÉRA-COMIQUE

The little-known myth of the tortoise-shell lyre

Opéra-Comique – 1, place Boieldieu
Metro Richelieu-Drouot

Above the four streetlamps gracing the façade of the magnificent Opéra-Comique (Comic Opera, opened in 1898), it's easy to miss four stone sculptures of a tortoise shell flanked by two arms and seven strings. A shell in gilded metal can also be seen above the first-floor balcony on either side of the windows. These motifs, chosen by architect Louis Bernier, recall the forgotten Greek myth of the tortoise-shell lyre.

The story goes that the young god Hermes, a true child prodigy, steals a herd of sacred cows from his half-brother Apollo. He slaughters one of them, and with the entrails and a tortoise shell, creates a lyre with seven strings. But he is soon forced to hand over the lyre to Apollo, a music lover, to make amends. Apollo finally gives the instrument to poet and musician Orpheus, who perfects it by adding two strings. Orpheus then meets Eurydice, falls in love and marries her. But alas, on their wedding day Eurydice dies, bitten by a snake. Orpheus then leaves for the Kingdom of the Dead to try to negotiate the return of Eurydice. With the sound of the lyre, he lulls the monstrous guard-dog Cerberus to sleep and wins over Hades, god of the Underworld. However, Hades sets a condition: Orpheus must not look at Eurydice while she is still in the Kingdom of the Dead. As they are almost at the doors of Hell, Orpheus, worried about not hearing Eurydice's footsteps behind him, turns around. This immediately triggers the foretold sanction: Eurydice disappears forever. Back among the living, the inconsolable Orpheus continues to play the lyre and charms the Maenads (or

Bacchanes), the disciples of Dionysus (or Bacchus). Jealous of the love that Orpheus still bears for his deceased wife, they tear her apart and throw her remains into the River Ebro. Sailing on the water, her head continues to sing in a plaintive voice (golden pattern to the left, above the balcony). Then, as in the painting by Gustave Moreau (1865 – Musée d'Orsay), the head, which rests on the poet's lyre and seems to be part of it, finds peace. The face displays gentleness and calm (golden motif on the right).

For more on the deeply symbolic meaning of the Orpheus myth, see the following double-page spread.

It seems that the meaning of the tortoise shells at first escaped Parisians who, impatient and irritated by the length of time the restoration work on the theatre was taking (11 years between demolition of the hall in 1887 and its reopening in 1898), made a rather unflattering association between the slowness of tortoises and that of the architect Louis Bernier.

Unlike Opéra Garnier and the many theatres nearby, the Opéra-Comique deliberately turned its back on the boulevard. At the outset, inaugurated as Salle Favart in the presence of Marie-Antoinette on 28 April 1783, it was very important for the company that enjoyed royal privilege to distance itself from the many popular entertainment venues that flourished locally, particularly on the Boulevard du Temple (nicknamed 'crime' boulevard, because of the number of plays themed on news stories, assassinations and thefts). No way were the 'king's actors' to be seen as 'boulevard actors'.

Geography of the Opéra-Comique

The Opéra-Comique was built between 1781 and 1783 for Comédie-Italienne, a theatre company of Italian actors who staged Italian plays. Rossini, who ran the theatre from 1824 to 1826, lent his name to a nearby street. Likewise, Place Boieldieu (named after the 'French Mozart' of the first quarter of the 19th century) and Marivaux (famous dramatist), Grétry (Belgian composer) and Favart (family of French playwrights) streets surrounding the Opéra-Comique also have links with it.

Myth of Orpheus

Orpheus had received a lyre from Apollo with seven strings, to which he added two strings in memory of the nine Muses, the sisters of his mother Calliope. He bewitched man and beasts with his songs, gave a soul to inanimate things and delighted the gods. This gift was very useful to him when he descended to the Underworld in search of his wife, the nymph Eurydice. Charmed, Cerberus and the Furies agreed to let the couple go. On one condition: Orpheus must not turn around to look at Eurydice until he had left their sinister kingdom. We know that Orpheus couldn't stop himself from doing so ... Swearing off women after this ordeal, he was killed by the Maenads, or Thracian women, for rejecting their advances. His head, thrown into the Hebrus, was washed up on the island of Lesbos. His lyre was placed among the constellations by the king of the gods Zeus, at the request of Apollo and the Muses, who gathered the scattered limbs of the ill-fated man to be buried at the foot of Mount Olympus.

Hidden symbolism of the myth of Orpheus

In the general context of Greek myths, which symbolise the psychological work that man must do to fight against his instincts and grow spiritually, Orpheus is one of the most important figures. Under the guise of seeking out life's intensity, Orpheus is in reality diverted from the essential desire for spiritualisation and seeks only the satisfaction of earthly desires. He represents the secretly hidden desire in everyone to yield to physical impulses.

The myth relates that Orpheus' wife Eurydice is bitten by a snake, dies and descends to the Underworld. Orpheus also descends and, having lulled Cerberus, the monstrous three-headed dog guarding the entrance, to sleep with his enchanting music, approaches the god Hades and manages to get the better of him. The god lets Orpheus depart with his beloved on condition that she follows him and that he avoids turning around or speaking to her until they have both returned to the world of the living.

As Orpheus is about to leave the Underworld, no longer hearing his beloved's footsteps, impatient to see her and afraid that her love will escape him, he turns around, losing Eurydice forever. Through this famous story, the myth of Orpheus sends an exceptional message.

The love (general symbol of spiritual elevation) that Orpheus bears for Eurydice corresponds to his sublime side. The death of Eurydice following a snakebite, conversely, corresponds to the death of this sublime side, to the death of the soul of Orpheus. The snake symbolises vanity (frequently found in artists – Orpheus is a musician), which makes him believe that the earth and its pleasures are owed to him. Fearing that such pleasures could escape him if he was content to love only one woman with all his soul (Eurydice), Orpheus can't give up his many desires, but he sets off to look for Eurydice. By going to Hell, he symbolically plunges into his subconscious.

Having been given a lyre by Apollo, Orpheus can both sing sublimely (a symbol of spiritual elevation) and use his lyre and his song to charm monsters. Here Orpheus charms Cerberus (which symbolises the act of flattering perverse instincts, each of the dog's three heads corresponding to a perversion of vital impulses: vanity, debauchery and domination) instead of killing the monster (which would symbolise victory over itself and these instincts). So he succumbs to his inclinations, instead of rising up.

Yet Orpheus repents on his way to meet Hades. Faced with this regret, a crucial factor, Hades gives him a second chance. But on one condition – he must not turn around before crossing the threshold of the Underworld.

Symbolically, he must not regret the world or the past of perverse seduction, which has distanced him from Eurydice (the meaning of her death), into which he had lapsed.

But in the end Orpheus gives in to the temptation to turn around and Eurydice disappears forever. In other words, Orpheus regrets his past sexual and material debauchery, and he will remain permanently attached to Eurydice. Licentiousness, unbridled rampaging passions, far from being liberating, is just another form of enslavement and obsession with the primitive energy of desire.

STAINED-GLASS WINDOW OF 21, ⑨
RUE NOTRE-DAME-DES-VICTOIRES

Best viewed in the evening

21, rue Notre-Dame-des-Victoires – Metro Bourse

A very fine but forgotten stained-glass window embellishes the façade of 21, rue Notre-Dame-des-Victoires. Listed as a historic property since 1994, the window was specially commissioned at the end of the 19th century from master glass-maker Eugène Grasset and painter Félix Gaudin to decorate the debating chamber of the new wing of the Paris Chamber of Commerce at 2, place de la Bourse. Entitled *Le Travail, par l'Industrie et le Commerce, enrichit l'Humanité* (*Work, through Industry and Trade, enriches Humanity*), it represents Work personified as a man holding a hammer, accompanied by two women, Industry and Trade. The upper part of the window shows the river port of Ivry, built on the initiative of the Chamber of Commerce. This stained-glass, originally shown at the Universal Exhibition of May 1900 in the Chamber of Commerce's pavilion, was definitively installed in the building at place de la Bourse in November 1900. A better view can be had in the evening when the window is lit from inside, as in broad daylight the details are almost impossible to make out.

MEMORIES OF THE ASSASSINATION OF JEAN JAURÈS

A murder in the Bistrot du Croissant

146, rue Montmartre – +33 9 74 73 50 22
bistrotducroissant.fr
See opening hours on the website
Metro Bourse

As the frontage indicates, the *Bistrot du Croissant* is a historic place: it was right here in the café that Jean Jaurès was assassinated on 31 July 1914. Inside there is a mosaic, a small statue of the hero and some contemporary press cuttings describing the event.

The table at which he liked to linger has also been preserved. The staff will be pleased to show you the rather sombre stain, still there after all these years, on the pale wood of the table – from the blood he lost in the attack. He had risen before collapsing a few metres away, where the mosaic is now.

RUE RÉAUMUR FAÇADES ⑪

First prize in façades competition 1897–1898

116, 118, 124, 126 and 134, rue Réaumur
Metro Bourse or Sentier

A succession of lofty and prestigious buildings constructed for the large textile manufacturers and printers at the beginning of the 20th century, rue Réaumur was opened up in 1895–96 between rues Saint-Denis and Notre-Dame-des-Victoires.

Inaugurated in 1897 by Félix Faure, this street displays a profusion of very decorative façades that reflect the new planning regulations at the end of the 19th century (extended roofs, bow windows allowed).

The architects mainly used a metal framework hidden behind stone frontages, into which the architects inserted vast glazed bays that let in the natural light needed for the activities of the locality.

Several façades won prizes at the annual architectural competition launched in 1897–1898.

Note especially No. 116 (built by Walwein, for which he received the gold medal in 1897), No. 118 (built by Montarnal in the Art Nouveau spirit and an award winner in 1900), and No. 126 and 134. The industrial building at No. 124, however, deserves special attention: built in 1905, it is different from the other designs of architect Georges Chedanne.

The façade shows the all-metal framework of the building (note the steel beams supporting the metal bow windows), which does not detract in the slightest from the Art Nouveau delicacy of the ensemble.

CERAMIC PANEL, AU PLANTEUR

Vestige of colonial France

10–12, rue des Petits Carreaux
Metro Sentier

Many passers-by fail to notice a splendid ceramic panel signed Crommer (1890) and titled *Au Planteur* on the first-floor of the building at 10–12, rue des Petits Carreaux.

Between two first-floor windows, a black man wearing only red and white striped shorts can be seen serving coffee to a white man dressed in colonial style, seated on sacks of goods. This is presumably the celebrated *planteur* (plantation owner).

Above the panel is the name of the establishment: *Au Planteur*, which offered exotic products including coffee.

Another sign below, *Aucune Succursale*, literally means 'no branch', i.e. the owner had no other sales outlets. The façade was listed as a Historic Monument in 1984.

STAINED-GLASS WINDOW OF THE SOCIÉTÉ IMMOBILIÈRE DE LA CHARCUTERIE FRANÇAISE

Aesthetic charcuterie

10, rue Bachaumont
Metro Sentier

Currently occupied by private societies and lawyers' offices, the building at 10, rue Bachaumont was built by Jules Michel for the Company of French Pork Butchers. Access is unfortunately controlled by an entry phone but through the glazed entrance to the building you can glimpse its superb hallway with walls covered in old signs from butchers' shops serving as commemorative plaques to the society's contributors, as well as paintings and a beautiful stained-glass window dedicated to the profession. If you're lucky the door might open unexpectedly and you can have a quick look inside to admire the bust of a former president of the corporation by Alfred Boucher. But be discreet as this is private property.

Parisian records

– Shortest street: rue des Degrés, 2nd arrondissement (5.75 metres), is actually a flight of 14 steps (with no entrances to buildings or houses) Longest street: rue de Vaugirard, 6th–7th arrondissement (4,360 metres)
– Widest avenue: avenue Foch, 16th arrondissement (120 metres)
– Narrowest street: rue de Venise, 4th arrondissement (2 metres), followed by rue du Chat-qui-Pêche, 5th arrondissement (2.50 metres)
– Highest point: Montmartre (129.75 metres – rue Saint-Rustique, 13th arrondissement) and not in the 20th arrondissement as many claim (128 metres)
– Narrowest house: 39, rue du Château-d'Eau, 10th arrondissement (1.2 metres)

A short covered route for rainy days

The lack of pavements until the 19th century was the main reason for the popularity of covered arcades, from the Directoire period to the Second Empire: when it rained, the streets quickly became very muddy. The construction of these arcades solved this problem, allowing people to stroll in the dry. Even today, the resourceful Parisian can make the most of them: on a day when they've forgotten their umbrella, they can walk from the Louvre to rue de Provence and rue Cadet, practically sheltered from the rain, by taking the Palais-Royal, rue des Colonnes (covered) and the passages des Panoramas, Jouffroy and Verdeau. The Passage des Panoramas, at No. 47, is home to Maison Stern (printers and engravers), a beautiful shop that has remained unchanged since 1830.

PLANT DECORATION OF THE JEAN SANS PEUR TOWER

One of the masterpieces of medieval French sculpture

20, rue Étienne Marcel
tourjeansanspeursite.wordpress.com
Wednesday, Saturday and Sunday 1.30pm–6pm
Metro Étienne Marcel

A unique Parisian example of medieval military architecture (the Sens and Cluny hotels are not military, and the Conciergerie and Fontaine du Vertbois have been extensively redesigned), Jean Sans Peur tower is supported by the remains of the wall of Philippe Auguste (see page 130).

It was built between 1409 and 1411 to allow the Duke of Burgundy Jean sans Peur (John the Fearless), who had just murdered King Charles VI's brother Louis d'Orléans, to take refuge there, safe from possible reprisals.

The duke's room was at the top of this 23-metre-high fortified tower, protected by battlements and trapdoors. Under the chamber was another chamber, then an empty space about 10 metres high in order to avoid attack or the risk of the floor catching fire.

The most remarkable element of this tower is the exceptional plant decoration on the vault of the spiral staircase. Once polychrome, this is a masterpiece of medieval French sculpture organised around three plants, each symbolising a member of the Burgundy family. Emerging from the four corners of the wall and the central pot, the oak represents Philippe le Hardi, father of Jean sans Peur, and the power of the dukes of Burgundy. In the middle of each wall are branches of hawthorn (ubiquitous in Flanders, a symbol of strength and hardness, but also purity) that symbolise his wife Marguerite de Flandre (Margaret III, Countess of Flanders). In the centre, hops, symbol of their son Jean sans Peur (see below), curling around the branches of the paternal oak.

Jean sans Peur and the origin of beer

Although it was Hildegard of Bingen (1099–1179) who discovered the aseptic and preservative virtues of hops that allowed beer to be kept better and longer, it was Jean sans Peur who made hops the main ingredient of beer. They replaced the herbal blends then used in brewing and standardised the taste. He also created the Order of the Hop in 1406; in 1435 an edict imposed this recipe and the word 'beer' appeared for the first time as distinct from 'ale'.

Jean sans Peur was eventually assassinated in 1419 by the Armagnacs, supporters of the Orléans family. In 1477 on the death of Charles the Bold, son of Philip the Good and grandson of Jean sans Peur, Louis XI integrated Burgundy into the Kingdom of France.

Vestiges of Egypt in Paris

Contrary to received wisdom, the Parisian infatuation with Egypt dates from before Bonaparte's expedition. From the mid–18th century, young artists sent to Rome were marked by Egypt: at the time researchers were looking for the Etruscan origins of Roman art. Pope Benedict XIV had opened an Egyptian museum at the Capitoline and an Egyptian room had been installed at the Villa Borghese in Rome. The young French artists thus came back home loaded with engravings by Piranesi, who had set himself up as promoter of this style. During the Revolution, with the help of the Freemasons, the Republic identified with the immoderation, cult of the dead and mysteries of Egyptian art. Bonaparte's Egyptian expedition of 1798, only followed a fashion already well established. The Napoleonic era nevertheless had enormous influence. Some streets were renamed and a number of monuments commemorate events of the expedition.

Other than the Louvre pyramid and its museum collections, the Concorde obelisk is the most famous souvenir. Donated by Mehmet Ali, in 1831, its twin was left in Luxor: it was also offered to France but the second half of the gift was officially declined until 1994 ...

Near place du Caire, rue d'Aboukir, rue du Nil, rue de Damiette and rue d'Alexandrie also owe their names to Egypt. Two fountains can also be attributed to this fashion. The famous Fontaine du Fellah, rue de Sèvres (near Vaneau Metro) symbolises an Egyptian farmer (fellah). Built between 1806 and 1809, the statue was damaged and replaced by a copy in 1844. The Fontaine du Palmier, place du Châtelet, has a capital in the form of a palm tree surrounded by four sphinxes. There is also the Egyptian retro-style bathroom of Hôtel de Bourrienne, the west façade of Cour Carrée which includes a fantastical representation of the goddess Isis, Hôtel de Beauharnais (now the German embassy) at 78, rue de Lille, the Temple du Droit Humain (see page 387), the Louxor cinema (junction of boulevards Magenta and de La Chapelle), pillars with palm-tree capitals on avenue Ledru-Rollin under the former railway line and an Egyptian tabernacle in Saint-Roch church. In all there are over a hundred sphinxes scattered around the city and a couple of dozen Egyptian-inspired tombs in Père-Lachaise cemetery, the country often being associated with eternity.

Finally, there are still two Egyptian mummies in a cave under the Bastille (see page 125).

EGYPTIAN SYMBOLS OF THE PASSAGE DU CAIRE

(15)

Egyptian revival in Paris

2, place du Caire – Metro Sentier

Passage du Caire, the oldest of the Parisian alleyways (1798) as well as the longest and certainly one of the most animated, was inspired by the great souk of the Egyptian capital. Built on the site of the Filles-Dieu convent, it is said that some of the paving comes from the tombstones of the nuns. Apart from its name it bears no relation to the splendour and riches of Egypt, having been deliberately designed to attract more down-market traders. It does however open onto place du Caire, where the façade of No. 2 is covered with hieroglyphs and decorated with columns with lotus capitals and three heads of the goddess Hathor. The influence of the capitals of the Egyptian temple of Dandarah is very clear. Probably constructed by the architect Berthier, the building dates from 1828 and the sculptures are by Gabriel-Joseph Garraud.

CARICATURE OF BOUGENIER'S NOSE

'As full of nose as he is of spirit'

2, place du Caire
Metro Sentier

The building at 2, place du Caire, in addition to its Egyptian character (see the previous double-page spread), has another unusual feature: look carefully at the hieroglyphics of the carved frieze and you'll see the caricature of a certain Henri Marcellin Auguste Bougenier (not Bouginier, as is often said), as the 1882 *Dictionnaire général des artistes de l'école française* specifies. Bougenier, who was born in Valenciennes on 2 January 1799 and died in Paris on 4 February 1866, was a pupil of Baron Gros who exhibited religious paintings at the salons of 1844, 1845 and 1851 before becoming a photographer. In the middle of the Romantic period this was considered outmoded Neoclassicism. So, endowed with 'as much nose as spirit', Bougenier saw himself enhanced by an imposing nose that's still there today. This nose is the last example of a joke that appeared on many city walls. Victor Hugo himself mentioned Bougenier's nose in a chapter of his epic historical novel *Les Misérables*.

The miracle court

Place du Caire was one of 12 'miracle courts' (Cour des Miracles) in 19th century Paris. The gathering place of thugs and outlaws of all kinds, this was also the stage-set for many true-false beggars who came here to practise their art. At the end of the day, when work was done, they would discard their trappings (crutches, false wooden legs, false stumps) and go home. For those who dared to venture into these infamous places in the evening, the spectacle was amazing: the blind suddenly regained their sight and the deaf spun round at the sound of their name being called by one of their associates ... The name 'miracle court' was soon adopted.

Origin of quartier de Bonne Nouvelle

The Cour des Miracles ('Miracle Court') in Place du Caire has existed since the 13th century. In the 17th century, Louis XIV's police lieutenant, Nicolas de la Reynie, cleaned it up for the first time. People heard the 'good news' and named the neighbourhood accordingly.

DIFFERENCES IN LEVEL OF THE LAND AROUND SENTIER

Remains of Charles V's fortifications

Passage Sainte-Foy
Rues de Cléry and d'Aboukir
Grands Boulevards
Metro Sentier

© domllorens

Some topographical details of the Sentier district are very interesting evidence of the existence of the fourth and fifth-century Parisian fortifications between the 14th and 17th centuries: the walls built by Charles V and those known as 'Fossés jaunes' (yellow ditches). Both used earth ramparts and ditches, which resulted in some incredibly uneven ground and differences in level.

From rue Sainte-Foy, passage Sainte-Foy leads to 263, rue Saint-Denis via a steep flight of steps which compensates for the difference in level between rue Sainte-Foy and rue Saint-Denis. More than just ordinary rough ground, this is evidence of the rampart on which Charles V's wall was built.

The routes of rues de Cléry and d'Aboukir are also clear markers: the more elevated rue de Cléry was built on the outer side of the ramparts whereas rue d'Aboukir follows the ditch built in front.

All the Grands Boulevards, notably boulevards Saint-Martin, Saint-Denis, Bonne-Nouvelle and Poissonnière, were also built on the ramparts and the roadway frequently climbs and descends for no apparent reason, while neighbouring streets remain at the same lower level. The road is simply crossing the former bastions of the walls of Charles V and the Fossés Jaunes: boulevard Bonne-Nouvelle crosses bastion No. 6. Just after Porte Saint-Denis the road climbs, with the left-hand pavement overhanging. Boulevard Saint-Martin, on the other hand, cuts through bastion No. 7, with pavements overhanging the roadway by almost 3 metres. The steps in passage du Pont-aux-Biches give access to the rampart, 7 metres higher up. And rue René-Boulanger follows closely the path of the outer wall of the bastion. The recesses and projections of the façades of No. 42–48, boulevard du Temple, are the exact shape of bastion No. 8. A little further on, boulevard Beaumarchais, built on the rampart itself, forces rues des Tournelles and Saint-Gilles to climb steeply in the last few metres before they join it. On the other side of the road, steps have had to be constructed to descend to rue Amelot.

Scarp: inner wall of a fortification with ditch.
Counterscarp: outer wall of a fortification with ditch.

For further information and a map of the route of Charles V's city walls, see the following double-page spread.

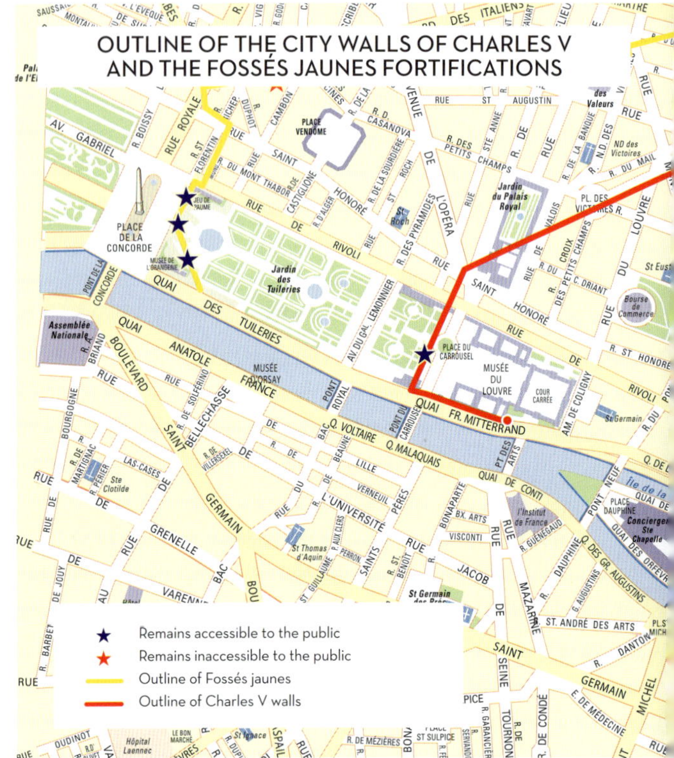

The city walls of Charles V (1356–1420) and the Fossés jaunes (1543–1640)

After the defeat by the English at Poitiers in 1356 and the fear of an attack on Paris, Étienne Marcel, provost of the merchants, vowed to improve the city's defences. The artillery that was coming into use in the 14th century changed the situation: it was too costly to build a wall 30 metres high (the height cannon balls could reach). The alternative was to build wide fortifications. Those of Charles V, including the ditches, extended over 87 metres and had an embankment 30 metres wide at the base and 3 metres high, on top of which was built a wall 6 metres high and 2 metres thick. A century later, from 1529, François I decided to construct a wall with bastions. To the east and south, they were placed alongside Charles V's wall using, where possible, the *voiries*, i.e. the mass of all kinds of rubbish dumped outside the walls by the residents over 150 to 200 years. The dump was higher than the walls,

compromising the defensive system. To the west, a new fortified wall, known as the *Fossés jaunes* (yellow ditches) because of the yellow earth, was built from the present place de la Concorde (east side) to porte Saint-Denis. The new ramparts enclosed 300,000 citizens within 1,000 hectares. Other than the traces that can be seen in and around the Sentier district (see previous double-page spread), some vestiges of these two walls are still visible:

– A section of wall (scarp and counterscarp) of Charles V's fortifications under place du Carrousel at the Louvre.

– Bastion No. 1 of the Tuileries: part of the bastion can be seen in the basement of the Musée de l'Orangerie (Fossés jaunes).

– A section of counterscarp at Bastille metro station, in the direction of Bobigny, line No. 5 (platform and access corridor).

NB: two other vestiges are not accessible to the public: in the basement of No. 39, rue Cambon and in the cellars of the Bibliothèque de l'Arsenal.

Are there any 'maisons closes' left?

On 13 April 1946, the famous 'bawdy houses' (*bordels*) were made illegal throughout France.

Thousands of prostitutes found themselves literally in the street. Although the 195 Parisian brothels were closed, some traces still remain of a time that is missed by some, in particular the important role they played in social order.

The most common relic is the street numbering: to be easily spotted the brothels feature plaques with a larger number than usual, or the shape of the windows and certain ornamental details may also give a clue to interested parties.

Thus you can still seek out these plaques that reveal the former use of an establishment ... such as 36, rue Saint-Sulpice with its unequivocally large numbering.

Men in cassocks, plentiful in the neighbourhood, were among the clients of a certain Miss Betty, and at 15, rue Saint-Sulpice, where the name of the tenant Alys is still on the tiled floor and the mosaic of the former brothel's hammam on the second floor (now private). In the 9th arrondissement, 9, rue Navarin — *Chez Christiane* — was appreciated by fans of sadomasochism. The fine neo-Gothic façade has not changed.

At 122, rue de Provence, the well-known *One Two Two* has kept the façade only, and 50, rue Saint-Georges — *Chez Marguerite* — has kept in two staircases a wood-painting showing the capture of a Sabine woman, naked, and a sculpture of women draped in the long tunics of antiquity.

Le Chabanais, at 12, rue Chabanais in the 2nd arrondissement, still has its two lifts which spared visitors embarrassing meetings: one could go up while the other went down ...

The whorehouse at 32, rue Blondel is probably the one with the finest vestiges (unfortunately very difficult to see, as the current

trade in rue Blondel is not very much different from what it used to be) ...

Finally, at 6, rue des Moulins (1st arrondissement), female cherubs have survived (and at 33, rue Radziwill (1st arrondissement), the double staircase and double entrance (also at 48, rue de Valois) ensured that customers did not cross paths (see page 48).

EROTIC MOSAICS
OF A FORMER BROTHEL

The most beautiful vestige of a Parisian brothel

32, rue Blondel
auxbellespoules.fr/reservation
Metro Strasbourg-Saint-Denis or Réaumur Sébastopol

Just register for one of the monthly lecture tours offered by Aux Belles Poules, named after a former brothel that had its heyday in the 1920s, and discover its history amidst a beautiful setting of erotic mosaics. This genuine masterpiece of Art Deco, which led to the old establishment being listed as a Historic Monument, is the only almost completely preserved relic of the decor of a Paris brothel.

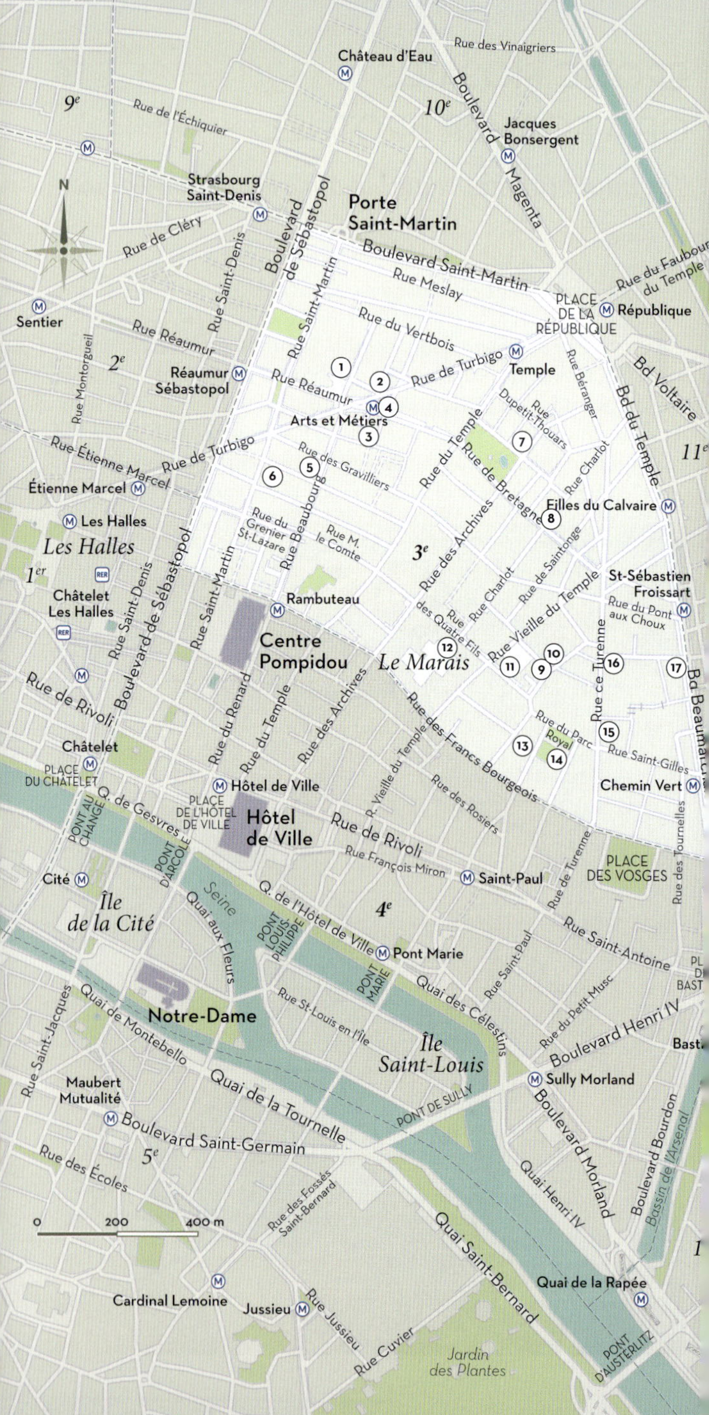

9e
10e
11e
2e
3e
1er
4e
5e
1
Rue des Vinaigriers
Château d'Eau
Rue de l'Échiquier
Strasbourg
Saint-Denis
Jacques
Bonsergent
Boulevard de Magenta
N
Rue de Cléry
Rue Saint-Denis
Boulevard de Sébastopol
Rue Saint-Martin
Porte
Saint-Martin
Boulevard Saint-Martin
Rue Meslay
PLACE
DE LA
RÉPUBLIQUE
Rue du Faubourg
du Temple
République
Sentier
Rue Réaumur
Rue du Vertbois
Bd Voltaire
Bd du Temple
Rue Montorgueil
Réaumur
Sébastopol
Rue Réaumur
Rue de Turbigo
Temple
Rue Béranger
1
2
Arts et Métiers
4
3
Rue
Dupetit-Thouars
7
Rue Charlot
Rue Étienne Marcel
Rue de Turbigo
Rue des Gravilliers
6
5
Rue du Temple
Rue de Bretagne
Filles du Calvaire
8
Étienne Marcel
Rue du
Grenier
St-Lazare
Rue du Beaubourg
Rue M.
le Comte
Rue des Archives
Rue de Saintonge
Les Halles
Les Halles
Rue des Quatre Fils
Rue Charlot
St-Sébastien
Froissart
Rue du Pont
aux Choux
Châtelet
Les Halles
Rambuteau
Rue Vieille du Temple
Boulevard de Sébastopol
Rue Saint-Denis
Rue Saint-Martin
Centre
Pompidou
Le Marais
12
11
9
10
16
17
Bd Beaumarchais
Rue de Rivoli
Rue du Renard
Rue du Temple
Rue des Archives
Rue des Francs Bourgeois
Rue du Parc
Royal
15
13
14
Rue de Turenne
Rue Saint-Gilles
Chemin Vert
Châtelet
PLACE
DU CHÂTELET
Hôtel de Ville
PLACE
DE L'HÔTEL
DE VILLE
Hôtel
de Ville
R. Vieille du Temple
Rue des Rosiers
Rue de Rivoli
PLACE
DES VOSGES
Rue des Tournelles
Q. de Gesvres
Rue François Miron
Saint-Paul
Rue Saint-Paul
Rue Saint-Antoine
Cité
PONT AU
CHANGE
PONT
D'ARCOLE
Q. de l'Hôtel de Ville
4e
Rue de Turenne
PL
D
BAST
Île
de la Cité
Seine
Quai aux Fleurs
PONT
LOUIS-
PHILIPPE
PONT
MARIE
Pont Marie
Rue St-Louis en l'île
Quai des Célestins
Rue du Petit Musc
Boulevard Henri IV
Bast
Rue Saint-Jacques
Quai de Montebello
Notre-Dame
Île
Saint-Louis
Sully Morland
Boulevard Morland
Boulevard Bourdon
Bassin de l'Arsenal
Maubert
Mutualité
Quai de la Tournelle
PONT DE SULLY
Quai Henri IV
Boulevard Saint-Germain
Rue des Écoles
Rue des Fossés
Saint-Bernard
Quai Saint-Bernard
Quai de la Rapée
0   200   400 m
Cardinal Lemoine
Jussieu
Rue Jussieu
Rue Cuvier
Jardin
des Plantes
PONT
D'AUSTERLITZ

3rd arrondissement

CNAM LIBRARY ①

'What is most perfect in Gothic'

270–292, rue Saint-Martin
+33 1 40 27 27 03 – bib.services@cnam.fr
Check opening hours at:
bibliotheques.cnam.fr/opac/library/BIBLIOTHÈQUE CENTRALE/CNA02
Open to CNAM students and auditors
Closes at 7 pm during the summer and autumn breaks, in July and September;
closed for the summer holidays in August
You may be able to have a look around the library if you ask politely
Metro Arts et Métiers

The sublime and little-known reading room of the central library of the Conservatoire National des Arts et Métiers (CNAM – National Conservatory of Arts and Crafts) has been installed since 1851 in the former Gothic refectory of the Benedictine priory of Saint-Martin-des-Champs.

The site had a religious vocation from the 8th century, when a chapel dedicated to St Martin was built in the fields (hence the name 'Champs') further north, where around AD 384 St Martin cured a leper by kissing his face. Founded in 1060, the priory became a Benedictine abbey in 1079. Following its heyday in the 13th century, it gradually declined until the Revolution, when it closed. The refectory, built around 1230 by Pierre de Montreuil, the renowned architect of Sainte-Chapelle, is 42.8 metres long and 11.7 metres wide, and is supported at the centre by seven extremely slender columns that give an unprecedented lightness to the structure. Recognised as a true technical and aesthetic feat, the refectory was considered to be 'what is most perfect in Gothic'. In 1794, at the instigation of Catholic priest Abbé Grégoire (1750–1831), the Conservatoire des Arts et Métiers was founded. The walls of the refectory, converted into a munitions warehouse, were protected and panelled up to the windows, before it was opened as a predominantly scientific library in 1851.

CNAM's amazing acoustics

In the Musée des Arts et Métiers (which occupies the buildings where the monks of the former priory of Saint-Martin-des-Champs were housed, as well as the old priory church), the room where the objects used by Lavoisier for his experiments are located has amazing acoustics. When two people turn their backs and face each other from opposite walls, they can easily talk without anyone in the centre of the room hearing. It's said that the room was used in this way by the monks of the former abbey to take confession from those who were contagious.

From 1140, the priory had its own enclosure (rebuilt in 1270) of which three features remain: part of the old wall and one of the 18 towers of the enclosure, rue du Vertbois, one of the four towers at the corner of rue du Vertbois and rue Saint-Jean-Martin and another of the towers inside 7, rue Bailly (private).

THE ANGEL OF
57, RUE DE TURBIGO

A wondrous angel

57, rue de Turbigo – Metro Étienne Marcel

Unknown even to many local residents, the huge caryatid of the angel (on three entire floors) fronting the building at 57, rue de Turbigo was said to have been carved by Auguste Émile Delange on the occasion of an 1851 project in honour of Augustin Fresnel (1788–1827). Fresnel had invented the step lens (now known as the Fresnel lens) used in lighthouses to increase the light's range, so his tribute was to be a lighthouse.

Delange, perhaps because of his name, designed a square tower bearing the angel of rue Turbigo. The project was not retained, but in 1859 the architect adopted the angel idea for this building.

According to another explanation put forward by Raymond Queneau in 1955, the angel owes its existence to the prophetic dream of its owner who had seen this angel with a little purse in its hand. The next day the owner won the lottery and had the angel represented on the façade.

Other sources think that rather than an angel, the caryatid is an Art-Déco version of a Nike, the Greco-Roman 'Winged Victory'.

Spreading its two wings as if to welcome visitors and protect the tenants, the angel appeared in an Agnès Varda short film in the 1980s (*Les Anges cariatides*) as well as in the sci-fi comedy *Peut-être* (*Perhaps*) by Cédric Klapisch.

NEARBY

House at 3, rue Volta ③

Metro Arts et Métiers

Long considered the oldest house in Paris (some postcards still make this claim), the house at 3, rue Volta in fact dates from 1644, as discovered in 1979, following in-depth research.

Built in 1407, the house known as the 'Grand-Pignon', at 51, rue de Montmorency, is believed to be the oldest in Paris (see page 88).

ARTS ET MÉTIERS METRO STATION

A station worthy of Jules Verne

Arts et Métiers is probably the most remarkable metro station in the Paris network. Being on a branch line, No. 11, the station is little used by Parisians.

Refurbished in October 1994 for the bicentenary of the Conservatoire National des Arts et Métiers (CNAM, National Conservatory of Arts and Crafts), located just above, the station was planned and executed by François Schuiten, the celebrated Belgian illustrator and author of *La Fièvre d'Urbicande* (strip cartoon album in the series *Cités obscures*). The station is completely covered with copper sheeting and features a series of portholes, giving the impression of being in a submarine.

NEARBY

Rue Transnonain plaque ⑤

Metro Arts et Métiers

At 79, rue Beaubourg, near the corner of rue Beaubourg and rue Chapon and between the two nameplates of rue Beaubourg, you can still see an old plaque with the earlier name of this part of the street: rue Transnonain.

The street, open since the 13th century, was successively known as rue de Châlons, then Trousse-Nonnain, Trace-Putain, Tasse-Non-nain and Transnonain, in memory of the prostitutes who lived in the neighbourhood.

The nameplate probably survived in memory of a massacre that took place on 15 April 1834, when General Bugeaux violently repressed rioters protesting against the regime of Louis-Philippe I. Government troops opened fire and killed all the occupants of what used to be 12, rue Transnonain (two numbers next to the nameplate). The massacre was immortalised in a lithograph by Honoré Daumier.

ALCHEMICAL SYMBOLS AT HOUSE OF THE GRAND-PIGNON

The home of the famous alchemist Nicolas Flamel

51, rue de Montmorency
Metro Rambuteau

Having belonged to the renowned alchemist Nicolas Flamel (1330–1418), hence the name of the restaurant located here (Auberge de Nicolas Flamel), house of the 'Grand-Pignon' (Great Pinion) at 51, rue de Montmorency, logically enough bears some alchemical symbols that most visitors miss. Some are underneath the old French phrase which runs across the front of the house above the entrance – the phrase recalls that, thanks to the rent from the shops on the ground floor, the most deprived were welcomed free on the upper floors … The only condition was to recite an Our Father and a Hail Mary every day for the remaining dead. Note also the initials in Gothic letters (N and F) of the sponsor of this house, a series of 15th century medallions depicting angel musicians, a sage reading a book (recalling the alchemists' motto *Ora et labora* – pray and work) and a saint in a boat with a serpent-shaped helm. In these medallions, the angel musicians represent alchemy itself. Alchemists adjust their chemical operations in accordance with the harmony of the vibrations of the soul, and alchemy is sometimes called the 'music of the gods'.

The medallions depicting a saint in a boat and a tamed serpent probably refer to St James the Elder, who sailed to Galicia (the present-day Santiago de Compostela is named after him). Here, the boat symbolises the ark that contains the secrets of alchemy that Flamel discovered after making his own pilgrimage to Santiago de Compostela.

For the philosopher, each step of the way was equivalent to an alchemical operation on whatever he was meditating and operating on, both in his physical laboratory and in the inner laboratory of his soul, going hand in hand (see page 98). The allegory of the tamed serpent expresses the mastery of the inner fire of man, which in Eastern traditions is called Kundalini This is why alchemists are sometimes called the philosophers of fire.

Tombstone at the Cluny Museum

Nicolas Flamel died in Paris on 22 March 1418 and was buried in Saint Jacques de-la-Boucherie church. His tombstone was set in front of a pillar bearing an effigy of the Virgin Mary. Since Paris City Council bought it from an antique dealer in 1839, this tombstone can be seen at the Cluny Museum. The dealer had picked it up himself from a fruit and vegetable vendor on rue Saint-Jacques-de-la-Boucherie, where it was used as a market stand.

BOUNDARIES OF THE TEMPLE ENCLOSURE

What remains of the Templars?

Rue Eugène Spuller
Metro Temple

Just in front of the 3rd arrondissement town hall (mairie) on rue Eugène Spuller, the silver markers unexpectedly integrated into the cobblestones and bitumen (replacing the former blue lines), marks the location of two turrets from the great tower (50 metres high) of the famous Temple enclosure. Here in the small tower, which adjoined the large tower but was not connected to it, Louis XVI and his family were imprisoned on 13 August 1792 before being transferred to the large tower on 26 September (followed by Marie-Antoinette and her children on 26 October). Louis XVI left the Temple tower on 21 January 1793 for the scaffold, which had been erected in Place de la Révolution (now Place de la Concorde). Marie-Antoinette was transferred to the Conciergerie on 1 August 1793. Little Louis XVII, according to the official version, died in the Temple tower on 8 June 1795. As the tower had become a pilgrimage site for royalists, it was demolished between 1808 and 1810 on Napoleon's orders.

While the great tower stood between the gates of square du Temple garden and the north-western side of the town hall, the square occupies the site of the palace of the Grand Master of the Knights Templar. A plaque at the corner of rue Dupetit-Thouars and rue Gabriel Vicaire shows the plans of today's streets and buildings juxtaposed on plans of the old Temple enclosure.

> The collegiate church in the Temple enclosure was modelled on the Church of the Holy Sepulchre in Jerusalem.

© Parismarais

Other remains of the Temple enclosure

The house of the Order of the Temple in Paris was the seat of the Templar province of France and the largest commandery in the country. It was built extra muros on old marshes which the Templars had drained, and hence became known as the Marais district. It was called the New Temple City, in contrast to the Old Temple which had been the first house of the Order in Paris. Contrary to popular belief, there are some remains of the Temple where Louis XVI was imprisoned:

– The doors of the porte cochère (carriage gate) of 1, rue Saint-Claude have been recovered from the door of the palace of the Grand Master of the Temple.

– At 73, rue Charlot there are the remains of a tower (private and inaccessible site) built around 1240 which stood on the east corner of the enclosure wall of the Temple Enclosure (part of it can be seen from the other side of the block, at 32, rue de Picardie).

– The doors of the large tower are preserved at Château de Vincennes. Rue du Temple, rue Vieille-du-Temple, boulevard du Temple, Temple métro station, the covered market known as Carreau du Temple, and square du Temple are other reminders of the existence of the Templar enclosure.

Rue des Blancs Manteaux (Street of the White Coats) owes its name not to traditional Templar dress, but to that of the mendicant monks, known as Serfs of the Virgin Mary, who occupied the old monastery on that street.

For more on the Templars, the execution of the last Grand Master Jacques de Molay and the reality of Baphomet, see page 40 and page 149.

The Knights Templar: myth and reality

The Order of the Poor Knights of Christ and of the Temple of Solomon (*Pauperes Commilitiones Christi Templique Salomonici*) – more commonly known as the Order of the Templars or the Order of the Temple – was the most famous religious-military Order of the Middle Ages. Founded upon returning from the First Crusade (1096) with the declared purpose of protecting Christian pilgrims to the Holy Land, the Order would exist for over two centuries. Officially recognised by Pope Honorius II in January 1128, the Order of the Temple quickly became the most highly regarded charitable order in Christendom, growing rapidly in both numbers and power. Distinguished by a white robe (revealing that members followed the Cistercian Rule) bearing a red cross pattée, they formed the elite fighting force of the Crusades. The non-combatant members of the Order ran a vast financial empire extending throughout Christendom (even inventing the letter of credit, which was the first step towards the modern banking system). Ultimately, the Knights Templar had forts and churches throughout Europe and the Holy Land. This magnificent organisational structure had a double goal: the formation of what would today be called a United States of Europe, and the provision of free and obligatory education (in keeping with the principles of the Templars themselves). Thus, the Order became established at two levels: one was outwardly visible to the whole world; the other was a more inward, esoteric existence. The 'secular' arm, as it were, comprised dynamic men of action and soldiers, while the esoteric arm was made up of the Order's true elite: the wise men and priests who formed the 'rearguard' to a body of knights and warriors. The two groups answered solely to the Grand Master of the Order and not to any king or pope. It was this which led to them being suspected of heresy, even if all they were doing was observing a rule of obedience. Similarly, the secrecy surrounding the Templars' ceremonies caused people to imagine that they engaged in heretic worship – something which was never proved because 'civilians never enter into the houses of the military'. The Order adhered rigorously to Apostolic Catholicism, even if some of its members had an intellectual interest in other cultures and theologies, and Gnosticism in particular. Gnostic symbols are sometimes to be found in the churches and castles the Templars built. The spiritual mentor of the Order, Saint Bernard of Clairvaux, had initially selected nine members of its elite to go to Jerusalem, where King Baldwin III would allow them to establish their premises in the underground stables beneath the ruins of the Temple of Solomon. Certain traditions have it that they supposedly discovered the Cup of Solomon there, which had been hidden or lost since the time of Jesus Christ. The Templars are believed to have brought this Grail to the West, which from that point onwards extended its dominion over the whole world, just as the Order itself grew to dazzling heights. With the loss of the Holy Land, the support the Templars enjoyed from Europe's monarchs began to wane. The French king, Philippe IV, who had no way of paying off a substantial debt to the Order, would begin to put pressure on Pope Clement V to take measures against the Templars. Evidence was forged and rumours spread, both with regard to sexual practices and religious unorthodoxy. It was said, for example, that the Templars worshipped a bizarre demonic figure called Baphomet, of which little was ever known exactly – except that it was a figure of pure invention (see page 149). Finally, in 1307, a large number of Templars in France were arrested and tortured until they made false confessions. They were then burnt at the stake or sentenced to service on the galleys. Philippe IV continued to pressure Pope Clement V, who finally dissolved the Order on 22 March 1312. In Portugal, however, the king, Dom Dinis, considered the Templars to be innocent and afforded immediate protection to the sizeable number who had fled there from France. After the dissolution of the Order, the king immediately founded another that incorporated the old Templars: the Military Order of the Knights of Christ, also known as the Order of Christ. The abrupt disappearance of most of the 'infrastructure' created in Europe by the Order of the Temple would give rise to a number of more or less extravagant legends and suppositions.

'LES OISEAUX' VEGETABLE GARDEN

Birds of good omen

Entrance via 39, rue de Bretagne or rue de Beauce
Saturday and Sunday 11am–1pm or, during the week, when a gardener
is present
potagerdesoiseaux.blogspot.com
Association responsible for the gardens: potagerdesoiseaux@gmail.com
Metro Filles du Calvaire

On the site of a former stable, just beside the Marché des Enfants-Rouges (Red-Children Market), an attractive vegetable garden was opened in September 2004 in response to city residents' keen interest in growing their own food. A relaxed and congenial place run along the lines of 'shared gardens' (see page 512), 'Les Oiseaux' vegetable garden's (Potager des Oiseaux) 120 m^2 consists of ten rectangles divided into three plots, run by the association 'Jardiniers du IIIe'. There are some 60 members who come along to garden, chat, drink coffee, pass on helpful hints – in short, mutual encouragement. You can have a look round and pick up some advice on the way to shop at the market next door. Better still, acquire a key and some tools and get your hands dirty, by joining (e-mail the address on the opposite page).

The word *potager* (kitchen or vegetable garden) comes from 'plants for the pot' that grow there, such as onions, cabbages and turnips.

Legend of the Marché des Enfants-Rouges

39, rue de Bretagne
Tuesday–Saturday 8.30am–7pm, Sunday 8.30am–2pm
Property of the City of Paris since 1912, the Marché des Enfants-Rouges (fruits, vegetables, restaurants ...) has been listed as a historic monument since 1982. Enthusiastically defended by the local residents, it recently escaped demolition in order to build parking spaces and reopened in 2000 after a six-year renovation project. It may owe its existence to an incredible legend according to which a medium predicted last century that the neighbouring houses would collapse if anything destroyed the Enfants-Rouges market. The name of the market, which was set up in 1615, comes from the orphans dressed in red (symbol of Christian charity) who were taken in by the hospital-orphanage founded by Marguerite de Valois in 1536 for 'orphans without father or mother' left at the Hôtel-Dieu de Paris hospital.

Aborted plans for a 'place de France'

Rues de Normandie, de Bretagne, de Poitou and de Saintonge are all named after French provinces. They recall a project of Henri IV for a semi-circular place de France, from which streets bearing the names of the various regions would radiate.

MARKS OF THE FIEF OF COUTURES-SAINT-GERVAIS 

Pre-Revolutionary traces

Corner of rue de Thorigny and rue des Coutures-Saint-Gervais
Corner of rue de Thorigny and rue Debelleyme
Metro Filles du Calvaire

Traces of an era before the French Revolution can be seen at the junctions of rue de Thorigny and rue Debelleyme, and the junction of rue de Thorigny and rue des Coutures-Saint. The letters F, C, S, G are engraved in stone around a cross, at a height of about 2 metres. These record the existence of the former fief (parcel of land held by a feudal lord) of Coutures-Saint-Gervais, which belonged to the Religious Hospitaller nuns of Saint-Gervais, hence the name.

The FCSG fief was bordered roughly by rues Vieille-du-Temple, de la Perle, de Thorigny, Sainte-Anastase and Turenne.

Rue des Coutures-Saint-Gervais

Rue des Coutures-Saint-Gervais is in no way a reference to a sartorial tradition but to one of the great challenges posed by Parisian geography: that of transforming the marshy land of the appropriately named Marais district into ground suitable for cultivation: the 'coutures'. The street ran along the 'coutures' of the estate belonging to the Hospitaller Sisters of Saint-Gervais (see above).

NEARBY

Saint erased 

Metro Filles du Calvaire

On rue des Coutures-Saint-Gervais and rue de Thorigny the names of rue des Coutures-Saint-Gervais and the former rue Saint-Gervais is also carved in the stone. Note that the 'ST' of 'Saint-Gervais' did not withstand the Revolutionary Committee of Public Safety's decision on 21 December 1794 to remove the word 'holy' from all the city streets.

For around a year and a half the word 'saint' was being erased from Saint-Dominique, Saint-Martin, Saints-Pères, Saint-André-des-Arts, and so on, as can still be seen on some of the surviving street names.

RUE DE LA PERLE SEALED MEDALLIONS

Cagliostro's Hermetic Freemasonry

20, rue de la Perle – Metro Saint-Paul or Filles du Calvaire

The building at 20, rue de la Perle is a 19th century construction that would be indistinguishable from its neighbours if not for three mysterious medallions bearing esoteric allegories of an alchemical and Masonic nature. On the first medallion, a square and compass are interlaced, from which hangs a plumb line, and down to the left is a figure resembling a Phoenician ship with a raised serpent as a figurehead. On the right is a still apparatus used for alchemical and chemical experiments. On the second medallion, a human head appears between two branches of holly intertwined and tied in the centre by a ribbon. Above the head is a six-pointed star. On the third medallion, a fire is lit at the top of a justice tower. At the base of a portal a geometric shape suggests a vase, and on the sides there is a strange craft with wheels (left)

and a bridge (right). This allegorical ensemble refers to the presence here of Hermetic Masonry derived from ancient Egyptian mysteries, which the Italian adventurer and self-styled magician Count Alessandro di Cagliostro organised and brought back from the brotherhood of Copts in the Sinai desert. In France, Cagliostro founded the Loge Sagesse Triomphante (Triumphant Wisdom Lodge) at Lyon on 27 July 1786, under the auspices of the Egyptian Coptic and androgynous Masonry (he was the 'Grand-Copte' of this rite in which both men and women participated). This order which Cagliostro founded aimed to 'know, teach and propagate Masonry in its purity and its primitive form'. Cagliostro, during his second stay in Paris, lived a few steps away at 1, rue Saint-Claude.

On the first medallion, the Phoenician ship marks the crossing of the mare incognita, a name given by ancient alchemists to the philosophical mercury they obtained during the 'great navigation' (i.e. alchemical operations). Distilled (purified) water is indicated by the presence of the still on the other side. At the top, the square and the interlaced compasses represent the peak of the presence of Hermetic masonry, and the rose at the top of the compass is the Philosopher's Rose, which becomes a sign of immortality. On the second medallion, the human bust represents the god Hermès, founder of Hermetic science, surmounted by the luminous star of the Initiate who is reborn illuminated by the Spirit of triumphant Wisdom. Finally, on the third medallion, the lit lighthouse serves to represent the 'oven' of philosophers, at whose base is the crucible where the coarse elements 'cook' in order to extract the quintessence which is vital for the evolution of the Great Alchemical Work. This progress is represented by the wheeled machine transforming the elements to render them subtle. To reach this state of perfection, a bridge is needed to bring the alchemist closer to this sacred Fire and away from the condition of the ordinary mortal.

CARAN FAÇADE RELIEF

A very strange relief, little known even to local residents

Archives Nationales – CARAN
11, rue des Quatre Fils
Metro Rambuteau

Built in a contemporary style between 1986 and 1988 by architect Stanislas Fiszer, the CARAN (Centre d'Accueil et de Recherche des Archives Nationales) completes the remarkable quadrilateral of the

Parisian National Archives site. Unknown to most Parisians and even local residents, a surprising bronze relief was designed by the Czech painter and sculptor Ivan Theimer, at 11, rue des Quatre Fils. Opened around 1300 in the New Town of the Temple, the street took its name from one of its inns evoking a famous *chanson de geste* (folkloric song): *La Chanson des quatre fils Aymon* (Song of the Four Sons of Aymon).

The song tells of the conflict between Aalard, Renaud, Guichard and Richard, the four sons of Duke Aymon of Dordogne, and Emperor Charlemagne, whose vassals they were. It all began when the four brothers were presented at Charlemagne's court in Paris to be knighted. Everything went well until a game of chess turned into a brawl, and the eldest of the Aymon sons, Renaud, killed his opponent, Charlemagne's favourite nephew, in exasperation. The four brothers fled on the back of Bayard, the magical horse that Renaud had received from Charlemagne during his enthronement, and took refuge in the Ardennes. Pursued by their father, they built their own castle, Montessor.

Driven off a few years later, by Charlemagne's troops, they were helped by their cousin Maugis, who later allowed them to build a castle and offered Renaud the hand of his sister Aélis (Alice) in marriage. The castle was then besieged by Charlemagne's troops, and Renaud successively competed against his cousin Ogier and Roland, one of Charlemagne's 12 warriors, hero of the eponymous song. Renaud and Maugis then made a pilgrimage to Jerusalem, where they fought alongside the Crusaders, and on their way back to Palermo, helped King Simon of Puglia repel an invasion by the Saracens.

Charlemagne, weary of fighting, finally made peace with the four brothers on condition that Bayard was returned to him. The horse, which had been thrown into the Meuse with a stone around its neck, survived and took refuge in an Ardennes forest. After another pilgrimage to the Holy Land and the death of his wife, Renaud decided to work with the builders of Cologne Cathedral, but members of the Masonic brotherhood killed him and threw his body into the Rhine.

Two of the brothers are sculpted in the round, probably Renaud and Richard who are at the forefront of the story, while the other two, Aalard and Guichard, are engraved on the background panelling. And Bayard, the enchanted horse who had wonderful gifts, such as the ability to adjust his size to the number of riders, is shown as a totemic animal responsible for protecting Renaud and his brothers.

Ivan Theimer also designed the very strange monument to human rights on the Champ de Mars (see page 238).

One of the world's four temples of positivism

5, rue Payenne
Opening hours and days discretionary, information at +33 1 44 78 01 97
Metro Saint-Paul

A listed historic monument, the Chapelle de l'Humanité is the only Positivist temple in Europe. It was inaugurated on a misunderstanding: the Positivist Church of Mexico which bought the place in 1903 believed it to be the house of Clotilde de Vaux (see opposite). In fact, she had probably died at No. 7. No. 5 was a private mansion that François Mansart had built for himself and in which he died in 1666. Today, the first floor houses a chapel of Humanity, a faithful reproduction on a smaller scale of Auguste Comte's plan. It comprises 14 pointed arches corresponding to the thirteen months of the calendar as redefined by Comte, the fourteenth arch being dedicated to Héloïse, who was held in high regard by the philosopher. The allegory on the altar represents *Humanity Holding the Future in its Arms* by Eduardo de Sá. There is also a bust of Auguste Comte by Antoine Etex.

The street frontage has been transformed by the architect Gustave Goy: you can see there a statue of Clotilde de Vaux as 'virgin mother' and a bust of Auguste Comte with the inscription: *L'amour pour principe et l'ordre pour base, le progrès pour but* (Love as a principle and order as the basis, progress as the goal).

There are only three other Positivist temples in the world, all three of which are in Brazil: Rio de Janeiro, Porto Alegre and Curitiba.

Auguste Comte's house in the 6th arrondissement can also be visited (see page 219).

© Jean-Pierre Dalbéra

A misunderstanding?

The Positivist Church of Brazil, which bought the place in 1903, thought it was the home of Clotilde de Vaux, a French intellectual, known to have inspired Auguste Comte's secular and positivist 'Religion of Humanity'. She probably died at No. 7, while No. 5 was a private mansion architect François Mansart had built for himself, and where he died in 1666.

Positivism inspiring Brazil's motto

Although the social theorist Saint-Simon had already used the term 'positivism', it was the philosopher Auguste Comte (1798–1857), secretary of the movement for six years, who made it widely known. Comte's positivist doctrine is linked to confidence in the progress of humanity through science and to belief in the benefits of scientific rationality as opposed to metaphysics. The word comes from references to 'positive' or 'exact' sciences such as mathematics, physics, etc. In 1845, Auguste Comte fell hopelessly in love with Clotilde de Vaux and his scientific positivism took a religious form that was intended to reconcile the principles of scientific rationality with human love. Positivism, little heard of today, had enormous influence in the 19th century, particularly in South America: notably being behind the motto *Ordem e Progresso* (Order and Progress) on the Brazilian flag.

SYSTÈME DE COMMÉMORATION.   19

CULTE CONCRET DE L'HUMANITÉ,

POUR

PRÉPARER L'OCCIDENT AU CULTE ABSTRAIT, SEUL DÉFINITIF.

	TYPES MENSUELS.	TYPES HEBDOMADAIRES.
L'ANTIQUITÉ.	Janvier. . . . . . . MOÏSE . . . . (*la théocratie initiale.*)	Numa, Bouddha, Confucius, Mahomet.
	Février. . . . . . . HOMÈRE . . . . (*la poésie ancienne.*)	Eschyle, Phidias, Plaute, Virgile.
	Mars. . . . . . . ARISTOTE . . . (*la philosophie ancienne.*)	Thalès, Pythagore, Socrate, Platon.
	Avril. . . . . . . ARCHIMÈDE . . . (*la science ancienne.*)	Hippocrate, Apollonius, Hipparque, Pline l'Ancien.
	Mai. . . . . CÉSAR . . . . (*la civilisation militaire.*)	Thémistocle, Alexandre, Ulpien, Trajan.
LE MOYEN AGE.	Juin. . . . . . . SAINT-PAUL . . . (*le catholicisme.*)	Saint-Augustin, Hildebrand, Saint-Bernard, Bossuet.
	Juillet. . . . . . CHARLEMAGNE . . (*la civilisation féodale.*)	Alfred, Godefroi, Innocent III, Saint-Louis.
LA PRÉPARATION MODERNE.	Août. . . . . . . DANTE . . . . (*l'épopée moderne.*)	Arioste, Raphaël, Tasse, Milton.
	Septembre. . . GUTTEMBERG . . (*l'industrie moderne.*)	Colomb, Vaucanson, Watt, Montgolfier.
	Octobre. . . . . SHAKESPEARE . . (*le drame moderne.*)	Calderon, Corneille, Molière, Mozart.
	Novembre. . . . DESCARTES . . . (*la philosophie moderne.*)	Saint-Thomas-d'Aquin, le chancelier Bacon, Leibnitz, Hume.
	Décembre. . . . FRÉDÉRIC . . . (*la politique moderne.*)	Louis XI, Guillaume-le-Taciturne, Richelieu, Cromwell.
	Final. . . . . . . BICHAT . . . . (*la science moderne.*)	Galilée, Newton, Lavoisier, Gall.

Jour complémentaire. . . . . Fête générale des MORTS.

CENTRAL PAVILION OF THE TUILERIES

The most important relic of the Tuileries Palace

Square Georges Cain – 8–14, rue Payenne
Metro Chemin Vert

The most important relic of the former Tuileries Palace is found in the charming Square Georges Cain. After the entrance to the square, on the right, is the pediment of the central pavilion of the palace, with its clock acquired in 1901 from the entrepreneur Achille Picart. He had won the contract for the demolition of the Tuileries by tender on 4 December 1882, and had initially installed this same pediment at the entrance to his demolition company. The idea of this square was to create a kind of open-air museum of the remains of demolished monuments from the capital and its surroundings. In addition to the Tuileries pediment, which stands on part of the door of Saint-Germain-en-Laye Castle, framed by columns from the palace, there is a rose window in the square of a ceiling from the Hôtel de Ville (City Hall, destroyed during the Commune) and the remains of the Hôtel de Thou, which was destroyed during the construction of rue Danton in 1898 (formerly 6 and 8, rue des Poitevins), as well as Merovingian sarcophagi. Construction of Tuileries Palace was begun in 1564 for Catherine de' Medici (Henri II's widow) in front of the Louvre. The tile factories (tuileries) that had stood on the chosen spot since the Middle Ages gave the new royal residence and gardens their name. The palace's 266 metre long façade linked the two wings of the Louvre towards the gardens, in front of the street now separating the Carrousel gardens from the Tuileries. Enlarged under successive reigns, the palace became the residence of many sovereigns, including Henry IV, Louis XIV, Louis XVI, Louis XVIII, Napoleon I and Napoleon III, until its destruction by fire in May 1871.

Electronic nightingale

While resting on one of the benches in the square you may hear the song of a nightingale. This is actually the work of Erik Samakh. The song is triggered by a solar sensor which reflects the climatic parameters that influence bird behaviour, especially at dusk.

For more on the other relics of the Tuileries Palace, see the following double-page spread.

Other relics of the Tuileries

9, rue Murillo: fragments of the grand staircase of Percier and Fontaine as well as constructions of the Renaissance architect Philibert Delorme, installed by architect Gustave Clausse in the courtyard of his 1870 building. He occupied the ground floor and the first floor, built of stone, and rented out the upper floors, for which he had used brick. Clausse also installed a Florentine bust, perhaps of Alphonse d'Este, and two Venetian capitals in the courtyard.

- Parc Monceau: two fragments of columns next to each other. Jardins du Trocadéro: a window on the courtyard.

- Cour de l'École des Beaux-Arts: Eugène Müntz, who was the National School of Fine Arts collections curator, brought in a significant number of relics.

- Jardin du Ministère de l'Éducation Nationale (110, rue de Grenelle – not open to the public): column shafts and capitals.

- École Spéciale d'Architecture (254, boulevard Raspail): resembling the Beaux-Arts de Paris, in reaction to which Émile Trélat had participated in the foundation of this private architectural school, and several relics were moved there.

- Tuileries Garden: two vestiges (a Delorme arcade and a corner span of the Bullant façade) were installed in 1884 at the foot of the Musée du Jeu de Paume but have been dismantled.

- Courtyard of Hôtel de Fleury (former headquarters of the École des Ponts et Chaussées at 28, rue des Saints-Pères): the superb arcade by Delorme was rebuilt in 2011 at the Cour Marly of the Louvre.

- Beautiful statues that used to grace the pediment of the present-day square Georges Cain (see previous double-page spread), including two statues by Philippe de Buyster, are now in the hall under the Arc de Triomphe of the Carrousel du Louvre.

- Cité des Fusains (22, rue de Tourlaque, see page 485): fragments of columns.

– Château de la Punta, former property of Duke Jérôme Pozzo di Borgo, above the Bay of Ajaccio, which took over entire façades of the demolished palace (see photo opposite and *Secret Corsica* by the same publisher).

– Manoir des Gandines (Essarts-le-Roi in Yvelines): several columns and bas-reliefs. Château Esterhazy (from the name of the family owners) in north-western Hungary: grid of Carrousel courtyard (note that the castle gardens are a copy of those at Versailles).

– Park of Villa Magali, in Saint-Raphaël (Var): 43 fragments of the Tuileries Palace (and the Hôtel de Ville) were acquired by proprietor Léon Carvalho, who was a former director of the Opéra-Comique. Another vestige is preserved in the Saint-Sébastien gardens at Saint-Raphaël.

– Villages of Bolbec and Barentin (Seine-Maritime): Tuileries vestiges that had been brought to the Suresnes villa of English fashion designer Charles Worth, and were dispersed there following the extension of a hospital. Those in the green (open-air) theatre of Barentin were removed because of their poor condition.

– Marly-le-Roi: for the park of his Verduron estate, Victorian playwright Sardou collected from the Tuileries a carved plaque with a central solar emblem and column drums, with fleur de lys and royal emblems.

– Domont: stonemason Stéphane Dervillé installed several remains in his Ombreval castle.

– Berlin (Steglitz-Zehlendorf – Schwanenwerder island): columns and parts of the wall (see *Secret Berlin* by the same publisher).

– *Le Figaro* newspaper acquired marbles that were made into paperweights and offered to some subscribers.

– Quito (Ecuador): some balustrades from the Tuileries were bought from France and installed at the presidential palace.

AMIS DE L'INSTRUCTION LIBRARY

19th century Paris

54, rue de Turenne
Saturday 3pm—6pm, outside school holidays and by appointment
bai3@orange.fr – bai.asso.fr
Metro Chemin Vert

In 1861 in the Marais district, workers and artisans gathered together books of their choice and established the Amis de l'Instruction library (Friends of Instruction). Its innovation was to allow books to be borrowed and taken home, providing the general public for the first time with the opportunity of studying at their leisure.

The wonderfully old-fashioned name of the library illustrates perfectly the utopia of 'popular instruction' that motivated its founders. An interesting detail is that women, who were also allowed to consult the books, were charged half price.

Since the library remained quite private, only its members and some of the inhabitants of the district were aware of its existence. Most of the original 20,000 volumes have been preserved, but home borrowing has now been prohibited in an effort to preserve these works. Novels, essays and periodicals from the period may, however, be studied at the library, in a setting and ambience from another century that reinvigorates the senses.

NEARBY
Delacroix' Pietà ⑯
Saint-Denys-du-Saint-Sacrement church
68 bis, rue de Turenne
Daily 7.30am-7.30pm except on Monday, 7.30am–10am
Metro Saint-Sébastien – Froissart

Few Parisians know that a major work by Delacroix is housed in Saint-Denys-du-Saint-Sacrement church. Many experts consider *Pietà*, painted between 1840 and 1844, to be one of the artist's masterpieces. Besides those held by Paris museums, the churches of Saint-Paul-Saint-Louis (4th arrondissement) and Saint-Sulpice (6th arrondissement) also possess Delacroix paintings.

The leaves of the carriage doors at 1, rue Saint-Claude ⑰

Metro Saint-Sébastien – Froissart

The leaves of the carriage doors at 1, rue Saint-Claude are said to have been salvaged from the door of the palace of the Grand Prior of the Temple. This house accommodated Cagliostro in 1783 and 1785.

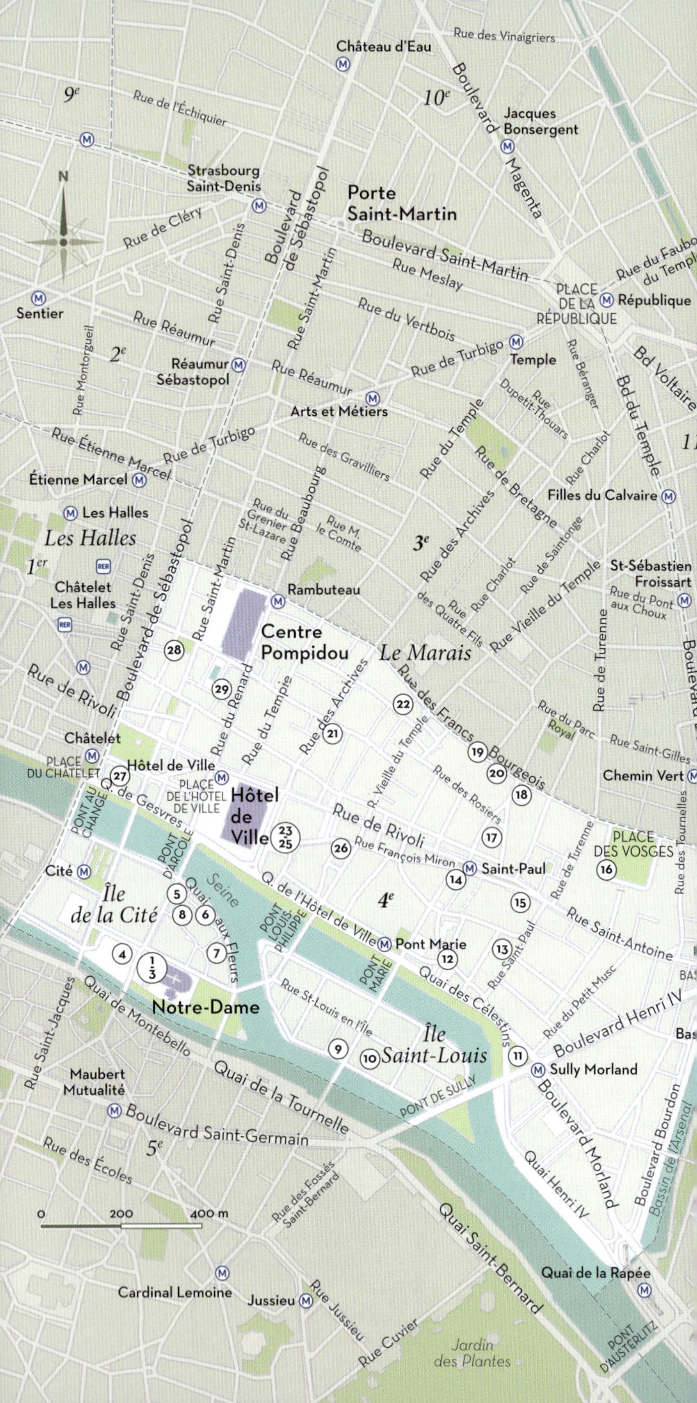

Rue des Vinaigriers
Château d'Eau
9e
Rue de l'Échiquier
10e
Boulevard Magenta
Jacques Bonsergent
Strasbourg Saint-Denis
Porte Saint-Martin
Rue de Cléry
Boulevard de Sébastopol
Rue Saint-Denis
Boulevard Saint-Martin
Rue Meslay
Rue du Faubourg du Temple
PLACE DE LA RÉPUBLIQUE
République
Sentier
Rue Montorgueil
Rue Réaumur
Rue Saint-Martin
Rue du Vertbois
Rue de Turbigo
Temple
Bd Voltaire
2e
Réaumur Sébastopol
Rue Réaumur
Bd du Temple
Arts et Métiers
Rue Béranger
Rue Dupetit-Thouars
Rue Petit-Thouars
11
Rue Étienne Marcel
Rue de Turbigo
Rue des Gravilliers
Rue du Temple
Rue de Bretagne
Rue Charlot
Étienne Marcel
3e
Rue des Archives
Rue de Saintonge
Filles du Calvaire
Les Halles
Rue du Grenier St-Lazare
Rue Beaubourg
Rue M. le Comte
Rue Charlot
St-Sébastien Froissart
Les Halles
Rue des Quatre Fils
Rue du Pont aux Choux
1er
Châtelet Les Halles
Rambuteau
Rue de Turenne
Rue Saint-Denis
Boulevard de Sébastopol
Rue Saint-Martin
Centre Pompidou
Le Marais
28
Rue de Rivoli
29
Rue du Renard
Rue du Temple
Rue des Archives
Rue des Francs Bourgeois
Rue du Parc Royal
Rue Saint-Gilles
22
Châtelet
21
R. Vieille du Temple
19
Chemin Vert
27
Hôtel de Ville
20
PLACE DU CHÂTELET
Rue des Rosiers
18
PLACE DE L'HÔTEL DE VILLE
Hôtel de Ville
Rue de Rivoli
17
PLACE DES VOSGES
Q. de Gesvres
23 25
Rue François Miron
26
Saint-Paul
16
PONT AU CHANGE
PONT D'ARCOLE
Quai aux Fleurs
14
Rue de Turenne
Cité
Q. de l'Hôtel de Ville
4e
15
Seine
5
Île de la Cité
8 6
PONT LOUIS-PHILIPPE
13
Rue Saint-Antoine
4
1 3
7
PONT MARIE
Pont Marie
12
Boulevard Henri IV
Notre-Dame
Quai de Montebello
Rue St-Louis en l'île
Quai des Célestins
Rue du Petit Musc
Bas
Rue Saint-Jacques
9
10
Île Saint-Louis
11
Sully Morland
Maubert Mutualité
Quai de la Tournelle
PONT DE SULLY
Boulevard Morland
Boulevard Bourdon
Bassin de l'Arsenal
Boulevard Saint-Germain
Quai Henri IV
5e
Rue des Écoles
Rue des Fossés Saint-Bernard
Quai Saint-Bernard
0   200   400 m
Cardinal Lemoine
Jussieu
Rue Jussieu
Rue Cuvier
Jardin des Plantes
Quai de la Rapée
PONT D'AUSTERLITZ

Once a month, Christ's crown of thorns is presented to the faithful

Notre-Dame de Paris cathedral – Place Jean-Paul II (Parvis Notre-Dame)
+33 1 42 34 56 10 – notredamedeparis.fr
Every first Friday of the month and Fridays during Lent at 3pm
and Good Friday 10am–5pm
Metro Cité

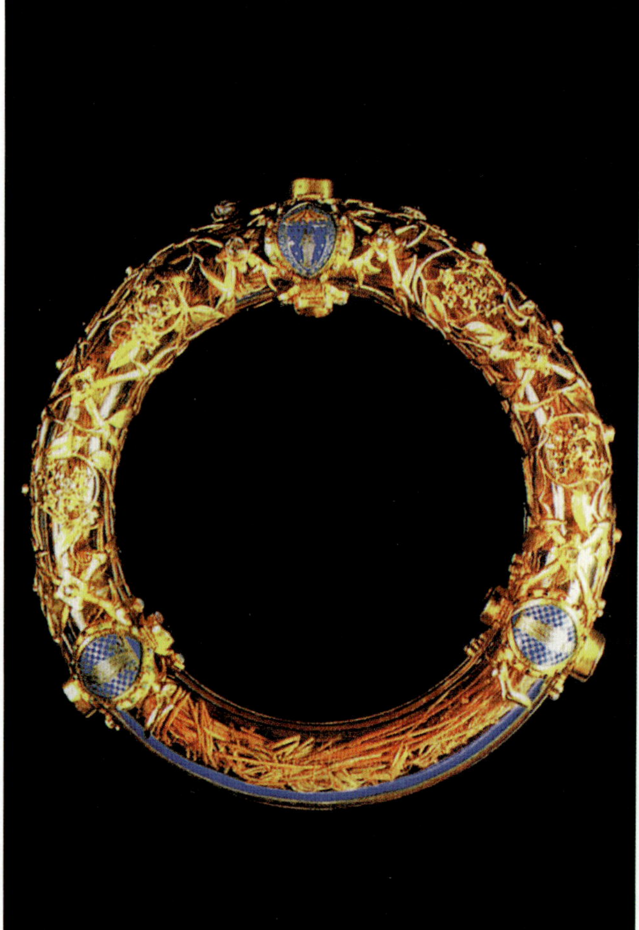

© Chevaliers du Saint-Sépulcre

Oddly enough, the immense majority of Parisians are totally unaware that Christ's crown of thorns, considered to be Christianity's second most important relic after the Holy Shroud of Turin, is presented in Notre-Dame cathedral once a month for veneration by the faithful. Contrary to common belief, the nearby Saint-Chapelle no longer has any relics: the other objects related to Christ's Passion (a nail and a fragment of the Cross itself) are also at Notre-Dame.

The first Friday of each month, in an atmosphere of profound devotion, the Knights of the Holy Sepulchre perform the duty of displaying the sacred crown to the crowd of worshippers. If most of those gathered are tourists who are blithely indifferent to the occasion, the fervour of the few Parisians present is impressive: when their turn comes to kiss the relic, it is by no means rare to see tears of emotion roll down their cheeks.

The first reference to this holy relic dates from the year 409, when Saint Paulinus of Nola mentions it as one of the relics at the Mount Zion basilica in Jerusalem. Transferred to Byzantium to preserve it from being pillaged by the forces of the Persian Empire, the relics were then sold to the Venetians in 1238 by the Latin emperor of Constantinople, Baldwin II, who was experiencing financial difficulties. The French king Saint Louis (1126–1270) purchased them in 1239 and ordered the construction of a suitable chapel in Paris to house them: the Sainte-Chapelle (some of the stained-glass windows in the chapel depict this event).

After the Revolution, however, the relics were entrusted to the canons of the Notre-Dame chapter. In the 19th century, two reliquaries were built to house the crown of thorns, one commissioned by Napoleon I and the other by Napoleon III. They now lie empty, but are on display in the cathedral treasury (open to the public daily, 9am–6pm, except Sunday mornings). The authenticity of the relics is of course difficult to prove, although on the one occasion when the reliquary in which they now reside was actually opened, in 1940, it was observed that while the leaves were dried, the ring of braided rushes was still green!

THE ALCHEMIST
OF NOTRE-DAME DE PARIS

Notre-Dame, an alchemical cathedral?

Notre-Dame de Paris cathedral
Metro Cité

As the inscrutable Fulcanelli explains in *The Mystery of the Cathedrals* (*Le Mystère des Cathédrales*, 1926) Notre-Dame has a series of sculptures inspired by alchemy. There's even one of an alchemist among the gargoyles on the balcony joining the two towers, seemingly observing the nave opening up before him.

Fulcanelli wrote of the figure: 'The whole cathedral is a silent but illustrated glorification of the ancient science of Hermes (Hermeticism); it also preserves one of its oldest craftsmen. Notre-Dame de Paris has, in fact, kept its alchemist: near the axis at the centre of the majestic building, in the angle of the northern tower, in the midst of a procession of chimeras, stands the bust of an old man made of stone. It is he, the alchemist of Notre-Dame.'

Another set of sculptures on the west portal of Notre-Dame is identified by Fulcanelli as *Alchemy or Hermetic Philosophy*. He comments (in the same work): 'Alchemy is represented by a woman whose head touches the clouds. Seated on a throne, she holds a sceptre – a symbol of her sovereignty – in her left hand, while in her right hand are two books, one closed (esotericism) and the other open (exotericism). Between her legs and resting on her chest, she holds a nine-step ladder, *scala philosophorum*, a symbol of the patience her followers must show during the nine successive operations of Hermetic Work.

On her left, a woman raises a distilling flask. It contains the quintessence of the surrounding toxic plants. It is an evil from which, through art, a good can be extracted.

On her right, another woman holds an astrolabe, an astronomical instrument (referring to the occult influence of planets on metals, or rather on the essence animating them).

These three characters all depict the idea of allowing the invisible to manifest itself, as well as the nature and understanding of its subtle laws (or primordial rules governing the visible and invisible universe).'

For more information on alchemy, see page 102.

BISCORNET'S IRONWORK ON PORTAIL SAINTE-ANNE

The Devil's blacksmith?

Notre-Dame de Paris cathedral
Metro Cité

Made up of abundant arabesques of remarkable finesse and great lightness, ranging from drawings of flowers and foliage to animal forms, the ironwork of Notre-Dame's Sainte-Anne portal is so perfect that it's said to have been inspired by the Devil himself.

According to legend, when the cathedral was under construction, the clerics of the future diocese commissioned a blacksmith named Biscornet to work on the ironwork scroll work of the doors.

The colossal order went far beyond his abilities, so he was obliged to summon the Devil to his aid. Biscornet thus made a pact with the Prince of Darkness and signed the diabolical contract with blood from his index finger.

Satan then played the part of the blacksmith, quickly completing the work requested by the clerics of Saint-Denis with diabolical mastery and perfection. As soon as it was finished, the wretched blacksmith died of a heart attack and his immortal soul went to hell, as he'd sold it to the Devil.

In fact, according to an anonymous article published in a Parisian newspaper in 1833, the blacksmith Biscornet was identified as Gobineau de Montluisant, apparently an outstanding ironworker from

Chartres. But metalwork was often linked to the Devil in the Middle Ages because it calls for the mastery of fire, indispensable in the forge and also associated with the underworld. This is what spurred the legend: metalwork was by definition a diabolical undertaking, and as the Devil was represented by a head with two horns (see opposite) it wasn't long before a man known as Biscornet was said to have made a pact to sell his soul.

The portal bears an 'asylum ring'. In the Middle Ages, grasping this type of ring on the door of a church gave the right to asylum.

When 'Biscornet' means 'two-horned'

Etymologically, Biscornet means two-horned, so it's just an allegorical name for the horned Devil, as represented at that time (see below).

Why does the Devil often take the form of a two-horned goat?

Blacksmiths, associated with the Devil, are commonly involved in initiatory rites such as those of the Kabyric mysteries in ancient Greece. The Cabeiri or Kabeiri, a name likely originating from the verb *kaiein* (to shine), were ancient Greek deities considered to be the sons (or grandsons) of Hephaestus (Vulcan in Roman mythology), god of the underground fire who was worshipped at volcanic sites such as Lemnos in present day Greece. The 'cabeiri goat' was a symbol associated with these deities and, from there, the superstitious popular imagination conceived the fantastic form of the Devil as a goat, an animal with two horns.

Why does the Devil smell of sulphur?

Sulphur is a naturally occurring element frequently found in volcanic regions, such as the Kawah Ijen volcano in Java, Indonesia, known for its sulphur blocks that labourers carry up from the depths of the crater. As volcanoes are associated with underground fire, sulphur was soon linked to the Devil himself.

> The Devil in the form of a two-horned goat appears at Notre-Dame's Portal of the Last Judgement, which bears a carved illustration of the judgement of God – where the righteous will inhabit the New Jerusalem descended from heaven to Earth, and where the unrighteous and sinners will be in the hands of the Devil, as shown here.

NEARBY

Names of former streets in Notre-Dame courtyard 

Metro Cité

Several paving stones scattered around the courtyard are engraved with street names: rue de Venise, rue Chaudron, etc. These names correspond to the streets that ran by here before Baron Haussmann, in 1865, developed the square to occupy a space six times larger than when the cathedral was built.

> A different layout from the classic stones is also marked on the paving, indicating the contours of the old basilica of Saint-Étienne, an early Christian church that preceded Notre-Dame on Île de la Cité.

COBBLESTONES OF 6, RUE DE LA COLOMBE

Traces of the first Gallo-Roman enclosure of Paris

6, rue de la Colombe
Metro Cité

An inscription on the pavement at 6, rue de la Colombe records the discovery of traces of the base of the Gallo-Roman wall, embodied in a 2.7-metre-wide cobblestone track across the street. The Gallo-Roman walls of Lutèce were built during the first half of the 4th century AD to resist barbarian invasions.

With a length of 1,500 metres, they included the greater part of the island of Lutèce. This was enlarged (by including the neighbouring islets), filled in (from 3 to 7 metres depending on the area) and surrounded by quays, and thus became Île de la Cité. The wall of the enclosure was 2.5 metres thick and 7 to 8 metres high, with a round path inside and a crenellated wall outside.

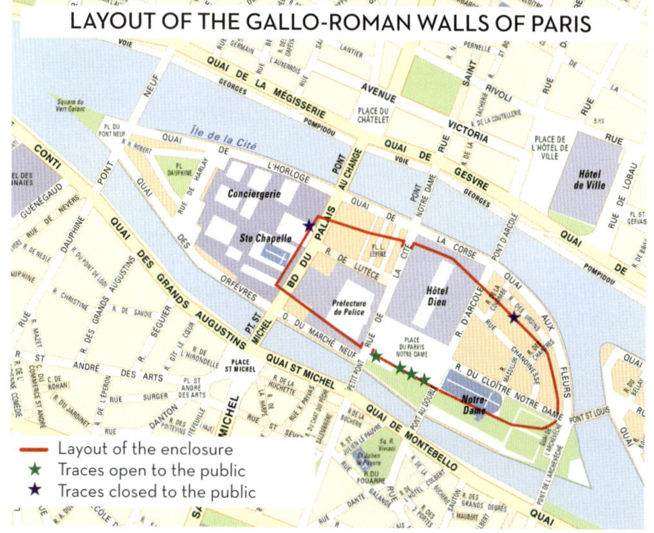

Other remains of the Gallo-Roman walls of Paris

Place du Parvis-Notre-Dame, where other remains (65 metres in total) were discovered between 1967 and 1970 during the construction of an underground car park. They can be seen in the archaeological crypt. In the Palais de Justice de Paris, in the 1st arrondissement, some remains, closed to the general public, have also been uncovered. At 18–20, rue Chanoinesse the officers might show you one of these remains if asked, including the aptly named 'butcher's stone' (see below for the tale of the barber who lived there).

A barber who slashes his customers

At 18–20, rue Chanoinesse, where there are remains of the first Gallo-Roman walls of Paris (see above), two houses once stood whose occupants had developed a formidable scheme. In one, a barber was actually cutting the throat of some of his clients who had come to be shaved, including students who were staying with the canons of Notre-Dame (hence the name of the street). He then passed the bodies to his sidekick, a pastry chef, who used the flesh to make pâtés that he sold to the canons! The barber and the baker were burned alive in 1387. The pastry chef is said to have prepared his sinister pâtés on this very stone from the wall – the reason why it's sometimes called the 'butcher's stone'.

THE MOCK MEDIEVAL HOUSE OF FERNAND POUILLON

An architectural forgery

1, rue des Ursins – Metro Cité

Few Parisians will have noticed that this medieval-looking house in fact dates from the 1960s. It owes its existence to the talent of the French architect Fernand Pouillon who successfully incorporated many elements from the past into this modern dwelling. The architect lived here himself for nearly a year.

Fernand Pouillon: a convict architect decorated with the Legion of Honour

Born in 1912 at Cancon (Lot-et-Garonne), Fernand Pouillon studied architecture at Marseille. Although his first buildings in Marseille and Aix date from before the Second World War, he remains best known for the reconstruction of the Vieux-Port of Marseille, ravaged by the Nazi occupation. The scandal surrounding the bankruptcy of the property company, Le Comptoir du Logement, led to him being sent to prison, from which he later escaped. After a period spent hiding in Italy, he then presented himself of his own accord at his trial and was sentenced to three years. During his imprisonment he wrote two books, the most famous being *Les Pierres sauvages* (*The Wild Stones*). He later worked on major urban projects in Algeria (including the 200 columns of 'Climat de France') and was awarded the Legion of Honour by President François Mitterrand. He died in 1986 at his château de Belcastel in the Aveyron region.

NEARBY

9 and 11, quai aux Fleurs: the memory of Héloïse ⑦ and Abélard

Metro Cité

At No. 9, quai aux Fleurs, a plaque evokes the memory of Héloïse and Abélard, the celebrated star-crossed lovers, whose story somewhat resembles that of Romeo and Juliet in Verona. The buildings at No. 9 and 11 also feature stone medallions depicting the couple on their façades.

The tombstones at 26, rue Chanoinesse ⑧

Metro Cité

In the courtyard at No. 26, rue Chanoinesse, some slabs covering the ground bear Gothic-looking inscriptions. These slabs are in fact tombstones from a religious establishment once located on the Île de la Cité.

ADAM MICKIEWICZ, CHOPIN AND BIEGAS MUSEUMS

A full immersion in Polish artistic life

6, quai d'Orléans
+33 1 55 42 83 83 – ibpp.eu/fr/musees/a-lattention-des-visiteurs
See opening hours on the website
Metro Pont Marie or Maubert-Mutualité

The Polish Library (Bibliothèque Polonaise) has been housed since 1853 in the heart of Île Saint-Louis in a handsome listed 17th century building that belongs to the Société Historique et Littéraire Polonaise. Founded in 1832 by Polish immigrants fleeing from the brutal repression of an insurrection against the Russian occupiers of their country, this society had as its aim 'gathering into one body and disseminating writings and documents related to the history of Poland, its present and future, with the goal of fostering and consolidating world sympathy to the Polish cause.'

The library today possesses over 200,000 works and publications, including some rare items such as the personal letters of Frédéric Chopin, the minutes of the Polish Diet in the 18th century, a very precious 16th century edition of Ptolemy's Map of Slavic Lands, and the three original editions (printed in Basel, Nuremberg and Amsterdam) of Copernicus' *De revolutionibus orbium coelestium* (*On the Revolution of the Celestial Spheres* – 1534). In a deliciously romantic atmosphere, three small museums have also been installed in this building. On the first floor, in a small salon, personal souvenirs, portraits, and engravings of Frédéric Chopin have been gathered together. On the second floor is a museum devoted to Adam Mickiewicz, the great Polish romantic poet,

born in 1798 in what is now Lithuania, occupying three rooms full of personal objects, manuscripts of his poems, and documents relating to his activities as a publicist and politician, as well as portraits and sculptures of Mickiewicz carried out by artists of his day. The visit ends on the top floor with the Boleslas Biegas museum, presenting the work of this Polish painter and sculptor who lived at the end of the 19th century and beginning of the 20th, along with several paintings and sculptures by other contemporary Polish artists.

OPENWORK BELL TOWER OF SAINT-LOUIS-EN-L'ÎLE CHURCH

To limit wind resistance …

Saint-Louis-en-l'Île church
9 bis, rue Saint-Louis-en-l'Île
Metro Sully-Morland or Pont Marie

Dedicated to Saint Louis, King of France as Louis IX from 1226 to 1270 (he came to pray on what became the Île de Saint-Louis, then occupied by cattle, and took the cross from here on a crusade to Jerusalem in 1269), the church of Saint-Louis-en-l'Île was built from 1656 to replace a chapel dating from 1623 that had grown too small.

On 2 February 1701 a storm destroyed the roof of the old building, killing a number of worshippers. So the new church had to be completed, for which a royal lottery raised funds (as for Tréguier in Brittany).

The building, finally consecrated in 1726 after several trials and tribulations, had a bell tower at the transept crossing, but it was struck by lightning in 1740.

In 1765 the current bell tower was built, with openings, to withstand the wind – the church had been built in the middle of the Seine, often subject to strong blasts as witnessed by the storm of 1701.

BASE OF A TOWER FROM BASTILLE PRISON

One of the last vestiges of the Bastille

Square Henri Galli
Metro Bastille

Stuck between the traffic of boulevard Henri IV and quai Henri IV (officially in square Henri Galli), this remains one of the few vestiges from the Bastille (see the following double-page spread). In 1898–99, during the construction of métro line 1, the foundations of the Tour de la Liberté (Liberty Tower, where the Marquis de Sade, among others, was incarcerated), which was one of the eight towers of the Bastille, were discovered at 211 and 236, rue Saint-Antoine. These remains were moved to their present location to preserve them. The inscription on the plaque at the base translates as: 'Remains of the Bastille foundations / Liberty Tower / discovered in 1899 / and transported to this location.'

© FLLL

Strange detour of Métro line 1

Instead of running straight as you might expect, line 1 bends strangely between Saint-Paul and Bastille, thus avoiding the foundations of the Tour de la Liberté.

No, 14 July doesn't commemorate the storming of the Bastille!

Although 14 July has been a day of national celebration in France since 1880, it doesn't commemorate the storming of the Bastille but the Fête de la Fédération (Festival of Federation) which took place a year later, on 14 July 1790, on the Esplanade du Champ-de-Mars and attended by Louis XVI. The festival was supposed to celebrate reconciliation and unity among all French people.

Egyptian mummies below the Bastille?

In the early 19th century, around the same time as the Concorde obelisk and a giraffe named Zarafa, the Viceroy of Egypt offered King Charles X of France a dozen carefully packaged mummies. After being exhibited in the Louvre for a while, the mummies failed to adapt to the Parisian climate and began to gave off a foul smell. In 1827 a decision was made to bury them in the Louvre gardens. Three years later, 32 victims of the 1830 July Revolution who had fallen here were buried in the same place. At the end of these revolutionary days, Charles' successor Louis-Philippe decided to offer a more dignified burial to the insurgents: the bodies were moved under the Bastille, without bothering too much that some of them were better preserved than others ...

It wasn't until 1940 that the vault was repaired that the body count was noted to be two higher than the number of insurgents officially buried ...

Nobody knows what happened to the other mummies. The vault in question can be seen from the river promenade along the Canal Saint-Martin, under the boulevard Richard Lenoir.

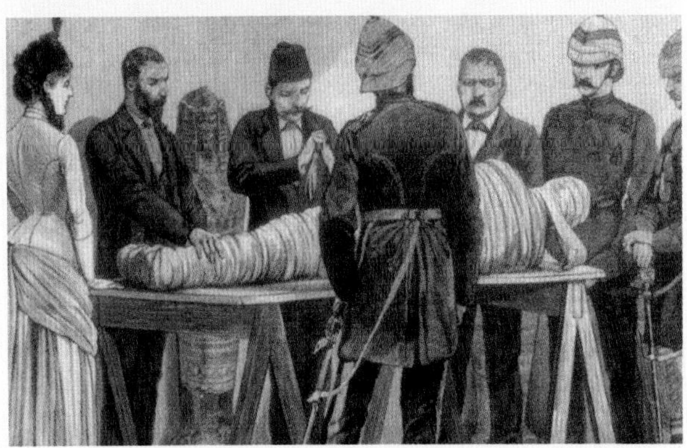

Other remains of the Bastille in the neighbourhood

On the platform of Bastille Métro station (line 5 – direction Bobigny) some stones remain from the counterscarp (outer wall) along the ditch of the prison enclosure. Yellow lines on the station platform trace the layout of the old fortress.

– The Métro entrance at the corner of boulevard Bourdon reveals another rampart of the fortress.

– At the beginning (north side) of the Bassin de l'Arsenal dock, on the right side looking at the Seine, you'll find a whole section of the wall of the prison ditch, now a retaining wall for the boulevard Bourdon.

– Remains of a Bastille cell: The cellar of the restaurant at 47, boulevard Henri IV occupies the site of a Bastille prison cell. The site is private and closed to the public.

– Cobblestones outlining the Bastille: At the beginning of rue Saint-Antoine, on the place de la Bastille side, you'll notice that some cobblestones seem to be oddly positioned in relation to the rest of the square. They mark the former location of part of the prison, as shown on the map on the wall plaque at 3, place de la Bastille.

Other remains of the Bastille elsewhere

The private contractor Palloy was responsible for the demolition of the Bastille. He didn't hesitate to sell stones, some of which were carved in the shapes of the fortress. Palloy also made models that were sent to the capitals of all French *départements* (administrative regions). Relics of the Bastille can be found in many places:

– Most of the stone was used to build the Pont de la Concorde, so 'the people can continuously trample on the old fortress'.

– In Sceaux, a suburb south of Paris, part of a house was built with stones from the Bastille, at 37, rue des Imbergères.

– The carillon is in the Musée Européen d'Art Campanaire (European Museum of Carillon Art), L'Isle-Jourdain (Gers *département*).

– One stone is kept at Pontoise town hall and another at Saumur town hall.

– Another stone is preserved on the wall of the Caisse d'Epargne building in Aix-en-Provence.

– La Fayette presented a key to the prison to George Washington. This is now in Mount Vernon Museum, Virginia, not far from Washington, D.C.

THE EMBEDDED CANNONBALL

'King of the French' rather than 'King of France'

Hôtel de Sens – Bibliothèque Forney
1, rue du Figuier
Metro Pont Marie

You need a particularly keen eye to spot the cannonball embedded at a height of several metres in the wall of the Hôtel de Sens. This cannonball, as the date inscribed on the wall indicates, was fired during the riots of 27, 28, and 29 July 1830 (known as the 'Trois Glorieuses' or the July Revolution).

The liberal members of the French parliament, a majority of whom were monarchists, took charge of the popular insurrection, saving the monarchy at the price of a change of dynasty. King Charles X was forced to abdicate in favour of the House of Orléans, the junior branch of the Bourbon family. The French gave themselves a new king in the person of Louis-Philippe I, crowned 'King of the French' and no longer 'King of France'. The July Monarchy (1830–1848) was proclaimed on 9 August 1830.

NEARBY

Remains of the enclosure wall of Philippe Auguste ⑬

Rue des Jardins-Saint-Paul
Metro Sully-Morland

The sports field of Charlemagne school enjoys a breathtaking view of the apse chapel of Saint-Paul church and a particularly well-preserved section of wall from the Philippe Auguste enclosure (80 metres long) between two towers, which was exposed after the Second World War. The Montigny tower, to the north, was torn down during the widening of rue Charlemagne, which crossed the enclosure at the site of the old Saint-Paul postern door.

For more on the Philippe Auguste enclosure, see the following double-page spread.

© Sam Spade

Philippe Auguste's defences (1190–1215)

The third wall in chronological order to encircle Paris was intended to encompass not only all of the city's existing dwellings, but also its surrounding fields, meadows, and orchards in order to ensure food supplies in case of siege. Its dimensions were considerable for the period, protecting an area of 250 hectares by ringing it with a wall measuring 5,400 metres in length. This wall had a height of 8 to 10 metres, with a thickness of 3 metres at its base and 2.30 metres at the top, including a walkway protected by crenellations. It had 65 defensive towers and 4 bigger towers located near the Seine River. Eventually, the city began to outgrow this wall, with various constructions being built against its inner or outer sides. Due to this, although much of the wall remains, it is rarely visible from the street. Places with public access, where the wall is clearly visible, include:

Right Bank

11, rue du Louvre, opposite the Bourse du Commerce

16, rue Étienne Marcel: beside the Jean sans Peur Tower (see page 68)

57–59, rue des Francs-Bourgeois: the Crédit Municipal tower

Rue des Jardins-Saint-Paul: the wall and two towers are well preserved

Left Bank

30 bis, rue du Cardinal-Lemoine

Rue Clovis

4, cour du Commerce-Saint-André: a tower in a shop

27, rue Mazarine: remains in an underground car park (see page 223)

13, passage Dauphine: a tower in a language school

There are also plaques (but no actual remains) recalling the existence of the wall at No. 113, rue Saint-Denis, No. 172, rue Saint-Jacques, No. 9, rue Mouffetard and No. 44, rue Dauphine.

© LPLT

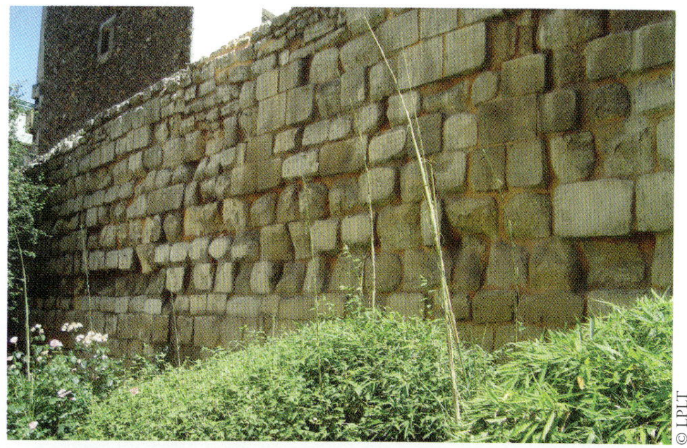

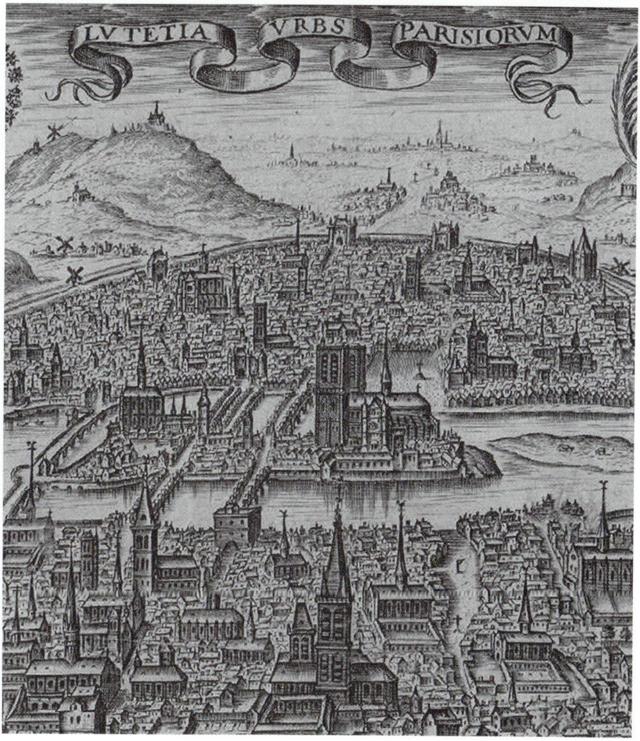

A dozen other remnants of Philippe Auguste's wall exist, but are located in private properties and inaccessible to the general public.

CERAMICS OF 133, RUE SAINT-ANTOINE

Really new Art Nouveau

133, rue Saint-Antoine – Les Chimères restaurant
Daily 7am–2am
Metro Saint-Paul

At the Saint-Paul exit, at the back of *Les Chimères* restaurant at 133, rue Saint-Antoine, a beautiful Art Nouveau ceramic panel depicts two peacocks resting on intertwining flowers.

The panel seems to date from the 1900s. Not so; as this is the work of designer Olivia Decaris, who in 2021 took inspiration from Art Nouveau to create floral motifs and arabesques, recreating the charm of early 20th century brasseries.

The earthenware tiles were hand-painted at Céramiques du Beaujolais, located in Arnas, near Lyon.

Don't miss the two lovely carved chimeras on the outside wall, added to the house in 1728. This used to be the mansion of Pierre Séguier (1588–1672), Minister of Justice, Chancellor of France and academician.

GRAFFITI AT SAINT-PAUL-SAINT-LOUIS CHURCH 

Message from the Paris Commune

Saint-Paul-Saint-Louis church, 99, rue Saint-Antoine
Daily 8am–8pm
Metro Saint-Paul

On the second pillar on the right side of the nave is a curious inscription: 'REPUBLIQUE FRANÇAISE OU LA MORT' (FRENCH REPUBLIC OR DEATH). This message probably dates from the Paris Commune (18 March to 28 May 1871), the time when, after the defeat of Napoleon III by the Prussians at the Battle of Sedan and the fall of the Second Empire, Republican convictions were increasingly strong.

The white marble of the high altar of Saint-Paul-Saint-Louis church, moved and remodelled at the time of Louis-Philippe, comes from fragments of the emperor's tomb at Invalides (see page 244).

The shells of the two fonts were offered by Victor Hugo when his daughter Léopoldine married in 1843.

NEARBY

Graffiti from 1764

Metro Chemin Vert

A curious passer-by might spot this striking graffiti on the wall of 11, place des Vosges: 1764 NICOLAS. It was engraved by a writer called Nicolas Restif de la Bretonne (1734–1806), who worked in the printing trade and was also a police informer.

He gained notoriety for engraving names, dates, etc. all around Paris, especially on the parapets of the nearby Île Saint-Louis. The graffiti there has not withstood the ravages of time, unlike that in Place des Vosges, which is protected by arcades.

SYNAGOGUE IN RUE PAVÉE

17

A rare Art Nouveau synagogue

10, rue Pavée
+ 33 1 48 87 21 54 – aciahdan@gmail.com
Visit only by appointment
Metro Saint-Paul

The only Art Nouveau building in the Marais neighbourhood and the last religious monument to be built here, the synagogue in rue Pavée is a curious sight. Its tall curved façade designed by Hector Guimard (see page 434) stands out from the nearby buildings. It remains one of the rare institutional and architectural traces of the immigrants who settled in this part of Paris. On Saturday mornings, on the Sabbath, when one sees the Orthodox Jews in traditional costume with side curls and kippas, quietly filing into the building for the ritual reading of the Torah, it is easy to believe that you have been transported back to the beginning of the last century. It was in 1913, as a response to the influx of Ashkenazi Jewish refugees from Central Europe since the end of the 19th century, that the Russo-Polish association, Agoudas Hakehilos, decided on the construction of a new synagogue on a narrow plot of land located in rue Pavée.

The choice of Hector Guimard as architect might seem surprising. It is hard to imagine the Parisian master of Art Nouveau joining forces with Orthodox Russian Jews, but it was in fact emblematic of their affirmation of a specifically French Yiddish culture. It was also Hector Guimard who designed the furnishings (lights, chandeliers, wall lamps, benches), as well as the stylised vegetal décor and ironwork railings. The building itself is made of hollow conglomerate on a concrete frame. The harmony between the rigour of a construction in reinforced concrete and the elegance of the façade's curves and counter-curves is complete.

The synagogue, which did not cost the wider Parisian community anything, was inaugurated on 17 June 1914. No representatives of the official French Jewish institutions attended, preferring to ignore this initiative on the part of immigrant Jews which they neither hindered nor assisted. The synagogue in rue Pavée, along with all its liturgical elements, was listed as a historic building on 4 July 1989.

PLANS OF
THE HISTORIC LIBRARY
OF THE CITY OF PARIS

18

*A spectacular painting from the Exposition
Universelle of 1889*

Hôtel de Lamoignon
24, rue Pavée
Daily 8am–6pm (closed on Sunday)
Metro Saint-Paul

Few Parisians know that in the modern wing (also called the Bourgeois wing) of the History Library of the City of Paris (Bibliothèque Historique de la Ville de Paris), dedicated to the history of the capital and installed since 1969 in the Hôtel de Lamoignon (17th century), there is a spectacularly magnificent painting by Eugène Bourgeois (1855–1909) based on drawings by the city architect Émile Hochereau (1828–1905).

Entitled *La Place de la Bastille et ses environs en 1889* ('Place de la Bastille and its surroundings in 1889'), it depicts the square and its surroundings with impressive precision.

Note especially the many factory chimneys whose smoke shows them to be working and thus reminders of the industrial past of the

district, the former Roquette prison (since demolished) on the left, the place des Vosges and, to the right of the Jardin des Plantes, the former warehouses of the (second) Paris wine market, completed in 1845.

The warehouse, which covers an area of 13.4 hectares, was bounded by rue Saint-Victor (now rue Jussieu), rue Cuvier, quai Saint-Bernard and rue des Fossés-Saint-Bernard.

In this map and plan consultation room, open to the public, you can browse through the daily papers as in any library.

On registration (free on presentation of a valid ID), you'll also have access to the Reading Room, to the left of the entrance; it presents a counterpart to the previous panorama.

The canvas *Paris en 1789*, which is the work of Fédor Hoffbauer (1839–1922), a painter and architect specialising in representations of the city, decorates the back of the room – in the centre the notorious Bastille prison can be seen.

The 1889 Bastille painting by Bourgeois was presented at the Pavillon de la Ville de Paris during the Exposition Universelle, in conjunction with *Paris en 1789*, to illustrate the dynamic urban development in the French capital during the 19th century.

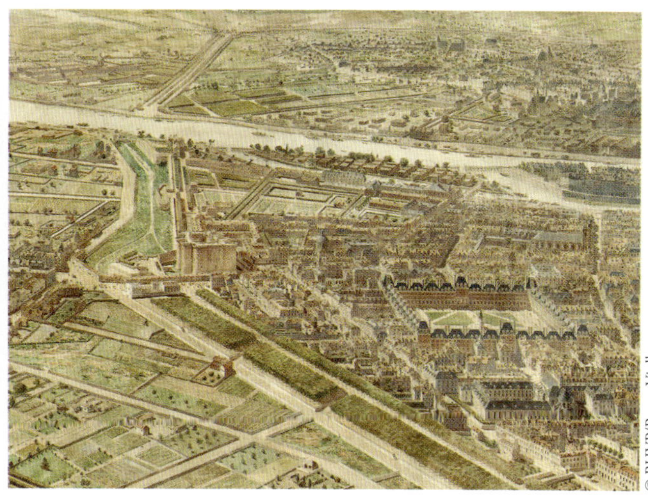

VESTIGES OF THE SOCIÉTÉ DES CENDRES

The industrial past of the Marais

39, rue des Francs-Bourgeois
Monday–Friday 11am–8pm, Saturday–Sunday 10am–8pm
Metro Rambuteau

Above the entrance to the building at 39, rue des Francs-Bourgeois (now a shop) the discreet inscription 'Société des Cendres' recalls the industrial past of the premises. Until 2002 this was the working site of one of the last factories in the Marais. In the centre of the shop, the 35 metres-high red brick chimney, which can also be seen from the Francs-Bourgeois-Rosier garden immediately next door, is the most significant remnant from this little-known site.

Far from being a mortuary enterprise, as its name might suggest, the Société des Cendres (Ash Society) would process 'ashes' here; more precisely, it would salvage gold, silver and even platinum from the different types of dust that constituted jewellers' waste.

Created in 1859 in order to deal with the waste produced by the jewellery profession, the Société des Cendres of the Marais functioned as a sort of cooperative whose clients (more than 500 precious metal professionals) were also shareholders. The headquarters on the rue des Francs-Bourgeois were constructed in 1867, a time when the Marais, which had been abandoned by its wealthier inhabitants for the Faubourg Saint-Germain, was given over to industry. The society now operates at Vitry-sur-Seine.

Besides the internal chimney and the plaque dedicated to the society on the street façade, there are other remains from this bygone age. On the same façade, above the plaque, another inscription details the company's activities: 'Gold and silver smelting, treatment of ashes, testing and analysis." Inside, a staircase, which leans partly on the wall of Philippe Auguste, provides access to the basement. Here tools from the period have been preserved and short films explain how these activities were carried out.

Customers would arrive at the premises with 50-500 kilos sacks containing dust that they had collected over the previous months. This waste was burnt and crushed before being sifted and washed then subjected to mercury-based chemical treatment, allowing the precious materials to be separated out. Suspicious customers would often remain on site to keep an eye on their dust, which was potentially rich in gold or silver. For sacks weighing 50 kilos and above, at least 250 grams of gold were required to make these operations profitable.

NEARBY

Vestiges of Couture Sainte-Catherine [20]
S.C. inscription

Corner of rue des Francs-Bourgeois and rue Pavée
Metro Rambuteau

At the base of the quadrangular turret of Hôtel de Lamoignon, on the corner of rue des Francs-Bourgeois and rue Pavée, two very discreet inscriptions are composed of the letters 'S.C'. Like the initials F.C.S.G. (see page 97), which recorded the boundaries of the fief of Coutures-Saint-Gervais, S.C. records one of the boundaries of the Censive* of Sainte-Catherine du Val des Ecoliers (Couture Sainte-Catherine), in other words, the boundaries of the lands of the Abbaye de Sainte-Catherine (the term couture comes from the word 'culture', a reminder that this part of the Marais was marshland that had to be drained for cultivation). The censive covered almost 7 hectares.

**Censive (parcel of land) is the name given to a seigneurial fief when the owner is a commoner, unlike the fief where the owner is a noble.*

A bleeding host

22–26, rue des Archives
Open during the frequent exhibitions, whose schedule can be found in Parisian entertainment listings magazines
Metro Hôtel de Ville

Endowed with four galleries flanked by flamboyant vaults, the small Billettes cloister is the only medieval cloister that remains in Paris. Dating from 1427, it belonged to the former monastery housing the Frères Hospitaliers de la Charité de Notre-Dame, also known as the *Billettes* (little beads) in reference to the heraldic figures that adorned their habits. The adjoining church, rebuilt several times, dates from 1756 and from 1812 has been used by members of the Evangelical faith, while the monastic buildings were converted into a school at the end of the 19th century, and the cloister, property of the Paris City Hall, was preserved and twice restored in the late 19th and 20th centuries.

If the general atmosphere that emanates from this timeless place is rather peaceful, its history is another matter altogether. In 1290, on Easter Sunday, a Jewish moneylender named Jonathas is said to have demanded of some poor woman that she bring him a consecrated host as repayment for her debt. Seizing this host, the man is supposed to have stabbed it several times with a knife, whereupon it began to bleed abundantly. He then threw it into a fire from which it emerged

undamaged, flying across the room. Finally, the moneylender plunged the host into a pot of boiling water which was then changed into blood, while the host itself rose unto the air, now bearing the face of Christ! Jonathas is said to have been burned alive for his misdeed ... Once this story spread, the house of Jonathas quickly became a place of pilgrimage, and in 1294, a bourgeois citizen was granted authorisation to erect a chapel on this very spot where 'God was boiled'. In 1299, King Philippe-le-Bel installed the Frères de la Charité de Notre-Dame here to perform church services.

The Miracle of the Billettes (the monks of the Charity of Notre Dame were known as 'Billettes') is commemorated by a stained-glass window in the Chapel of Catechisms at Saint-Étienne-du-Mont church.

The charge against Jews of desecration of the host (consecrated bread) was a recurring theme of anti-Semitic propaganda in the Middle Ages. To profane a consecrated host was to profane the body of Christ himself, who was present in the Eucharist according to the dogma of transubstantiation. This was a mortal sin.

NEARBY

Remains of Hôtel de Noyon façade 

Metro Rambuteau

To the right of 57, rue des Francs-Bourgeois, a door opens onto a private courtyard. From the outside you can see, on the right side of the wall behind the door, a curious piece of work that contrasts with the smooth surface on which it rests. It comes from the façade of the former Hôtel de Noyon, built in 1638, which stood at the back of the courtyard. This section of wall is all that remains of the hôtel, demolished in 1885.

In the courtyard of 55, rue des Francs-Bourgeois you can still see some remains of the enclosure wall of Philip Augustus: the 8-metre-high tower and traces on the ground date from the late 12th century.

A movable façade

The façade of the Blancs-Manteaux church is taken from Saint-Éloi church, part of the Barnabites convent built in 1701 on Île de la Cité and demolished in 1863 during the construction of boulevard du Palais. That same year architect Victor Baltard, who was working on the extension of Blancs-Manteaux, joined the Barnabites façade to that of Blancs-Manteaux as a finishing touch.

Rue des Blancs-Manteaux owes its name not to the traditional attire of the Templars (see page 91) but to that of mendicant monks known as Servants (or Servants) of the Virgin Mary who formerly occupied the monastery.

23

MERCIES AT SAINT-GERVAIS-SAINT-PROTAIS CHURCH

Spectacular popular performances, sometimes censored

Place Saint-Gervais and 13, rue des Barres
paris.fraternites-jerusalem.org
Metro Hôtel de Ville

In the early centuries of monastic life, monks and nuns worshipped standing in the church choir in a kind of individual compartment separated by wooden partitions called parcloses.

As the services became longer and more frequent during the day, folding wooden seats were introduced around the 11th century to let the clerics rest. The seats, fixed between the partitions, were fitted with a support and a small projection on the underside called a misericord (from the Latin misericordia, meaning mercy).

Once the seat was turned, the tired cleric could lean on it while giving the appearance of standing, hence the name 'mercy seat', as in a way it shows compassion by reducing discomfort.

Although the partitions and backs of the seats are usually decorated

with religious themes, the misericords occasionally move away from specifically Christian iconography, as at Saint-Gervais-Saint-Protais. Carved between the first part of the 16th and early 17th centuries, these depict the daily life of this district in the heart of the city, at the time vibrant with commercial and professional activity. Sailors, wine merchants and masons all based their brotherhoods in the church.

Some picturesque scenes are carved in the wood: a shoemaker trimming his leather with shoes lined up above him, a sommelier surrounded by barrels, a stonemason and an architect, a peasant picking squashes, a boat with a boatman (now gone), two chefs turning a chicken on a spit, a scientist sitting on a chair reading a book on a desk, and what looks like a surgeon kneeling next to a prone woman.

Some misericords, like this one, are badly damaged, either because of the wear and tear of time or because of the scissor blows from those who found these representations shocking.

This censorship is more widely found in the second category of themes on the misericords, covering moral or religious principles, or metaphors of everyday life and society.

To represent these diverse and varied subjects, the artists freely integrated symbols and legendary figures from the iconography of the time into their works.

In this way they evoke (in no particular order): gluttony and impurity, with a sow leaning over a wide tub; chastity, with a fire-resistant salamander (a popular heraldic figure at the time, Francis I having added it to his weapons and associated it with his motto: 'I feed on the good fire; I extinguish the bad'); lust, with a dog lying down and raising a thigh to lick itself; pleasure, with a mermaid slicking back her hair; vanity (allegorical representation of the fragility of human life), with a young boy sleeping on a skull; the three ages of life, with the three related crescent moons (the figure of Diane de Poitiers, a favourite of Henry II) whose concavities profile three faces evoking youth, virility and middle age; strength and courage, with a lion's head; absolution, with a woman kneeling with joined hands in the penitential court, facing a confessor, and a third figure carrying a large key symbolising the divine power with which the priest is invested to absolve his flock; indecency, with a fool holding a marotte ('bauble' on a stick), kneeling to defecate in front of an occupied house; the baseness of human impulses with another fool wearing a pointed hood, who wants to frolic with a woman struggling to keep him at bay, but also a communal bathtub in which a woman is joined by a man.

There are also the interwoven monograms of the church patrons, St Gervais and St Protais, as well as the Saint-Gervais feudal elm emerging from the well, a legend that once lent a certain fame to the district.

THE ELM TREE ON THE PARVIS OF SAINT-GERVAIS-SAINT-PROTAIS

At night, the women in the neighbourhood secretly took pieces of its bark

Place Saint-Gervais – Metro Hôtel de Ville

If the elm tree in front of the Saint-Gervais-Saint-Protais church is not particularly eye-catching, it does have an astonishing history. Cut down during the French Revolution, the original elm that stood in this spot symbolised several things: from the beginning of the Christian era it was considered sacred due to its red sap, like the blood of the martyrs; it was also the place where justice was rendered after Mass, beneath its branches. In addition, people gathered here to drink and dance on feast days, and business deals were concluded. It is said, moreover, that women living in the neighbourhood used to come secretly in the night to take away pieces of the tree's bark, useful against fevers ... Rather than the existing tree, which only dates from the beginning of the 20th century, it is the multiple references scattered throughout the neighbourhood to this famous older elm that help to keep the tradition alive.

St Gervais and St Protais: a church for two non-existent saints

St Gervais and St Protais probably never existed. They were 'invented' by St Ambrose, Bishop of Milan, in the year 386. Guided by a vision, he found the legs of two saints hitherto unknown: Gervais and Protais. After this discovery of relics, as often happens in such cases, a story was invented to tell of their life and spread their cult, with the main purpose of increasing the number of saints (and therefore relics) whose example people could follow and pray to. According to the official hagiography, they were the sons of St Vitalis and St Valeria, early Christian martyrs under Nero (reigned AD 54 to 68).

Front steps of Saint-Gervais-Saint-Protais church: last traces of the second wall surrounding Paris

Measuring 1,700 metres in length, the wall built in the 11th century enclosed three natural *monceaux* (hillocks), safe from river floods, on which the churches of Saint-Germain-l'Auxerrois, Saint-Merry, and Saint-Gervais were located.

The front steps of the Saint-Gervais-Saint-Protais church and the route of rue des Barres are the only physical signs today of this wall's existence, and more specifically, of height variation formed by the monceau Saint-Gervais.

NEARBY

The elm of the balcony ironwork

Metro Hôtel de Ville

Early 18th century ironwork featuring an elm tree can be seen on the balconies of houses from 2 to 14, rue François Miron. Four stalls in Saint-Gervais-Saint-Protais church also bear its image.

Ourscamp House

11 16, rue François Miron – paris-historique.org
Monday–Friday 1pm–6pm, Saturday 1pm–7pm, closed on Sunday
Metro Hôtel de Ville

In its basement, the Association du Paris Historique houses one of the most beautiful Gothic cellars in the capital. Dating from the 12th century, this cellar owes its survival to local residents, who used it as a storage space and filled it right up to the chapiters, thus preserving them. At No. 11 and 13, rue François Miron, two 15th century houses have kept their gables and frame walls, although the latter actually date from their renovation in the 1960s.

SARAH BERNHARDT'S DRESSING ROOM

A memory of the 'Golden Voice'

Théâtre de la Ville – 16, quai de Gesvres
Can be visited during intervals by members of the audience
Metro Cité or Hôtel de Ville

Sarah Bernhardt's dressing room at the Théâtre de la Ville, is sadly a mere replica, the real dressing room of the artist (1844–1923) having been destroyed in 1968 when the theatre was renovated. Some of the original items were nevertheless salvaged: you can still see a settee with the head of a sphinx, her famous bathtub, and various personal objects.

Regarded as one of the greatest actresses of the 19th century, Sarah Bernhardt is best known for being the first to tour the world.

NEARBY

Gateway at 22, rue Quincampoix (28)
Metro Les Halles

The gateway to the building at 22, rue Quincampoix has not always stood in this spot. Just above the door, the following inscription can still be seen on a black marble medallion: 'Bureau des Marchandes lingères, 1716'. It reminds us that this gate once belonged to the Hôtel des Marchandes lingères, situated on the nearby place Sainte-Opportune. At the start of the 20th century, as part of a neighbourhood regeneration project, the gate was moved to the Square des Innocents, before being relocated again in 1977 to the place Edmond Michelet and finally placed in its current position.

What do the colours of the giant tubes at the Centre Pompidou mean?

The colour scheme of the giant tubes at the Centre Pompidou is no coincidence: blue for air conditioning, yellow for electrical cables, green for water pipes and red for elevators and escalators.

The origin of 'la grève'

Faire la grève (to go on strike) is an expression derived from the former place de la Grève in Paris, now called place de l'Hôtel de Ville. This square, located by the Seine, was one of the principal landing places for boats during the Middle Ages (a *grève* is a gravel or sand beach, by the sea or a body of water). Men seeking employment were readily hired here for loading and unloading vessels. In the course of time, workers dissatisfied with their wages and labour conditions tended to gather at place de la Grève to express their grievances.

THE 'DEVIL' OF SAINT-MERRY CHURCH

An invention of 19th century occultists

Saint-Merry church – 76, rue de la Verrerie
Metro Châtelet

At the top of the pointed portico of Saint-Merry church, a very surprising sculpture about 30 centimetres high is traditionally said to represent the Devil sitting in a cross-legged position, with an erect male penis and a female breast. An enduring legend says that this sculpture represents the Devil, and dates back to the origins of the church in 1526, although it was built on the site of an older church dating from the 11th century (1005), when the parish of Saint-Merry was founded.

In fact this sculpture, installed between 1840 and 1847 during extensive 19th century restoration works by a Companion of the Duty of Freedom, a French-inspired Masonic association, represents the god Astaroth. In the 19th century, French occultist Éliphas Lévi celebrated Astaroth as a 'Sabbatic Goat' – a hermaphroditic winged human figure

with the head and feet of a goat covered with numerous esoteric symbols. Also known as the Goat of Memphis, later called Mendes, the Caprin or Kumara of Egypt, the birthplace of the Western initiatory tradition.

Astaroth, much loved by the ancient Jews, Sidonians and Philistines, is an androgynous deity (half man, half woman), as can be seen on the Saint-Merry sculpture, which was later demonised. It represented the divine intelligence that did not admit hypocrisy, deceit and distortion of ideas, and therefore was perfectly appropriate on a church façade.

According to some, Astaroth was worshipped by the Templars under the name Baphomet, whereas this term was unknown in the Middle Ages. Baphomet only appeared rarely in the prose and poetry of some Occitan troubadours, giving a name to a creation of poetic imagination. For more on Baphomet, see opposite.

What in fact is Baphomet?

The Templars are sometimes said to have worshipped a mysterious skull that produced oracles and dictated the so-called Secret Rule containing the most unimaginable blasphemies. This legend obviously springs from the imagination of 19th century Romantics, because there is no evidence and no mention before them of the existence of a satanic skull. The word Baphomet wasn't part of contemporary medieval vocabulary. Unknown to the Church and the Temple, it was coined by Occitan troubadours and cropped up occasionally in their poetic fables. If the Templars ever possessed a relic of a skull (they were great collectors of sacred relics), it should be interpreted differently. The skull, even if it refers mainly to death in Catholicism, has a double meaning: it contains the brain and therefore what is 'higher' in man. It is therefore the most sacred part of the body, and a symbol of the discovery of supreme knowledge. The word itself comes from the Arabic *ouba-al-fometh*, which means 'mouth of the Father', and in this sense is connected with supreme knowledge, which comes from the Father himself. The Father, incorporating the Son and the Holy Spirit, is also the Light of Wisdom to which some have given the meaning, from Late Greek, of Baphêtous. This is the meaning of the phrase in the poem *Ira et Dolor* (Wrath and Pain), written in 1265 by an Occitan troubadour: '*E Baphomet obra de son poder*' – 'And Baphomet made its power shine'. In the Moorish language of the Iberian Peninsula, inherited from the Muslims, the word used was *Abufihamat* (pronounced Buphimat), which meant 'Father, Source, Understanding'. An expression derived from it, Ras-el-fah-mat, means 'Head of Knowledge' and refers to the mental capacity of man who has reached a degree of perfection in consciousness. The expression 'I build a head' refers to this process, as used by some Sufi schools of the Iberian Peninsula that medieval Christians pejoratively called Bafometarias and Carvoarias (black works), in the popular sense of 'Black and Evil'. Secret knowledge was taught and practised there which, for the ignorant Christian, could only be likened to 'things of the Devil'. The 'baphometic' skull actually represented an illumination, just like the Celtic goddess Brigid when she presided over Imbolc, a purification festival celebrating the end of winter – a symbol of the illumination of the world after sterile darkness. For the same reason, St Brigid (Brigit/Brigitte) is sometimes depicted with a candle in her hand and a cow at her feet to evoke lactation, here a reference to the renewal of life in spring.

5th arrondissement

1er
Châtelet
Hôtel de Ville
PLACE
DE L'HÔTEL
DE VILLE
Rue de Rivoli
3e
Le Marais
St-Paul
PLACE
DES VOSGES
Bd Beaumarchais
N
Cité
St-Michel
Notre-Dame
Île
de la Cité
4e
Pont Marie
Île
Saint-Louis
PLACE
DE LA
BASTILLE
Bastille
11e
10
11
y
orbonne
9
Q. de Montebello
Q. de la Tournelle
PONT DE SULLY
Bd Henri IV
Sully Morland
Boulevard Saint-Germain
Saint-Jacques
Maubert
Mutualité
Rue des Écoles
R. des Fossés
Saint-Bernard
Institut du Monde Arabe
Seine
Quai Saint-Bernard
Rue de Lyon
12
14
Cardinal Lemoine
7
Panthéon
5e
13
15
Jussieu
16
Rue Cuvier
18
Jardin
des Plantes
Quai de la Rapée
12e
Gare de Lyon
PONT
D'AUSTERLITZ
Rue d'Ulm
Rue Lhomond
4
5
2
Rue Mouffetard
Rue Monge
Place Monge
19
Rue Geoffroy Saint-Hilaire
17
Rue Buffon
PONT
CHARLES
DE GAULLE
Gare d'Austerlitz
Rue Claude Bernard
Censier
Daubenton
Boulevard de l'Hôpital
-Royal
3
20
Boulevard Saint-Marcel
St-Marcel
13e
Les Gobelins

VAL-DE-GRÂCE CLOISTER

The forgotten cloister

Musée du Service de Santé des Armées
1, place Alphonse Laveran
+33 1 40 51 51 92
Wednesday–Sunday 11am–6pm
Valid identification required
RER Port-Royal

A visit to the museum of the French army's health service is a very good excuse to admire the little-known but magnificent cloister of the former abbey of Val-de-Grâce, built between 1624 and 1669.

The church itself was the result of a vow made by Queen Anne of Austria, in thanks for having given birth to a son after 23 years of marriage, in 1638. On 1 April 1645, the future King Louis XIV therefore laid the first stone for a building whose construction was prolonged until the end of the 1660s. Mansart, then Le Mercier, and finally, Le Muet, assisted by Le Duc, all contributed to the design of the church, which is decorated with numerous statues, as well as four paintings by Philippe de Champaigne. The abbey was transformed into a military hospital in 1793 and is still the property of the French Army.

The museum itself is intended to help the visitor understand the multiple relationships between medicine and the military, but its chief point of interest is its location, beneath the vaults of one of the upper galleries overlooking the beautiful cloister. Note the superposition of the two galleries that compose it.

NEARBY

Garden of the École Normale Supérieure ②

45, rue d'Ulm – RER Luxembourg
Open daily during class hours
A very pleasant garden graced with a small ornamental pond.

LUMIÈRE DE L'ŒIL

A museum of old-fashioned lighting

4, rue Flatters
+33 1 47 07 63 47
lumiara@aol.com – lumieredeloeil.com
Tuesday–Friday 2pm–7pm, Saturday 11am–5pm
Metro Gobelins

For almost 25 years Monsieur Ara has restored and sold old-fashioned lighting at Lumière de l'Œil. Gas, oil and electric lamps, glass fixtures, wicks, sleeves, beaded fringes and other accessories are crammed into a tiny room, waiting for a buyer.

At the back of the shop is a small museum with oil, kerosene, spirit and gas lamps from around the world, the oldest of which date back to the 18th century. It is a unique collection in France because, as this enthusiast will proudly tell you, all the lamps are in working order.

RUE LHOMOND TORTOISE ④

A discreet nod to administrative slowness

21, rue Lhomond
Metro Place Monge

On the façade of the building at 21, rue Lhomond, completely rebuilt at the end of the 20th century, is quite a discreet plaster tortoise that many locals might have missed.

It seems to be a mocking message for the Services Territoriaux de l'Architecture et du Patrimoine (STAP, Territorial Services for Architecture and Heritage), which intervened during the works because the building is 'in the field of view of a listed building or listed as a Historic Monument' – namely the Panthéon.

The Bâtiments de France architect in charge of the file is thought to have been very demanding, giving the owner a hard time and delaying approval of the project.

Having brought the new building into line with the requests of Bâtiments de France, the architect, marked by this gruelling experience, decided to add this pretty tortoise to the gable as a humorous nod to the slow grind of administration and to test the responsiveness of STAP controls.

No reaction has been heard to date, and it's generally agreed that the tortoise looks great on the gable and is now part of the fittings.

THE GARDEN
AT 33, RUE LHOMOND

Beautiful relic of a former monastery

33, rue Lhomond – Metro Place Monge

By asking one of the residents you can sometimes access the beautiful garden at 33, rue Lhomond. Here, on 2 November 1808, the monastery was bought by Benedictine Sister Françoise de Bèze and four other nuns commissioned by their congregation. It had belonged to the Dames Religieuses de Sainte-Aure until the Revolution drove them away. Gradually the Benedictines took over the quadrangle formed by Lhomond, Amyot, Tournefort and Pot de Fer streets. Their priesthood continued until the end of the 1970s. Since there was no renewal of vocations, the remaining elderly sisters retired to the monastery of the congregation in Rouen, the buildings were sold. The chapel of the Benedictines and the basilica of Christ the King were demolished. They were replaced by a modern real-estate complex.

The original arrangement still contains the charming garden from which you can see the old monastery, now rebuilt, as well as the tombs-

tone of Françoise de Bèze and a marble panel with the coat of arms of the Benedictine Nuns of Perpetual Adoration of the Blessed Sacrament. The Basilica of Christ the King was built at the initiative of Sister Olive, a young Breton nun who had a revelation during which Jesus commanded her to raise 'a throne under the symbol of a consecrated temple with its own name: Christ the King, Prince of Peace, Master of the Nations'. The sanctuary, designated a basilica, was consecrated on 16 June 1956 by Cardinal Feltin, who indicated in his homily that 'Paris would now have two summits of piety to the Divine Master, Montmartre with its perpetual adoration to the Heart of Christ, and Montagne Sainte-Geneviève with its perpetual adoration to the Christ-King'.

Les Misérables *at 33, rue Lhomond*

In his epic novel, Victor Hugo recounts the escape of Jean Valjean and Cosette, pursued by Inspector Javert. In the first version of the novel, published in 1862, it was here in the garden of the Benedictines that he first set the convent of the religious order 'Bernardines de l'Obédience de Martin Verga', before changing it in the final version to Saint-Antoine in what is now the 12th arrondissement.

CURIE MUSEUM

The glory days of radium

1, rue Pierre et Marie Curie
+33 1 56 24 55 33
musee@curie.fr
Wednesday–Saturday 1pm–5pm
Metro Place Monge or Cardinal Lemoine
RER Luxembourg

Located on the ground floor of the Curie pavilion, the intriguing Curie museum occupies the former laboratory and office of Marie Curie. This 'Radium Institute' was built between 1911 and 1914 by the University of Paris and the Institut Pasteur after the discovery of polonium* and radium by Pierre and Marie Curie. The guided tour is strongly recommended for its numerous fascinating anecdotes. In the entry hall, glass display cases present the first instruments for measuring radioactivity as well as a history of radium. Visitors thus pass from the serious scientific research to the fanciful notions of the general public which, for

example, even went as far as attributing radium with cosmetic virtues, as claimed by a Miss France at the time!

The second room is none other than Marie Curie's office, left in the state it was found upon her death in 1958 by her son-in-law, Frédéric Joliot: there are some personal items belonging to Marie and her daughter, Irène Joliot-Curie. As for the laboratory, it had a relatively high level of radioactivity and required decontamination before it could be opened to the public in 1992. The rear door opens onto the garden leading to the Institut Pasteur, specialising in medical and biological research. Conceived by Marie Curie, the principal purpose of this garden is to allow researchers from both institutes to meet informally.

** The name given to this element by Marie Sklodowska-Curie in tribute to her native Poland.*

The family with five Nobel Prizes

Of Polish origin, Marie Sklodowska-Curie was in 1903 the first woman to present a thesis in physics (she received the highest grade). The same year, she was also the first woman to receive the Nobel Prize in physics, together with her husband Pierre Curie and Henri Becquerel, for their discovery of radioactive elements. In 1911, after the death of Pierre, she was awarded, on her own, the Nobel Prize in chemistry for her work on radium. She remains to this day the only woman to have received two Nobel Prizes. Then, in 1935, her daughter Irène and son-in-law Frédéric Joliot obtained a Nobel Prize in chemistry for their research on artificial radioactivity.

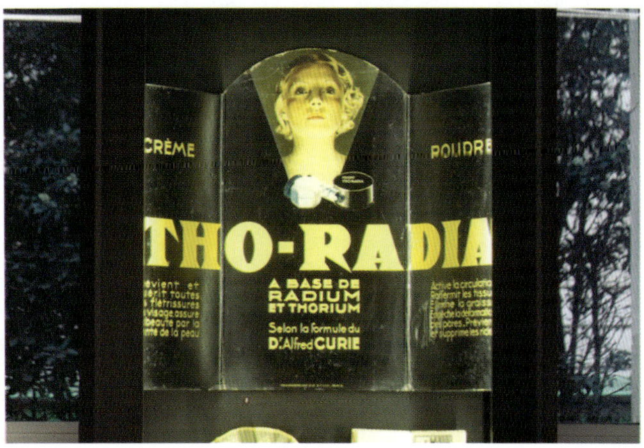

THE JUBE
OF SAINT-ÉTIENNE-DU-MONT

The last jube

30, rue Descartes – Place Sainte-Geneviève
saintetiennedumont.fr
Closed on Monday
Metro Cardinal Lemoine

The Saint-Étienne-du-Mont church, whose construction was begun in 1517 by François I and only completed in 1627 (which explains the rather fanciful mixture of Gothic and Franco-Italian styles making this a unique monument) possesses the last jube, that can be seen in Paris. An architectural marvel sculpted by the artist Biard l'Aîné, the jube is formed by a single arch with a span of 9 metres traversing the choir, accessed by two spiral staircases in openwork stone. This piece of art, unmatched in its lightness despite the richness of its sculpted ornamentation (ivy, angels, palm trees, foliated patterns, interlacings, mascarons and worshippers), has by some miracle escaped destruction, the parishioners themselves having requested its demolition in 1735! The church also possesses some very fine stained-glass windows at the rear of the sacristy illustrating scenes from the Bible, as well as the relics of Saint Geneviève, the patron saint of Paris. Pascal and Racine are both buried here, behind the choir.

What is a jube?

The jube is a transversal gallery separating the choir from the nave of a church, from where the Holy Scriptures would be read. Most of them vanished with the introduction of pulpits. The word stems from the Latin expression *Jube, Domine, Benedicere* (command, Lord, to bless).

SYMBOLISM OF
LA DAME À LA LICORNE

Hidden symbols of a medieval spiritual path

Cluny Museum
Metro Cluny – La Sorbonne

As explained in 1883 by Edmond du Sommerard in a supplement to his catalogue for the Cluny Museum, the tapestries of *La Dame à la Licorne* (*The Lady and the Unicorn*) were commissioned in 1457 by the patriarch of the Le Viste family, originally from Lyon but living in Paris. Jean Le Viste, who died in 1500 and was buried at Célestins church in Paris, was close to the Hermetic traditions of his time, so the tapestries were probably an artistic means of communicating his esoteric beliefs. It reflects the symbolism of the Provencal concept of courtly love, dear to the ideal of chivalry immortalised by troubadours and minstrels. *Fedeli d'Amore* (Love's Faithful, a group of poets practising an erotic spirituality), very popular at the time, inspired Jean I (died 1383), founder of the Le Viste line. Dante's *Divine Comedy*, published 63 years earlier, which propagates these ideals, had alrcady found fame throughout Europe (see *Secret Florence*, by the same publisher). Some link the Le Viste family to Prince Zizim, son of Mehmed II and brother of Bajazet, who married a Christian woman during his stay in Bourganeuf, which would explain the origin of the crescent on the family coat of arms, as well as in the tapestries.

If the lady who accompanies the unicorn represents someone from the Le Viste family, the occult message is that above all she represents the Virgin Mary, mother of Jesus. In turn, the unicorn in medieval courtly

iconography represents, with its single horn, the Holy Spirit – the divine penetrating the human, through whose grace Jesus was born of the Virgin. Western iconography positioned the horn in the middle of the mythical animal's forehead to spiritualise its original sexual symbolism. The unicorn became a symbol of purity, which is why medieval illuminations and tapestries show that it can only be captured with the help of a pure virgin, on whose knees it constantly takes refuge before being captured and then killed by hunters. This process was interpreted in the Middle Ages as a symbol of the purity of the Virgin Mary's conception of Jesus Christ and of the death of the Saviour on the Cross. In these scenes, Mary is seated in a walled garden (Latin *hortus conclusus*), or in an enclosed rose garden (as on the tapestries of the Cluny Museum), as in the rosarium hermeticum where only a lucid and pure being such as Jesus can enter, or even Perceval in his Quest for the Holy Grail, which contains the unicorn's milk – the elixir of spiritual immortality.

Basically, the divine manifests itself through the development of bodily senses so that the human being can become totally receptive to spiritual influences through enlightened consciousness. This is why the six *Lady and the Unicorn* tapestries are dedicated to the human senses: *La vue (Sight)– L'ouïe (Hearing) – Le goût (Taste) – L'odorat (Smell) – Le toucher (Touch) – À mon Seul Désir (To my Desire Alone)*, the last piece evoking the union of the soul (the Lady) with the spirit (the Unicorn) in such a way as to go beyond worldly pleasures as she places her jewellery in a box.

According to the Primordial Tradition, these tapestries also correspond to the influences of the planets on human senses, in the following form:

– *Touch* – physical consciousness – the Sun (the Lady is receptive to fertilisation by touching the unicorn's horn).

NB: As touch is traditionally the coarsest sense it should be in first place, according to the scale 'from densest to subtlest'.

– *Taste* – vital consciousness – the Moon (the Lady stares at the unicorn and reaches out to the vase of creation).

– *Sight* – emotional awareness – Mars (the Lady tenderly looks at the unicorn reflected in her mirror).

– *Smell* – psychomental awareness – Saturn (the Lady hangs up a wreath of carnations, scenting the standing unicorn).

– *Hearing* – mental awareness – Venus (the Lady plays music and enchants the attentive unicorn before her).

– *To my Desire Alone* (intuition) – intuitive consciousness – Mercury (ecstasy) – spiritual consciousness – Jupiter (the Lady receives the unicorn's homage near the tent or tabernacle, home of the Eternal as revealed to the Virgin).

SALVADOR DALI'S SUNDIAL

A nod and a wink from the master

27, rue Saint-Jacques – Metro Cluny – La Sorbonne

The sundial on the wall of 27, rue Saint-Jacques, designed by Salvador Dalí in 1966, was a gift for friends who kept a shop on the corner. The engraving is of a woman's head resembling a scallop on top, an allusion to the street named after the Santiago de Compostela pilgrimage. One of the routes started from the Tour Saint-Jacques in Paris.

Traces in Paris of the pilgrimage to Santiago de Compostela

One of the four French pilgrimage routes leading to the shrine of Saint James in Santiago de Compostela has its point of departure in Paris, at the former Saint-Jacques-de-la-Boucherie church, of which the last vestige is Saint-Jacques tower. The pilgrims then left the city by way of rue Saint-Jacques, rue du Faubourg-Saint-Jacques, and rue de la Tombe-Issoire. The present-day Cluny Museum was on this route and it is therefore not surprising to see numerous scallops carved on the façade. The Saint-Jacques-du-Haut-Pas church, in rue Saint-Jacques, also owes its existence to the pilgrimage.

NEARBY
Charnier Saint-Séverin

Rue des Prêtres-Saint-Séverin
Metro Cluny – La Sorbonne

On the right-hand side of the Saint-Séverin church, a pretty garden is curiously surrounded by a Gothic-style gallery housing small alcoves, which make it look like a cloister. This place, at first sight charming, bears the name of 'charnier Saint-Séverin': it is the vestige of a medieval charnel house first opened in the 15th century. Its galleries and niches were meant to receive the remains of Parisian dignitaries, while the ground in the middle was filled with bones from the city's mass graves when their sites were needed for other purposes.

The oldest tree in Paris

Metro Cluny – La Sorbonne

The oldest tree in Paris can be found opposite Notre-Dame, on the Left Bank of the Seine, in square René Viviani (25, quai de Montebello). This *robinia* (false acacia) tree was planted in 1636 and survives in part thanks to a 'crutch' made from concrete that no doubt prevents it from collapsing completely. Its name is derived from Jean Robin, who was the first to introduce this American tree to France, in 1602.

The flag over La Tour d'Argent

Some Parisians will have noticed that a flag sometimes flies above *La Tour d'Argent* restaurant. This indicates that the owner is on the premises.

SQUARE PAUL LANGEVIN MASONIC SIGN

The hidden symbols of a Freemason physicist

Square Paul Langevin
Metro Cardinal Lemoine

The small garden in Square Paul Langevin is overlooked by a huge bas-relief panel representing figures which are clearly of Masonic inspiration, as well as the man who gave his name to the square. Paul Langevin (Paris, 23 January 1872 – Paris, 19 December 1946) was a brilliant physicist, whose Freemasonry membership has not been proven. The panel, which had decorated the Palais de l'Industrie at the 1889 Exposition Universelle, was transferred here to illustrate the human and spiritual journey of Paul Langevin.

The first medallion on the left depicts the emblem of universal Freemasonry: the square and compass superimposed, surrounded by acacia leaves, all topped with a ribbon forming an 8 (the symbol of infinity) traditionally known as the 'ribbon of love', which indicates the union of opposites such as the Sun and the Moon, spirit and matter, masculine and the feminine, the square and compass, etc., and which, interwoven, symbolise the primordial state of the perfect androgynous being who succeeds in achieving the union of opposites, which is necessary for spiritual growth.

In Masonic symbolism, the compass (associated with the active Spirit) refers to 'measure in research' and the square (relating to passive matter) indicates 'rectitude in action'. When the two tools are interwoven they express the idea of neutrality (neither good nor evil), a necessary condition for attaining spiritual enlightenment. This enlightenment is represented in Masonic hierarchy by the 3rd degree of Master Mason, where the compass are placed on the square, indicating that spirituality has defeated the profane, as seen here in the garden.

For Paul Langevin, the compass also evokes his personality as a remarkable physicist, while the square recalls the courageous resistance fighter who was even chairman of the Anti-Fascist vigilance committee.

Acacia: a Masonic symbol of immortality

The presence of the acacia branch is also very significant: this is the plant chosen by universal Freemasonry to designate the Master Mason, Masonic initiation and immortality, achieved by the state of innocence and purity known as *Akákia* by the ancient Dorians and Ionians. The word acacia is derived from the Greek *aké*, which means point or sharp end, a meaning then given to *lonkhē*, lance or spear. The ancient form to designate this was *akantha*, which means the plant that has thorns: acanthus, acacia, from which *akákia*, a term derived from *aké*. These thorns represent the painful trials which must be faced and overcome by the initiate on the path that will lead to the rank of Perfect Master.

FAU DE VERZY
AT ARÈNES DE LUTÈCE

An unexplained mystery

In front of 7, rue des Arènes
Metro Place Monge

The Fau de Verzy tree in the grounds of the Lutetian arena, opposite 7, rue des Arènes, was planted in 1905. Less well known than the Robinia false acacia in square René Viviani, but considered to be the oldest tree in Paris (see page 165), it is now about 1 metre high with a circumference of about 2.5 metres. It is one of the most remarkable in the city and the plant world as a whole.

The Fau de Verzy is a contorted beech, so called because its trunk and branches are crooked and twisted, with the outer branches bending to the ground.

While in summer the leaves can create a curious igloo shape, the tree best unveils its awesome architecture in winter, when all the twists and turns are fully exposed.

The tree owes its name to the forest of Verzy, near Reims, which is the world's main reserve of dwarf beeches with its 1,000 specimens. Fau was the name for beech in Old French (derived from the Latin *fagus*).

Two other sites in Europe have a few hundred specimens – the Süntel region near Hanover (Germany) and in Dalby Söderskog, near Malmo (Sweden). Dwarf beeches are also found in Moselle, Brittany, the Auvergne region, the Vosges mountains of France and in Denmark.

No scientific explanation has been agreed for the existence of these exceptional trees that live for about 350 years and, apart from their distinctive shape, sometimes have branches and trunks that merge with each other (the phenomenon of anastomosis).

NEARBY

A vestige of the crossing-point of the Bièvre in Philippe Auguste's wall 

30 bis, rue du Cardinal Lemoine
Visits first Wednesday of every month at 2.30pm
Metro Jussieu or Maubert-Mutualité

Once a month, the post office at the corner of rue du Cardinal Lemoine and boulevard Saint-Germain organises a visit to its basement: there you can see an interesting remnant of Philippe Auguste's wall. At this very spot, a branch of the Bièvre river (supplying the gardens of the Saint-Victor abbey with water) crossed the wall, through the so-called Bièvre arch.

Mineral Collection of La Sorbonne 

4, place Jussieu
+33 1 44 27 52 88 – Tuesday–Saturday 1pm–6pm
Metro Jussieu

Located since 1970 in a basement of the Jussieu university science faculty, the Mineral Collection of La Sorbonne has 24 panoramic display cases containing a selection of 2,000 minerals from its holdings of 24,000 specimens, with special lighting and a constant temperature to preserve them from deterioration. This choice allows the public to view the most beautiful pieces in a relatively small space. Based on rarity, quality and beauty, the selection presents the surprising riches offered by the mineral world with the aim of awakening the interest of a public often ignorant of the subject, but able here to discover what lies behind mysterious names such as *cummengéite, cuprosklodowskite* or *phantom quartz*. Those who are passionate about minerals can pursue matters further by visiting the Mines Mineralogy Museum, in the 6th arrondissement (see page 186), which has over 80,000 samples! Affected by the plan to remove dangerous asbestos from the Jussieu science faculty, the museum moved to new premises in June 2006, and now has disabled access.

Relief of the burning bush

25, rue Jussieu
Metro Jussieu

The unassuming relief of the burning bush, which dates from 1896, recalls the 17th century cabaret sign *Le buisson ardent* (Burning bush), famous for its grilled crayfish buissons (pyramids). In the Bible (Exodus: 3), the burning bush episode is the revelation of the monotheistic God to Moses in the land of Midian. In this scene, the Lord calls Moses from within this bush that burns without being consumed. The episode is said to have taken place on Mount Sinai, where St Catherine's Monastery today offers a wild mulberry as the biblical burning bush.

BONNIER DE LA MOSSON 'CABINET DE CURIOSITÉS'

A little-known gem

Media library of the National Museum of Natural History
38, rue Geoffroy Saint-Hilaire
+33 1 40 79 36 33
bcm@mnhn.fr – mnhn.fr
Wednesday, Thursday and Friday 9am–7pm, Tuesday 1pm–7pm, Saturday
10am–7pm
Admission free
Metro Place Monge or Jussieu

Hidden behind the white wall of the media library in the National Museum of Natural History, this *cabinet de curiosités* (chamber of curiosities) is a little-known gem that is the work of a wealthy art lover, Joseph Bonnier de la Mosson (1702–1744). A knowledgeable collector, Bonnier ruined himself gathering together their contents, to the point that his creditors recovered part of the amounts he owed by auctioning off the collections after his death in 1745.

Bonnier nevertheless managed to acquire one collection, the so-called '*Cabinet des insectes et autres animaux desséchés des plus remarquables*' (The most remarkable set of insects and other dried animals), which he had installed in the King's garden. Dismantled in 1935, the display cases were restored and moved to their present location in 1979. They were listed as a historic monument in 1980. Today, the cabinet is composed of five magnificent display cases carved in Dutch wood, decorated with entwined serpents and surmounted by animal heads bearing real horns. They present a collection of multicoloured insects and butterflies, gaudy birds, dried animals, horns of narwhales (once believed to be those of the legendary unicorn) and rhinoceroses, tarantulas, giant millipedes, etc. It is strongly recommended that you consult the detailed list of these curiosities. This can be found in catalogue 069.95 BON, available at the reception desk.

The 'cabinet de curiosités', precursor of the museum

In the 16th century, with the development of exploration and the discovery of unknown lands, many scientists, art lovers and persons of wealth began to collect curiosities originating in these new places. This led to the emergence of 'cabinets de curiosités' as a sort of mirror of the world, gathering together a multitude of rare and strange objects that not only reflected human endeavours, but also the three natural kingdoms: animal, vegetable and mineral. By the mid-17th century, the fad for these collections of curiosities began to wane, in favour of what would be called in the following century 'cabinets d'histoire naturelle', and then, the first museums.

THE DODO RIDE

A prehistoric ride

Jardin des Plantes
Wednesday, Saturday and Sunday: from 1pm to the garden's closing time,
Monday, Tuesday, Thursday and Friday: from 3pm to the garden's closing time
Creator and owner: M. Samy Finkel
Metro Place Monge or Jussieu

Set up in 1992 in the middle of the Jardin des Plantes, this 1930s-style carousel was specially conceived for this location on the theme of animals that have now vanished or are threatened by extinction. It thus gathers together members of rare or extinct species, such as the famous dodo from Mauritius, the Tasmanian wolf, the sivatherium (an elk-like precursor of the giraffe), and the triceratops (one of the last dinosaurs).

Although children are not always aware of the history of the animals they've climbed upon, they seem to be delighted to ride in a gondola carried by a panda, in the shell of a horned tortoise, or on the back of a Madagascan aepyornis (the biggest bird ever recorded).

Microclimate in the Alpine garden at the Jardin des Plantes

The Alpine garden at the Jardin des Plantes is an amazing place first conceived in the 1930s. Constructed 3 metres below the level of the rest of the botanical gardens, and thus protected from both heat and cold, by means of the interplay of rocks and irrigation it mimics the microclimates of several mountainous regions. Within a confined space, there are temperature differences of up to 20°C. The garden can thus take pride in over 2,000 different plant species, including the famous but rare edelweiss, all cohabiting in an area measuring less than 4,000 m².

Buffon's *gloriette* (gazebo), at the summit of the maze in the Jardin des Plantes, is the oldest metallic construction in France. Born in the town of Montbard, Buffon directed the famous foundry there, which produced the steel used to build these metal structures.

NEARBY

The human foot in the Fontaine aux Lions

Metro Place Monge or Jussieu

The lion fountain located in the Jardin des Plantes near the gate in rue Geoffroy Saint-Hilaire, was built by Henri Jacquemont in 1863. Astonishingly, a lion is seen here devouring what appears to be a human foot ... The sculptor, particularly keen on naturalism, also conceived the sphinxes for the fountain in place du Châtelet, the lions in place Félix Éboué (12th arrondissement), and the dragons in place Saint-Michel.

HORSE HEAD SCULPTURE

Relic of the former horse market

11–13 bis, rue Geoffroy Saint-Hilaire
Metro Gobelins

On the façade of the pavilion at 11–13 bis, rue Geoffroy Saint-Hilaire, dating from 1760, you can still see a beautiful horse's head and the inscription '*Marchand de chevaux, poneys, doubles poneys, de toutes provenances et chevaux de trait*' (Trader of horses, ponies, large ponies from all over and draft horses). The place was built at the request of Police Lieutenant Sartine to house the horse market surveillance officers. The market closed in 1907.

There's also a superb sculpture of a horse's head at 67–69, rue Pigalle, which marks the site of a post for horses (see page 308).

At 27, rue de Grenelle (see page 266) a manger that held their food still stands in front of a garage door.

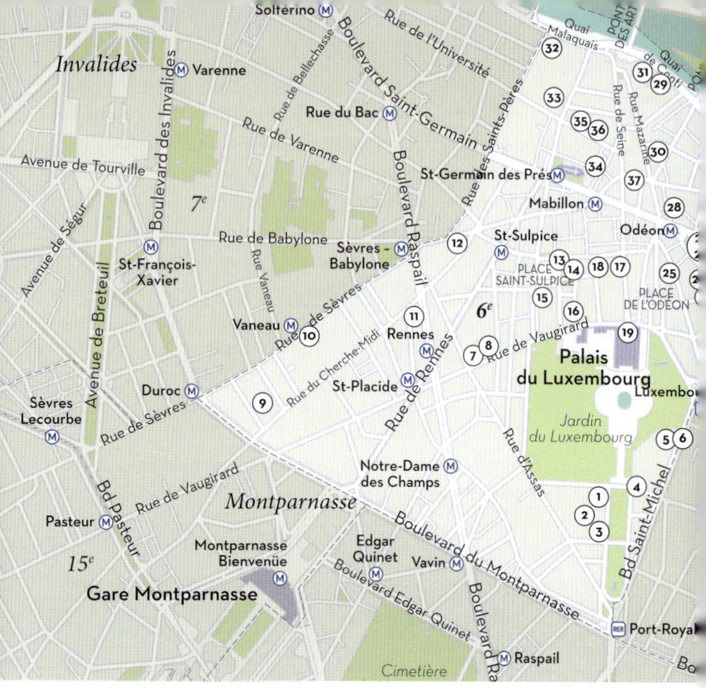

6th arrondissement

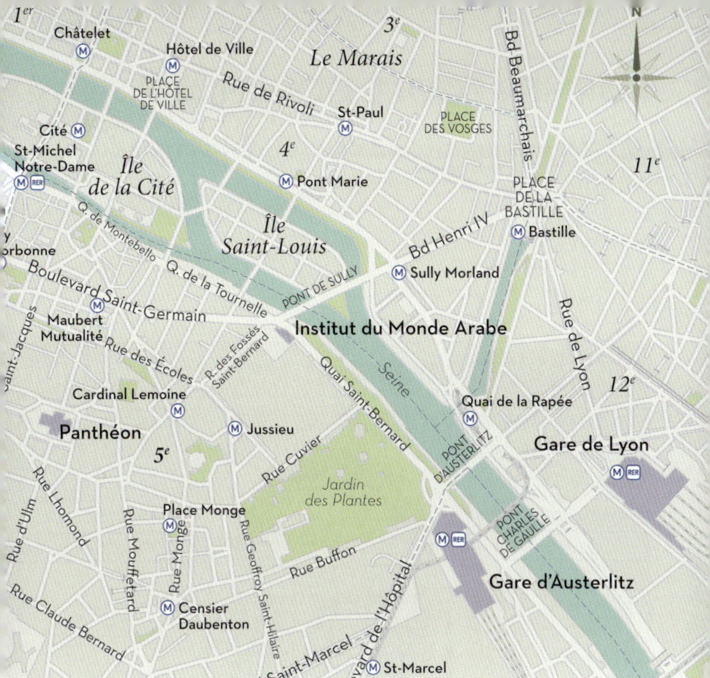

1er
Châtelet
Hôtel de Ville
PLACE
DE L'HÔTEL
DE VILLE
Rue de Rivoli
3e
Le Marais
St-Paul
PLACE
DES VOSGES
Bd Beaumarchais
N
Cité
St-Michel
Notre-Dame
Île
de la Cité
4e
Pont Marie
11e
PLACE
DE LA
BASTILLE
Bastille
y
orbonne
Q. de Montebello
Q. de la Tournelle
Île
Saint-Louis
PONT DE SULLY
Bd Henri IV
Sully Morland
Boulevard Saint-Germain
Maubert
Mutualité
Rue des Écoles
R. des Fossés Saint-Bernard
Institut du Monde Arabe
Rue de Lyon
Saint-Jacques
Cardinal Lemoine
Quai Saint-Bernard
Seine
Quai de la Rapée
12e
Panthéon
5e
Jussieu
Rue Cuvier
Jardin
des Plantes
PONT
D'AUSTERLITZ
Gare de Lyon
Rue d'Ulm
Rue Lhomond
Rue Mouffetard
Rue Monge
Place Monge
Rue Geoffroy Saint-Hilaire
Rue Buffon
boulevard de l'Hôpital
PONT
CHARLES
DE GAULLE
Gare d'Austerlitz
Rue Claude Bernard
Censier
Daubenton
Saint-Marcel
St-Marcel

The finest Islamic building in Paris after the Great Mosque

Now the École Nationale d'Administration
2, avenue de l'Observatoire
RER Luxembourg or Port-Royal

Constructed in 1894–1896 to a design by the architect Maurice Yvon, this building at the corner of avenue de l'Observatoire and rue Auguste Comte is one of the finest examples of Islamic architecture in Paris. Possessing a superb Moorish-style entrance on avenue de l'Observatoire, it has an attractive interior patio and a magnificent library that have maintained their original appearance. It is strange that this gem is not better known. Originally built to house the École Coloniale, which trained those who would administer France's overseas colonies, it now houses the ENA, which trains those who administer France itself.

Islamic architecture in Paris

The first official contacts between France and the Orient came in 1669–1670, when ambassadors were exchanged between the courts of Louis XIV and the Ottoman emperor. Subsequently, the publication of Antoine Gaillard's translation of The Arabian Nights at the beginning of the 18th century made the Orient all the rage in the capital. Around the middle of that century French travellers rediscovered the beauties of Egypt (see page 70), with the result that travel throughout the whole of the Muslim world became more common. The Spanish Alhambra and the mosques of Cairo would have an equal influence on the architects of the famous Marseilles church of Notre-Dame-de-la-Garde and even on the design of the crematorium at Père-Lachaise cemetery. Other than the beautiful Great Mosque in the 5th arrondissement, the most striking example of the influence of Islamic architecture in Paris is probably the former École Coloniale at 2, avenue de l'Observatoire (see above). Other fine examples are to be seen at 4 bis, avenue Hoche (a large Moorish-style salon built in 1892); 68, rue Ampère (a Moorish-style salon, 1895); 44, rue Servan (in the 11th arrondissement, 1870-1890, façade adorned with material probably recycled from the pavilions for the Universal Exposition); 9, rue Fénelon (a private house with an Arab-style vestibule and ceramic decoration produced by the Gillet ceramic works); and 16, rue Bardinet (in the 14th arrondissement, dating from 1908). At 18, rue des Mathurins you can also see the typical Arab-style windows of what used to be a hammam, while the Maison du Maroc in the Cité Universitaire has a magnificent carved wood ceiling from Morocco itself. Finally, two buildings in which the influence is less marked can be seen at 35, rue de Charenton (in Moorish-Gothic style and dating from 1840) and 4, rue de la Cossonnerie (an elephant head that reveals a Muslim-Indian influence).

FRANÇOIS TILLEQUIN MUSEUM

A rare experience

Collections from the analysis laboratories of the Faculty of Pharmacology
4, avenue de l'Observatoire
By appointment for specialist professional groups (+33 1 53 73 98 04)
Open to the general public during the 'Journées du Patrimoine' (September)
and the 'Fête de la Science' (October)
RER Luxembourg or Port-Royal

A visit to the Museum of Medical Specimens is a rare experience. This fine hall – complete with carved wooden decoration, old-style display cabinets and historical flasks and carboys – even incorporates materials recycled from a pavilion constructed for the Universal Exposition of 1889. Within this timeless ambience, the museum has more than 25,000 different compounds and 'simples' (natural substances that were dried and then used in the preparation of medicines). Professor Tillequin, who is usually the guide for those visiting the museum, is a veritable mine of information, supplying endless anecdotes regarding the substances present. For example, you learn that theine is the same as caffeine. Similarly, the subtle differences between various sorts of coffee (Arabica, Robusta, etc.) are explained, as is the truth about Brazilian guarana and Amazonian curare. The cabinet dedicated to Vin Mariani is particularly interesting. One day, Mariani, a Corsican, created a drink based on coca leaves (the source of cocaine) and wine. The beverage was a great success, in part due to Mariani's undeniable talent for marketing; he used to send bottles of the drink to the great and powerful, publishing in his advertisements letters of thanks from the more famous of them. In the United States, a local chemist took his inspiration from this concoction to produce one of his own, in which coca leaves were replaced by an extract of coca beans and wine by a fizzy drink. In 1892, the rights to this recipe were bought by Asa Chandler, and Coca-Cola was born. Just behind this display is another with quinine bark, a substance which is still used to treat malaria. It was first brought back to Europe by the Jesuits, and an illustrious early user was Louis XIV, who had contracted malaria in the marshy areas around Versailles.

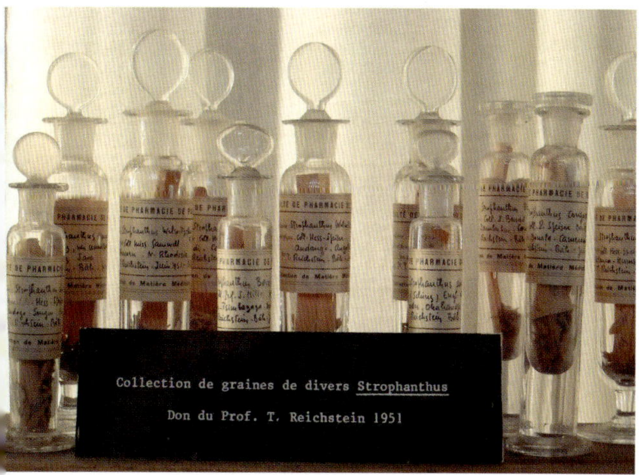

BONATICAL GARDEN OF THE FACULTY OF PHARMACOLOGY

Garden of Simples

4–6, avenue de l'Observatoire
Monday–Friday 9am–7pm; sometimes closed because of the Vigipirate security plan
RER Luxembourg or Port-Royal

Originally intended for students of pharmacology (the study of medicinal plants is part of their first-year course), this stunning and slightly neglected botanical garden is now open to the public. It has a rather nostalgic and romantic atmosphere, which makes it the perfect place for a first date (or perhaps to ask for a first date). The garden is reached by the entrance at 4, avenue de l'Observatoire, from where you follow the pathway and then turn left. Formerly, the Paris École de Pharmacie was located in rue de l'Arbalète, which was also the site of the city's first 'Garden of Simples', created by Nicolas Houel, a 16th century apothecary. When the Faculty of Pharmacology was transferred to avenue de l'Observatoire, the garden too was replanted (in 1880). Originally its surface area was almost 8,000 m², but now it occupies about half that. Nevertheless, it is still delightful to wander around the plant beds and old-style greenhouses, which contain about 500 different species of medicinal plants, toxic plants and plants that are used in the production of perfumes and cosmetics.

Each one is identified with a little label fixed into the ground; however, the abundance of weeds sometimes makes these difficult to read.

NEARBY

The elephants ④ *at 1, avenue de l'Observatoire*

RER Luxembourg or Port-Royal
Directly opposite the former École Coloniale (see page 179) stands a very attractive building which, in spite of its exuberant façade, is easily missed by passers-by. Note, in particular, the carved elephant decoration on the first floor.

War-wounded Palm trees

The palm trees which during the summer months are placed near the large pond in the Jardin du Luxembourg are war veterans. The holes in the trunks of some of the trees were caused by shell shrapnel during the First World War.

LIBRARY
OF ÉCOLE DES MINES

One of the capital's lesser-known libraries

60, boulevard Saint-Michel
+33 1 40 51 91 39
bib.minesparis.psl.eu/bibliotheques/bibliotheque-paris
bibliotheque@mines-paristech.fr
RER Luxembourg

Founded in 1794, the library of the Parisian École des Mines was installed in 1815 in the Hôtel de Vendôme.

The superb reading room was inaugurated during Marshal Foch's presentation of the Croix de Guerre (First World War Cross) at the school in 1926.

The library is open to all on free registration, but you could also ask to look into the reading room to see one of the capital's lesser-known collections.

Resources include scientific works relating to the school's fields of study and research: energy, mechanics, materials, economics, management, society, mathematics, history of science, scientific culture, arts, humanities, languages.

It holds approximately 200,000 documents, including a collection of ancient, rare and valuable books in more than 30,000 volumes dating from the early 16th century to 1940.

MINES MINERALOGY MUSEUM

A magnificent and timeless collection

60, boulevard Saint-Michel
+33 1 40 51 91 39 – musee.minesparis.psl.eu/Accueil/Infos
See website for opening hours
RER Luxembourg

The Mineralogy Museum of the École des Mines, founded in 1794, is a timeless gem housed in the beautiful Hôtel de Vendôme. In its 19th century display cases, arranged along a beautiful 100-metre-long wooden gallery, it presents one of the largest collections in the world, unique in France, of more than 80,000 minerals and crystals.

You can spend hours looking around, but it is best to seek out the volunteers who regularly move around the museum to show you the most spectacular pieces.

For example, the radioactive thorianite cube, a wonderful hauerite crystal, constantly protected from the light by a wooden display case whose lid has to be lifted; or some of the cut gems from the jewels of the Crown of France allocated to the school in 1887.

NEARBY

Édouard Branly Museum ⑦

Institut Catholique de Paris (ground floor)
21, rue d'Assas
+33 1 44 39 52 00 – icp.fr/vie-du-campus/paris/musee-edouard-branly
Visit by appointment only
Metro Rennes or Saint-Placide

The three rooms occupied by the laboratory of Édouard Branly, inventor of radio conductors and former professor of physics at the Catholic University, have been converted into a museum. The exhibits include some of his inventions: the first remote control device and his magnificent 'Nautilus Chamber', a Faraday cage coated with copper to block external electrical fields. You can also see the professor's study overlooking the Carmelite monastery, unchanged since Branly's day.

CRYPT OF SAINT-JOSEPH-DES-CARMES CHURCH

Blood-stained flagstones

70, rue de Vaugirard
sjdc.fr
Visits to the crypt: Saturday at 3pm – For any visit at another time, contact
Mme Nicole de Monts: nicole.demonts@wanadoo.fr
Metro Rennes

Every Saturday at 3pm, groups of five or six people can visit the macabre and little-known crypt of Saint-Joseph-des-Carmes. Before the Revolution, the Carmelite monastery was a peaceful place nestling in a garden where the monks produced the distillation of lemon balm that became well-known as 'Eau des Carmes'. This is still on sale today under the name 'Eau des Carmes Boyer'. The monastery church was also famous for its cupola, which had been the first in Paris.

After a law of 17 August 1792 ordered the closure of all monasteries and convents, the building was converted into a prison, whose inmates included some 160 clerics (three of them bishops). Having refused to take the oath of allegiance to the republican Constitution, which the Assembly had introduced for the clergy in 1790, these clerics would ultimately be massacred in prison.

You can still see the steps to the garden where, summoned on Sunday 2 September 1792, these so-called 'réfractaires' were killed by the pikes and bayonets of a mob led by Commissaire Maillard. The accounts of that event subsequently written by the few survivors can be read on the website bxmartyrsde1792.com.

When rue de Rennes was laid out in 1867, it sliced through the monastery garden and resulted in the destruction of the Martyrs Chapel and of the well where the bodies had been thrown. Subsequent excavation recovered their remains, and these are now preserved in the church crypt. Aligned in rows, a number of the skulls bear clear traces of the murderers' blades.

The model of the demolished garden chapel also brings to mind the horrible scene (some of the blood-stained flagstones have survived).

The visit ends with a message that Josephine de Beauharnais, herself imprisoned here during the Revolution, wrote on the wall of her cell: 'Liberty, when will you cease to be an empty word? It's seventeen days now since we were locked up. They tell us that we'll get out tomorrow. But isn't that just a vain hope?'

After the guided tour, you can wander around the garden and church, which are open to the public all day and contains a very fine *Virgin and Child* by Bernini.

CHAPEL OF THE SŒURS AUXILIATRICES DU PURGATOIRE

A neo-Byzantine cupola

Accueil Barouillère
14, rue Saint-Jean-Baptiste-de-La-Salle
+33 1 53 69 61 00
Telephone for appointment
Metro Duroc, Vaneau or Falguière

In 1856 Eugénie Smet, Sister Marie de la Providence, founded the Congregation of the Auxiliary Sisters in Paris, adopting a Rule based on the spiritual exercises of St Ignatius Loyola. The Barouillère house is the mother house of this order.

You can meditate and pray here in a 19th century chapel surmounted by a neo-Byzantine cupola; the edifice has recently been restored, inspired by the theme of hope. Contemporary in style, the altar combines wood and perspex and is particularly interesting. You can also visit the rooms where the founder of the order lived and worked until her death on 7 February 1871. These have been left just as they were and are imbued with a pleasant sense of calm and quiet.

© Pierre Frey

NEARBY

Relics of Saint Vincent de Paul ⑩

Lazarist Church of Saint-Vincent-de-Paul – 95, rue de Sèvres
+33 1 45 49 84 84 – Metro Duroc or Rennes

The chapel of the Lazarist Fathers in rue de Sèvres has, since 1830, housed the relics of Saint-Vincent-de-Paul. These are contained in a dazzling silver shrine – made by the silversmith Odiot and paid for by the people of Paris – which dominates the chapel choir. Steps adorned with bas-reliefs lead to an impressive scene: the skeleton of the Saint, with the face and hands modelled in wax. The body is clothed in priestly vestments and the hands hold the cross said to be the actual one with which Saint Vincent attended Louis XIII on his deathbed.

SCULPTURE
OF A TELEPHONE OPERATOR

A reminder of the 'telephone girls'

37, rue du Cherche-Midi
Metro Rennes or Sèvres-Babylone

At 37, rue du Cherche-Midi, just raise your head to see an amazingly sympathetic sculpture of a woman's head. Look more closely at her right ear – she's wearing an earpiece, slightly masked by her hair. Above the face, the inscription J'ÉCOUTE (I LISTEN) is a reminder that one of the Parisian telephone exchanges stood here.

These exchanges date from a time when telephones were not dial-up – the subscriber's instrument was still connected to an exchange by a pair of wires. Before the telephone was automated in the late 1970s, the link wasn't direct and to reach a subscriber you had to call the central exchange, which then established the connection. In this central exchange, the 'telephone girls' were seated in front of a huge board, each of them in charge of around a hundred subscribers.

In Paris, the girls lived not far away in an 111-room boarding facility at 41, rue de Lille, built in 1905 (pretty Art Nouveau façade, small inner garden).

Note also the high relief representing a telegraph post at the top left of the façade.

LIBERTY STATUE OF CÉSAR'S *CENTAURE*

Unknown reproduction of a famous statue

Carrefour de la Croix-Rouge
Metro Saint-Sulpice

Some local residents might have noticed the testicles on César Baldaccini's sculpture Centaure, but few will have spotted the miniature statue (the size of a hand) hidden in the half-man, half-horse creature's breastplate. This is one of the six Statues of Liberty in the city, the most famous being those of Île aux Cygnes (16th arrondissement) and the Jardin du Luxembourg (a copy of which is now kept at Orsay Museum). The Arts et Métiers Museum also has a model, probably by Bartholdi himself, and the last copy stands on the walkway by the Seine at Beaugrenelle (15th arrondissement).

Statues of Liberty in France

In addition to the six Statues of Liberty in Paris (see opposite), there are at least six other representations of the famous New York statue in France: in Roybon (Isère), Barentin near Rouen (seen in Gérard Oury's film *Le Cerveau* with Bourvil and Jean-Paul Belmondo), at place de la Liberté in Poitiers, in Colmar, in Nice and in Saint-Cyr-sur-Mer (see *Secret Provence* by the same publisher). The original statue in New York was donated by private French subscription in 1886. It was executed by Frédéric-Auguste Bartholdi and its metal frame designed by Gustave Eiffel. The statue is hollow and covered with riveted copper plates. Its official name is *La Liberté éclairant le Monde* (*Freedom Illuminating the World*).

Turnaround of the Statue de la Liberté in Paris

The Parisian Statue of Liberty, unveiled on 4 July 1889, American Independence Day, on the occasion of the Exposition Universelle, is more than a copy – it's the original model for her big sister in New York. This statue followed the first plaster model, donated by the Comité des Américains de Paris, which was installed in place des États-Unis in the 16th arrondissement on 4 July 1885.

For reasons of protocol, at the unveiling the statue was facing east towards Pont de Grenelle, as it was much easier to inaugurate on land at the western end of Île aux Cygnes.

Bartholdi nevertheless insisted she should be looking in the direction of the United States, but an inauguration that would have had to be carried out by boat was unpopular.

The statue was finally turned to face west for the 1937 Exposition Universelle.

GNOMON IN THE CHURCH OF SAINT-SULPICE

An astronomical instrument 'used' by The Da Vinci Code

Place Saint-Sulpice
pss75.fr/saint-sulpice-paris
Daily 8am–7.45pm
Metro Saint-Sulpice

Now attracting numerous pilgrims eager to verify what is said in *The Da Vinci Code*, Saint-Sulpice church contains a real 18th century gnomon. Standing in the north transept, this astronomical instrument consists of a vertical upright that, in sunlight or moonlight, casts a shadow on a horizontal surface which makes it possible to determine how high the sun or moon are above the horizon. The gnomon consists of a white obelisk about 12 metres high. This is surmounted by a sphere from which a copper line runs down to the floor level and then continues some 40 metres across the choir and north transept.

Commissioned in 1727 by the parish priest, who wanted a more accurate means of determining the March equinox and thus the date of Easter Sunday, this instrument was designed by the clockmaker Henri de Sully, who had wanted to create a way of marking twelve noon within the city of Paris. However, he died before he could complete the task, and his work was subsequently modified, in 1743, by the astronomer Charles Le Monnier, assisted by the engineer Claude Langlois; these changes led to the creation of the famous pink copper line fitted into the floor between bands of white marble. Today, the sundial is only partially functional, as one of the 'lenses' set in the window for the passage of sunlight was badly placed; however, the way it works is explained in detail in a text on a lectern not far from the gnomon.

Given the various claims made about this famous meridian in Dan Brown's book, another text has been added alongside this explanation for the benefit of the curious. It begins: 'Contrary to the far-fetched allegations made in a recent novel of some success, the meridian line of Saint-Sulpice is not the extant trace of a pagan temple which, it is claimed, once stood here ... '

For more on the purpose and operation of meridians, see following double-page spread.

The marble columns of the Virgin Chapel in Saint-Sulpice were installed in 1747, but they date back to Roman times. They come from the ancient site of Leptis Magna in Libya.

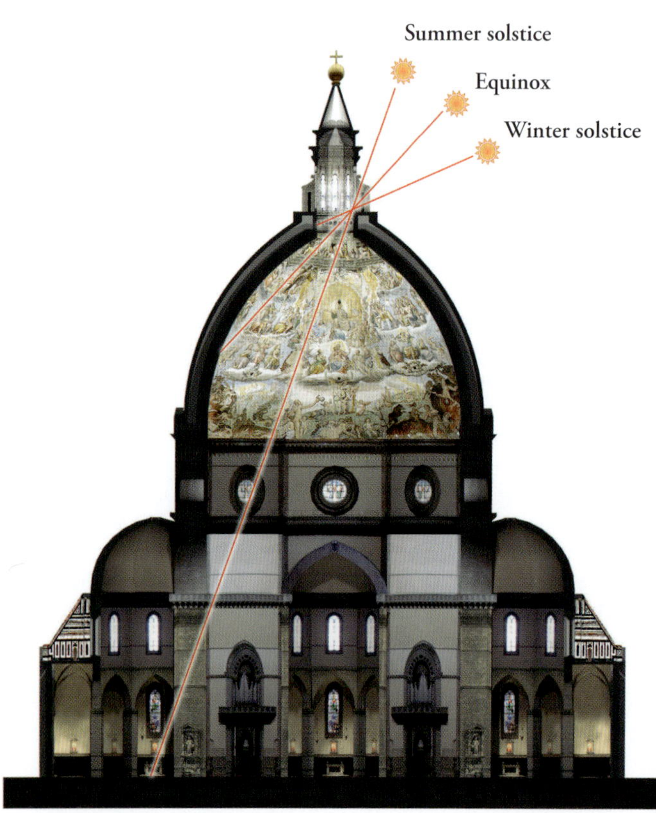

The technical name for a leap year is a bissextile year. The term comes from the fact that the additional day was once placed between 24 and 25 February. In Latin, 24 February was the sixth (sextus) day before the calends of March, hence the name bis sextus, to indicate a supplementary sixth day. The calends were the first day of each month in the Roman calendar.

How does a meridian work?

Instead of using the shadow of a gnomon, meridians use a small hole placed at a certain height, through which the sun's light falls onto a meridian line (i.e. one aligned exactly north-south). The fact that the sun's rays perform the function of the shadow in a traditional sundial means that the opening is sometimes referred to as a 'gnomonic opening.'

The higher the opening, the more efficient the meridian, hence the interest in using cathedrals; the circumference of the hole had to be no more than one thousandth of the height above the ground. Obviously, the opening had to be installed on the south side of the building in order to let in the rays of the sun, which lies to the south in the northern hemisphere.

The meridian line should run from the point which stands perpendicularly below the axis of the opening, not always easy to determine using the instruments available to scientists in the past. The length of the line depends on the height of the opening; in some cases, where the building was not long enough to trace the entire meridian line across the floor (as was the case at Saint-Sulpice), an obelisk was added at its end, so that the movement of the sun's rays could then be measured up the vertical. In summer, when the sun is highest in the sky, the sun's rays fall onto the meridian line closer to the south wall (where that line begins) than they do in winter, when the sun is lower over the horizon and the rays tend to strike towards the far end of the meridian line.

The main principle behind the working of the meridian is that at noon, solar time, the sun is at its apex and, by definition, its rays fall straight along a line running exactly north-south. So, the exact moment when those rays strike the meridian line, which does run north-south, indicates the solar noon.

Furthermore, the exact place on the meridian line where the rays fall makes it possible to determine the day of the year: the point right at the beginning of the line is reached solely on the day of the summer solstice, while the exact end of the line is reached on the day of the winter solstice. Experience and observation meant that the meridian line could be calibrated to identify different days of the year.

Once this was done, the line could be used to establish the date of various movable feasts, such as Easter – one of the great scientific and religious uses of meridians. Similarly, the different periods corresponding with the signs of the Zodiac could be established, which explains why such signs are indicated along the length of a number of meridian lines.

Why was October 4 followed immediately
by October 15 in the year 1582?
The measurement of time and the origin of the
meridians

The entire problem of the measurement of time and the establishment of calendars arises from the fact that the Earth does not take an exact number of days to orbit the Sun: one orbit in fact takes neither 365 nor 366 days but rather 365 days, 5 hours, 48 minutes and 45 seconds. At the time of Julius Caesar, Sosigenes of Alexandria calculated this orbit as 365 days and 6 hours. In order to make up for this difference of an extra 6 hours, he came up with the idea of an extra day every four years: thus the Julian calendar – and the leap year – came into being.

In AD 325, the Council of Nicaea established the temporal power of the Church (it had been called by Constantine, the first Roman emperor to embrace Christianity). The Church's liturgical year contained fixed feasts such as Christmas, but also movable feasts such as Easter. The latter was of essential importance as it commemorated the death and resurrection of Christ, and so the Church decided that it should fall on the first Sunday following the full moon after the spring equinox. That year, the equinox fell on March 21, which was thus established as its permanent date. However, over the years, observation of the heavens showed that the equinox (which corresponds with a certain known position of the stars) no longer fell on March 21. The 11 minutes and 15 seconds difference between the real and assumed time of the Earth's orbit around the Sun was resulting in an increasing gap between the actual equinox and March 21. By the 16th century, that gap had increased to ten full days and so Pope Gregory XIII decided to intervene. Quite simply, ten days would be removed from the calendar in 1582, and it would pass directly from October 4 to October 15. It was also decided, on the basis of complex calculations (carried out most notably by the Calabrian astronomer Luigi Giglio), that the first year of each century (ending in 00) would not actually be a leap year, even though divisible by four. The exceptions would fall every 400 years, which would mean that in 400 years there would be a total of just 97 (rather than 100) leap years. This came closest to making up the shortfall resulting from the difference between the real and assumed time of orbit. Thus 1700, 1800 and 1900 would not be leap years, but 2000 would ...

In order to establish the full credibility of this new calendar – and convince the various Protestant nations that continued to use the Julian calendar – Rome initiated the installation of large meridians within its churches. A wonderful scientific epic had begun.

The meridian of Santa Maria del Fiore: the highest in the world

From the fifteenth to the 18th century almost seventy meridians were installed in churches in France and Italy. Only ten, however, have a gnomonic opening that is more than 10 metres above floor level – that height being crucial to the accuracy of the instrument:

S. S. Maria del Fiore (Florence)	90.11 m
S. Petronio (Bologna)	27.07 m
St-Sulpice (Paris)	26.00 m
Monastery of San Nicolo l'Arena (Catania, Sicily)	23.92 m
Cathedral (Milan)	23.82 m
S. Maria degli Angeli (Rome)	20.34 m
Collège de l'Oratoire (Marseille)	17.00 m
S. Giorgio (Modica, Sicily)	14.18 m
Museo Nazionale (Naples)	14.00 m
Cathedral (Palermo)	11.78 m

Why were meridians installed in cathedrals?

To make their measurements more precise, astronomers required enclosed spaces where the point admitting light was as high as possible from the ground: the longer the beam of light, the more accurately they could establish that it was meeting the floor along an exactly perpendicular plane. Cathedrals were soon recognised as the ideal location for such scientific instruments as meridians. Furthermore, the Church had a vested interest, because meridians could be used to establish the exact date of Easter.

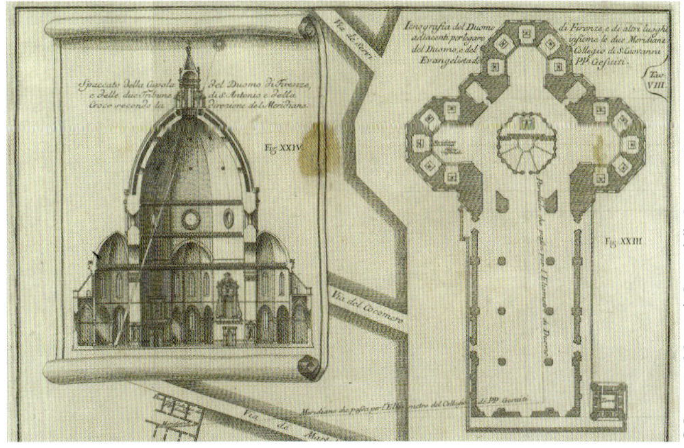

INITIALS 'SP'
AT SAINT-SULPICE

Priory of Sion: purely and simply the invention of an impostor

West transept rose window
Saint-Sulpice church – Place Saint-Sulpice
Daily 7.30am–7.30pm
Metro Saint-Sulpice

On the rose window in the west transept of Saint-Sulpice church are two interlaced initials, 'SP' or 'PS', which amateur occultists or fanciful novelists attribute to the 'Priory of Sion', said to be the name of a mysterious secret society.

This sect never existed. It was the invention of Pierre Plantard (1920–2000), a controversial figure who created it in December 1953 after serving a six-month prison sentence for breach of trust while he was a public servant. On 7 May 1956, he handed over the statutes of his imaginary sect to the sub-prefecture of Saint-Julien-en-Genevois and then, between 1964 and 1967, he anonymously sent the Bibliothèque Nationale de Paris well-developed genealogical studies on Merovingian Frankish kings. He traced their origin to Jesus and Mary Magdalene, who would have been married. The curator of the National Library denied the authenticity of these documents and in 1993 Plantard, who was a rejected Freemason and an outspoken racist, confessed his imposture to the Paris police. He died abandoned by all in 2000.

The initials are in fact those of St Peter and Bishop St Sulpice, the two patrons of the church.

In the church, a painting by Émile Signol (1804–1892) also causes wild imaginings on an alleged inverted 'N'. It shows the sign of the cross (Titulus Crucis) of Jesus, on which is written 'Jesus of Nazareth, King of the Jews', as often, in three languages: Hebrew, Greek and Latin, which were common in the Middle East 2,000 years ago. But these inscriptions are completely reversed: Jesus was Hebraic and, as Hebrew is read from right to left, the very imaginative artist painted the Greek and Latin phrases along the lines of reading and writing Hebrew. In this way he implied the submission of Rome and Athens to Jerusalem, where Christ died and rose again.

NEARBY

Cloister of the old Séminaire de Saint-Sulpice   (15)

9, place Saint-Sulpice
Metro Saint-Sulpice

The tax office in the 6th arrondissement attracts little attention. You should, however, take a look at the cloister of this Florentine-style seminary. The first seminary, dating from 1645, was closed during the Revolution and then destroyed under the Empire. Rebuilt from 1820, the new seminary also housed a hospital for cholera patients. The last students left in 1905.

THE LAST STANDARD METRE

The absolute reference

36, rue de Vaugirard
Metro Saint-Sulpice or Mabillon

The metre, born of the spirit of the Enlightenment and the French Revolution, was defined for the first time in 1791 by the Academy of Sciences as a replacement for units of measurement referring to human beings (thumb, foot ...). As human beings are inherently different in nature, the sovereign was often used as a reference, which was obviously a strong monarchical symbol. The metre was definitively adopted by France in 1795 as an official length measurement.

From 1796 to 1797 the Convention had 16 stone-carved standard metres set around Paris in order to familiarise people with this new measuring system. The standard metre under the arcades of rue de Vaugirard, to the right of the porch of number 36, is the only one still at its original site. The other standard metre in Paris was moved in 1848 from 13, place Vendôme, left of the entrance to the Ministère de la Justice. It was sealed in a wall section belonging to the Bureau International des Poids et Mesures (BIPM: International Bureau of Weights and Measures).

NEARBY
MACL inscription

(17)

4, rue de Tournon – Metro Mabillon or Odéon

On the facade of 4, rue de Tournon, the small inscription 'MACL' simply records that the *Maison est Assurée Contre l'incendie* (House is Insured Against Fire). During the Revolution some people, perhaps inspired by the brothels on nearby rue Saint-Sulpice (see page 78), exploited these initials to give the meaning *Marie-Antoinette Cocufie Louis* (Marie-Antoinette Cuckolds Louis) before, under the Restoration, they took another meaning: *Mes Amis, Chassons Louis* (My Friends, Drive out Louis – for Louis XVIII). In this sense, these inscriptions are reminiscent of those found on a Venice bridge, where at La Fenice opera house at the beginning of the film Senso the audience screams at the Austrian occupying forces '*Viva Verdi*', which stands for *Viva Vittorio Emmanuele, Re d'Italia* (Long Live Victor Emmanuel, King of Italy). (See *Secret Venice* by the same publisher)

There are other MACL inscriptions in Paris, for example at 6, rue Pernelle (4th arrondissement), 9, rue Henri Monnier (9th) and rue du Capitaine Lagache (17th).

How was the metre defined?

It's too often forgotten that the metre is a French invention: it was defined in 1791 by the Académie des Sciences de Paris as being the 10-millionth part of a quarter of a terrestrial meridian. By this definition the Earth had a circumference (equal to the length of one meridian) of 40,000 km. After the establishment of the first standard metre (see opposite), 17 states signed the Convention du Mètre (Metre Convention) in 1875. In 1889 the BIPM had a rod constructed from a platinum-iridium alloy (as variations within the alloy were supposed to be minute) concretely defining the size of one metre. This bar still exists and is kept at the Pavillon de Breteuil in Sèvres (Hauts-de-Seine).

In 1960, with the rise of laser technology, the General Conference on Weights and Measures defined the metre – rather obscurely for the layman – as being 1,650,763.73 wavelengths of the orange-red radiation emitted by the krypton-86 atom.

Even more esoterically, the 1983 conference finally redefined one metre as the distance travelled by light in vacuum during a time interval of 1/299,792,458 of a second.

The speed of light in a vacuum being the same at all points according to the theory of relativity, this definition is considered to be more accurate.

NUMBER 1096, RUE GARANCIÈRE ⑱

Street numbering from the time of Louis XVI

2, rue Garancière
Metro Saint-Sulpice

A little to the left of the street numberplate at 2, rue Garancière, 1096 can still be deciphered as pale figures against slightly blackened stone. This is a left-over from the first attempt to number the streets of Paris under Louis XVI, which was followed during the Revolution with numbering by district (in 1789 Paris was divided into 60 districts), rather than by street, which explains the very high numbers – such as 1096.

The current system (see below) was adopted in 1805 on Napoleon's initiative.

How are street numbers organised in Paris?

Since 1805, the buildings in Paris have always been numbered with even numbers on the right and odd numbers on the left, starting from the beginning of the street.

For streets more or less parallel to the Seine, this follows the direction in which the Seine flows (from east to west, in the case of Paris). For streets more or less at right angles to the Seine, the beginning of the street is always nearest the river.

At first the numbers of the streets parallel to the Seine were painted in red on a yellow background, and those of streets at right angles in black on a yellow background (see example at 167, rue Saint-Jacques). Since 1847, the number has had to be written on porcelain plaques with white numbers enamelled on a blue background. These are still used today.

Curiously, the Charenton, Reuilly and Picpus streets in the 12th arrondissement do not follow this numbering system.

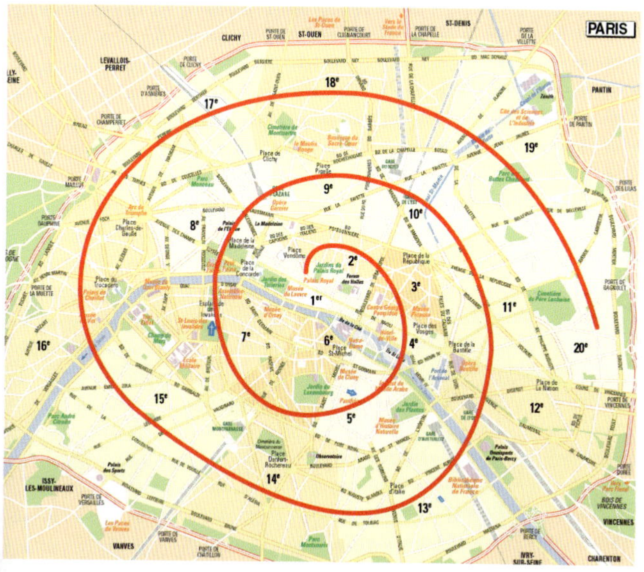

Organisation of Parisian arrondissements

Starting from the city centre (Louvre district) which forms the 1st arrondissement, the 20 arrondissements follow one another, spiralling in a clockwise direction. This arrangement dates back to 1860 and the annexation of the suburbs beyond the Mur des Fermiers Généraux (the wall that surrounded Paris from 1778 to 1860, initially built so that tax farmers could collect tax on goods entering the city). Some villages were completely annexed (Belleville, Grenelle, Vaugirard, La Villette), some were shared between Paris and other communes such as Auteuil (16th and Boulogne), Les Batignolles-Monceau (17th and Clichy), Bercy (12th and Charenton), La Chapelle-Saint-Denis (18th, Aubervilliers, Saint-Denis and Saint-Ouen), Charonne (20th, Bagnolet and Montreuil), Montmartre (18th and Saint-Ouen), Passy (16th and Boulogne), and others were only partially annexed: Aubervilliers, Bagnolet, Gentilly (Glacière district in the 14th, and Maison-Blanche in the 13th), Issy (Javel district in the 15th), Ivry, Montrouge (Petit-Montrouge district in the 14th), Neuilly (Ternes district in the 17th), Pantin, Le Pré-Saint-Gervais, Saint-Mandé (Bel-Air and Picpus districts in the 12th), Saint-Ouen and Vanves. Before 1860, Paris had 12 arrondissements: the 13th took time to accept its number. In addition to superstition about the number 13, at that time the expression *'marié à la mairie du treizième'* ('married at the 13th town hall') meant living in sin.

VISITING THE FRENCH SENATE

The treasures of the Senate building

Palais du Luxembourg
15, rue de Vaugirard
Bookings: +33 1 42 34 20 01
Admission free
Metro Saint-Sulpice or Mabillon

To designs by the architect Salomon de Brosse, work on the palace began in 1615 at the behest of Queen Marie de Médicis, who wanted a building in a style that reminded her of the Pitti Palace in Florence. Now housing the French Senate, this is one of the finest — even if least known — of the public buildings of the Republic. Too often people forget that it is very easy to visit the palace, without having to wait for the Journées du Patrimoine when it attracts huge crowds. Article 33 of the French Constitution lays down that parliamentary sessions must be open to the public; in fact, any citizen can attend the sessions of either the Senate or the National Assembly. However, while places are expensive and very hard to come by at the Assembly, the Senate is much more readily available (at no charge whatsoever) for anyone who wants to fulfil their conscientious duties as a citizen (see box for conditions of admission). Before housing the Senate in 1799, the Palais du Luxembourg had been used as a museum (1750–1780) and even as a prison during the Revolution.

A visit to the modern-day building will give you the chance not only to see senators in full rhetorical flight or fast asleep (both educational experiences), but also to admire the artistic wealth of the place: the 57-metres-long conference chamber, formerly the Throne Room, which was built in 1852 by Alphonse de Gisors; the famous Library, decorated in 1845 by Delacroix; and the 18th century salons by Germain Boffrand.

© Sénat/L. Poyet

How to visit the Senate

– With valid identification, go to 15, rue de Vaugirard on a day when the Senate is sitting (generally Tuesday, Wednesday or Thursday, plus other days – even at night during the annual budget debate). For days and times of sittings, +33 1 42 34 20 01. Tickets to the public gallery (*tribune*) are available on a 'first come, first served' basis.

– Other days when the doors are open to the public (generally Saturdays): the Journée du Livre d'Economie (January), the Journée du Livre d'Histoire (June), etc. These are announced on the Senate website: senat.fr.

– Individual visits organised one Saturday a month, 10.30am–2.30pm, by the Centre des Monuments Nationaux (+33 1 44 54 19 49).

– Group visits: more information at senat.fr

– Journées du Patrimoine (generally the third weekend in September).

A striking portrayal of Death

15, rue de l'École de Médecine
Metro Odéon

Inside the René Descartes Faculty of Medicine, after passing through the cloister, on the left, in a corner, stands a strikingly realistic sculpture. Created by Allouard in 1910, it bears the classic attributes of Death, including the scythe, and tramples underfoot the symbols of human pride and vanity: a crown, a treasure chest, a sword, jewellery and trinkets, a sceptre...

NEARBY

Refectory of the Couvent des Cordeliers ㉑

15, rue de l'École de Médecine
Information on the temporary exhibitions held here at mam.paris.fr
refectoiredescordeliers.rivp.fr – +33 1 77 75 11 00
Metro Odéon

All that remains today of the famous Monastery of Les Cordeliers is this refectory, a fine example of Flamboyant Gothic built at the end of the 15th century. A place of religious devotion, the monastery is best known for the fact that, from 1790 to 1794, it was home to the (in)famous Club des Cordeliers, whose members included Danton and Marat; after his assassination by Charlotte Corday, the latter was buried in the monastery gardens. Covering an area of more than 900 m², the fine refectory is lit by vast Gothic windows and has an impressive timberwork roof. Now the property of the City of Paris, it is a listed historic monument and is used for temporary exhibitions and other events.

The name 'Cordeliers' refers to a mendicant order of Franciscan monks who took this name in reference to the rope belt they wore.

HISTORIC LIBRARY OF THE ÉCOLE DE MÉDECINE

One of the finest secrets of Paris

12, rue de l'École de Médecine
Open only to students of medicine, dentistry and pharmacy, as well as to academic staff and healthcare professionals, but you may be able to take a quick look at the entrance if you ask politely
Monday–Saturday 9am–8pm
Metro Odéon

Located on rue de l'École de Médecine, the site of the medical faculty and a few steps from the Odéon, the Bibliothèque Interuniversitaire de Santé (BIU Santé – Inter-university Library of Health) is one of the finest secrets of Paris. Opened in 1891, the great room of the magnificent library is a little-known gem with its long wooden tables, green lights, vast paintings evoking the history of medicine and shelves of books and archives – a heritage from the long tradition of teaching the science of care.

The library was designed by architect Léon Ginain (Prix de Rome 1852) who also built the Notre-Dame-des-Champs church and the Palais Galliera. He was elected to the Académie des Beaux-Arts (Academy of Fine Arts) in 1881. Ambitious, he designed a library 6 metres longer than Sainte-Geneviève's.

In 1908, with the constant arrival of new documents, a higher level was achieved. The first traces of the medical library in Paris date from the Middle Ages. It was located on rue de la Bûcherie, then rue de Beauvais. The library evolved in the 18th century thanks to donations from doctors, and then again during the French Revolution.

The library remains a world reference resource, especially for the conservation of its original holdings. It offers 100 study spaces where 550,000 books, 20,000 periodicals and 1,300 manuscripts retracing the history of epidemics, diseases and many other ills can be consulted.

STATUE ON
THE ÉCOLE DE MÉDECINE'S
GRAND STAIRCASE

A spectacular allegory of Nature

12, rue de l'École de Médecine
Monday–Saturday 9am–8pm
Metro Odéon

Heading to the Inter-university Library of Health (see previous double-page spread), don't miss the beautiful staircase – at its foot is the remarkable sculpture *La Nature se dévoilant devant la Science* (Nature unveiling herself before Science). The statue depicts a young woman, an allegory of Nature, sensually removing her veil in front of Science in order to discover its beauty and secrets.

After a first version in white marble in 1889 was created for the new Faculty of Medicine in Bordeaux, Louis-Ernest Barrias (1841–1905) created a second version in 1899 (white marble, red marble, onyx, malachite and lapis lazuli) for the Conservatoire National des Arts et Métiers in Paris. This version is currently on display at the Musée d'Orsay.

The white marble version at the medical school was exhibited at the 1902 Paris Salon art exhibition and installed at its present location. A plaster copy is also kept at the Musée de Grenoble.

The initial project for the medical school was due to Jacques Gondoin (1737–1818), a young architect supported by Louis XV, who on returning from Rome commissioned a building to house the Collège Royal and Académie Royale de Chirurgie. Louis XVI laid the first stone in 1774.

The central part of the façade facing rue de l'École de Médecine, the peristyle, the Grand Amphithéâtre (a fine painting by Antoine Esprit Gibelin on the theme of surgery – visiting is sometimes possible on request) and its façade in the Cour d'Honneur, all date from this early period.

In 1876 architect Paul-René-Léon Ginain (1825–98) was commissioned to carry out extension works.

SECRETS OF THE MUSEUM OF THE HISTORY OF MEDICINE

'A table made from brains, blood, bile, liver, lungs and petrified glands ...'

Université de Paris-V – René Descartes
12, rue de l'École de Médecine
+33 1 76 53 16 93
musee.histoire-medecine@u-paris.fr
Visits: 2pm–5.30pm except on Thursdays, Sundays and public holidays
Guided tours for groups (maximum 20–25 people) by appointment
Bookings: Sonja Poncet: sonja.poncet@u-paris.fr
Metro Odéon

Housed in a beautiful space built between 1905 and 1907, the Museum of the History of Medicine is a magnificent small museum whose collections, the oldest in Europe, were gathered by Dean Lafaye in the 18th century.

Decorated with wooden panelling, in which are the embedded portraits of famous doctors and surgeons, the room is 25 metres long by 8 metres wide, and is on the second floor of the Medical School, where formerly a library was housed, and it gave way to the museum when it opened in 1955.

It contains a spectacular collection of surgical instruments and an important collection of pieces covering the various branches of the surgical art up to the end of the 19th century. Scalpels, drills, and saws are next to works of art such as a silver and agate circumcision kit from the 17th century. Other pieces are also of historical interest, such as the scalpel of Felix, surgeon to Louis XIV, or the kit of Doctor Antommarchi, who performed the autopsy on Napoleon.

To fully appreciate and understand the museum, a close look at the labels of the objects presented, as well as the sketches accompanying some of them is highly recommended. Some send shivers down your spine, such as the trepanation boxes, the Percy retractor 'which was used, during amputations, to hold the flesh in order to make a slightly stump' or the instruments for cleft palate operations.

Many visitors never notice that at the back of the room beside the stairs, there is a small table with a foot on it (see next page).

© Emile Barret

The label says that the table consists of 'brains, blood, bile, liver, lungs and petrified glands on which stands a foot, four ears and severed vertebrae, also petrified'. It was made by Efisio Marini, an Italian naturalist physician, and donated to Napoleon III.

Finally, don't miss the sketch, with the aid of supporting objects, showing lithotritie or lithotripsy: an operation without anaesthetic during which kidney stones were removed through the urethra ...

NEARBY
House of Auguste Comte ㉕

10, rue Monsieur Le Prince
+33 1 43 26 08 56 – augustecomte.org
See opening hours on the website
Metro Odéon

Restored in the 1960s thanks to Paulo Carniero, Brazilian ambassador to UNESCO, Auguste Comte's apartment now looks as it did at the time of the death of this philosopher, the founder of Positivism (see page 102). Lasting some 5 to 10 minutes, the visit is a perfect opportunity to learn something about Positivism, and perhaps put a few questions to the staff on duty that day. There is nothing strange about the fact that the apartment was restored by a Brazilian: most adherents of Positivism today are to be found in Brazil, a country in which there is great interest in the spiritual and the esoteric.

© Nicolas Velut

A surprising concrete building: 1, rue Danton ㉖
Metro Saint-Michel

Built by François Hennebique for himself, the structure at 1, rue Danton is surprising because it is entirely made from concrete even if it looks as if it were in stone. Reinforced concrete was, in fact, invented by Hennebique's company, which took out a patent in 1892; the company moved into these premises in 1898.

REMAINS OF OIL-POWERED STREET LIGHT SYSTEMS

From oil to light

8, rue des Grands-Augustins
Metro Saint-Michel

The two vertical marks and small niche on the facade of 8, rue des Grands-Augustins are the discreet remains of the lighting systems for oil street lamps which operated until the beginning of the 19th century.

The City of Paris was concerned with street lighting as early as the 13th century, mainly for security reasons. In 1258 Étienne Boileau, provost of the merchants of Paris, ordered the facades of bourgeois buildings to be illuminated with candles, a measure which was barely applied. In 1667, La Reynie (1625–1709), first lieutenant-general of Paris, had lanterns distributed (still candlelight) to be placed in the centre and at each end of a street. In 1763, M. de Sartine replaced the candles with oil lamps. The lanterns were suspended over the middle of the street, 5 metres above ground. This is why the traces on the wall have two large vertical holes, used in operating the pulleys. The oil lantern hung at the end of a wire connected to a pulley, itself connected to a wire coiled inside a cabinet in the niche on the wall.

Gas lighting was introduced at the beginning of the 19th century and, from 1880, gas gave way to electricity.

NEARBY

Cour de Rohan (28)

Access through cour du Commerce-Saint-André or rue du Jardinet (before 8pm)
Metro Odéon

Made up of three small communicating courtyards, the charming cour de Rohan owes its name to the Hôtel des Évêques de Rouen (Bishops of Rouen), with the name of the city being corrupted into 'Rohan'. It has been linked with cour du Commerce-Saint-André since 1791, and traces of the city walls dating from the time of Philippe Auguste (at No. 3 and 7) can still be seen. A tower from those walls – now a private residence – stands within the Maison de la Catalogne in Cour du Commerce-Saint-André.

The second courtyard has an old 'shoe step' in wrought iron, which served to help women and old people to mount their horses. The third courtyard, which gives onto rue du Jardinet, has an old well complete with pulley and waterspout.

HÔTEL DES MONNAIES PYRAMID

The one The Da Vinci Code *forgot*

11, quai de Conti
Metro Pont-Neuf, Louvre-Rivoli or Odéon

In the second courtyard on the left as you enter the Hôtel des Monnaies (built in the mid-18th century on the orders of King Louis XV), there is a remarkable vertical sundial that is little known to Parisians.

It was designed in 1777 by two members of the Academy of Sciences: Father Pingré (1711–1796), a monk who turned to astronomy, and Edmée Sébastien Jeaurat (1724–1803), a mathematics teacher and surveyor.

Standing 7.80 metres tall, the sundial features just one hour line, that of midday: along with the obelisk-gnomon at Saint-Sulpice (see page 196) and the cannon at the Palais-Royal (when it was in operation), it is one of the three sundials in Paris indicating midday by the sun's path.

NEARBY

Vestige of Philippe Auguste's city walls in an underground car park 

27, rue Mazarine – Metro Mabillon

The first level of this underground car park contains an important vestige of the Philippe Auguste city walls (see page 130). There is pedestrian access, and a plaque marks the location of the wall fragment.

MAZARINE LIBRARY

A forgotten gem

23, quai de Conti
+33 1 44 41 44 06
webmaster@bibliotheque-mazarine.fr
bibliotheque-mazarine.fr
Monday–Saturday 10am–6pm
Annual closure: 1–15 August
Metro Saint-Germain-des-Prés or Pont-Neuf

ndissolubly linked to its creator, Cardinal Mazarin, whose coat of arms features on the pediment of the building, and on the woodwork of the reading room, as well as on the red leather of the bindings, the Mazarine library is sublime. Contrary to expectations, public access is simply by presenting an ID card and two photos.

The library was originally the cardinal's personal collection that he'd gathered in his mansion. Opened in 1643 to scholars, it became the oldest public library in France. In order to avoid the dispersion of his collection after his death, Mazarin attached it to the Collège des Quatre-Nations (College of the Four Nations). The left wing was reserved for the library, which was transferred in its entirety, including furniture.

Attached since 1945 to the Institut de France, which occupies the buildings of the former college, the Mazarine library has, in addition to its collections of old books, a magnificent neoclassical staircase leading to the impressive reading room, 65 metres long and 8 metres high. Punctuated by 32 aisles of shelving and 18 windows, the artworks were largely confiscated during the Revolution.

32

SECRETS OF THE ÉCOLE DES BEAUX-ARTS

All the magic of Paris

14, rue Bonaparte – Metro Saint-Germain-des-Prés
+33 1 47 03 50 74 – beauxartsparis.fr

Occupying 2 hectares of land in the very heart of the Saint-Germain-des-Prés area, the École des Beaux-Arts is one of those places that are an essential part of the magic of Paris. Some of the structures date

back to the 17th century, and all around are works by the art students themselves, giving the place a uniquely romantic atmosphere. The oldest part of the art school is the chapel and connected buildings; these were built at the beginning of the 17th century for the monastery of the Petits Augustins friars and paid for by Queen Margot; the money was said to have been acquired dishonestly (*mal acquis*), hence the name of the nearby quai Malaquais.

When the chapel was deconsecrated in 1795, Alexandre Lenoir (1761–1839) used it to house a Musée des Monuments Français; when that closed in 1816, the building became part of the École des Beaux-Arts. Today, it houses various copies of works from the French and Italian Renaissance, including the *Gates of Paradise*, the original of which were produced by Ghiberti for the Baptistery of Florence Cathedral, and Xavier Sigalon's copy of Michelangelo's *Last Judgment*.

The glazed courtyard (1832) was the inspiration for Labrouste's design for the Reading Room at the Bibliothèque Imperiale (now the Bibliothèque Richelieu). The so-called Amphithéâtre d'Honneur – also known as the Award Amphitheatre – is famous for the Paul Delaroche painting *La Renommée distribuant des couronnes* (*Fame Distributing Crowns*).

The study hall, the exhibition space and the examination building are by the architect François Debret, whose work here was continued by his pupil and brother-in-law, Félix Duban; they were also responsible for the restoration of the entrance courtyard, the chapel courtyard and the magnificent cour des Mûriers (Mulberry Courtyard), an authentic Florentine-style cloister. The final extension to the École des Beaux-Arts came in 1883, with the purchase of the Hôtel de Chimary and its annexes at 15 and 17, quai Malaquais. Conveniently, the porter at the rue Bonaparte entrance often mistakes visitors for students, so you can inspect the magnificent cloister – just to the right of the entrance – without being disturbed.

LECTURE HALL OF THE ACADÉMIE DE MÉDECINE

A place little known to Parisians

16, rue Bonaparte
+33 1 42 34 57 70 – academie-medecine.fr
Public lectures (check programme on the website) held on Tuesday at 2.30pm
(reservation mandatory, contact accueil@academie-medecine.fr)
Metro Saint-Germain-des-Prés or Mabillon

The Tuesday afternoon sessions, usually devoted to public health issues, offer a chance to experience first-hand this bastion of medicine, situated right next to the Beaux-Arts. The assembly hall, a true Italian-style theatre, has regained its subtle colours and period splendour, but on the old-fashioned lecterns, simple labels indicate that this is where the greatest names in medicine gather, in a spirit of camaraderie, at their designated places. The Hall of Busts (featuring ironwork and marble mosaics) displays, in impeccable order, the great figures from the history of medicine and the Academy. The Reading Room, a more intimate space, is reserved for researchers; the library is one of the largest medical libraries in the world and houses some of the most precious treasures in the history of medicine.

Founded in 1820 by Louis XVIII, the Academy, officially intended to answer questions from the government, increasingly plays a role in raising awareness and providing scientific guidance on health matters. It also makes a significant contribution to medical research through the prizes it awards each year on behalf of its donors.

NEARBY

Recess of rue de l'Échaudé 

Corner of rue de l'Échaudé and rue de l'Abbaye
Metro Saint-Germain-des-Prés or Mabillon

The house at the corner of rue de l'Échaudé and rue de l'Abbaye has a curious opening, allowing easier access for horse-drawn carriages, which stood quite high.

Québec in Saint-Germain-des-Prés

Place du Québec, at the intersection of boulevard Saint-Germain, rue de Rennes and rue Bonaparte, owes its name to the fact that the first Bishop of Québec, François de Montmorency-Laval, was consecrated in 1674 in Saint-Germain-des-Prés church just opposite. It houses a very strange fountain that local residents might have had trouble explaining – the tangle of tiles is supposed to represent the ice melting in Canadian rivers. *Le Québec* café complements the Canadian presence in the neighbourhood.

VISCONTI WOOD

The least-known green space in Paris

Access sometimes possible via 26, rue Jacob
Metro Saint-Germain-des-Prés

If you're lucky enough to know someone living at 26, rue Jacob (otherwise, you can always ask nicely), you may have the huge privilege of accessing one of the most secret and surprising green spaces in Paris.

Over about 2,000 square metres, strictly out of sight of the street, the Visconti wood is a set of adjoining gardens that includes those of 34, rue de Seine and 20, 22 and 26, rue Jacob.

The Visconti wood is what remains of the gardens created during the subdivision of the small Pré-aux-Clercs from 1550 to 1600.

In the depths of the wood is hidden a striking little temple with Doric columns. For more on this, see following double-page spread.

The oldest tree in Paris?

A tenacious legend refers to the old tree within the Visconti wood as the oldest tree in Paris. This tree is a catalpa, a species known to not live long. The circumference of the tree (1.7 metres), on the other hand, is exceptional and suggests that, although the tree may not be the oldest in town, it's still very old.

The oldest tree is actually a Robinia false acacia planted in square de Saint-Julien-le-Pauvre in 1601.

TEMPLE OF FRIENDSHIP

One of the least unknown and romantic places in Paris

20, rue Jacob
Private, not open to visitors
Metro Saint-Germain-des-Prés

Concealed from the street, hidden in the heart of Visconti wood (see previous double-page spread) at the bottom of 20, rue Jacob, is an impressive little temple with Doric columns, classified in the Additional Inventory of Historic Monuments. The glory days of the temple, thought to have been built in the early 19th century, were in the early 20th century, thanks to the leaseholder from 1908 to the 1960s, Natalie Clifford Barney. The free and progressive personality of this woman turned it into a renowned literary salon attended by Colette, Hemingway, Proust, Joyce and Paul Valéry.

In 1966 a former prime minister wanted to convert the temple to a studio and transformed its nature. It was, however, restored to the original style in 1974, thanks to a photo taken in 1909.

It can just be seen from the courtyard of 22, rue Jacob that the temple has a pediment with a wreath of flowers and fruits encircling the initials 'DLV'. Below this is written '*À l'Amitié*' (To Friendship).

The inscription DLV is mysterious: does it mean the number 555 in Roman numerals or, rather, *Dieu-Le-Veut*, a motto frequently found in Freemasonry, as the Temple of Friendship also served as a meeting place for some Freemasons?

NEARBY

Star on the building at 12, rue de Buci ㊲

Metro Mabillon

Here the stroller in quest of local interest will find a curious star carved into the façade of the building. In fact, this is a Masonic symbol, the 'Flaming Star' indicating the second level in the hierarchy of Freemasonry. In 1732 the building housed the first Masonic lodge in Paris.

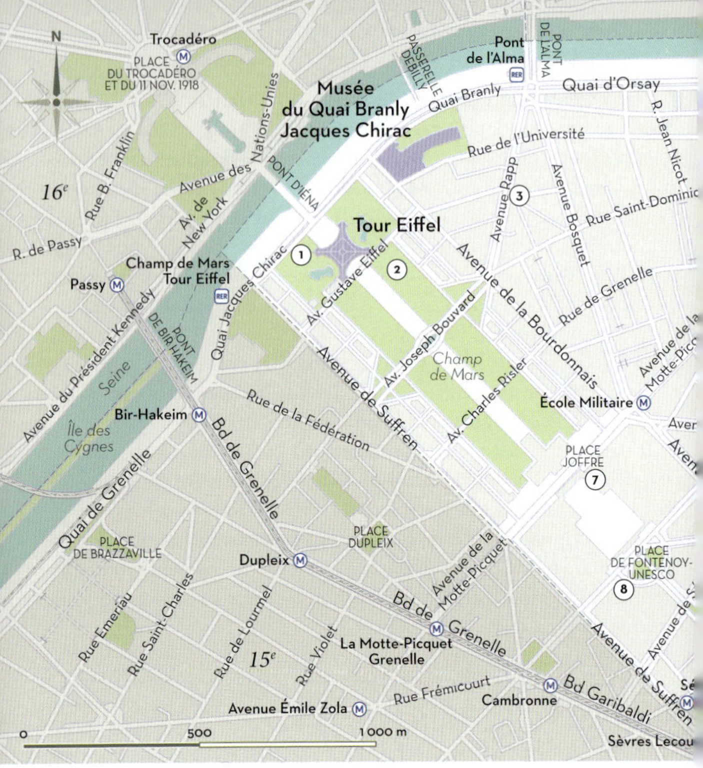

7th arrondissement

PONT ALEXANDRE III
Quai d'Orsay
Invalides
1er
Palais Royal
Musée du Louvre
Assemblée Nationale
Q. A. France
PONT DE LA CONCORDE
PASS. L SEDAR SENGHOR
Quai Aimé Césaire
Seine
Boulevard Saint-Germain
Rue de l'Université
Invalides
Rue de Constantine
Rue Saint-Dominique
Musée d'Orsay
Q. V. Giscard d'Estaing
PONT ROYAL
Q. Voltaire
PONT DU CARROUSEL
Rue Fabert
Musée d'Orsay
Solférino
Rue du Bac
Rue de Lille
Quai Malaquais
La Tour-Maubourg
Rue de Bourgogne
Rue de Verneuil
Rue de l'Université
Rue des Saints-Pères
Varenne
Rue de Bellechasse
Rue Jacob
Invalides
Musée Rodin
Rue de Grenelle
Rue du Bac
Bd Saint-Germain
St-Germain des Prés
7e
Rue de Varenne
Tourville
Rue Barbet de Jouy
Rue du Bac
Boulevard Raspail
Mabillon
St-François-Xavier
Rue de Babylone
Sèvres – Babylone
St-Sulpice
PLACE SAINT-SULPICE
Avenue de Breteuil
Boulevard des Invalides
Rue Vaneau
Vaneau
Rue de Sèvres
Rue du Cherche-Midi
Rennes
Rue de Rennes
6e
Rue de Vaugirard
Duroc
St-Placide
Jardin du Luxembourg
quesne

CHIMNEY OF
THE EIFFEL TOWER

An intriguing turret behind the western pier of the Eiffel Tower

RER Champ-de-Mars

Tucked behind the western pier of the Eiffel Tower, few may have noticed a brick-built pillar surrounded by bushes.

This dates from the work on the tower's foundations (1887) and was a chimney linked by a duct to the old machine room under the south pier.

When the family name of Eiffel Tower scientists cannot exceed 11 letters ...

Many Parisians have never seen it, but on the first floor of the Eiffel Tower, just above the arch formed by the feet of the tower, Gustave Eiffel had engraved 72 names of scientists, engineers or industrialists who honoured France from 1789 to 1889. Although these names were originally written in gold letters 60 cm high, they were painted over at the beginning of the 20th century before restoration in 1986.

On the four sides of the tower you can still read the names of these scientists. But no woman is included, and at least one other detail besides their scientific contribution justifies their inscription – because of the limited space between the beams their family name can't be longer than 11 letters.

So out went Charles Sainte-Claire Deville (geologist and meteorologist), Boussingault (chemist and agronomist), Henri Milne-Edwards (zoologist) and Quatrefages de Bréau (biologist, zoologist and anthropologist), although he'd been considered.

© gede

MONUMENT TO THE DECLARATION OF THE RIGHTS OF MAN AND OF THE CITIZEN

An enigmatic Masonic monument

Champ-de-Mars – Metro École Militaire

The young people who often play football in front of its steps have certainly never noticed one of the most intriguing monuments in Paris. Commissioned in 1989 by the City of Paris to celebrate the bicentenary of the French Revolution, the monument to the Declaration of the Rights of Man and of the Citizen on the Champ-de-Mars owes its many esoteric references to Michel Baroin, the former Grand Master of the Grand Orient, who organised this anniversary. Designed by Czech sculptor Ivan Theimer, the monument is in the classic cubic form of ancient Egyptian and Jewish temples carved from stone. It stands on a podium reached by seven steps, counting the base.

On either side of the entrance are copies of Jakin and Bohaz, the two traditional columns of the ancient Temple of Solomon that bear no weight, as here. Symbolically, they carry the vault of the universe. Just like the Temple of Solomon, the main door of this Parisian monument is made from bronze.

An impressive number of allegories relating to the initiatory mysteries of ancient Egypt have been carved into it, transforming it into a condensed version of occult traditional knowledge.

It forms an amalgam resembling an initiatory anagram that can only be deciphered by those who possess the keys to initiation: a series of Egyptian gods, pyramids of various styles, and mysterious temples and symbolic Parisian buildings is a veiled allusion to the transfer to Paris of the initiatory tradition of Egypt. This tradition reached its peak under Napoleon Bonaparte, sometime after the Revolution that not only changed the political and social situation of France, but also that of Europe and America. Hence the 12 stones inlaid with the names and seals of European Community member cities in 1989.

Also at the entrance is the famous phrase attributed to French painter Nicolas Poussin (1594–1665): *Et in Arcadia ego*, which means 'I [Death], I am also in Arcadia [the land of delights]', which can be interpreted as a message that by divine wisdom, death does not prevent the Enlightened from accessing Arcadia.

The image of the deified paradise is depicted by two other engravings accompanying a phrase which translates as 'The French people recognise the supreme being and immortality of the soul' and 'Unity, indivisibility of the Republic. Liberty, Equality, Fraternity, or death', with the Masonic delta and pendulum, and paradise in the background.

Above the entrance, a circular opening without a window shows a snake biting its own tail – the celebrated ouroboros. The snake is the symbol of global knowledge, and coiled around like this it symbolises the universe of Knowledge, and the unity of Being.

Next to it is the sculpture of a lizard, which the Old Testament (Proverbs 30:24) describes as one of 'four things which are little upon the earth, but they are exceeding wise' recalling the symbolism of the snake. Its long hours of immobility in the sun are a symbol of contemplative ecstasy, and the lizard will therefore symbolise the soul humbly seeking the light. At the back of the monument, two obelisks lend an Egyptian aesthetic to the whole. They are covered with inscriptions and symbols, most of them from the Masonic alphabet adopted by the French rite.

On the obelisk to the right, a parallel is made between the sculptures of the Tables of the Law given by God to Moses, and the Declaration of the Rights of Man.

Two bronze statues also grace the monument. One is a citizen raising his arms, personalising the humanity, piety and tolerance we must feel towards each other.

The other is a woman with a branch who guides a child, an allegory of Motherhood and Education: a well-educated young generation is the cornerstone of civilisation and universal progress.

The vertical Hebrew texts decorating the man's tunic and the horizontal French text point to the Old Testament (Exodus 34:1) – both refer to the two tablets of the Law cut by Moses after the destruction of the first, and to the Covenant of God with his people who must obey the Law and be humanly just with their neighbours.

For more on the ouroboros above the monument door, see page 28.

THE GIANT PHALLUS AT 29, AVENUE RAPP

A door adorned with a giant inverted phallus

RER Pont de l'Alma

A prize-winner in a 1901 competition for façade design, the building at 29, avenue Rapp is considered to be Lavirotte's masterpiece. Surmounted by a female head (perhaps a portrait of the architect's wife) and flanked by Adam and Eve driven out of Paradise, the main doorway is relatively well known to Parisians; however, there are few who have noticed that the door itself takes the form of an inverted phallus.

To see this, just focus on the central part of the wooden door (the carving itself is significant), with the central glass panel and the two oval-shaped glass panels at the top.

A fervent champion of sexual symbolism, Lavirotte also used the motif of a penis inside a vulva in the ironwork of the ground-floor window balconies.

Contrary to what is widely believed, the owners of the building were Lavirotte himself and a certain Charles Combes. It was never the home of the ceramicist Alexandre Bigot, whom many think used the façade to advertise his skills; however, there is no doubt that he did adorn the building with his famous stoneware ceramics, specially adapting them for use in architecture. Lavirotte himself lived on the fifth floor of the nearby building at 3, square Rapp.

Jules Lavirotte

One of the most famous architects of Parisian Art Nouveau, Jules Lavirotte (1864–1929) was undoubtedly the most flamboyant. He not only banished straight lines and right angles from designs in which curves predominate, but he also made free use of sexual symbolism – something which did not prevent him from becoming the only architect to win the 'City of Paris' façade design award three times. However, in 1907 he abandoned Art Nouveau, claiming that the imitations of his work were mere pastiches which betrayed the essence of the original movement. His most famous buildings are to be found at 29, avenue Rapp, 3, square Rapp, 12, avenue Sédillot and 34, avenue de Wagram (Hotel Céramic, see page 289). Other, less spectacular, buildings by him can be seen at 134 and 151, rue de Grenelle, 23, avenue de Messine, 169, boulevard Lefebvre and 2, rue Balzac at Franconville (95) (Villa Dupont).

Other ceramic phalluses

The building at 12, avenue Sédillot was the first fully designed by Lavirotte. That at 3, square Rapp contains quite clear sexual symbols (most notably, the ceramic phalluses in the window balconies of the fourth floor).

WOLF SCULPTURE

A rebus that isn't word play

Cour d'Honneur des Invalides
Metro Varenne, La Tour-Maubourg or Invalides

Entering the Invalides courtyard on the Seine side, a lucarne in the shape of an eye at the bottom left of the courtyard is strangely surmounted by a sculpture of a wolf's head that seems to be holding the window in its paws. Two feet can also be seen at the base of the skylight, as well as weapons. According to the sign welcoming visitors at the entrance to the courtyard, the group is thought to be a rebus dreamt up by Louvois (1641–91), who was Minister of War and the Buildings Superintendent of Louis XIV, in order to establish symbolic control of a building in his charge by playing on the parallel between *loup voit* (wolf sees) and *Louvois*.

For some specialists, however, the 60 dormers of the courtyard are a specific symbol relating to the military history of Louis XIV from 1643 to 1697. The wolf that could be part of a rebus was made in 1735 by Guillaume Coustou, more than 40 years after Louvois's death. It

actually corresponds to the mythological wolf companion of Arès (or Mars), god of War. Not far away, we find Pallas (Minerva), goddess of War, sitting near her traditional owl. There are three other wolves carved in the courtyard – accompanied by the symbolic crescent of Islam, they represent the Turkish enemy (the grey or blue wolf is the mythological ancestor of the Turkish nation) during three events: the Battle of Kahlenberg (1683), the Battle of St Gotthard (1664) and the Battle of Djidjelli (1664).

The sculptural ensemble of the Invalides courtyard is a masterpiece of military symbolism. It draws its repertoire from a collection of scholarly symbols by Cesare Rippa as well as from the work of the Petite Académie (ancestor of the Académie des Inscriptions et Belles Lettres) on medals.

The statue of Napoleon in the courtyard is the one that stood on top of the Vendôme column from 1833 to 1863. Exhibited for a time in Courbevoie (see page 245), it was thrown into the Seine at the fall of the Second Empire, then retrieved in 1876, and placed here in 1911.

NEARBY
Graffiti of a shoe ⑤
Metro Varenne, La Tour-Maubourg or Invalides
On the first floor of the Invalides courtyard (access to the back of the courtyard on the Seine side), the 'corridor of Quesnoy' lets you see, behind the statue of the Grenadier, above the right parapet, the graffiti of a shoe with a *talon rabattu* (folded heel), a type of footwear reserved for the nobility under Louis XIV. Another similar graffiti is located right next to the parapet on the west corridor.

NAPOLEON'S ACTUAL TOMBSTONE

Secrets of the Emperor

West exterior of Invalides church
Metro École Militaire
RER Pont de l'Alma

To the left of the Invalides church, looking from the main entrance on rue de Tourville, at the foot of a tree behind a small grove, the three sections of Napoleon's actual tombstone are very discreetly placed. The tombstone was brought back from Saint Helena Island in 1840, along with the mortal remains of the Emperor, aboard the ship *La Belle Poule*, which arrived at Cherbourg on 30 November 1840. The body was transferred six days later to the steamer Normandie, which delivered its precious cargo to the vessel La Dorade at the port of Val-de-la-Haye, near Rouen (see *Secret Normandy* by the same publisher). It was therefore La Dorade and not La Belle Poule that sailed up the Seine to Courbevoie. From Courbevoie, the funeral chariot passed through the Champs-Élysées to reach the Invalides.

The white marble of the high altar of the Saint-Paul-Saint-Louis church, which was moved and remade in the time of Louis-Philippe, comes from fragments of the Emperor's tomb at Invalides.

Two more little-known relics of the return of Napoleon's body

In the business district of La Défense (Terrasse des Feuillantines, La Défense 1), a little-known monument was erected to the glory of Napoleon in 1940, to celebrate the 100th anniversary of the return of his remains to France. The stele was moved to its present location in 1980 following the development of this part of La Défense, although a new stele had to be built on that occasion, as the old one had weathered too much. The original stele is now in the Musée Roybet Fould at Courbevoie, which also has another relic relating to Napoleon: sawdust from his coffin. As the coffin was about to be placed in the hearse, Courbevoie carpenter Jean-Nicolas Tacaille had to plane a few centimetres from the wood to make it fit.

NEARBY
Graffiti for Napoleon ⑦
École Militaire – Avenue de la Motte-Picquet
Metro École Militaire

On the main façade of the Military School, behind the last column on the right of the main entrance, about 3 metres from the ground, you can read some discreet graffiti that has survived the passage of time:
'VIVE LA FRANCE
VIVE NAPOLÉON
(PARTI) SEUL POUR ILE S. HELENE'
The site of the graffiti is particularly well chosen, partly because Napoleon was a student at the school, but also because his remains, as well as his tombstone (see opposite), were installed nearby at Les Invalides in 1840. Did the author of the graffiti, who probably engraved it in 1815 (the year of Napoleon's departure for Saint Helena) or shortly after, have a flash of inspiration?

WORKS OF ART
AT UNESCO

Picasso, Miró, Calder, Giacometti, Tadao Ando ...

United Nations Educational, Scientific and Cultural Organization
7, place de Fontenoy
+33 1 45 68 10 00
Access only by appointment: book your tour on website
unesco.org/fr/guided-tours?hub=171411
Identification required
Metro La Motte-Piquet or Ségur

© UNESCO/Dominique Roger

A hidden Zen garden, a panoramic terrace, works by the greatest of modern artists ... UNESCO is crammed with art; on the walls hang more than 500 different works. There is even a remarkable space designed by the Japanese architect Tadao Ando, who was to have built the Musée Pinault of the Île Seguin.

As soon as the building was completed in 1958, famous artists were invited to make a contribution to the interior décor. Pablo Picasso, Joan Miró, Henry Moore, Alexander Calder, Jean Arp and Isamu Noguchi all responded, creating works especially for the site. In the foyer to the Conference Halls stands the largest work Picasso ever painted; a tragic *Fall of Icarus*, this acrylic on wood panel measures 10 metres by 9 metres. Outside, the work by Noguchi is probably the most famous of the contributions. The Japanese artist started with a few sculptures for the terrace, but ultimately transformed the place into an authentic 'Japanese garden', a marvel of quiet and greenery. Other names encountered here are Giacometti, Brassaï, Appel, Tàpies, Chillida and Bazaine. But it was not only painters and sculptors who made a contribution: no less than twelve architects played a part in the design of this Y-shaped building, which rests on 72 trapezoidal pillars in reinforced concrete and has three curved glass façades whose lines echo the semicircle of place de Fontenoy. The three main architects were Marcel Breuer, Pier Luigi Nervi and Bernard Zehrfuss, with input from Walter Gropius (the father of Bauhaus) as well as from Le Corbusier, Lucio Costa, Sven Markelius, Ernesto Rogers and Eero Saarinen. One room was designed by the American Philip Johnson, one of the first exponents of the 'International Style' of which the UNESCO building is an example.

More recently, in 1995, the Japanese architect Tadao Ando worked here on what is his sole completed project in France. This is a 'meditation space' in the form of an inclined concrete cylinder, where thoughts, like the flowing water, can run on forever.

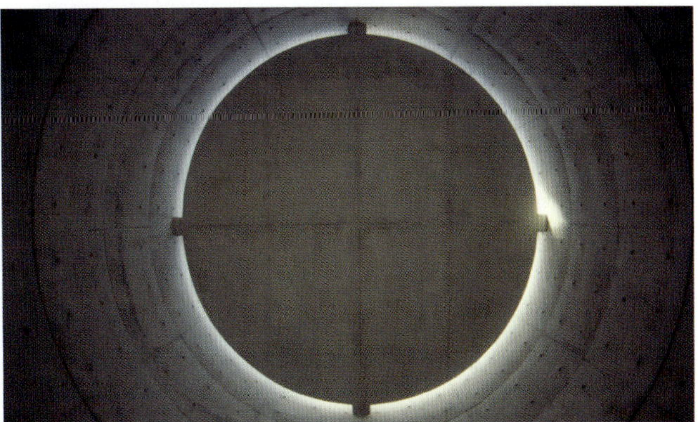

TINTORETTO'S *LAST SUPPER*

A little-known masterpiece by Tintoretto

Saint-François Xavier church
Marriage Sacristy
Saturday 9am–12pm, or by appointment: +33 1 44 49 62 62
sfx-paris.fr
Metro Saint-François-Xavier

The Marriage Sacristy in the church of Saint-François-Xavier unexpectedly contains a masterpiece by Tintoretto (1518–1594), one of the great masters of the Venetian Renaissance.

This *Last Supper* was painted in 1559 for the chapel of the Scuola del Santissimo Sacramento (Confraternity of the Holy Sacrament) in the Venetian church of San Felice. The inscription in the lower left names those who, at the time of the commission, were at the head of the confraternity, which was dedicated to the protection and veneration of the consecrated host. Thus we learn that the *gastaldo* (chamberlain) was Girolamo Diletti, the *vicario* (vicar) Salvador di Orsini and the *scrivano* (secretary) Marco de Marco. The painter also included their portraits in the picture. However, only those of the vicar and secretary (at the far right and left of the scene) survive; that of the chamberlain was removed by order of his successor after Diletti was accused of ill management of the confraternity's funds.

Though Tintoretto painted *The Last Supper* a number of times, this was not – as some say – because it was his favourite subject, but because it was much in demand among his clients. Anxious that his patrons should never feel they were getting 'mass-produced' works, the artist did however tend to focus on a different moment in the gospel narrative each time he painted the scene. The San Felice work, for example, hinges on the identification of the apostle who will betray Christ. Jesus has just caused great agitation by announcing that there is a traitor amongst them; the apostles are looking at each other, trying to identify who the wretch might be. The painter also involves the spectator in the scene, by revealing something hidden from those within the picture: Judas faces away from us, but we see that behind his back he is clutching the purse with his 30 pieces of silver.

NEARBY

Religious plants in the garden of Saint-François-Xavier presbytery ⑩

39, boulevard des Invalides

Metro Saint-François-Xavier

Open during the Parisian Fête des Jardins and every Thursday evening in summer (for fathers left alone in the city while their families are on holiday), this is a charming priest's garden which focuses on plants that have some sort of relation with the Church. These include: honesty (*monnaie-du-pape*), curate pears (*poirier du curê*), 'red cascade' spindle trees (*fusain bonnet de prêtre*) and of course daisies (called *pâquerettes* in French because they flower around Easter, *Pâques*).

VALENTIN HAÜY MUSEUM

An atmosphere reminiscent of a cabinet of curiosities

5, rue Duroc
+33 1 44 49 27 27 – avh.asso.fr
Visit by appointment only, contact m.duhen@avh.asso.fr or
museevalentinhauy@avh.asso.fr
Admission free
Metro Duroc

Set up in 1886, the Valentin Haüy Museum is named after a man who founded a school for the blind in 1785; it charts the history of the blind and of the various methods developed to enable them to read and write – from the invention of raised cursive script to the introduction of Braille. This fascinating museum collection also includes a number of objects, machines and works of art created either for or by the blind or partially sighted.

A small area dedicated to the blind

The Valentin Haüy Museum is conveniently located just next door to the National Institute for Young Blind People, in boulevard des Invalides.

A couple of steps away lies rue Valentin Haüy itself, which is officially part of the 15th arrondissement, and rue Maurice de la Suzeranne, which cuts across rue Duroc; the street is named after the founder of the Association Valentin Haüy, who as the result of an accident lost his sight at the age of nine.

Système Braille

	a	b	c	d	e	f	g	h	i	j
Signe majuscule										

k	l	m	n	o	p	q	r	s	t

u	v	x	y	z	ç	é	à	è	ù

â	ê	î	ô	û	ë	ï	ü	œ	w

	1	2	3	4	5	6	7	8	9	0
Signe numérique										

,	;	:	.	?	!	"	(	*	)

Apostrophe	Trait d'union	Italique	Fin de vers

SAINT-DOMINIQUE-SAINT-MATTHIEU CHAPEL

A hidden country chapel

30, rue Vaneau
Ask for the mass schedule at cdas@diocese-paris.net
Metro Vaneau

Once a week, on Sunday from 10.30am to 11.30am, the door of 30, rue Vaneau opens onto a small corridor containing mythological bas-reliefs. At the bottom, a charming little courtyard gives access to one of the most secret chapels in Paris.

Built in 1910 on a previous place of worship for the sisters of the Mercy de Sées, and restored in 1929, Saint-Dominique-Saint-Matthieu chapel has seven superb stained-glass windows made in 1995 by Jean Bazaine. The windows recall the seven daily prayers of believers: matins and laudes, prime, terce, sexte, none, vespers and compline.

The church also keeps a tapestry of the same author behind the altar, and an icon of St Matthew dating from the 14th to the 15th centuries.

NEARBY

23, rue Oudinot and 50, rue Vaneau ⑬

Metro Vaneau

If a resident opens the door, take the opportunity to glance around this little corner of paradise with its low houses and cobbled passages.

GARDEN OF THE FOREIGN MISSIONS SOCIETY

A sublime secret garden

128, rue du Bac
+33 1 44 39 10 40
missionsetrangeres.com
28ruedubac@gmail.com
Accessible during 'Journées du Patrimoine' (Heritage Days) on guided tours
or during 'Fête des Jardins', by appointment only
Metro Rue du Bac or Sèvres-Babylone

© Eric Henry

Behind the buildings at the corner of Bac and Babylone streets lies the most secret garden in the district. The garden, which is one hectare in total and adjoins the Matignon garden, belongs to the Foreign Missions Society (Société des Missions étrangères), which dates back to the 17th century when Bishop Bernard de Sainte-Thérèse founded a seminary here to prepare missionaries for distant lands. Absent from Paris for too long and probably poorly supported, the bishop never managed to run his seminary. He gave it to the nascent society, legally recognised in 1663 for training French priests and lay people destined for the Missions of Asia.

Today's garden is the result of combining several plots that were private vegetable gardens in the 17th century. The seminary directors were careful to buy them one after another, especially on the occasion of succession. It took 70 years to extend the garden to its present dimensions. The plan, executed by a disciple of Le Nôtre and approved by Le Maître, is of a French garden with rectilinear paths and 'green carpets'. Since it was established, the garden has undergone no major changes and is still tended with care.

The garden features some curiosities including rare plants such as the Souliena rose discovered by Jean-André Soulié [1858–1905], a Chinese bell donated in 1858 by Rear-Admiral Rigault de Genouilly on behalf of the French expeditionary corps in Canton. There is also an oratory with a roof like a Chinese hat, built in a corner of the garden around 1844, and statues recalling the life of priests of the Foreign Missions of Paris who had been active for over three centuries in South-East and East Asia.

Origin of the name rue de Babylone

Rue de Babylone owes its name to Bernard de Sainte-Thérèse (see above), who was appointed Bishop of Babylon (present-day Iraq) in 1638.

FORMER CHAPPE TOWER

The last Chappe tower in Paris

103, rue de Grenelle
Metro Varenne

At the rear of the courtyard at 103, rue de Grenelle, an impressive tower has been preserved. This was used by Chappe in the 18th century for his experiments to establish telegraphic links in France during the Revolution (see page 518 for *modus operandi*).

The tower at the rue de Grenelle was part of the line linking Paris to Strasbourg that came into service in 1798. This 500-km line had 44 signalling stations (48 when it closed in 1852), including eight in Paris. The starting point of the line was initially at the top of the south tower of Saint-Sulpice church, but it was moved in 1823 to Notre-Dame-des-Victoire church, and then in 1834 to Saint-Eustache church.

At the entrance to the tower, on each side of the front door, you can see Chappe's original tombstone. Remember that the Chappe telegraph between Paris and Lille was used to announce the reconquest of Condé-sur-l'Escaut (commune in northern France on the border with Belgium) in 1793 at the expense of the Austrian occupiers. The other is surprisingly surmounted by an ouroboros (see page 28).

A statue of Chappe was installed in 1893, not far away at the corner of rue du Bac and boulevard Saint-Germain, to mark the centenary of the invention of the telegraph.

The statue was melted down during the Second World War. Not only did Germany need metal for its war effort, but the statue also obstructed traffic. Finally, before the war it was also judged to be one of the four ugliest statues in Paris!

For more on the operation of the Chappe telegraph and other former sites of Chappe towers in Paris, see the following double-page spread and page 518.

Abside de l'Eglise de Montmartre.

Vecinto exterior del coro de la Iglesia de Montmartre.

Other Chappe towers in Paris

Besides the tower at 103, rue de Grenelle, there were eight Chappe towers on the Paris–Strasbourg line, at the following locations:
– Petits Pères church (Notre-Dame-des-Victoires) (on the bell tower)
– Saint-Eustache church (on the bell tower)
– Saint-Pierre de Montmartre church (on the bell tower, see photo opposite)
– Saint-Sulpice church (left tower and right tower)
– Louvre (Pavillon de l'Horloge / Clock Pavilion, see below)
– Ménilmontant (Belleville) (40, rue du Télégraphe, where there is a plaque, see page 519)
– Ministère de la Marine (on the roof) NB: another telegraph tower stood by the Saint-Roch church, marking the departure of the private line of the 'Vigigraphe' of Laval and Peytes-Montcabrier (1799–1803), a Chappe telegraph competitor based on a decimal code that was abandoned after trials in 1799.

Télégraphe métro station in the 20th arrondissement is linked to the installation of the Chappe telegraph on the heights of Belleville. A plaque was also fixed at 40, rue du Télégraphe specifically on the site of Chappe's experiments, which was considered to be the highest point in Paris (see page 519). Chappe's tomb, at Père-Lachaise cemetery, features an awesome miniature reproduction of his telegraph (see page 518).

16

GLOVED HAND
OF THE STATUE OF THE LAW

Masonic statue in front of the Assemblée Nationale

Place du Palais-Bourbon
Metro Assemblée Nationale

Created in 1852 by French sculptor Jean-Jacques Feuchère (1807–1852), the statue of the Law, which sits opposite the entrance to the National Assembly at Place du Palais-Bourbon, was installed on this square in 1854. With her right hand she raises the golden sceptre of power and presents from the left the *Déclaration des Droits de l'Homme et du Citoyen* (Declaration of the Rights of Man and of the Citizen) of 1789. Under the pedestal, the scales and sword of justice can be seen (symbols of fairness and strength), as well as the mirror around which the snake wraps itself, representing prudence. You'll realise that the statue's right hand is gloved, likely to be a Masonic symbol. White gloves are worn by Masons as a sign of distinction but also of purity: they mean that their hands are clean because they did not participate, symbolically speaking, in the assassination of the great architect of the

Temple of Solomon, the Phoenician Hiram Abiff, who was thought to be the founder of traditional Freemasonry.

After his admittance to the Masonic brotherhood, the Apprentice Mason receives two pairs of white gloves, one for him and the other for 'the lady he loves most'. In this respect, Swiss occultist Oswald Wirth comments: 'The white gloves received on the day of his initiation evoke to the Mason the memory of his commitments. The lady who will show him the gloves, if he is about to fail, will appear to him as his living conscience, the guardian of his honour. What higher mission could he entrust to the lady he loves most?' And he points out that Goethe, initiated in Weimar on 23 June 1780, paid homage to Madame von Stein with these symbolic gloves, showing her that what might seem an insignificant gesture was anything but, as it could only be made once in the entire life of a Freemason.

The golden sceptre of the statue is grasped by a hand giving a blessing, indicating that the light of Justice symbolically grants its grace indiscriminately to all. The universal character of the Law is confirmed on the pedestal by the scales and behind them the Eye of the Great Architect of the Universe, a reference to the Justice of God whose Law is sovereign over all human contingencies, impartial in his judgements, and right in his decrees.

Why does quai d'Orsay only begin at number 33?

The numbering of quai d'Orsay curiously begins at number 33. In 1947, although the beginning of the quay was indeed named quai Anatole France, it was out of the question to change the address of the Ministère des Affaires Étrangères (Ministry of Foreign Affairs) for which Quai d'Orsay had become a synonym.

Why does Mickey wear white gloves?

Mickey's gloves are also a Masonic reference imagined by Walt Disney, who had the 33rd degree of the ancient and accepted Scottish Rite, and was an officer of the DeMolay Order, an order of Masonic inspiration whose name comes from Jacques De Molay, the last Grand Master of the Templars (see page 40).

The DeMolay Order is a secret Mason-sponsored organisation for young men between 12 and 21 years of age. Founded in the USA on 18 March 1919 by Frank Sherman Land, the Order has been officially sponsored and supported since 1921 by Freemasonry. The actor John Wayne (1907–79), the writer John Steinbeck (1902–68) and Bill Clinton (1946–) were members.

17

SHRAPNEL MARKS

Bullet holes in the ministry wall

231, boulevard Saint-Germain
Metro Solferino or Assemblée Nationale

The former Ministry of War, which now houses the General Staff of the Armed Forces, bears disturbing witness to how close the First World War came to the centre of Paris. The damage to the walls was caused by shrapnel during the heavy bombardment of Paris on 11 March 1918. An inscription in the stone recounts details of the event.

If you are particularly interested in traces of past warfare, you will find numerous examples within the city. For example, shell damage can be seen on the Théâtre de l'Europe in the 6th arrondissement and on the façade of the Law Courts in the 4th.

Even more astonishing is the small cannonball still embedded in the walls of the Hôtel de Sens (see page 128); this dates from the days of the 1830 revolution.

HOUSE OF LATIN AMERICA GARDENS

A hidden gem

217, boulevard Saint-Germain
mal217.org
Metro Rue du Bac

Visible from the street, the beautiful French gardens of the House of Latin America (Maison de l'Amérique Latine) are open to the public either for exhibitions in the lounges or for lunch on the restaurant's magnificent terrace, which is also open to the public. La Maison de l'Amérique Latine has occupied two mansions since 1946: Hôtel de Varengeville, built in 1704 by architect Jacques Gabriel V, and Hôtel Amelot de Gournay, built in 1712 by architect Germain Boffrand. The two are now connected by their ground-floor lounges overlooking the gardens. Although the Varengeville was damaged in 1876 by drilling in the construction of boulevard Saint-Germain, the Amelot of Gournay remained intact.

The hotel, and the gardens, are listed in the Additional Inventory of Historic Monuments.

© Maison de l'Amérique Latine

NEARBY

Garden of the School of Political Sciences ⑲

56, rue des Saints-Pères
Open during term
Metro Saint-Germain-des-Prés

Known familiarly as 'Sciences-Po', the renowned Parisian School of Political Sciences (École des Sciences Politiques) has, as one of its premises, a 17th century town mansion that was formerly the residence of Gabriel de Mortemart, father of the Marquise de Montespan. In theory, the magnificent garden is reserved for students and teachers, but sometimes a polite request can get you in to see it.

Protestant Library ⑳

54, rue des Saints-Pères
+33 1 45 48 62 07
shpf.fr – shpf2@wanadoo.fr
Wednesday–Friday 9.30am–5.30pm
Metro Saint-Germain-des-Prés

Founded in 1885, the Protestant Library is a fine room open to the public. Though primarily a library, it also holds small exhibitions regarding Protestantism and its history. The location is no accident, as the building stands some 50 metres from the old embassy of the Netherlands, which in the days of religious persecution was where Parisian Protestants came to attend church services. The fine room is in a pre-Baltard style (Victor Baltard being the architect of the famous metal structures of Les Halles) and measures 21 metres in length and 11 metres in width. The library itself comprises more than 180,000 volumes, some of them extremely rare, together with various manuscripts, medallions, periodicals, etc.

© marionbarat

RUE DE GRENELLE MANGER

A reminder of the presence of horses in Paris

27, rue de Grenelle
Metro Saint-Sulpice

The entrance door of 27, rue de Grenelle is decorated with a strange metal bar with downward spikes. In the 19th century this was a manger to store hay for feeding horses, which in those days were used for many administrative and commercial tasks: postal deliveries, ambulances, funeral services, etc.

There is still a superb sculpture of a horse's head at 67–69, rue Pigalle, which records the existence in such places of a post for horses (see page 308).

CARROUSEL BRIDGE TELESCOPIC STREET LIGHTS

Street lights that grow 10 metres at night

Pont du Carrousel
RER Musée d'Orsay

The four bronze art deco lampposts on the Carrousel bridge (Pont du Carrousel, built in 1935) were forged and wrought by the iron sculptor Raymond Subes in 1938. They were not installed until 1946.

During the war, bronze was a very sought-after metal to be rendered for military use, and Subes had the presence of mind to hide the lampposts in his workshop.

In order not to interfere with the view of the Louvre during the day, the lampposts are different heights day and night. As soon as darkness falls, to light up the entire bridge, they come to life and extend from 12 to 22 metres high.

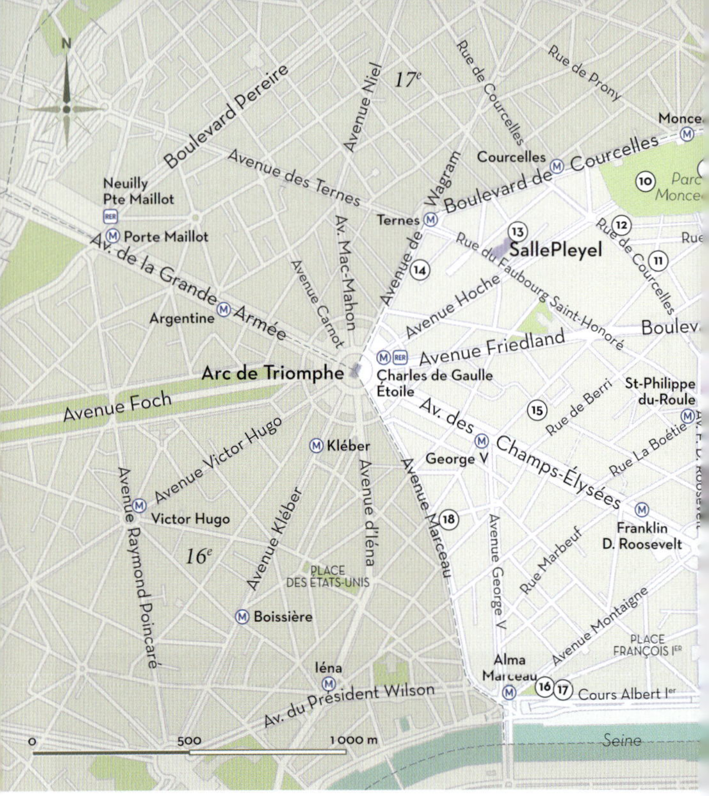

8th arrondissement

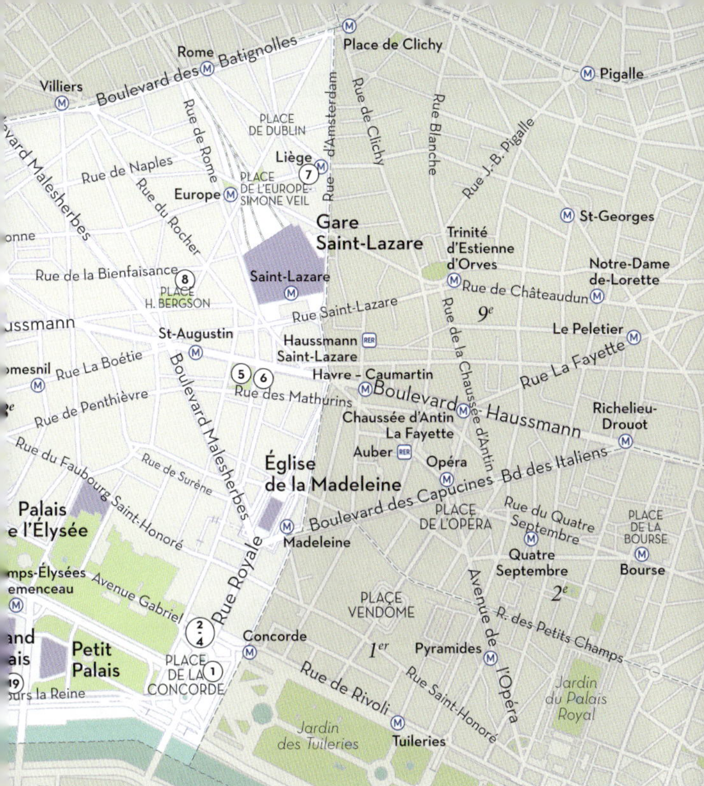

Rome
Boulevard des Batignolles
Place de Clichy
Pigalle
Villiers
Rue de Clichy
Rue Blanche
Rue J.-B. Pigalle
PLACE
DE DUBLIN
Rue d'Amsterdam
Liège
PLACE
DE L'EUROPE-
SIMONE VEIL
Europe
St-Georges
Rue de Naples
Rue de Rome
Rue du Rocher
Boulevard Malesherbes
Gare
Saint-Lazare
Trinité
d'Estienne
d'Orves
Notre-Dame
de-Lorette
Rue de la Bienfaisance
Saint-Lazare
Rue de Châteaudun
PLACE
H. BERGSON
Rue Saint-Lazare
9e
Haussmann
St-Augustin
Haussmann
Saint-Lazare
Le Peletier
Rue La Boétie
Havre – Caumartin
Rue La Fayette
Rue de Penthièvre
Boulevard Malesherbes
Rue des Mathurins
Boulevard Haussmann
Richelieu-
Drouot
Chaussée d'Antin
La Fayette
Rue de la Chaussée d'Antin
Rue du Faubourg Saint-Honoré
Rue de Surène
Église
de la Madeleine
Auber
Opéra
Bd des Italiens
Palais
e l'Élysée
Boulevard des Capucines
PLACE
DE L'OPÉRA
Rue du Quatre
Septembre
PLACE
DE LA
BOURSE
mps-Élysées
Avenue Gabriel
Madeleine
Quatre
Septembre
Bourse
emenceau
Rue Royale
Avenue de l'Opéra
2e
PLACE
VENDÔME
R. des Petits Champs
and
ais
Petit
Palais
Concorde
1er
Pyramides
Jardin
du Palais
Royal
19
PLACE
DE LA
CONCORDE
Rue de Rivoli
Rue Saint-Honoré
urs la Reine
Jardin
des Tuileries
Tuileries

THE OBELISK-SUNDIAL

The world's largest sundial

Place de la Concorde
Metro Concorde

Presented to France in 1831 by Mehmet Ali as a gift from Egypt, this obelisk was raised in place de la Concorde on 25 October 1836 in a ceremony attended by King Louis-Philippe. One of the two famous obelisks raised by Ramses II at the entrance to the Luxor temple, it has, since 1999, been part of the largest sundial in the world. In 1913, the astronomer Camille Flammarion, founder of the Société Astronomique de France, submitted to the Paris City Council a plan to lay out within place de la Concorde 'the world's largest sundial', using the obelisk as the gnomon (see page 196) and carving the indications of the hours into the street paving itself. However, due to the 1914–1918 war the project was abandoned.

Twenty years later, in 1938, Daniel Roguet, the architect of the Juvisy Observatory, resurrected Flammarion's idea. Work began in spring 1939, but once again the project was interrupted by a war.

Some traces of what was done are still visible: at the foot of the obelisk facing towards rue Royale are five radiating lines carved into the ground, one of them still with its original metal facing.

The project was finally completed more than 50 years later, under Philippe de la Cotardière and Denis Savoie, with the sundial being officially opened on 21 June 1999.

Marked in bronze, the lines of the dial radiate from the foot of the obelisk and extend to the various divider strips in the square.

At their end, Roman numerals from VII to XVII indicate the solar hour.

NEARBY

The general mobilisation order, 2 August 1914 ②

1, rue Royale
Metro Concorde

The walls of Paris bear various traces of war and episodes of bloodshed. Just to the left of the restaurant Maxim's you can still see a copy of the general mobilisation order dated 2 August 1914. Protected by a dusty glass panel, the poster reads: "The Mayor (Doctor Phillippe Maréchal) of the 8th arrondissement informs his constituents that a general mobilisation has been declared. The first day of the mobilisation has been set for Sunday 2 August (from midnight to midnight)." It seems, however, that the present poster is actually a photocopy dating from the 1970s.

PLAQUE IN PLACE LOUIS XVI

In memory of the king guillotined on site

Junction of place de la Concorde and rue Boissy d'Anglas
Metro Concorde

Surprising as it may seem, a stone plaque indicating Place Louis XVI survives at the junction of place de la Concorde and rue Boissy d'Anglas. It records the name taken by place de la Concorde between 1826 and 1828, at the Restoration, in memory of the decapitation of the king in this very square on 21 January 1793.

Place de la Concorde has changed its name many times, reflecting the instability of political regimes after 1789: it was successively called place Louis XV, then place de la Révolution after 10 August 1792, place de la Concorde under the Directory, the Consulate and the Empire, and again place Louis XV, and then place Louis XVI under the Restoration, then place de la Charte in 1830, and finally place de la Concorde under the July monarchy.

At numbers 4, 6, 6a and 8, place de la Concorde there are also examples of the old Parisian numbering system (see page 206).

Since when did Paris' streets have names?

Until 1728 there were no street signs or maps. Note that with around a thousand streets at the time (1,337 during the Revolution), it was sometimes difficult to find your way. In 1728, the Paris police ordered a plaque to be attached to the first and last houses of each street with its name in black on a yellow background.

The following year the plaques were replaced by an engraved stone embedded in the wall (there is still one notable plaque at quai Voltaire, at the corner of rue des Saints-Pères), before the appearance of metal plaques with white letters on a black background in 1823, and then in 1844 the enamelled plates with white letters on a blue background which are still around today.

FIFTH COLUMN OF HÔTEL DE CRILLON

Memories of the Liberation

10, place de la Concorde
Metro Concorde

A close look at the façade of the Hôtel de Crillon reveals that the fifth column from the left, when facing the building, is a darker colour than the others.

This column was in fact destroyed (then replaced by a column less resistant to pollution than the original from the 18th century) during the Liberation in improbable circumstances.

On 25 August 1944, the day of the Liberation, a Leclerc company tank was stationed in place de la Concorde, opposite the Hôtel de Crillon, when shots were heard apparently coming from the hotel roof. A French officer then shouted to watch out for Germans and the "fifth

column", an expression in common use since the Spanish Civil War of 1936 (see below) to designate infiltrated enemy partisans. But the tank driver didn't understand the allusion and shelled the 5th column of the hotel …

Where does the term 'fifth column' come from?

In 1936, during the Spanish Civil War, nationalist forces were moving in four columns towards Madrid, which had remained in the hands of the Republicans (who brought together Communists, Socialists, Republicans and Anarchists), the nationalist radio announcing that their "fifth column" was already there, which was false. This psychological manipulation unsettled the defence by raising suspicions, even though the nationalist attack on Madrid failed.

EXPIATORY CHAPEL

In memory of the king

Square Louis-XVI
+33 1 44 54 19 33
See opening hours on the website: chapelle-expiatoire-paris.fr/visiter/
informations-pratiques
Metro Saint-Augustin

© Myrabella

Located in the charming square Louis-XVI, at the corner of boule-vard Haussmann and rue d'Anjou, this expiatory chapel was built in 1816–1826 to commemorate Louis XVI. Remarkably quiet for some-where right in the heart of Paris, it recalls a particularly dramatic period in French history. After he had been guillotined in place de la Concorde, the king's body was brought here for burial in what was then the Cemetery of La Madeleine. Opened in 1721, that cemetery was at the time best known as the burial place of the 133 people who, in a sad presage of things to come, were crushed to death in rue Royale and place Royale (now place de la Concorde) during the firework display held on 30 April 1770 to mark the marriage of the future Louis XVI and Marie-Antoi-nette, Archduchess of Austria. The cemetery was also used to bury the 900 Swiss soldiers of the Royal Guard at the Tuileries who were massa-cred when the palace was attacked on 10 August 1792. Subsequently it was also the burial place of those guillotined between 26 August 1792 and 24 March 1794, on which date the cemetery was closed because of complaints regarding the pestilential odour.

Guillotined on 21 January 1793, Louis XVI was – like all those who had died a similar death – buried with his severed head between his legs, his body then being covered with quicklime. He was, however, accorded the right to an open coffin and buried in an individual grave (by the rue d'Anjou wall of the cemetery) rather than in a mass grave. The body of Marie-Antoinette was buried alongside him on 25 October 1793.

After the Restoration, King Louis XVIII had the bodies of his brother, Louis XVI, and his queen moved to the royal mausoleum of

Saint-Denis on 21 January 1815. He himself then paid for the re-purchase of the areas of this cemetery that had been sold to private individuals so that the present commemorative chapel might be built there.

Modelled on a Graeco-Roman necropolis, the structure occupies the entire 900 m² of the old Madeleine cemetery.

The courtyard leading up to the chapel proper is lined to north and south by a nine-arch arcade (see photo previous page), each bay of which houses an empty tomb; the number commemorates the 900 Swiss soldiers of the Royal Guard.

The altar in the crypt is in the form of a tomb and stands on the exact site of Louis XVI's grave. On January 21 each year a commemorative mass is celebrated here.

Traces of the monarchy in Parisian place names

Although France is now a republic proud of its political achievements, its capital still preserves numerous traces of the country's past as a monarchy, most notably in the name of streets and boulevards and in the innumerable statues, busts and royal monograms adorning the façades of buildings. Near the site where he chose to be buried, Clovis has a street named after him; Charlemagne has both a school and a narrow street, while Henri IV has a boulevard, a quai alongside the Seine, a footbridge, a bridge and a school, and Louis-Philippe has a bridge. The reference to Louis XIII is more indirect, given that rue Dauphine was named after him in 1607, when he was still heir to the throne. Similarly, the street and school named after Louis XIV are actually called Louis-le-Grand. Rue François Ier is not actually named for the king, but for the reconstructed façade of a building in so-called 'François Ier' style. The female members of the royal family are not forgotten. Cours la Reine owes its name to Marie de Médicis, who commissioned it, while rue Sainte-Anne is named after Anne of Austria and rue Thérèse after Queen Maria-Teresa. Finally, rue de Berry, rue de Provence, rue Monsieur, rue Madame, rue Mademoiselle, rue d'Artois and rue Monsieur-le-Prince are all named after members of the royal family, just as rue Mazarin, rue Richelieu and rue Colbert are named after royal ministers. Even Louis XVI receives due homage. Not only is there the expiatory chapel, but also the nearby rue Tronchet, rue de Sèze and boulevard Malesherbes, named after the three men who defended the king during his trial. Although it has since been renamed place de la Concorde, a stone plaque for place Louis XVI can still be seen at the corner of place de la Concorde and rue Boissy d'Anglas (see page 272).

NEARBY

Haut-reliefs at 34, rue Pasquier ⑥
Metro Havre-Caumartin

Note the haut-reliefs of sharks and camels adorning this 1930s-style building. The work of Alexander and Pierre Fournier, it was in fact built in the year 1927 for the Société Financière Française et Coloniale.

LIÈGE
METRO STATION

One of the most beautiful stations of the Paris metro

Entirely faced with ceramic tiles, this – together with the Arts et Métiers station (see page 86) – is probably the most beautiful of

the city's metro system. It used to be the "Berlin" metro station, but the name was changed during the First World War.

Closed for a long time, the station only reopened in 1968, with Welkenraedt ceramic decoration depicting the landscape and monuments of Liège in Belgium.

Since December 4, 2006, completion of the modernisation work has meant that the station no longer closes at 8pm.

NEARBY

Boundary marker at 4, rue de Laborde ⑧
City limits in the 18th century
Metro Europe or Havre-Caumartin

An unobtrusive plaque on the rear wall of the inner courtyard of 4, rue de Laborde bears the following inscription: "1729, in the reign of Louis XV. By order of the king it is expressly forbidden to build in this road outside the present boundary and limit, upon pain of the sanctions contained in the edicts of His Majesty from 1724 to 1726." Initially placed near rue de l'Arcade, this boundary marker set a limit to the area within which Parisians could build and was inspired by the need to maintain control over the population and guarantee supplies for the city. Clearly, people paid little heed to the ban, though its presence here is an interesting reminder of the limits of urban expansion at the time. All in all, 294 boundary markers of this kind were fixed to the walls of 18th century Paris. Another surviving plaque can be seen at 304, rue de Charenton in the 12th arrondissement.

What happened to rue de Berlin and rue de Hambourg?

The area above Saint-Lazare is known as the 'Quartier d'Europe' because all the streets are named after great European cities. However, the 1914–1918 war led to some changes in names here: rue de Berlin became rue de Liège and rue de Hambourg became rue de Bucarest. Similarly, after the Second World War, avenue de Tokyo in the 16th arrondissement became avenue de New York.

PARC MONCEAU PYRAMID

A forgotten Masonic symbol

Parc Monceau
Metro Monceau

A tour of Parc Monceau, following the paths around the edge of the park, is exactly 1 km. Ideal for joggers, many of whom know this very well.

Monceau park is full of curiosities: pretend Romantic ruins, truncated columns ... The most impressive is the stone pyramid with a door framed by two Egyptian heads. Louis-Philippe d'Orléans (1747–93), also called Philippe Égalité, cousin of Louis XVI and father of Louis-Philippe, was the first Grand Master of the Grand Orient of France in 1771.

He chose this park to establish his residence and ultimate home. He built a kind of Masonic garden whose realisation was entrusted to two Freemasons: the painter Louis Carogis de Carmontel and the architect Poyet. Apart from the now-defunct residence, which was secretly used as a temple, the park also had a "Valley of the Fallen". The Egyptian pyramid was erected as an explicit symbol of the Temple of Osiris and Isis, representing the Sun and Moon that illuminate the mountain of initiation, the one which the initiate climbs in the Masonic hierarchy, step by step up to the 33rd supreme degree.

Inside (inaccessible), eight columns imitating granite are buried to over one third of their height. Their capitals, formed by Egyptian heads, support an entablature of granite and bronze. The coffered vault is painted with bronze rosettes. To the right and left are two black marble tombs. Finally, in a niche in front of the door, a woman squatting on her heels presses her breasts to make water run out of a bowl.

Parc Monceau: 'In a single garden, all ages and places'

In 1778, Carmontelle began designing this park for the future Philippe Égalité.

It is the last remaining vestige of the various 'Anglo-Chinese' gardens (known at the time as 'fabriques') which were laid out during this period; the parks of Bagatelle, Bastille and Clichy have long disappeared (though, outside the city, there is still the fine "Désert de Retz").

Laid out so that it formed a long journey of 'initiation', Parc Monceau aimed to bring together all of knowledge, the most dazzling examples of human civilisation, in one place.

Thus Venice was represented by a bridge (extant), Italy by a vineyard (at the time, the country had yet to be unified so Venice was an independent State), Egypt by a pyramid (see opposite), China by a stone lantern (extant) and Rome by a naumachia (this man-made basin for fake naval battles still stands to the north side of the park), Holland by a windmill (no longer extant), and so on.

REMAINS OF THE HÔTEL DE VILLE ⑩

One of the few old structures in Parc Monceau

Parc Monceau – Near the naumachia
Metro Monceau

The Hôtel de Ville (Paris City Hall) designed by the Italian architect Boccador and built between 1533 and 1628 (with extensions and

additions between 1836 and 1850), was torched in the Paris Commune of May 1871 and reduced to ashes, but some remains were saved. It was rebuilt between 1874 and 1882 to the plans of the architects Théodore Ballu and Édouard Deperthes. The façade, in neo-Renaissance style, is inspired by the original building.

There are still some remains of the old Hôtel de Ville in Paris and elsewhere in France, although they are fewer in number than those of the Tuileries (see page 106). Along an alley in Parc Monceau near the naumachia (site of naval battles staged as mass entertainment), beside the small artificial pond, is a solitary but impressive arcade from the ruined building. Unlike many features of the park, the arcade is not neo-Romantic in design.

Other remains of the Hôtel de Ville

– Jardins du Trocadero (16th arrondissement): a skylight from the front elevation.

– Square Paul Langevin (5th arrondissement): next to Masonic medallions from the 1889 Exposition Universelle (see page 166), two Renaissance niches that lost their statues during the events of May 1968.

– Musée Carnavalet (4th arrondissement): high relief depicting Henry IV on horseback, in the courtyard of the museum that decorated the main door of the Hôtel de Ville. In the museum there are several other fragments. The museum itself is a composite of several other buildings, including the Nazareth Arch from the Palace of Justice, the façade of the former cloth merchants' offices (from the Halles) and the central section of the former Hôtel des Marets.

– Square Leopold Achille (4th arrondissement): frieze from the former vault of the main entrance, called the salamander frieze because of the sculpted salamanders in tribute to Francis I, and a statue of Pomona.

– Square Georges Cain (3rd arrondissement): next to the remains of the Tuileries (see page 104) is a rosette from the Hôtel de Ville ceiling.

– Château de la Punta (Corsica): as well as the many remains of the Tuileries (see page 106), the castle has a sculpture representing the four seasons that was part of a fountain in the Louis XIV court of the Hôtel de Ville.

– Parc de la Villa Magali, in Saint-Raphaël (Var département): 43 fragments of the Tuileries Palace and Hôtel de Ville were acquired by owner Léon Carvalho, a former director of the Opéra-Comique.

THE PAGODA – PARIS

An amazing gallery-museum housed in a pagoda

48, rue de Courcelles
+33 1 45 61 06 93 – info@pagodaparis.com
Visit only by appointment
Metro Courcelles, Saint-Philippe du Roule or Monceau

In the heart of the Monceau area, an astonishing Chinese pagoda stands alongside the buildings typical of Baron Haussmann's urban redevelopment.

Occupying the site of a Louis-Philippe town mansion, it was built in 1926 by the French architect Fernand Bloch for the Chinese antique dealer Ching-Tsai Loo, whose company is still the oldest gallery of Asian art in Paris and the only truly Chinese antique dealer within the city. With 600 m² of space spread over six floors, the pagoda provides a unique architectural setting for the business. Details of the refined interiors include: Chinese lacquered woodwork dating from the 17th and 18th centuries; a ceiling in Art Deco glass tiles; a superb wooden gallery of Indian carving dating from the 18th and 19th centuries; and a lift entirely finished in woodwork and lacquer. The overall impression is of a Zen-like atmosphere, of a space where the passage of time has left its mark ...

> Some of the gallery's rooms are also available to hire for cocktail parties, press conferences, fashion shows or receptions...

© Pagoda-Paris

NEARBY
Remains of Tuileries Palace ⑫
9, rue Murillo – Metro Monceau

The courtyard of the building at 9, rue Murillo features amazing remains of the Tuileries Palace, destroyed by fire in May 1871. These include fragments of the grand staircase of Percier and Fontaine, and constructions by Renaissance architect Philibert Delorme. The remains were installed here by architect Gustave Clausse in the courtyard of his 1870 building. He occupied the ground floor and first floor, built of stone, and rented out the upper floors, made of brick. Clausse also installed a Florentine bust, perhaps of Alphonse d'Este, and two Venetian capitals in the courtyard.

For other remains of the Tuileries in Paris and elsewhere, see page 106.

ALEXANDER NEVSKY CATHEDRAL ⑬

The church where Picasso married the Russian ballerina Olga Koklova

12, rue Daru – Metro Ternes
Tuesday and Thursday–Sunday 9am–12pm and 3pm–6pm, Wednesday 9am–12pm

Listed as a historic monument in 1983, Alexander Nevsky Cathedral is undoubtedly the most famous of the numerous Orthodox churches in Paris. The initial scheme was promoted by Josef Vassiliev, chaplain at the Russian embassy, and paid for by funds collected not only in Russia (Tsar Alexander II gave the princely sum of 150,000 francs in gold) but also from among the Russian community spread throughout Europe. Designed by the architects Kouzmine and Strohm, the Cathedral was intended to provide Paris with an Orthodox church worthy of the name and was consecrated on 12 September 1861. A great national hero, the Grand Prince Alexander Nevsky (1219–1263) was canonised

for his humanity as a ruler, his military success against aggressors, his great wisdom and the fervour of his Christian faith. Placed under the jurisdiction of the Patriarchate of Constantinople (Istanbul) in 1931, this church is the archdiocesan seat of the Russian Orthodox Church in Western Europe. In Byzantine-Russian style, it has a Greek-cross plan with a mosaic façade and five cupolas gilded "like the flames of candles" (the number symbolises Christ and the four Evangelists). The overall result is a building that stands out to striking effect within the urban landscape of Paris. Inside there are iconostases, icons and paintings with their traditional gold backgrounds. The services, maintaining a liturgy which has existed for some sixteen centuries, are celebrated to the chants of Orthodox priests amidst clouds of incense.

It is impossible to be present without sensing the fervour of the local Russian community who worship here.

The church, in fact, serves two parishes, so that each Sunday there are two Masses. One in French (in the lower church of the crypt) for the parish of Sainte Trinité, the other in Slav in the upper church for the parishioners of Saint-Alexandre-Nevski. One anecdotal curiosity regarding the church is that Picasso chose it for his wedding to the Russian ballerina Olga Koklova, where the guests included Jean Cocteau, Max Jacob and Guillaume Apollinaire. If, while respecting the silence of the place, you wish to attend a service, choose the great Easter Mass, which is certainly worthwhile, or the Mass held on 12 September to celebrate the feast day of the patron saint of the Russian community. That event is always followed by a pir, a magnificent Russian-style banquet.

NEARBY

Hôtel Céramic ⑭

34, avenue de Wagram – Metro Ternes
Designed by Lavirotte, this fine Art Nouveau hotel was built in 1904 and is entirely faced with ceramic stoneware. The interplay of volumes within the façade seems to herald modern architecture. Today, the building houses a comfortable three-star hotel, for which the façade serves as the best possible form of advertising.

Cité Odiot ⑮

26, rue de Washington – Metro Ternes
A haven of peace near the Champs-Élysées, the Cité Odiot stands on the site of the old city mansion of the goldsmith Jean-Baptiste Odiot, who made not only the shrine of St Vincent de Paul but also Napoleon I's imperial sword and sceptre. Far from the madding crowd, you can enjoy a space of wide lawns dotted with trees and lined by buildings dating from 1847.

THE SANDBOX

Souvenir of days gone by

2, place de la Reine Astrid
Metro Alma-Marceau

The cast-iron box which faces 2, place de la Reine Astrid takes us back to the days when sand was used to make roads less slippery from snow or ice in winter, and all year round to mop up horse urine before sweeping. The horse-drawn vehicles of all kinds having long since left the capital, and with salting (developed from 1917) being more efficient and cleaner, having replaced sanding, the sand boxes that dotted the streets have almost all disappeared.

There are five remaining, all of which are similar and can be dated to the period 1901–19, as indicated by the Art Nouveau style of their decoration. The boxes are 1.5 to 1.7 metres high and consist of a pyramidal base topped by a rounded cornice bearing the motto of the City of Paris, *Fluctuat Nec Mergitur* (Rocked [by the waves] but Does Not Sink) with a mesh lid, as the boxes were supplied with sand from above. The front faces are decorated with the city's coat of arms: the nave (sailing ship), placed in the interlocking of a laurel branch and an oak branch, surmounted by a five-tower wall crown, and completed at its base by the Legion of Honour, incorporated into the coat of arms following the decree of 9 October 1900.

On the sides of the boxes, the initials of the City of Paris are placed on a circle, at the intersection of two laurel branches. A hatch at the base is decorated with a scallop shell which opened to let the road-workers shovel sand to spread on the roadway.

In addition to the heritage conservation issue, the five remaining sandboxes have found a new mission. They are used as ventilation chimneys for underground changing rooms used by the maintenance workers of the City of Paris.

Other sandboxes in Paris

– 22, avenue de Saxe, 7th arrondissement
– 41, avenue Gabriel, 8th arrondissement
– Place Georges Guillaumin, 8th arrondissement
– 39, avenue Trudaine, 9th arrondissement

NEARBY

Façade of 40, cours Albert Ier ⑰

Metro Alma-Marceau

Given that cours Albert Ier is mainly used by motorists in a hurry, most Parisians have never noticed the building at No. 40, built by the famous master glassmaker, Lalique. It was designed in 1911 to serve as his home, but then became a studio and showroom. The façade is a magnificent amalgam of plant motifs. Note the door made up of carved glass sections that form the branches of a tree.

Façade of 30, avenue Marceau

Metro Alma-Marceau

Built for himself by André Granet, Gustave Eiffel's son-in-law, the house dates from 1913 to 1914 and is a superb example of Art Nouveau architecture. Particularly striking is the upper part of the façade, which is entirely covered in sculpture of branches and pine cones.

THE TORTOISE ON LA FAYETTE'S STATUE

Self-critical of slowness

Cours la Reine
Metro Champs-Élysées – Clemenceau

At the Grand Palais, on cours la Reine, the statue of La Fayette often goes unnoticed by Parisians, despite its size. At the top of the imposing base, by the horse's feet, the sculpture of a small turtle recalls the extraordinary history of this monument.

In 1899 France accepted an American project in recognition of the aid given by General La Fayette (1757–1834) in the American War of Independence (1775–1783). The sculptor who was commissioned, an American named Paul Bartlett, had to accept quite short deadlines, as he was supposed to finish the monument for the 1900 Exposition Universelle (World's Fair).

The sculptor managed to honour his commitment, and a provisional plaster model was inaugurated on 4 July 1900 at the Louvre. But casting in bronze was more laborious, and Bartlett took almost eight years to finally finish a largely reworked version, which is why, in a kind of self-criticism, he modelled a small turtle to mock his own slowness.

Work on the Grand Louvre expansion project finally led to the statue being moved from its prestigious location to its current home in 1985.

"

NEARBY
La Vallée Suisse 

Jardin de la Nouvelle France – Metro Champs-Élysées – Clemenceau

The Swiss Valley garden has gone by several names: Vallée Suisse, Jardin de Anne Sauvage, and finally Jardin de la Nouvelle France. It's an amazing little space, hidden on the slopes below place du Canada at the junction of avenue Franklin Roosevelt and cours la Reine. Adjoining Palais de la Découverte, this charming secret garden is a vestige of the Swiss Pavilion at the 1900 World's Fair. English-style, it seeks to imitate nature with a waterfall and artificial pond.

La Fayette: from American Independence to the Declaration of Human Rights

Born in Auvergne in 1757, General La Fayette soon joined forces with Washington and the American insurgents. With the expeditionary corps led by Rochambeau, he was a major contributor to the victory at Yorktown in 1781 and the independence of the United States of America. It was also thanks to La Fayette, along with Condorcet and Sieyès, that the Declaration of Human Rights adopted on 26 August 1789 was drafted. He is buried in Picpus cemetery in the 12th arrondissement (see page 362).

La Fayette behind the tricolour

The tricolour flag, composed of the blue and red of the City of Paris and the white of royalty, owes its existence to La Fayette, who imposed the tricolour cockade as part of the uniform of his troops on 17 July 1789.

9th arrondissement

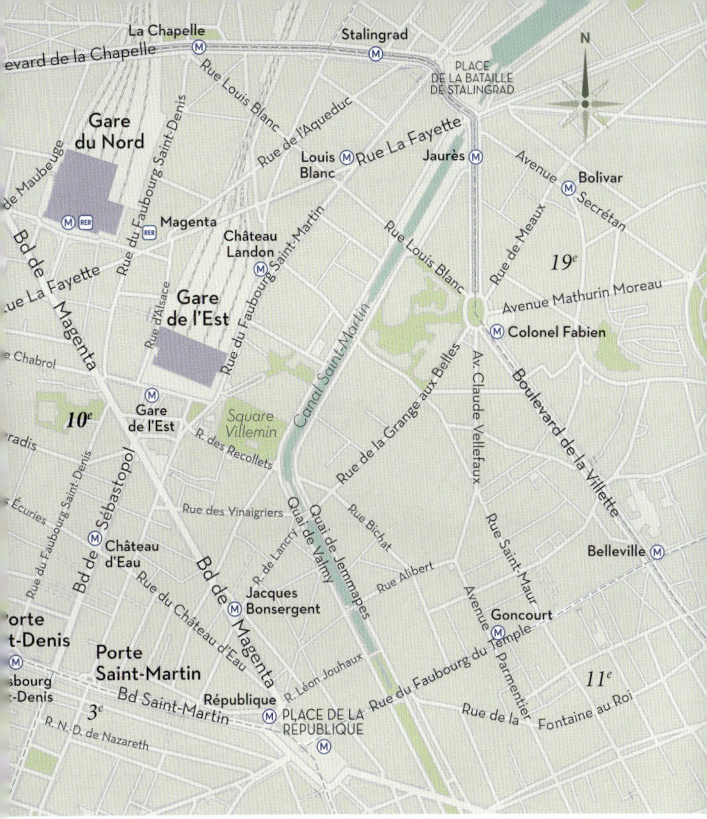

La Chapelle
Stalingrad
PLACE DE LA BATAILLE DE STALINGRAD
N
evard de la Chapelle
Gare du Nord
Rue Louis Blanc
Rue de l'Aqueduc
Rue La Fayette
Louis Blanc
Jaurès
Avenue Secrétan
Bolivar
de Maubeuge
Rue du Faubourg Saint-Denis
Magenta
Bd de la Fayette
Château Landon
Rue du Faubourg Saint-Martin
Rue de Meaux
Rue Louis Blanc
19e
ue La Fayette
Rue d'Alsace
Gare de l'Est
Rue du Faubourg Saint-Martin
Canal Saint-Martin
Avenue Mathurin Moreau
Bd de Magenta
Colonel Fabien
e Chabrol
10e
Gare de l'Est
Square Villemin
R. des Recollets
Rue de la Grange aux Belles
Av. Claude Vellefaux
Boulevard de la Villette
radis
Rue des Vinaigriers
R. de Lancry
Quai de Jemmapes
Quai de Valmy
Rue Bichat
Rue Saint-Maur
Belleville
Écuries
Rue du Faubourg Saint-Denis
Bd de Sébastopol
Château d'Eau
Rue du Château d'Eau
Bd de Magenta
Jacques Bonsergent
Rue Alibert
Avenue Parmentier
Goncourt
orte t-Denis
Porte Saint-Martin
République
R. Léon Jouhaux
Rue du Faubourg du Temple
11e
sbourg -Denis
3e
Bd Saint-Martin
PLACE DE LA RÉPUBLIQUE
Rue de la
Fontaine au Roi
R. N.-D. de Nazareth
Rue de la

GLASS ROOF OF
THE CENTRAL OFFICES
OF THE SOCIÉTÉ GÉNÉRALE

A bank in all its splendour

29, boulevard Haussmann
Open during office hours, and for 'Journées du Patrimoine' (Heritage Days)
Metro Opéra

The Société Générale was founded in 1864, and its main branch occupies a magnificent ensemble of seven interconnected buildings dating from the Second Empire. When the bank bought the premises in 1905, the architect Jacques Hermant demonstrated a clearly modern approach to structural conversion because he did everything possible to maintain the original façades, redesigning the interior space to create four underground levels for the vaults. The completed structure was opened in 1912. In the centre of the bank is a large circular counter, known as le 'fromage'; this stands under an immense cupola of iron and glass which measures 24 metres in diameter and was designed by Jacques Galland. The mosaic floors were the work of the Gentil & Bourdet company of Boulogne-Billancourt. Various parts of this bank (the exteriors; the glass and iron roof and hall; the main stairwell; the vault rooms) are all listed architectural features. Of particular note are the splendid strongbox rooms, the mosaics and the main door to the bank vault; weighing some 18 tons, this has 40 cm thick armour plating. Visitors should be discreet as this is a place of work.

Why are there so many banks in the Opera district?

Nights at the opera have long been a way for high society to show off its wealth: in the 19th century, women used to attend the Opéra Garnier wearing their finest jewels. Their value was such that they were kept in the vaults of nearby banks. This limited the risk ...

Glass and iron structures in the Opera District
Grand Hôtel, 2, rue Scribe

Galeries Lafayette, 40, boulevard Haussmann
Monday–Saturday 9.30am–7.30pm (Thursday until 9pm)

Printemps, 64, boulevard Haussmann
Monday–Saturday 9.35am–7pm (Thursday until 10pm)

There are three very fine glass and iron structures in this district which are much better known than the premises of the Société Générale. Each of them is an example of the luxurious Second Empire architecture associated with the massive urban-planning schemes undertaken by Baron Haussmann. Built in 1861, the Grand Hôtel has a vast hall that already hints at the use of colour in such structures. However, the real masterpiece here is the Reception Room, where a marvellous glass roof – a veritable blossom of gold and coloured glass – rests on double ranks of Corinthian columns. If it is not open, ask at the hotel's reception desk. Nearby, the two department stores of Le Printemps and Galeries Lafayette also have very fine glasswork. The roof at Galeries Lafayette rests on ten large metal pillars, while the glasswork on the sixth floor of Le Printemps is a fine example of Art Nouveau and was designed by Binet in 1911. The space now houses a tearoom and other areas used for receptions, etc.

NEARBY

Fragonard – Perfume Museum ②
9, rue Scribe
+33 1 40 06 10 09
Monday–Saturday 9am–5.30pm (4.30pm on Sunday) – Free guided tours only
Metro Havre-Caumartin, Opéra or Chaussée d'Antin

Set up by the Fragonard Perfume Company in 1983, this museum traces the history of perfume-making from the ancient Egyptians until the 19th century. A miniature factory demonstrates the different processes used in extracting essences from raw materials. Unfortunately, the visit is very commercially oriented, and ends in the Fragonard shop, like all the worst tourist traps for groups of happy spenders.

Operatic Street Names

The names of the streets around the Garnier Opera House – Auber, Meyerbeer, Halévy and Gluck – are no accident; each one is named after a 19th century opera composer. Scribe, a librettist, also has a street named after him. And Diaghilev, the Russian impresario who hired and fired choreographers and composers, has a city square that bears his name; it stands just behind the Opera.

Façade of the former hammam of the Mathurins ③

18, rue des Mathurins
Metro Havre-Caumartin

The majority of the many workers in the offices located in the Opéra district do not notice the astonishing façade at 18, rue des Mathurins, its Moorish appearance in sharp contrast with the surrounding Haussmannian buildings. The façade recalls the existence of an old hammam, which women accessed via another entrance at 47, boulevard Haussmann.

THE VINES OF RUE BLANCHE FIRE STATION

Wine-making firefighters

22–28, rue Blanche
For the dates when the grapes will be picked, ask at the fire station from around the beginning of September
Metro Trinité

I f the firefighters of rue du Vieux-Colombier in the 6th arrondissement are well known for the ball they hold on July 14, those in rue Blanche also have their own very special public festivity: for a few days every year, their fire station is transformed into a vineyard.

The superb climbing vine on the façade of the building yields a generous harvest, from which is made a (non-alcoholic!) wine that is 'mis en bouteille au château' and sold under the Château Blanche label. The quality of this 'cru' might be debatable, but the tradition dates back to 1926; for the last 30 years in particular, the grape-picking has been a lively, colourful event involving firefighters, local residents, street urchins and even the girls from the Moulin Rouge.

More than 150 kg of grapes are harvested in just a few days, and these are used to make fifty or so full bottles of Château Blanche (each numbered) and 150 small bottles for the fire station itself.

Undoubtedly more authentic than the much more touristy event in Montmartre, the grape harvest in rue Blanche also has a small celebrity connection (Gérard Depardieu is the owner of bottle 24 of the 1997 cuvée).

Still, the whole thing remains thoroughly convivial and the fire station chief is more than happy to talk to anyone about the curious traditions associated with the place. For example: to guarantee they will have children, the most recently married fireman and his wife must be the first to tread the grapes; the bottle labels depict the events of that particular year; and the name of the cuvée is that of the fireman who happens to be fire chief that year.

Origin of rue Blanche's name: plaster in Paris

It is the nearby quarries of Montmartre that resulted in rue Blanche getting its name: as the quarried plaster was being carted down to the barges on the Seine, it was not uncommon for small pieces to fall onto the road, which thus became covered in white dust.

It was due to the special heat-resistant qualities of this plaster that Paris avoided the catastrophic fires which so often ravaged cities like London: as early as the reign of King Philippe le Bel an edict was issued requiring every new house built in Paris to be faced with chalk.

The abundance of the material has also meant that the city's buildings have that uniformity of colour so appreciated by visitors.

STAIRWELL IN GUSTAVE MOREAU MUSEUM ⑤

Paid for by the artist, and built in what had been his home

14, rue de La Rochefoucauld
+33 1 83 62 78 72
Daily 10am–6pm, closed Tuesday
Admission free on the first Sunday of every month
Metro Saint-Georges or Trinité

© Celine Ylmz - Unsplash

Rather ignored by Parisians, the Gustave Moreau museum is very special in that it was planned, designed and built by the artist himself in what had been his home. Three years before his death, Gustave Moreau, who had already asked himself the question of what would happen to his work, undertook to transform 14, rue de La Rochefoucauld with the aid of the architect Albert Lafon. Having decided to keep the first-floor apartment where he had lived with his parents as a sort of family museum of personal mementos and keepsakes, he had Lafon build the large studio one can see today. The magnificent spiral staircase gives access to a space which now houses his masterpieces along with all his preparatory sketches and thousands of drawings (these are conserved in cabinets with sliding panels). Intended as the masterwork of the artist, this museum gives an insight into his private genius, allowing each phase in the mysterious process of artistic creation to be followed. This unique museum still maintains the special enchantment that is a defining characteristic of Gustave Moreau's art.

> Born in 1826, Gustave Moreau went on to become an artist whose work was inspired by themes taken from mythology, literature and the Bible. The profusion of drawings he left makes it possible to chart the development of someone who was initially an academic artist but went on to become a symbolist and a modernist, producing towards the end of his life works that verge on the abstract.

NEARBY

Square d'Orléans ⑥

Entrance at 80, rue Taitbout – Metro Notre-Dame de Lorette

Invisible from the street, this was the centre of a district of Romantic artists and writers which a contemporary newspaper christened *La Nouvelle Athènes*. One of the most unusual and peaceful parts of the district, the square d'Orléans was designed by the English architect Edward Cresy and took a whole twelve years to complete (from 1830 to 1842). The end result, based on the model of a London square, contained 46 apartments and six artist's studios. The central garden, the fountain and the four square buildings around English-style courtyards were an immediate hit with artists and celebrities, who set up house – and salon – here, forming a sort of literary/artistic phalanstery. The best-known residents included the ballerina Marie Taglioni, the composer Marmontel and – most famously of all – George Sand (whose apartment was on the first floor of No. 5) and Frederick Chopin (at No. 9).

LOUISE WALSER-GAILLARD LIBRARY

A little-known jewel

26, rue Chaptal
+33 1 49 70 92 80 – bibliotheque.walser-gaillard@paris.fr
Tuesday, Thursday and Friday 1pm–7pm, Saturday 10am–6pm, Wednesday 10am–7pm
Metro Pigalle or Blanche

Located in an old mansion constructed in 1780, which previously housed the School for Firefighting and Fire Prevention, the Louise Walser-Gaillard Library (formerly Chaptal Library) boasts a superb, little-known reading room. It can be found in the former stateroom, which has retained its murals, woodwork, fireplace and glass skylight.

NEARBY

Hands at 82, rue Blanche ⑧

Metro Blanche

The number of this building is indicated in a remarkable fashion, two hands on either side of the number seem to be stopping it from escaping.

Hôtel de la Païva ⑨

28, place Saint-Georges
Metro Saint-Georges

One of the most picturesque buildings in this neighbourhood, this dates from 1840 but is named after the woman who lived here in 1850–1851: Thérèse Lachman, Marquise de la Païva, famed for her love of diamonds. In so-called 'style troubadour', the building is a mix of neo-Renaissance and neo-Gothic, with opulent external decoration intended to compensate for the narrowness of the façade.

Number 3: a symbol of the church of La Trinité

The architect Ballu played repeatedly upon the symbolic significance of the number three when designing the church of La Trinité. The central porch is divided into three arches; the large water basin has three separate fountains, each with three smaller basins. The central fount is surmounted by a statue of a woman, symbolising Hope, whose arms embrace three children, each of which has three bronze jars at its feet.

Impact of the advent of elevators

Before the introduction of elevators in Parisian buildings, in 1895, the most sought-after floor was the first above ground level. This explains why the height of the ceilings decreases as you move up the building, being highest in the most expensive floor and lowest in the cheapest. That all changed after 1895, with the higher floors becoming much sought after: not only were they less noisy, but — being above the level of the trees — they also received more light.

FOUNTAIN WITH HORSE'S HEAD

The former horse post

67–69, rue Pigalle
Metro Pigalle

Invisible from the street, the impressive horse-headed fountain that is hidden in a small garden behind a graceless building at 67–69, rue Pigalle, is probably one of the best-kept secrets of the 9th arrondissement. This is, in fact, the last remaining watering-hole for horses in the capital. In the 19th century, horses were particularly common on the streets: they were used for postal deliveries, ambulances, funeral homes and many private businesses. It was in such places that the last postmaster of Paris, Adolphe Dailly, had installed his depot for the horses: they rented sheds to rest the horses and obviously had to water them.

The modern horse's head represents a stallion from a line of Percherons in the service of the Daillys. The original head is at the entrance of the building on the right. It can just be seen from the street. Behind this head, a discreet inscription reads '*poste aux chevaux* (horse hitching post)'.

Adolphe Dailly was the son of Claude-Gaspard Dailly, who had begun his profession as postmaster after marrying the eldest daughter of Jean-Baptiste Lanchère, a Parisian postmaster, in 1805. It was with the competition from railways, from the 1840s, that activity began to decline. In 1849, when his father died, Adolphe Dailly owned more than 400 horses: 200 in the old depot at 2, rue Pigalle, the rest distributed between the stables of Monceau, Bercy and Charenton.

In 1880, he moved his business to 67–69, rue Pigalle. Taken over by his son Louis, the activities then diversified as best they could: hire of horses by the day or hour, transport for the armed forces, sugar trade, removals with teams of six horses ... At the last available census in 1910, the Daillys owned only 257 horses. The horse post business disappeared completely with the death of Louis Dailly.

There is also a horse feeding trough at 27, rue de Grenelle (see page 266).

AVENUE FROCHOT

A cursed villa

Private gateway; admission is a matter of luck
Metro Pigalle

Though shut away behind a keypad-controlled gate, this little paradise can be admired through the wrought-iron railings. Laid out in 1830, the avenue is lined by opulent 19th century residences surrounded by greenery. The mix of architectural styles here (neo-Gothic, Flemish, medieval, Palladian or neoclassical) has attracted the attention of artists of various periods: Victor Hugo, Alexandre Dumas Senior, Toulouse-Lautrec and Victor Massé are some of those who succumbed to its charms. More recently, Django Reinhardt amused himself by burning some of his furniture in the fireplace of one of the houses, while François Truffaut used the avenue as the setting for a scene in his famous film *Les Quatre Cents Coups*.

A curious tale has been told of the house at No. 1 since the death of composer Victor Massé, who spent his last years here afflicted with multiple sclerosis. So it would seem that the house has brought nothing but ill luck to owners or occupiers. The director of the Folies-Bergères, who had bought it for himself, left it to his housekeeper, who was then savagely beaten to death with a poker. Having stood empty for thirty years, the house was bought by Sylvie Vartan, who lived here a very short time and then moved out abruptly. The next to buy the property was Mathieu Galev, and he too died – a victim of multiple sclerosis ... True story or urban legend?

To the left of the avenue, a pretty stained-glass window with Art Deco marine motifs, part of the former Théâtre en Rond, dates from 1837.

NEARBY

Cité Malesherbes   ⑫

Private road, accessible via 59, rue des Martyrs
Metro Pigalle

Laid out on the site of the former city mansion of the lawyer Lamoignon de Malesherbes, who was guillotined in 1794, the Cité Malesherbes contains some interesting buildings. Note the façade of No.11, covered with rich decoration in ceramic, enamelled earthenware and tufa. Commissioned by the painter Jollivet, this is the work of the architect Jal. At No.17 is the fine rotunda of the private home of the architect Amoudru. Note also the cornice to the balcony, decorated with a female mask and two medallions with silhouettes.

Gardens at 41–47, rue des Martyrs   ⑬

Metro Pigalle

Partially hidden from the street, this carefully-tended lawn with rose bushes dotted here and there offers a pleasant breath of the countryside. Take advantage of it for a welcome pause.

THE PRIVATE COLLECTION AT THE 'PHONOGALERIE' SHOP

A collection of talking machines

10, rue Lallier
+33 1 45 26 45 80 – +33 6 80 61 59 37
aro@phonogalerie.com – phonogalerie.com
Thursday, Friday and Saturday 2pm–8pm or by appointment
Metro Anvers or Pigalle

Jalal Aro is more than just a collector: he nurses back to life all sorts of instruments that have played a part in the history of sound recording. After a few years spent collecting the more amazing forms of 'talking machines' produced since the invention of the technology in 1877 (cylinder recorders, horn gramophones, music boxes), he opened a shop dedicated to all aspects of recorded sound. Here you can find advertising posters, musical postcards, old 78s and vinyl discs, and all sorts of rare and sophisticated apparatus for recording and playing sound. However, anything produced in the last thirty years is rigorously excluded. The proprietor will help you to choose the perfect gift (prices ranging from €5 to €15,000); he will also be happy to regale you with marvellously erudite anecdotes. Half-museum, half shop, 'Phonogalerie' is ideally situated between the cabarets and nightclubs of Montmartre and the artists' neighbourhood of *La Nouvelle Athènes*.

NEARBY

Cité Napoleon

58, rue Marguerite de Rochechouart – Metro Anvers

Invisible from the street itself, the Cité Napoleon is a rare and fine example of a familistery, completed in 1853. Built to provide accommodation for 400 working families, its aim was to offer low-cost housing for those of modest means; not only was the rent affordable, but a doctor paid regular visits, free of charge. However, the families were expected to observe very strict discipline, and an inspector called frequently to verify the morality of their behaviour.

The owl at 68, rue Condorcet

68, rue Condorcet – Metro Anvers

Under the balcony at 68, rue Condorcet, a sculpted owl perches atop a column. It is, in fact, a species known in French as 'grand-duc', and is a trademark identifying the building as the work of none other than the great Viollet-le-Duc. The architect designed this as his own home in 1862–1863, placing the owl under the windows to his studio.

Familisteries and phalansteries

The familistery was a concrete expression of the utopian socialism Charles Fourier outlined in his theory of the phalanstery, a communal settlement in which accommodation was organised around a covered central courtyard. The name itself comes from the term 'phalanx', which in classical antiquity referred to an elite corps of soldiers. As the very name 'familistery' suggests, it provided accommodation for families alone.

CERAMICS AT 24, RUE DU FAUBOURG MONTMARTRE

Beautiful forgotten tiling

24, rue du Faubourg Montmartre
Metro Le Peletier

Successive restaurants which have been installed since the 1990s in the former premises of Bernheim, the fishmonger, have kept the superb original ceramics linked to the theme of fishing and fish. The shop, founded in 1879, had decorated all its walls with ceramics from Sarreguemines. The best way to calmly admire them is of course to sit down and order lunch or dinner.

NEARBY

Museum of Freemasonry 

16, rue Cadet – +33 1 45 23 74 09
Tuesday–Friday and Sunday, 10am–12.30pm and 2pm–6pm,
Saturday 10am–1pm and 2pm–7pm
Metro Cadet or Le Peletier

Built in 1889 on the site of the Hôtel Cadet, the Museum of Free-masonry, in the Grand Orient de France headquarters, has a collection of more than 10,000 items (documents, Masonic symbols, badges of office, etc.) illustrating the history of the arrival and spread of the Order in France.

Cité de Trévise 

Off rue Richer and rue Bleue – Metro Cadet

Characteristic of the various development schemes of the 1840s, the Cité de Trévise housing development still maintains a certain charm, in spite of the traffic. The neo-Renaissance buildings stand around a tree-dotted square, in the centre of which is a pretty drinking-fountain in the form of three caryatids holding hands.

Branch of Banque Nationale de Paris ⑳

14–20, rue Bergère – Metro Le Peletier

Built in 1881 by Corryer, this was long the home of the Paris Comptoir National d'Escompte, one of the four banks whose fusion gave rise to BNP Paribas. The stairwell and the trading hall with its magnificent glass ceiling are worth a visit. The three large façade sculptures are by Millet and depict Prudence, Commerce and Finance.

First basketball match in Europe

At 14, rue de Trévise, the YMCA (Young Men's Christian Association – Association des Jeunes Hommes Chrétiens) had the first sports complex to be built in France. It was designed by the architect Bénard, a student of Gustave Eiffel, and opened in 1893. The first basketball game in Europe was played there in the same year. Invented in 1891 in the USA (Massachusetts), basketball allowed sports educators to continue giving classes even when it rained.

CHURCH OF SAINT-EUGÈNE-SAINT-CÉCILE

*Two patron saints, two liturgies,
two types of architecture ...*

6, rue Sainte-Cécile
Daily 7.15am–9pm
Check masses on dioceseparis.fr/-saint-eugene-sainte-cecile-.html
Metro Grands Boulevards or Bonne Nouvelle

This fine but little-known church is curiously dedicated to two saints: Saint Eugene (in honour of Napoleon III's wife, Eugénie, who was responsible for it being built in the first place) and Saint Cecilia (patron saint of music; the National Conservatoire is close by). Note that the church has no bell tower, so that the bells do not disturb the musicians.

Designed by Lussion and Boileau, who took their inspiration from 13th century architecture, the church was built in 1854–1855 to meet the needs of the new suburbs being created as Paris expanded. Wherever you stand in the interior you get an overall view of the entire space, which is brightly painted and flooded with light; note also the Second Empire chandeliers.

The entire structure, including the columns, is in painted cast iron, creating a very original polychrome interior. The columns are steel blue and Florentine bronze, whilst the vaults are dotted with stars and the ribbing is painted a variety of colours.

Another peculiarity of the church is that since 1989 masses here have been held according to two different liturgies – that introduced by Paul VI and that associated with Pope Pius V and celebrated in Latin. Up to 1998 the two liturgies were celebrated by two different priests, but now are the responsibility of a single priest. Thus it is not uncommon to find, in the same morning, a mass in French (with the celebrant facing towards the congregation), then – a couple of hours later – the same priest, now in gold and purple vestments, celebrating a Latin mass (complete with Gregorian chant) according to a rite that has him facing away from the congregation.

The Tridentine and the Pauline liturgies

– The Tridentine mass. This is associated with Pope Pius V and was the liturgy which the Roman Catholic Church followed from the period of the Council of Trent (1563) – hence the name Tridentine – to the Second Vatican Council. Though opposed by some (most notably Monseigneur Lefebvre in France), the Pauline liturgy is considered as a step towards modernisation, a sign of the Church adapting to the 20th century.

– The Pauline mass. This is now the standard liturgy of the Roman Catholic Church and was introduced by Pope Paul VI following the Second Vatican Council (1962-1965).

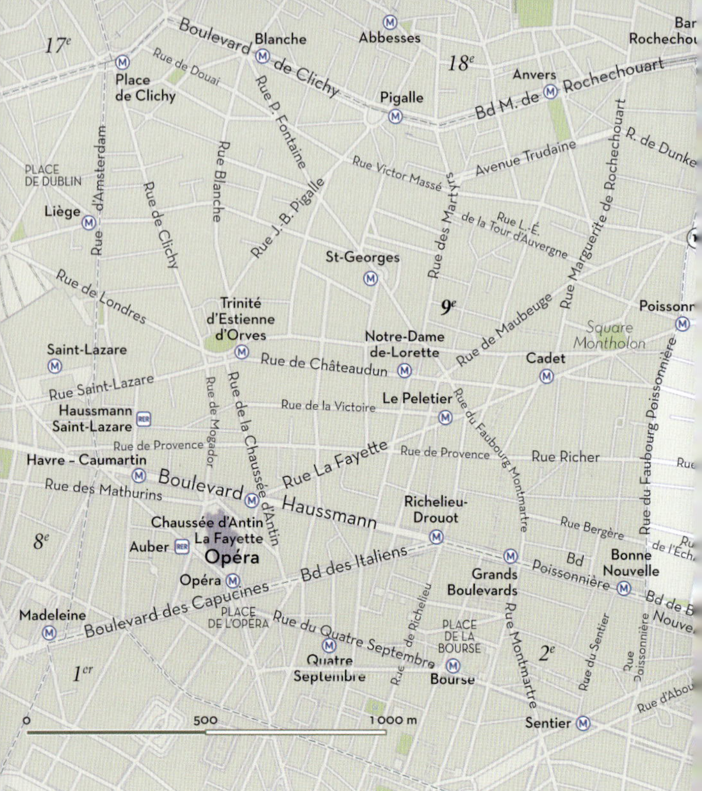

10th arrondissement

La Chapelle
Stalingrad
Boulevard de la Chapelle
PLACE DE LA BATAILLE DE STALINGRAD
N
Rue Louis Blanc
Rue de l'Aqueduc
Gare du Nord
Rue du Faubourg Saint-Denis
Louis Blanc
Rue La Fayette
Jaurès
Avenue Secrétan
Bolivar
Rue de Maubeuge
12
Magenta
Château Landon
Rue du Faubourg Saint-Martin
Rue de Meaux
19e
14
Rue d'Alsace
Gare de l'Est
Avenue Mathurin Moreau
Rue La Fayette
Bd de Magenta
Canal Saint-Martin
Rue Louis Blanc
Colonel Fabien
Rue Chabrol
1
2
Gare de l'Est
Square Villemin
R. des Recollets
Rue de la Grange aux Belles
Av. Claude Vellefaux
Boulevard de la Villette
Paradis
10
10e
4
5
es Écuries
Rue des Vinaigriers
Quai de Valmy
Rue Bichat
3
Rue du Faubourg Saint-Denis
Bd de Strasbourg
Château d'Eau
R. de Lancry
Quai de Jemmapes
Rue Alibert
Rue Saint-Maur
Belleville
9
8
Rue du Château d'Eau
Jacques Bonsergent
Goncourt
Avenue Parmentier
Porte St-Denis
Bd de Magenta
6
R. Léon Jouhaux
Rue du Faubourg du Temple
11e
Porte Saint-Martin
7
République
PLACE DE LA RÉPUBLIQUE
Rue de la Fontaine au Roi
asbourg nt-Denis
3e
Bd Saint-Martin
R. N.-D. de Nazareth

Unknown aspects of Parisian railway stations

There was a practical reason for the height and size of the glass roofs in most of Paris's railway stations: at the time they were built, trains were steam-powered and the high roofs were necessary to prevent passengers and staff being choked by noxious fumes.

The arrival of the railways in the city was not untroubled, and some engineers were very doubtful about the project. Arago, for example, predicted the most dire health risks for those who ventured into the Saint-Cloud tunnel. Furthermore, the railway companies were suspected of wanting to interfere in the city's business; as a result, it was decided to make Metro tunnels too low to take railway trains, in order to prevent the two systems ever being interconnected. Similarly, as railways followed the English system of driving on the left, it was decided that Metro trains were to drive on the right. It is no accident, therefore, that there is no direct Metro line linking the various mainline stations. Indeed, the route one has to follow from one station to another is sometimes bizarre. For example, travellers arriving at Gare d'Austerlitz and wanting to continue their journey from Gare de Lyon (just over the Seine) have to carry bag and baggage there themselves. There is no Metro link between the two stations. Perhaps now the time has come to remedy this situation.

The hollow columns of Gare du Nord

The metal columns bearing the structure of the Gare du Nord are hollow, allowing the rainwater that falls onto the roof to flow down directly into the drains below ground.

Apart from Paris, only four French cities have 'line-head' stations, where the tracks come to an end rather than running through: Marseilles, Lyons, Tours and Orleans.

The influence of Napoleon III on Parisian place names

The various military campaigns undertaken during the time of Napoleon III have left their mark on the toponymy of the city, with 31 roads and streets being named after cities or generals associated with the campaigns in the Crimea, Mexico or Italy – for example, avenues Bugeaud, Malakoff, Magenta, Alma and Mac-Mahon. In the church of Notre-Dame-du-Travail in the 14th arrondissement (see page 394), there is even a bell from the Crimean War.

THE BUNKER AT GARE DE L'EST ①

A bunker under the rail tracks

Gare de l'Est
Place du 11 Novembre 1918
Ask the station's communications department about the days when the station is open to visitors
Metro Gare de l'Est

Hidden under tracks 2 and 3 is an old bomb shelter which, strangely, is still intact. The place, from where the station was to be run in case of bombardment, is strikingly authentic: old train timetables lie on the floor as if they had just been dropped there, and the mechanical equipment appears to be in perfect working order (the Ministry of Defence still maintains the shelter). The signs reading *Notausgang* and other inscriptions on the walls reveal that the place was taken over by the Germans. However, one question remains: was this command centre ever used?

We know that construction work began on July 20, 1939, when the declaration of war was imminent, and that it was completed in 1941, during the Occupation. Hermetically sealed from the outside world, this concrete structure has a floor area of 120 m² and could accommodate up to 72 people.

The three main rooms – telephone exchange, machine room and traffic-control room – are separated by three massive anti-blast doors. Bottled oxygen was also installed, for use in case of poison gas, and there were even pedal-operated generators to provide power should the electricity be cut off.

© Jean-Jacques Le-Roux

S.T MARTIN

Phantom stations of the Paris metro

Although they no longer appear on the present-day map of the Paris transport system, a few stations still physically exist underground, some of them being put to uses very different from those for which they were built. The closure of most of these so-called 'phantom' stations dates from the start of the Second World War in 1939, when – due to the call-up of some of the transport staff – the Metro system was cut back. Later, when the war was over, it was decided not to reopen stations that had been little used or were too close to busier stations. As a result, the stations Arsenal, Croix Rouge, Champs de Mars, Saint Martin, Martin Nadaud and Porte des Lilas disappeared from the Paris Metro map; the first four, however, are on lines still in use, so if you keep your eyes peeled you may catch a glimpse of them from your train. Since being decommissioned, few of the stations have stood idle: Arsenal now houses facilities for the training of the network's electrical engineers and technicians; Saint Martin – whose walls are still decorated with fine, period advertisements in ceramic tile – was used as a shelter for the homeless, then in 1999 became a social solidarity facility run by the Salvation Army. For its part, Croix Rouge has had various roles: in the early 1980s, for example, an artist transformed it into a beach resort, complete with *chaises longues* (deck chairs) and umbrellas; it has also been used for fashion shows. The situation at Porte des Lilas is rather different, as part of the station is still functional within the Metro network. Behind the public platforms, however, facilities have been created for location filming. Depending upon the needs of the script, the station can become Pont Neuf, Pigalle or whatever is required. Renamed Porte des Lilas-Cinéma, this part of the station used to serve the line which ran here from Pré Saint Gervais, a stretch of the Metro which was opened in 1921 and closed in 1939; the shuttle along this line is still used for staff training and for the testing of new equipment. Two other stations – Haxo (between Porte des Lilas and Pré Saint Gervais) and Porte Molitor (located between lines 9 and 10) – suffered a different fate. No sooner were they built than they were abandoned, due to changes in the original plans for the transport system. The access stairways linking them with the street above were never even built.

ASSOCIATION FRANÇAISE DES AMIS DES CHEMINS DE FER

For those mad about trains

(Association of French Railway Enthusiasts)
Gare de l'Est
Place du 11 Novembre 1918
+33 1 40 38 20 92
Saturday 2.30pm–6pm
(Children must be accompanied by an adult), group visits on Wednesdays by appointment between 3pm and 6pm, closed in August
Metro Gare de l'Est

Founded in 1929, the AFAC (Association Française des Amis des Chemins de Fer) is housed in the amazing underground space beneath Gare de l'Est.

Upon entering, you are warmly welcomed by the club members operating the model train layouts. You will probably be invited to stand in the middle of one of these immense networks to understand the complex layout of rail signals, level crossings, marshalling yards, platforms, etc. – all reproduced to scale.

The association occupies two rooms. In one is a 1/87 scale model, while in the other are two layouts, one at a scale of 1/43.5 and the other at 1/32. Lovingly created by AFAC members, these three rail networks can accommodate a number of trains, with traffic being handled with all the rigour of an actual rail system. Louis Armand, a former chairman of the SNCF (French State Railways), was so impressed by the visit he paid here that he commented that the association was in some respects ahead of the SNCF itself!

Any member can run their own trains on these layouts, provided of course that they are compatible. This is one of the privileges you will enjoy if you join – and listening to the advice of your fellow members you may even learn how to build your own trains and carriages. A must for children!

THE SQUARE COURTYARD OF SAINT-LOUIS HOSPITAL

Place des Vosges – without the traffic

40, rue Bichat and 1, avenue Claude Vellefaux
+33 1 42 49 49 49
Daily 8am–6pm
Metro Goncourt

This sublime interior courtyard is entirely on a par with place des Vosges – with the added bonus of having no traffic. Not to be missed for anything ...

Now a listed building, the hospital was set up in response to the great plague of 1562, which caused more than 68,000 deaths in the capital: given the overcrowding in the Hôtel-Dieu hospital and the fact that the disease was so highly contagious, it was essential that there be a new Maison de Santé where patients could be isolated from the rest of the population.

The design that Henri IV chose for the building was by Claude Vellefaux, 'master mason employed on the building projects of the king,' and within a few years the Hôpital Saint-Louis was created. The central square measures 120 metres by 120 metres and is surrounded by a covered walkway, with each corner marked by large buildings in stone and bricks. There are also four other groups of free-standing buildings. The separation of each of the structures was intended to limit contagion and to prevent the patients from escaping.

The flowerbeds in the centre of the lawn are in the shape of a Maltese Cross. The Knights of Malta (now a hospitalier Order) occupy one of the buildings.

NEARBY

The waters of Belleville 

2, rue Juliette Dodu
Metro Goncourt or Colonel Fabien

Roughly opposite 2, rue Juliette Dodu, the curious building that barely rises above the ground and escapes the attention of most users of Saint-Louis hospital where it stands, is nevertheless classified as a Historic Monument. Built in the 17th century, it was a reservoir constructed to bring water from the Belleville springs to the city.

MUSEUM OF DERMATOLOGICAL CASTS

Museum of Skin Diseases

Hôpital Saint-Louis
1, avenue Claude Vellefaux
+33 1 42 49 49 86 – musee.moulages.sls@aphp.fr
Monday–Friday 9am–4.30pm, by appointment only and during 'Journées du Patrimoine' (Heritage Days)
Under 12s not permitted
Metro Goncourt

This Museum of Dermatological Casts (Musée des moulages dermatologiques) is extraordinary.

Set up by Doctor Alphonse Devergies in 1865 as a Museum of Skin Diseases, it received its first wax cast in 1867, the work of Jules Baretta.

The hospital also initiated the study of dermatology, so this collection was intended for teaching purposes, with almost 5,000 wax casts of heads or limbs showing the symptoms of skin diseases.

Produced over the period 1867–1958, these casts are exhibited in glass display cases against a black background and show the effects of such diseases as leprosy, gangrene, syphilis, naevus, scabies, dermatitis, eczema, shingles and pustules.

Materials added since 1958 are in the form of photographs.

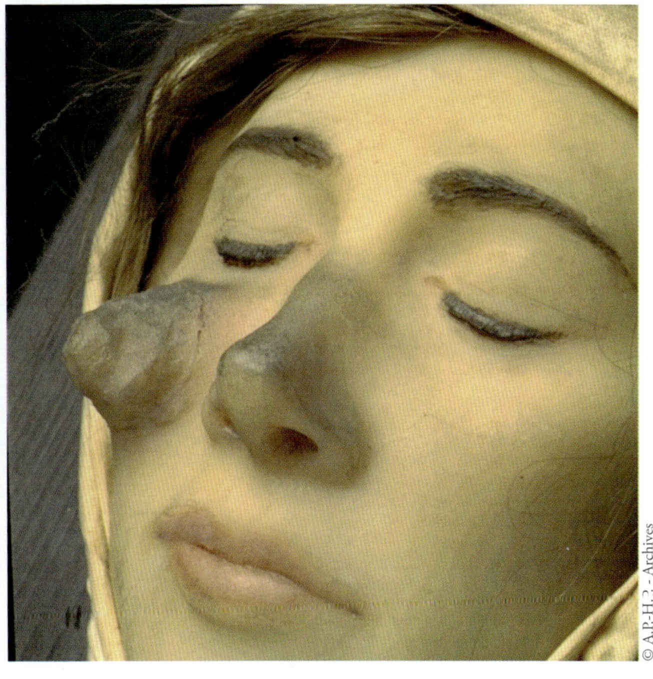

© A.P.-H.P. - Archives

LABOUR EXCHANGE

A hidden gem from the 19th century

3, rue du Château d'Eau
+33 1 44 84 50 21
Monday–Friday 8am–10.30pm, Saturday 8am–5.45pm
Visit on request at reception
Metro République

Built from 1888 to 1896 by Joseph-Antoine Bouvard (1840–1920), then architect of the City of Paris, the Bourse du Travail conceals a superb period room behind its imposing five-storey façade. Note especially the symbols of different trades (gilders, sculptors, grocers, carpenters, printers, bakers, charcutiers, painters, luthiers, goldsmiths, etc.) as well as a very pretty metallic verrière.

The land was occupied by a building from 1775 which had successively housed private individuals, then the 5th arrondissement town hall, then the Grand Café Parisien until 1880.

It offers a panorama in a vast rotunda, 120 metres in circumference and 17 metres high.

What is a labour exchange?

A labour exchange was originally an office run by trade unions where people could find work, following a project of Belgian economist Gustave de Molinari.

Worker unrest that grew in such places finally discouraged employers and employees from using them, and their function as a placement office for workers was gradually eroded.

Since then labour exchanges have become places where different trade unions gather, with reception rooms, mutual aid services, etc. Social work collectives or associations sometimes organise meetings there.

NEARBY

Ceramics at 8, boulevard Saint-Martin ⑦

Metro Strasbourg – Saint-Denis

Beautiful Art Nouveau ceramics by famous Czech artist Alphonse Mucha.

The smallest house in Paris ⑧

39, rue du Château d'Eau
Metro Jacques Bonsergent

The house at 39, rue du Château d'Eau is the smallest in Paris, at 1.1 metres wide and 5 metres high. It originated through a quarrel over the ownership of the passage between rue du Château d'Eau and rue du Faubourg Saint-Martin. To resolve the dispute, the passage would have been blocked by this house.

HIGH RELIEF OF
LA FRATERNITÉ DES PEUPLES

A manifesto for homosexuality?

72, rue du Faubourg Saint-Martin
(Town hall, 10th arrondissement – Salle des Mariages)
+33 1 53 72 10 10
Monday, Tuesday, Wednesday and Friday 8.30am–5pm,
Thursday 8.30am–7.30pm, Saturday 9am–12.30pm (civil status and library only)
Metro Château d'Eau

The 10th arrondissement town hall, opened in 1896, is one of the most beautiful in Paris. In the first-floor wedding hall, an awesome sculpture sits behind the mayor's altar depicting two men voluptuously kissing.

Far from being a hidden statement in favour of homosexuality, the sculpture by Aimé-Jules Dalou (1838–1902) is titled *La fraternité des peuples* (The Brotherhood of Peoples).

Also sometimes called *Le retour de l'enfant prodigue* (The Return of the Prodigal Child), it was bought by the city in 1884. Originally planned to be installed at the Hôtel de Ville, it shows Justice from above dominating the Fatherland, laying his hand on the shoulder of the Republic. Below, the father receives his son back from war and kisses him affectionately.

Under the father and son, the man breaking up arms symbolises the hope that the Republic will be a source of peace: the Third Republic was established after the war against Prussia (1870) and the violence of the Commune (1871).

The sculptures on the façade, erected in 1906, recall the various trades represented in the district.

NEARBY

An old faience shop: Boulenger de Choisy-le-Roi ⑩

18, rue de Paradis
Metro Château d'Eau

In the late 19th – early 20th centuries, rue de Paradis was considered the place in Paris to buy glassware, porcelain and ceramics. It was one of the last examples in the city of a street given over entirely to the interests of one particular economic activity. Built in 1889–1892 by the architects Georges Jacotin and Ernest Brunnarius, the building at

No. 18 housed the offices and the shop of the faience manufacturers Boulenger de Choisy-le-Roi. The company's moment of glory came during the creation of the Paris Metro, for which they provided about two-thirds of the wall tiles. Today, the interior and exterior of the building are still covered by immense ceramic tiles; since 1981 this has been a listed building. A polite request will get you a look inside, even if the building is not officially open to the public.

ART NOUVEAU FAÇADES AT 14 AND 16, RUE D'ABBEVILLE

Two superb Art Nouveau façades

Metro Poissonnière

The building at No. 14 was designed in 1901 by the architects Alexandre and Édouard Autant, with the ceramic decoration by Alexandre Bigot.

Note the extravagance of the plant motifs: the central bay of the building swarms with what look like real climbing vines, whilst the loggia on the fifth floor is decorated with leaves, chimeras and slim columns in green ceramic.

NEARBY

Garden of Fernand Widal Hospital ⑫

200, rue du Faubourg Saint-Denis – Metro and RER Gare du Nord
Intended for geriatric patients, this green area of 1,000 m² is a very welcome surprise within this bustling area of the city, offering the chance of a pleasant moment of relaxation.

ENAMELLED LAVA PANELS OF 9, RUE FÉNELON ⑬

Traces of an old painting workshop

9, rue Fénélon – Metro Poissonnière

Built in 1858 along the Saint-Vincent-de-Paul church, the building at 9, rue Fénelon features remarkable enamelled lava decorations. It housed the painting workshop of François Gillet, inventor of a process for creating polychromed decorations on enamelled lava. Several medallions represent famous ceramists, such as Bernard Palissy, among whom we find François Gillet and the painter Pierre-Jules Jollivet (1794–1871). An attractive frieze tells the story of the art of fire.

NEARBY

RER B ventilation shaft ⑭

145, rue La Fayette
Metro and RER Gare du Nord

The Haussmann building at 145, rue La Fayette, a few steps from the Gare du Nord, is unlike its neighbours. Have a good look and you'll realise that it has no proper front door: no code, no doorbell, no intercom. The windows on the upper floors don't give anything away about what lies inside. That's for a reason: far from being a classic apartment block, the building houses a ventilation shaft of the RER line B that passes nearby at Gare du Nord.

A beautiful example of RATP façadisme, this exercise in style neatly hides technical infrastructure behind conventional architecture.

11th arrondissement

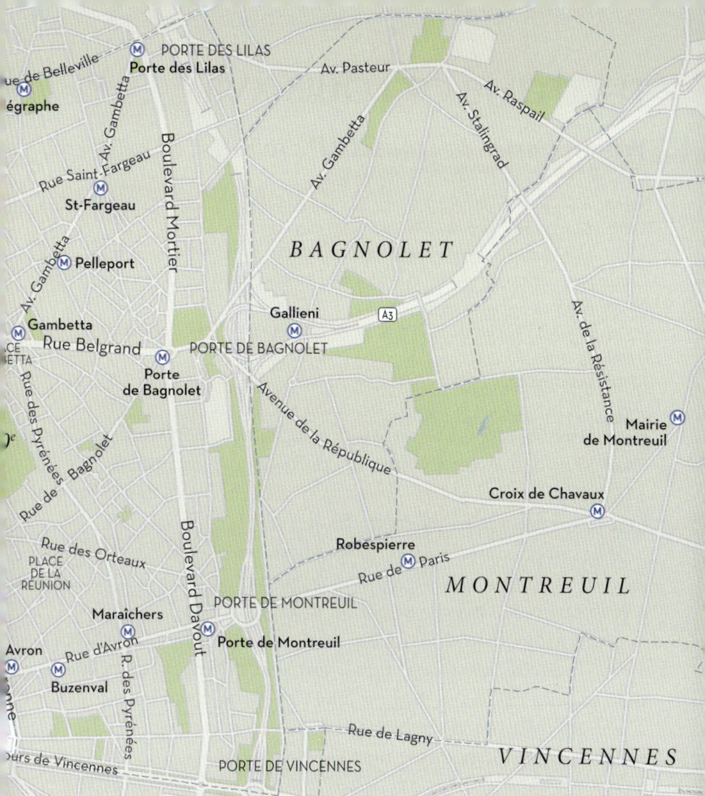

PORTE DES LILAS
Porte des Lilas
Av. Pasteur
Av. Raspail
ue de Belleville
égraphe
Av. Stalingrad
Rue Saint-Fargeau
Av. Gambetta
St-Fargeau
Boulevard Mortier
Av. Gambetta
Pelleport
BAGNOLET
Av. Gambetta
Gambetta
Gallieni
A3
Rue Belgrand
PORTE DE BAGNOLET
CE
ETTA
Porte
de Bagnolet
Av. de la Résistance
Rue des Pyrénées
Avenue de la République
Mairie
de Montreuil
Rue de Bagnolet
Croix de Chavaux
Rue des Orteaux
PLACE
DE LA
RÉUNION
Robespierre
Boulevard Davout
Rue de Paris
MONTREUIL
Maraîchers
PORTE DE MONTREUIL
Avron
Rue d'Avron
Porte de Montreuil
R. des Pyrénées
Buzenval
Rue de Lagny
VINCENNES
urs de Vincennes
PORTE DE VINCENNES

THE TOMB OF LOUIS XVII

Who is buried in Louis XVII's tomb?

Sainte-Marguerite Cemetery
Sainte-Marguerite church – 36, rue Saint-Bernard
+33 1 43 71 34 24 – secretariat@saintemargueriteparis.fr
Church: Monday–Saturday (except school holidays) 8am–7.30pm (8am–7pm
on Sunday)
To see Louis XVII's tomb, call or send an email to apply (or check the reception
desk)
Metro Ledru-Rollin

Closed in 1804, the cemetery attached to the church of Sainte-Marguerite contains a small tomb with the inscription "L XVII – 1785–1795". There is a mysterious story associated with this, as for a long time it was taken to be the tomb of Louis XVII.

The son of Louis XVI and Marie-Antoinette, Louis-Charles was shut away in the prison of Le Temple on August 13, 1792, when he was just seven years old. After the execution of his father on January 21, 1793, he was entrusted to the keeping of the cobbler Simon until January 1794. Thereafter all trace of him is lost, and the official story runs that the Dauphin fell ill and died on June 8, 1795 and was buried in secret. The mystery surrounding this death led to no fewer than 43 false "Dauphins" coming forward over the following years.

Research carried out at Sainte-Marguerite cemetery, traditionally used to bury those who had died in the prison of Le Temple, revealed that a child was buried there on June 10, 1795 – that is, two days after the supposed death of Louis XVII. A first exhumation was ordered in 1846, but the body discovered in the lead coffin was that of a youth aged 15–18. This gave rise to various rumours: some said that the prince had been saved from the prison by royalists, and that the body had been placed there to cover his escape; others argued that he had actually died in Le Temple but in 1794, and that no one was informed of the fact until a year later (in order to avoid a scandal, a burial was then held with another body).

The truth would seem to be that Louis XVII did actually die in the dungeons of Le Temple, and that his heart was removed and concealed during the autopsy. The prince's body was apparently then buried in Sainte-Marguerite cemetery, before being exhumed by order of the government of the day for reburial in the cemetery of Clamart.

Over the coming years his heart would pass from owner to owner, until in 1975 it was laid to rest in the crypt of Saint-Denis, the burial place of many of France's kings. DNA analysis carried out in 2000 confirmed the authenticity of the attribution to Louis XVII, and a funeral urn containing the heart was placed in the Bourbon Chapel of the cathedral on June 8, 2004.

However, one question still remains: who is buried in the tomb at Sainte-Marguerite?

Why is the heir to the throne of France called the Dauphin?

The origin of the name Dauphin to designate the heir to the throne of France (equivalent to the British title "the Prince of Wales") dates from 1349, when Humbert II, Lord of the Dauphiné (region of Grenoble), sold his lands to the future King of France on condition that the heir apparent bore the title Dauphin of Viennois. So the first Dauphin of France was the future Charles V, son of Jean le Bon. The origin of the word "Dauphiné" is itself obscure and there are many theories: the name of the ancient local people the Auffinates; a reminder that the Allobroges, the ancient inhabitants of the Viennois, came from Delphi (in Greece); a link with a Venetian ancestor by the name of Delfino; a resemblance to Vienne (from the Viennese); people's response on naming their land of origin; a derivation of Germanic wigo meaning prince; the evolution of a Celtic expression dalh pen which translates as sovereign of the country ...

STROLLING AND EXPLORING THE ALLEYS AND COURTYARDS OF FAUBOURG ST-ANTOINE

Starting point: Bastille or Ledru-Rollin metro station (depending upon whether you want to stroll up or down rue du Faubourg-Saint-Antoine)

The passage du Cheval-Blanc at No. 2, rue de la Roquette is a good place to start. Comprising a sequence of six fully-restored cobbled courtyards – named after the first six months of the year – this leads to the cité Parchappe area giving directly onto rue du Faubourg Saint-Antoine. Take the opportunity to glance into the cobbled court-yard of No. 33 in this street, the gate generally being open during the daytime; the Parisian radio station Radio Nova is located here. At No. 50 on the other side of the street (and therefore in the 12th arrondissement; Baron Haussmann's redevelopment scheme divided the street between two arrondissements), No. 9 passage de la Boule-Blanche houses the premises of the *Cahiers du Cinéma* under a fine glass roof draped with greenery. From here you can, during the week, pass through to rue de Charenton (the passage is closed at weekends). A little further on, at No. 56, rue du Faubourg-Saint-Antoine, is the cour de Bel-Air, which is even prettier since its restoration; in autumn the façade vines here are

full of grapes. This is home to the famous bookshop L'Arbre à Lettres, which is entered from No. 62, rue du Faubourg-Saint-Antoine. One of the houses in the courtyard also has a fine staircase in black wood which is known as 'L'escalier des Mousquetaires Noirs' (The Black Musketeers Staircase). At No. 66, take passage du Chantier, which still looks as it did in the 19th century, with large cobblestones, narrow pavements, and various workshops and shops; some of the premises still house woodworkers. At No. 71, on the 11th arrondissement side of the street, the cour des Shadocks (its unofficial name) is a fine example of what restoration can achieve, creating a place with its own, very special atmosphere. A little further, at No. 75, the cour de l'Étoile d'Or takes its name from the À l'Étoile d'Or sign. Here you can still see a small 17th century 'pavillon de plaisance'; a sort of pleasure pavilion, which used to stand between the courtyard and the garden beyond (the latter was paved and made into a second courtyard in the 18th century). Reference is often made to the face of a sundial dated 1751 which is supposed to be engraved on the right side of the pavilion's façade, but nowadays it is completely invisible. If you have still managed to avoid getting run over as you cross back and forwards over rue du Faubourg-Saint-Antoine, try your luck once more to see cour des Bourguignons at No. 74. Here, the workshops bristle with large signs but still house a good number of artists and craftsmen. The courtyard has a fine porch decorated with sculpture and carved medallions; the fine brick chimney rising above a large glass roof is now a listed architectural feature. Crossing the road (yet again!), take the time to glance into cour des Trois-Frères at No. 81–83; it is a veritable hive of industry; cour de la Maison Brûlée at No. 89 (the entrance has two fine mascarons); and finally cour de l'Ours at No. 95 (there is a relief of a bear carved on the façade). Moving away from the rue du Faubourg-Saint-Antoine, this stroll should also take in passage Lhomme in the nearby rue Ledru-Rollin (on the 11th arrondissement side). A verdant, cobbled street now occupied by art galleries and craft showrooms, this links rue Ledru-Rollin with rue de Charonne, where at No. 37 you can admire the last stop on our brief tour: cour Delépine.

Why are wood crafts located in Faubourg Saint-Antoine?

The establishment of wood crafts in the Faubourg Saint-Antoine district is due to the fact that the wood transported into Paris by river entered the city by the nearby fluvial port of La Rapée. Firewood and building timber were thus stored nearby, so it was only natural that people would soon have the idea of setting up wood-working crafts in the neighbourhood.

NEARBY

Mosaics of 1, passage Rauch ③

Metro Ledru-Rollin

Near Sainte-Marguerite cemetery, the animal mosaics above the doors (lion, dromedary, bear ...) recall the former site of a mosaic workshop. They were created in 1990 by *trompe l'œil* artist Leonor Rieti.

Cour du Coq ④

60, rue Saint-Sabin
Metro Chemin Vert

Closed by a wrought-iron gate decorated with a cock (in case you didn't notice the name written in full just above ...), Rooster Court owes its name to the attitude of its former owner, who was as 'proud as a rooster' to own this paved passage with a rural feel in the mid city. If the gate stays shut, you can still admire the tranquillity of the place through the openwork bars.

Marks from the 1724 census ⑤

Metro Ledru-Rollin

At the corner of rue de Charonne and rue du Faubourg Saint-Antoine, a discreet engraving on the façade of the building reads Cte I et Cte V. This is one of the marks (see page 513) of a census of Parisian houses commissioned by Louis XV in 1724 from Jean Bausire, the city's master builder, and his son Jean-Baptiste, to prevent individuals from building without a permit. 'Cte' stands for Committee, and 'I' and 'V' are markers used for these two streets during the census.

CERAMICS FROM THE OLD LOEBNITZ POTTERY

A vestige of the 1878 Exposition Universelle

4, rue de la Pierre Levée
Metro Parmentier

The beautiful ceramics of 4, rue de la Pierre Levée owe their presence to the former headquarters of the Loebnitz pottery, built in 1884 by Paul Sédille, who was also the architect of Magasins du Printemps (a store chain).

The building contained workshops on one side and staff accommodation on the other. Owner of an earthenware factory producing stoves and chimney plates, Jules Paul Loebnitz (1836–95) launched in 1860 into architectural ceramics and won a gold medal at the 1878 Exposition Universelle (World's Fair) for a 12-metre-high façade entirely in terracotta and faience.

The Porte des Beaux-Arts, with three panels representing architecture, painting and sculpture, can still be seen on the façade of the old factory. A fourth panel on the façade itself was added later by Loebnitz as a kind of sign.

Loebnitz decorated the Gare du Champ in Paris, the Gare du Havre, the Monte-Carlo Opera and the cupola of the monument to Joan of Arc in Rouen. He also worked with architect Félix Duban at the Château de Blois where, based on drawings by Viollet-le-Duc, he made tiles for floors, the fireplaces and bathrooms of the Loebnitz earthenware factory, which was having difficulty moving into the age of mechanisation and had to close in 1935. There are still ovens in the basement of the building.

Rue de la Pierre Levée menhir

Rue de la Pierre Levée owes its name to a menhir discovered there when opening the route in 1782.

NEARBY
Édith Piaf Museum   ⑦

5, rue Crespin du Gast
+33 1 43 55 52 72 – Visits by appointment only – Admission free
Metro Ménilmontant

Including stuffed toys, Marcel Cerdan's boxing gloves, letters, pumps and the famous black dress that the singer wore on stage, these mementos of Édith Piaf were all donated by her friends and family. Visits must be prebooked by phone. This small, two-room museum is the life's work of a dedicated fan of the French chanteuse; retiring and discreet, he is also one of those who maintains the singer's tomb at Père-Lachaise cemetery. Visitors cannot help but be touched and moved by this collection of heterogeneous objects lovingly brought together in what was for some time the singer's own home. Even if this small apartment was not Édith Piaf's only home in Paris, you come away feeling that some of her spirit and generosity still pervade the place.

WOODEN PAVERS
OF PASSAGE SAINT-MAUR

Some of the last wooden pavers in the capital

81, rue Saint-Maur
Accessible during the day via a carriage entrance. If this is closed, you can gain entry by ringing the doorbell of one of the shops located in the passageway
Metro Rue Saint-Maur

Saint-Maur passage, behind the carriage entrance to 81, rue Saint-Maur, is a lovely reminder of 19th-century Paris, when housing and industry coexisted in the courtyards and passages of this popular district.

Although the floor is entirely paved, you'll discover that the rectangular section under the porch is made up of different paving from those classical stones next to them.

These wooden blocks cut from fir trees are among the last remains of a paving method that peaked in the late 19th century for about 30 years.

Between 1801 and 1901, the population became almost five times larger (from 548,000 to 2,714,000) and travel, such as goods transport was mainly on foot or by horse: the years 1855 to 1900 were a true golden age of horse-drawn traction.

In 1900 some 80,000 horses were passing through the streets of Paris, pulling all kinds of vehicles including omnibuses and trams. And trotting on large cobblestone paving wasn't ideal for horses, nor for passengers or residents: there was the risk of slipping, resulting in injuries to the horses and potentially serious traffic accidents, loose stones clinging to the wheels, and of course a huge noise nuisance for all those living near the roads.

This is how the idea of wooden paving gained ground. An early attempt in 1842 proved inconclusive.

After exchanges with London where a wooden surface had been deployed on some major arteries and in the City (see *Secret London – An unusual guide*, by the same publisher), and a first trial in Paris at rue Croix des Petits Champs and rue de Richelieu, the capital launched a vast programme in 1881, prioritising the most prestigious and busy arteries: avenue des Champs-Élysées, avenue Marigny, place Beauvau, rue de l'Élysée, place de l'Opéra, rue Royale and the Grands Boulevards.

Although the new surface was at first appreciated, problems inherent to wood quickly appeared.

The blocks were slippery in the rain and would rot under the effects of weather and horse manure, emitting pestiferous odours and becoming sources of infection.

The rising waters of the 1910 floods detached the blocks one by one and the wood rotted, again posing hygiene problems.

The disadvantages of wooden paving and the development of new means of locomotion (cars, electric trams, bicycles) led the city towards other more suitable materials. The use of wood gradually diminished before it was definitively abandoned in 1938.

There are other wooden pavers at 17, rue de la Présentation (11th arrondissement), 47, rue Oberkampf (11th arrondissement), 74, boulevard Richard Lenoir (11th arrondissement) and 38, rue Notre-Dame de Nazareth (3rd arrondissement).

Blood on the streets

Corner of rue de la Roquette and rue de la Croix-Faubin
Metro Voltaire or Philippe Auguste

Very discreetly set into the tarmac, five granite flagstones commemorate a very macabre time in the city's history: in 1832 the guillotine was transferred from place de Grève (Hôtel de Ville), where it had stood since 1792, to the barrière d'Arcueil (located above the present Saint-Jacques metro station), where it stood until 1851. This new location put the guillotine some 5 km from the prison of La Grande Roquette, where the condemned were held, which meant that their journey to their execution took some time. Finally aware that this added to the torture of those about to be beheaded, the government decreed on 29 November 1851 that the executions should take place in the street at the entrance to the prison. To bear the weight of the guillotine, five large granite flagstones were set into the cobbles, forming a cross. The place would soon become known as the 'Abbaye de cinq-pierres' (playing upon the similar pronunciation of St Pierre [St Peter] and *cinq pierres* [five stones]). A total of 69 people were executed on this spot. When the prison was decommissioned in 1900, the guillotine was moved to a position in front of – then inside – the prison of La Santé. The former governor of La Roquette prison had the five flagstones ripped up and tried to sell them to the Carnavalet Museum, which was not interested. However, when he then set them back in the road surface, he made a mistake: which is why pedestrians nowadays walk across not a traditional Latin cross in black granite but what is in fact St Andrew's cross.

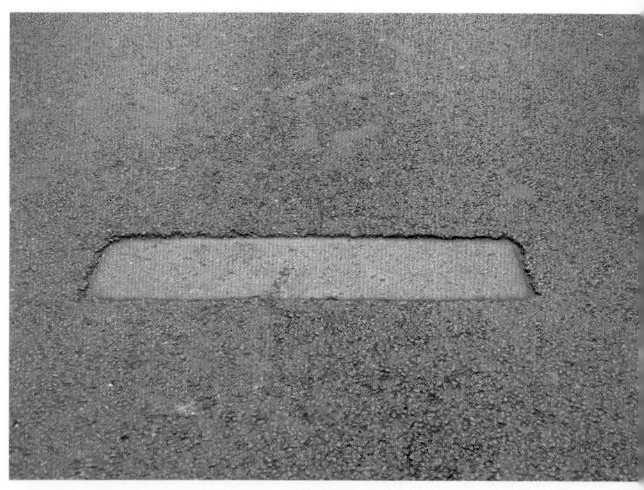

Invention of the guillotine

In a certain sense, three people could claim the "credit" for having invented the guillotine. The godfather of the instrument was undoubtedly Doctor Guillotin, who was the first to propose decapitation using a machine of which he would say: "Gentlemen, with my machine you can cut off a head in the blink of an eye and without feeling the least pain." Finally approved in 1791, the project was then entrusted to the great surgeon Louis, Secretary to the Académie de Chirurgie, who was appointed to resolve the various technical problems posed by this type of execution. He called for "tenders" from those who were to build it. This is where the joiner Schmidt comes into the story. He, too, made various modifications to the machine, testing it in cour de Rohan using sheep and bales of hay. Schmidt even managed to fraudulently claim paternity of the guillotine and register a patent that would earn him a fortune, thanks to the orders that flooded in from all over France: at one point a total of 83 guillotines were at work. However, Schmidt could not prevent this malevolent machine taking on the name of its real inventor.

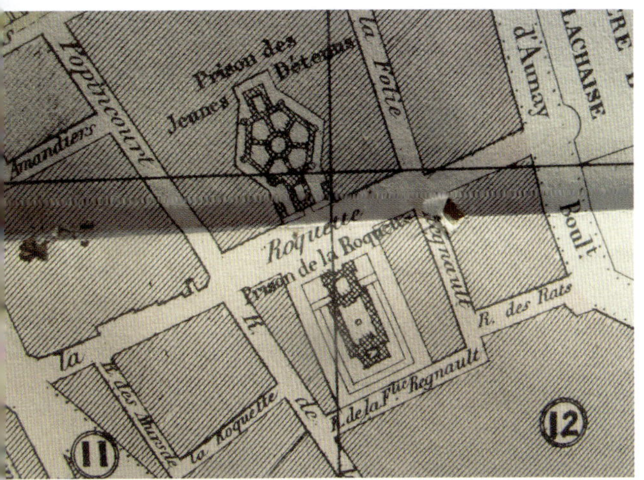

Garden of Dr Belhomme ⑩

159, rue de Charonne – Metro Charonne or Alexandre Dumas

This garden is a pleasant, little-known green space that opens onto three pretty pavilions. These buildings are the last traces of what was the Belhomme pension: a health home founded in 1769 by former glazier Jacques Belhomme (1737–1824) to treat the insane. At the Revolution, and while 37 patients were still interned in the boarding house, Belhomme offered to house for a fee the prisoners of the Terror who had enough money to pay for this discreet and practical means of escape from the scaffold. Probably taking advantage of the protection of the public accuser of the Fouquier-Tinville Revolutionary Tribunal (even though no evidence has been found), Belhomme welcomed such people as the Duchess of Orléans, widow of Philippe-Égalité, Portalis, who was one of the drafters of the civil code, or the deputy Rouzet who also fell in love with the Duchess of Orléans. Finally denounced by two patients who had no means of payment so had been left without food, he was arrested and imprisoned on 28 January 1794. He was released and returned to manage the pension in 1798. The rich boarders had left on 9 Thermidor II (27 July 1794), at the fall of Robespierre.

NEARBY
Rue des Immeubles Industriels ⑪

Metro Nation

Inspired by Fourier's notion of phalansteries, the industrialist Jean-François Cail commissioned the architect Leménil to build the 19 residential buildings that make up rue des Immeubles Industriels. Constructed in 1872–1873, they offered a novel model of accommodation for working families. Within one and the same building were workshops (in the basement and lower levels) and family homes (on the upper floors), the whole development being designed to be both modern and comfortable. A 200 horsepower steam engine provided the craftsmen (most of whom were woodworkers) with the energy necessary to drive their equipment. Unfortunately the only housing development of its kind in the capital, this experiment would be a great success; by the end of the 19th century there were almost 2,000 people living here.

The 19 buildings are admirably designed, with repetition making for elegance rather than monotony; the façades are adorned with painted and decorated cast-iron columns and the windows on the first floor have a fine arcade motif. The entire design won a Gold Medal at the 1878 Universal Exposition.

© FLLL

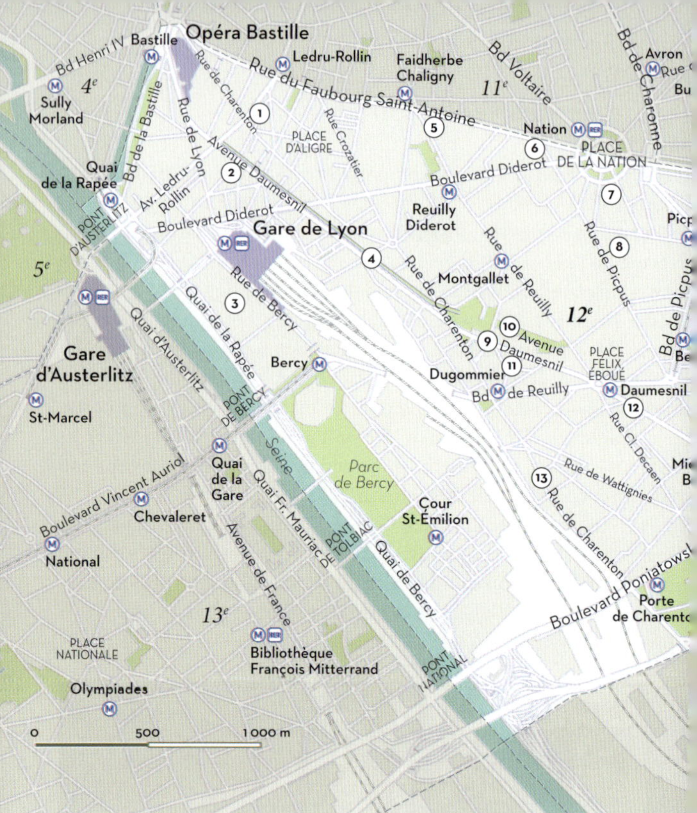

12th arrondissement

20e
Porte de Montreuil
MONTREUIL
VINCENNES
Boulevard Davout
Rue de Lagny
Rue de Fontenay
PORTE DE VINCENNES
RER Vincennes
rs de Vincennes
Porte
de Vincennes
Avenue de Paris
Bérault
St-Mandé
Château
de Vincennes
de Saint-Mandé
Château
de Vincennes
Boulevard Soult
Lac
de Saint-Mandé
Avenue des Minimes
Route de la Pyramide
SAINT-
MANDÉ
Avenue Daumesnil
rte
rée
Parc zoologique
de Paris
Bois de Vincennes
Avenue de Saint-Maurice
Lac
Daumesnil
Route de la Tourelle
14
17
iberté

FLOOD PLAQUE OF 1740 

No, not only the flood of 1910

28, rue de Charenton
Metro Ledru-Rollin

As recorded on the plaque on the façade of 28, rue de Charenton, near the entrance to the hospital of Quinze-Vingt, the Seine has brought other important floods, other than 1910, which remains the most famous because of its importance and the spectacular photographic testimonies. Along with those of 1658, 1711 and 1802, the flood of 1740 was one of the most important: more than 720 hectares were flooded. The plaque was placed by Constant Bouquet in front of his house.

Below, the flood plan drawn up by Philippe Buache, a cartographer and member of the Académie des Sciences (8.05 metres at Pont d'Austerlitz, which places it just behind the floods of 1658 and 1910), shows in a spectacular way the extent of the damage.

NEARBY

The Egyptian columns of viaduc Daumesnil

Metro Ledru-Rollin

Where it crosses avenue Ledru-Rollin, viaduc Daumesnil rests on curious columns with lotus flower capitals. These are a leftover from the 19th century craze for Egyptian artefacts (see page 70). The viaduct was originally built to serve the old Vincennes railway, which opened in September 1859.

NEARBY

The giant sliding gate at 94–96, quai de la Rapée ③

Metro Quai de la Rapée

Designed by Aymeric Zublena in 1992, the building at 94–96, quai de la Rapée has a very striking peculiarity: the entire façade is covered by an enormous sliding gate (weight: 84 tons; height: 25 metres; width: 33 metres). The spectacular opening and closing of the gate can be seen at around 7am and 7pm. For security reasons, access to the building has, for some years now, been by the rather anonymous entrance on avenue Ledru-Rollin.

SCULPTURES OF MICHELANGELO'S DYING SLAVE

Slaves of the law

Hôtel de Police, 12th arrondissement
23, rue de Rambouillet and 78–80, avenue Daumesnil
Metro Montgallet or Reuilly-Diderot

© Pauline Le Goff

The best view of an awesome work of art is on the other side of avenue Daumesnil, at the top of the arcades at the level of the Coulée Verte. At the junction of rue de Rambouillet and avenue Daumesnil, the top of the 12th arrondissement police station is in fact discreetly occupied (you have to look up to see them) by a series of 12 concrete sculptures of naked men, each 7 metres tall.

The work of Manuel Nuñez-Yanowski; each statue is a reproduction of Michelangelo's Dying Slave, whose unfinished originals are in the Louvre Museum. The only difference from the original: although the exuberantly bare torso was faithfully reproduced, the penis was omitted. At the time, according to the architect, 'that was shocking to politicians'. On the day of the installation, however women of a certain age exclaimed: 'It's a shame that the most interesting bit is hidden!'

Validated in 1985 under François Mitterrand, Nuñez-Yanowski's project was dropped until 1991, when the building was finally completed. The dying slaves on the roof of the police station are not a coincidence: quite the contrary. 'I wanted to show that it is not the bandits and criminals who are in prison, but police officers,' he explains, alluding to the fact that the police were 'slaves of the law'. He adds: 'In the specifications, bars were also provided on the windows of the ground floor.'

The statues all look in the same direction, towards place de la Bastille, an obvious reminder of the old prison.

DEAD END AT 18, RUE DE REUILLY

A clock that only gives the correct time twice a day

Metro Faidherbe-Chaligny

You have to ring the bell of one of the traders or ask a resident at 18, rue de Reuilly to enter one of the most beautiful passages in Paris. Passing under the vines, you reach the foot of a small pavilion whose lantern is decorated with a clock painted in trompe l'œil, where the time, which indicates 05.07 or 17.07, is correct only twice a day.

At 83, rue de Reuilly, impasse Mousset, even if less magical, still has a pleasant rural feel. Not far away, No. 67 opens on cour d'Alsace-Lorraine, another charming courtyard but without any greenery.

PLAN OF THE EUGÈNE NAPOLÉON FOUNDATION

(6)

In the shape of the necklace refused by the empress

254, rue du Faubourg Saint-Antoine
Visit by appointment only: contact@fondation-eugenenapoleon.org (bring a valid form of ID)
Metro Nation

Looking at an aerial photo of Paris you realise that the construction plan of the Eugène Napoléon Foundation seems quite bizarre. It takes the shape of the necklace that Empress Eugénie declined to accept in order to finance this foundation.

On 26 January 1853 the Paris municipal commission voted to use 600,000 francs in gold to purchase a diamond necklace for Empress Eugénie on the occasion of her marriage to Napoleon III. Two days later, however, the empress announced that she would refuse the necklace and wanted to use the money to create 'a free education facility for poor girls'. The money destined for the necklace was used for the buildings now on the site of the former fodder market in Faubourg Saint-Antoine. In tribute to the empress's generous gesture, the architect Hittorff shaped the buildings, opened in 1856, into a necklace.

In 1858 the establishment was named Maison Eugène Napoléon in honour of the young Prince Imperial, Louis-Eugène, only son of Napoleon III and Eugénie, born in 1856 and killed in southern Africa serving with British forces in a skirmish with the Zulus in 1879.

The foundation still fulfils its original role.

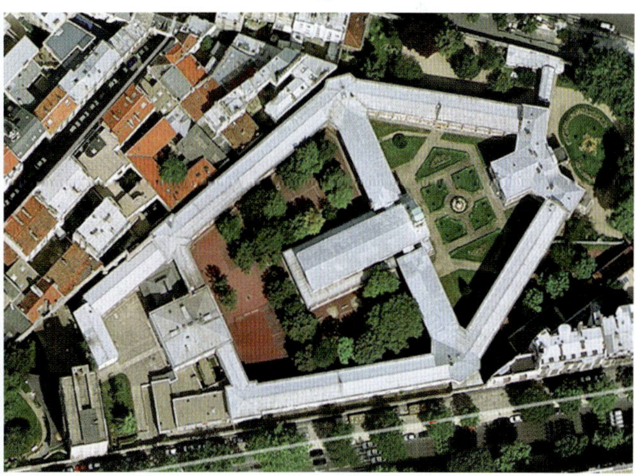

Alchemist of rue Fabre d'Églantine

9, rue Fabre d'Églantine
Metro Nation

Above the entrance to 9, rue Fabre d'Églantine, a curious high-relief shows a seated figure, legs crossed, gazing thoughtfully at an alembic (still). He holds a heavy book in his left hand and behind him is a furnace. Near the still a dog is sleeping. In the centre, behind the figure, a strange crocodile lies horizontally, and far behind is a phoenix.

The high-relief, clearly Hermetic in nature, shows an alchemist whose book represents the *Universalis Liber* (Book of the Universe), whose secrets he decodes as he delves into the Grand Work and advances in personal development.

The figure's pensive aspect suggests that this work on matter and self requires deep concentration and meditation on the solution, while waiting for distillation and dissolution to take place in the still. The sleeping dog, apart from representing the guardian of his faithful companion the alchemist, also indicates the primitive state (or animal state) that his master must transform into a rational and spiritual state.

Behind the alchemist is the furnace or athanor (from Arabic *at-tannur*), an object for perfecting both chemical elements and the human condition passing to a spiritual condition. If the still is the instrument of liquid distillation, a fundamental step to reach the quintessence of elements, the furnace, heated by the Hermetic fire, is the environment where the same elements are purified in order to be effectively distilled. The action of both results in steam, a sign of the ethereal 'spirit'. In its sense of perfecting and transformation, the athanor has often been compared to the Mountain of Initiation which is climbed gradually,

just as the alchemist will gradually transform during the process of the Great Work. It was also associated with the idea of a house enclosed and a temple. The ancient alchemists even used a hollow oak to represent an athanor, because early Druids attributed the oak with the significance of a temple, and it was, in fact, the sacred tree of their religion.

The crocodile behind the alchemist is the representation of the makara in Hinduism: a half-god, half-man traditionally attributed to the true spiritual illuminated.

At the bottom, the phoenix is the sign of the perfect transformation of dense elements into subtle ones, which is represented by the death and resurrection of this mythical bird in the fire that consumed it and causes it to be resurrected. For this reason it is usually accompanied by the Latin legend *Ignis Natura Renovatur Integra* (Through Fire, Nature is Reborn Whole).

Above the door of the building there is a window surmounted on either side by a hooded human head. These heads, which represent Innocence and Virtue, are also, in alchemy, the descendants of the King (Gold) and Queen (Silver), with the result of their chemical marriages, the Hermetic sign of the presence of the Philosopher's Stone (*Petra philosophorum*) lying just below in the character of the alchemist.

The 'King' and 'Queen' appear higher on the façade, on the third floor: dressed in medieval costume. The couple standing face to face represents the consciousness that results from the fusion of mercury and sulphur, in other words of the Soul and the Spirit, known in alchemy as a conjunction. Directly opposite the lady stands another knight looking at the couple, ready to intercede between the two if necessary. He represents mercury, a malleable element intermediate between a dense state and another subtle one, like the god Mercury who is the intermediary between the lower and upper worlds.

Below, a frown on the face, representing the beginning of the Great Work and the complete unknown as to its outcome, and that of a smiling hooded monk: the Great Work has been reached. Finally, the window frames are four mythical animal figures (a mixture of dogs and salamanders, those with wings) represent fixed elements (without wings) and volatile elements (with wings) indicating the relationship between sulphur (Fire, Spirit) and mercury (Water, Soul), and also the basic components of the processes of alchemy, the natural elements that are gradually perfected, until reaching maximum perfection.

At the height of the second floor, the small key that ends with a lily flower symbolises the Key of the Great Arcane – the Hermetic knowledge of universal Nature – gradually revealed by the alchemist who prays and works (*ora et labora*), until he himself achieves perfection in the image of the Creator.

PICPUS CEMETERY

An aristocratic cemetery

35, rue de Picpus
Monday–Saturday 2pm–5pm (except public holidays)
Admission fee during the 'Journées des Parcs et Jardins'
Metro Picpus

Picpus cemetery is now cared for by the priests and nuns of the Sacred Heart who, committed by their vows to perpetual veneration of the Holy Sacrament, here watch over the repose of the earthly remains of some 1,306 victims of the Terror. A visit here is a very solemn and moving experience. Guillotined between 14 June and 27 July 1794 in what was at the time called place du *Trône renversé* (Overturned Throne) – now place de la Nation – these 1,306 victims were buried in two of the three mass graves dug in the gardens of the former Convent of the Augustinian nuns. In 1795 the cemetery was then closed and filled in – shortly after the fall of Robespierre – and two years later was secretly repurchased by Princesse Amélie de Salm de Hohenzollern-Simaringen, whose brother had been one of those guillotined. In 1803, it was thanks to the Marquise de Montagu (née de Noailles) that the entire grounds of the former convent were bought by an association of the families of the victims, with one area being set aside for the creation of a private cemetery reserved for relatives of those guillotined. The mass graves cannot be visited although they can be seen through the railings, whereas the rest of the cemetery is open to the public. The tombs here are adorned by the armorial bearings of all the great French aristocratic families. One of the most famous is that of the Marquis de La Fayette, husband of the Marquise de Noailles and hero of the American War of Independence. This latter fact explains the presence of the American flag in the cemetery; in fact La Fayette was so attached to the country for whose independence he had fought that, at his request, the soil covering his tomb comes from America.

'Permission to die, Mother Superior?'

Amongst those buried in one of the mass graves of Picpus are sixteen Carmelite nuns from Compiègne, whose tragic story inspired Georges Bernanos' play *Dialogue des Carmélites*, which in turn inspired Poulenc's opera of the same title. Sentenced to execution, their courage would earn them a place in history: along the entire route to the guillotine, they sang psalms and canticles, without anyone managing to silence them. Just as she was about to mount the scaffold, each of the nuns kneeled before the Mother Superior (who had been given the sad privilege of dying last) and asked 'Permission to die, Mother Superior?', receiving the answer: 'Go, my daughter.' The Mother Superior, Mother Mary Lidoine, then mounted the scaffold in her turn, chanting the *Laudate Dominum*.

SALON DE LA FRANCE D'OUTRE-MER

Memories of the 1931 Exposition Coloniale

Town hall of 12th arrondissement (1st floor)
130, avenue Daumesnil
+33 1 44 68 12 12
Monday–Friday 8.30am–5pm
Metro Dugommier or Montgallet

Built in 1876 by Antoine-Julien Hénard, the 12th arrondissement town hall (*mairie*) is part of a series of commissions which were made early in the Third Republic (1870–1940).

It only took four years to build town halls to serve the 12th, 15th and 19th arrondissements. Although inspired by the Renaissance style of Louis XIII and Louis XIV, Hénard also decorated the building with columns, skylights and a bell tower.

In 1931, on the occasion of the International Colonial Exhibition (see page 370), Louis-Jean Beaupuy and René Durieux created a set of murals which were set up in the large living room of the first floor, where they can still be seen. What used to be a colonial salon has now taken the name Salon de la France d'Outre-Mer.

NEARBY

A fountain of sparkling water ⑩
Entrance to Jardin de Reuilly
Avenue Daumesnil and rue de Charenton
Metro Dugommier or Montgallet
To continue the battle against the environmental harms of plastic water bottles, in September 2010 the City of Paris unexpectedly installed a sparkling water fountain at the entrance to Reuilly garden, just in front of the 12th arrondissement town hall. Local residents are happy to drink freely sparkling water, which is just as good as that found in the shops.

Caryatids at 199–201, rue de Charenton ⑪
Metro Dugommier
The winner of a 1911 architectural award, this fine building was designed by the architects Brandon and Morlon. The unusual caryatids each represent a specific trade: a miner, a peasant, a craftsman and a sailor.

CHURCH OF SAINT-ESPRIT

A replica of the famous Hagia Sophia in Istanbul

186, avenue Daumesnil
+33 1 44 75 77 70
Daily 9.30am—7pm
Metro Daumesnil

Built in 1928-1935 to designs by the architect Paul Tournon, this church has a spectacular interior that cannot fail to impress. It is, in fact, a small-scale replica of the famous basilica of Hagia Sophia in Istanbul, with burgundy-red bricks facing a reinforced concrete structure built by François Hennebique.

At the time, the use of concrete was itself a demonstration of technical prowess – particularly in the creation of the cupola, whose height (33 metres) is a reference to Christ's age at his death. The crypt of the church measures 33 metres by 27 metres.

Over 70 artists worked on the decoration of the church, making it one of the most important examples of Christian religious art in the period between the two world wars. The church now figures in the supplementary register of listed buildings.

Other examples of Byzantine architecture in Paris

In the period between the two world wars, Cardinal Verdier launched a massive campaign to 're-Christianize' the area of Paris. The dozen or so churches which he commissioned were often inspired by Byzantine architecture, which at the time was considered the 'Christian' style 'par excellence'. Thus, along with the church of Saint-Esprit, there is the church of Sainte-Odile (2, avenue Stéphane Mallarmé, 17th arrondissement), the church of Sainte-Jeanne-de-Chantal (16th arrondissement) and the chapel of the Auxiliary Sisters (see page 190).

NEARBY

Boundary marker at 304, rue de Charenton 

Metro Porte de Charenton

An unassuming plaque is attached to the wall at 304, rue de Charenton. The inscription translates as: '1726 – Boundary marks from the reign of Louis XV by the King – expressly forbidden to build from the present boundaries and limits until the next village by the penalties imposed by the declarations of his majesty in the years 1724–26.' To control the population and supply of goods, this prevented Parisians building beyond that limit. The prohibition was obviously not respected, yet it indicates in an interesting way the limits of the city at that time. A total of 294 such markers were affixed to the walls of Paris in the 18th century. A similar plaque survives in the inner courtyard of 4, rue Laborde in the 8th arrondissement.

Curiously, the rues de Charenton, Reuilly and Picpus, in the 12th arrondissement, don't follow the classic Parisian numbering system, according to which numbers increase east to west (in the direction the Seine flows).

BUDDHIST PAGODA OF THE BOIS DE VINCENNES

Vestiges of the 1931 Exposition Coloniale Internationale

40, route de Ceinture du lac Daumesnil
+33 1 43 42 01 69
Metro Porte Dorée

Within a compound of almost 8,000 square metres on the shores of Lake Daumesnil, two pavilions preserved from the 1931 International Colonial Exhibition have found an alternative use, which is unexpected to say the least. The larger of the two, the Cameroon pavilion, was restored in 1977 as the Pagode du Bois de Vincennes Buddhist Centre. The former house of Togo next door is to contain a library on various Buddhist traditions. The pavilion, designed by architects Léon Carrière and Louis-Hippolyte Boileau, still stands on its original site. It houses an imposing golden statue of Buddha, 10 metres high under an exceptional shingled roof made from 180,000 pieces of chestnut hewn with axes. The headquarters of the International Buddhist Institute are also located here.

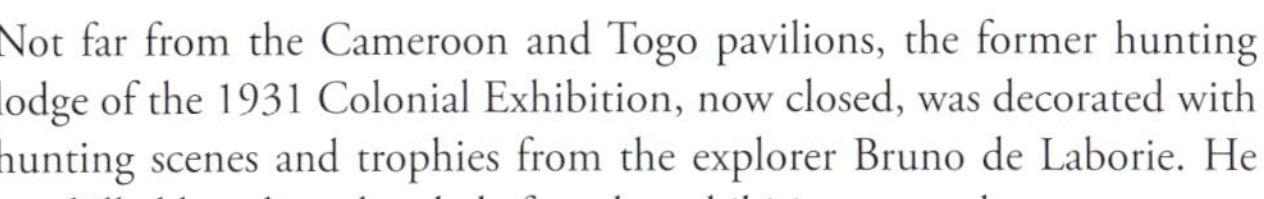

NEARBY

Former hunting lodge ⑮

Metro Porte Dorée

Not far from the Cameroon and Togo pavilions, the former hunting lodge of the 1931 Colonial Exhibition, now closed, was decorated with hunting scenes and trophies from the explorer Bruno de Laborie. He was killed by a lion shortly before the exhibition opened.

> For more on the various relics from the 1931 International Colonial Exhibition, see the following double-page spread.

Tibetan temple ⑯

Metro Porte Dorée

On the right of the Buddhist Centre, a Tibetan temple completed in 1985 was built to the plans of the architect Jean-Luc Massot, but especially to the precise and personal directives of the very venerable Kalu Rinpoche, the great Tibetan master who died in 1989.

Wooden elephant sculpture ⑰

Metro Porte Dorée

Right next to the Buddhist Pagoda (see opposite), is the imposing wooden elephant sculpture that stood in front of the Colonial Woods pavilion at the 1931 Colonial Exhibition where exotic wood varieties were exhibited.

The 1931 Colonial Exhibition

Organised in Paris at the Bois de Vincennes, Porte Dorée, the 1931 Colonial Exhibition was planned as early as 1925 to respond to the British Empire Exhibition of 1924, and to affirm the colonial power of France and its civilising mission in the colonies, while constituting an effective economic tool. Inaugurated on 6 May 1931 by the Minister of Colonies Paul Reynaud, President of the Republic Gaston Doumergue, Governor-General of the Colonies Léon Geismar and Commissioner General of the Exhibition Marshal Lyautey, the exhibition was held across 120 hectares of buildings recalling the architecture of all French colonies and protectorates, but also of some foreign countries such as the United States (see opposite). The United Kingdom refused to participate despite being invited, due to competition for influence with France over their respective colonial empires. The exhibition welcomed over 8 million visitors in all.

Vestiges of the 1931 Colonial Exhibition

– Former Colonies Museum became the Cité nationale de l'histoire de l'immigration in 2007.

– Statue of *La France apportant la paix et la prospérité aux colonies* (France bringing peace and prosperity to the colonies), designed by Léon Drivier, was placed on the grand staircase of the Colonies Museum. Now in place Édouard Renard, Porte Dorée, not far from its original location.

– Former pavilions of Cameroon and Togo, now Buddhist pagoda (see the previous double-page spread).

– Former hunting lodge: near the Cameroon and Togo pavilions.

– Sculpture of a wooden elephant from Colonial Woods pavilion: see the previous double-page spread.

– Former Notre-Dame-des-Missions church: sited in front of a replica of the Temple of Angkor Vat, the Art Deco church designed by Paul Tournon is now at 102, avenue Joffre in Épinay-sur-Seine. It was built by the architect himself.

– Metal sculpture of an elephant protecting its baby from a tiger, which stood not far from the Palais des Beaux-Arts, is now in Maurice Thorez Park in Choisy-le-Roi.

– Former cottage of George Washington was a copy of the one in Mount Vernon, Virginia (USA), where La Fayette slept. He had offered Washington a key to the Bastille prison, which is still there. The cottage, built on the site of the present-day rock of Vincennes Zoo, was moved to Vaucresson at 33, rue du Professeur Victor Pauchet.

– Wooden Sainte-Colombe church, at 23, rue Sainte-Colombe in Villejuif, was constructed from one of the exhibition buildings.

– Murals of the Salon de la France d'Outre-Mer (see page 364).

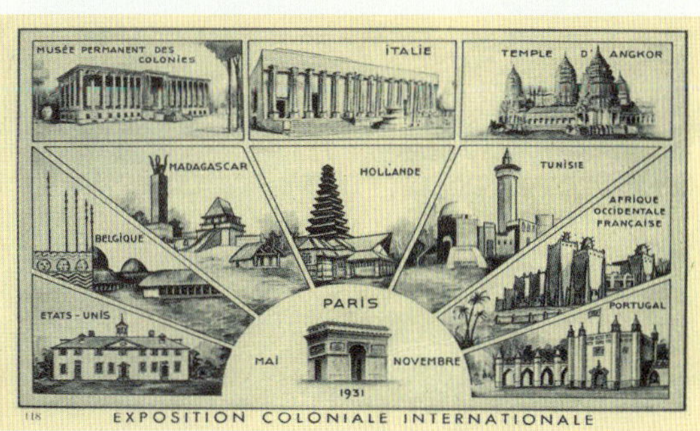

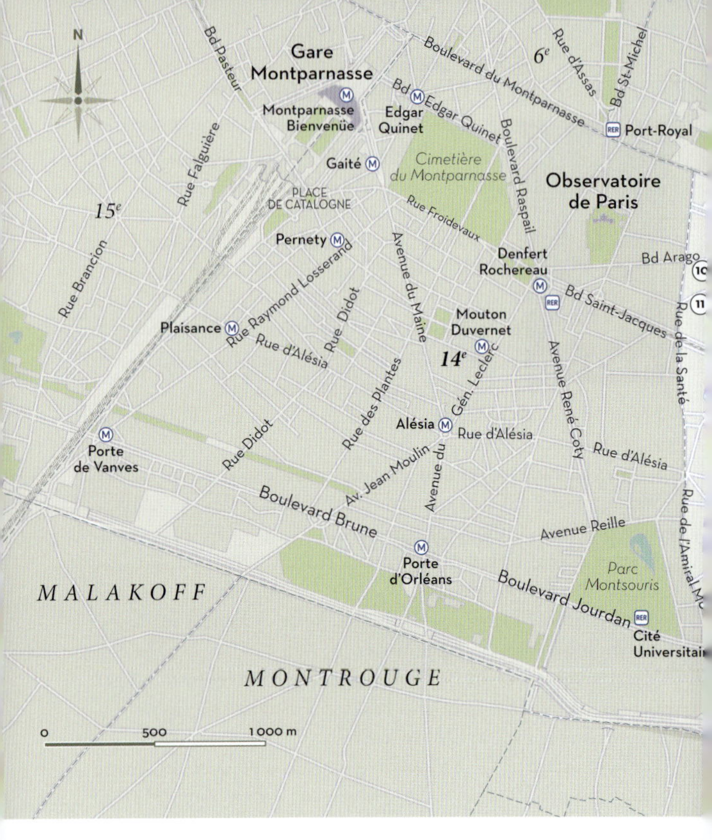

13th arrondissement

5e
Jardin des Plantes
Rue Buffon
Gare d'Austerlitz
Censier Daubenton
Boulevard Saint-Marcel
St-Marcel
Quai d'Austerlitz
Bercy
12e
PONT DE BERCY
Av.
Gobelins
Arago
des Gobelins
Boulevard de l'Hôpital
Campo Formio
Boulevard Vincent Auriol
Chevaleret
Seine
Quai de la Gare
Quai de Bercy
Cour St-Émilion
quare René e Gall
National
R. Jeanne d'Arc
Rue du Chevaleret
Avenue de France
PONT DE TOLBIAC
Q. Panhard et Levassor
PLACE D'ITALIE
13e
Blanqui
ste
Rue Bobillot
Place d'Italie
orvisart
Parc de Choisy
Rue de Patay
Bibliothèque François Mitterrand
PONT NATIONAL
Tolbiac
Rue de Tolbiac
Rue de Tolbiac
Olympiades
Avenue d'Italie
Avenue de Choisy
Avenue d'Ivry
Bobillot
Maison Blanche
Boulevard Masséna
Porte d'Ivry
PONT MASSÉNA
Boulevard Kellermann
Porte d'Italie
Porte de Choisy
NTILLY
IVRY-SUR-SEINE

A COUNTRY STROLL AROUND PORTE D'IVRY

The countryside in the 13th arrondissement

Metro Porte d'Ivry

Just like Tour Montparnasse or Tour Jussieu, the tower blocks of the Olympiades district do have one great advantage: when you are inside them, you do not see them. Still, even if you are not lucky enough (!) to live there, you can still find traces of the countryside within the city; not by spying down upon it, but by strolling around it. Leaving the Porte d'Ivry metro station and walking back up rue Nationale towards rue de Tolbiac, you soon reach passage Nationale, a small unpretentious street which it is a pleasure to stroll along. A bit further on, you come to the charming cul-de-sac Bougoin, which is open to those who manage to be both curious and discreet. Still further on, at 36, rue Nationale, is another little cul-de-sac, bedecked with flowers and plants. And at 56 bis, avenue Nationale is the entrance to impasse Nationale. If you then walk down the street on the even-number side, you come to passage Bourgoin: lined with low houses, each complete with garden, this even has a small area for pétanque — right in the centre of Paris!

VILLA PLANEIX ②

An exercise in style

26, boulevard Masséna
Visits by appointment, at weekends only
Contact Hélène Planeix at +33 9 79 28 02 41
Metro Porte d'Ivry

This is perhaps Le Corbusier's most complex composition of architectural volumes, with the architect meeting the challenge posed by creating a living space of a total area of 300 m² on a site measuring only 200 m². Commissioned by the self-taught artist Antonin Planeix, the villa was built in 1924–1928. At the time, this was an area of market gardening and 'land was still cheap', says Antonin Planeix's granddaughter, Hélène Planeix, who still lives here. Due to its slope, the site was a difficult one, with walls adjoining other houses. Initially, Le Corbusier designed the house to stand on pilotis 4.5 metres high, intending to use the upper level for the apartment and the artist's light-filled studio. 'However, my grandfather had already gone way beyond his budget, so asked the architect to stop at the ground floor and use the space for two studios that could then be rented out.'

Despite these changes, the main apartment has maintained all the characteristics of Le Corbusier's style, with 8 metres of the living-room walls given over to windows, and non-weight-bearing partitions cleverly converted into storage units. The bathroom is tucked away in a specially designed curved wall.

Joan of Arc in Paris and in the 13th arrondissement

There are five statues of the Maid of Orleans in Paris. Apart from the famous gilded statue by Frémiet in rue des Pyramides, these are to be found in: rue Jeanne-d'Arc (13th arrondissement), on the esplanade of Sacré-Cœur (18th), outside the church of Saint-Augustin (the 8th) and on the façade of Saint-Denis-de-la-Chapelle (18th). There is also a bust of Joan of Arc in rue Saint-Honoré, by the plaque marking the

place where she was wounded by an English arrow. The 13th arrondissement honours the saint not only with a statue and with a square and street named after her, but also in various other ways: rue de Patay is named after one of her important victories, rue Domrémy after the village where she was born, and rue La Hire and rue Xaintrailles after knights who fought alongside her.

TEMPLE FOR RESIDENTS OF CANTONESE ORIGIN

Temple in an underground car park

37, rue du Disque
Access is easiest from avenue d'Ivry, opposite No. 66
+33 1 45 86 80 99
Daily 9am—7pm
Admission free
Metro Porte d'Ivry

© domllorens

While the Buddhist temple of the Teochew Association is located on the Dalle des Olympiades (see below), this temple for residents of Cantonese origin is actually built below it: rue du Disque is in fact more of an underground car park than a street as such, and it has the odour of trash cans to prove it. However, the interior of this, the only other Buddhist temple in Paris, is in sharp contrast to its setting: the visitor is warmly welcomed, and the atmosphere is just right for personal reflection or for initiation into the world of Chinese Buddhism.

NEARBY

Temple of the Teochew Association

44, avenue d'Ivry
Daily 9am–12pm and 2pm–6pm – Office hours 3pm–4pm
Admission free
Metro Porte d'Ivry

In around 1975 hundreds of thousands of Chinese fled Vietnam to settle in the four corners of the earth. About 80,000 of them were Teochew (pronounced Ti-chew) from Guangdong Province who came to Paris, where they settled and prospered in the 13th arrondissement. In 1985 the community founded the French Teochew Association's Centre for Buddhist Meditation, with the aim of providing 'mutual assistance to further the social integration of its members and promote the cultural identity of the Teochew.'

This place of worship for both Thai and Chinese Buddhists is open to everyone, irrespective of their religious beliefs. It is reached by passing along the market gallery (where the merchandise on display already gives you a sense of another culture) and then turning left onto the Olympiades concourse (known as the 'Dalle des Olympiades') and finally turning right. Inside the temple there is an altar dedicated to Buddha, where you can meditate or make offerings of incense and fruit. However, some just come here for a cup of tea and to leaf through the newspapers. If your Chinese is good enough, you can also catch up on the local gossip.

Square des Peupliers

74, rue du Moulin des Prés
Metro Tolbiac

Created in 1926, this small area of rich vegetation has a number of pretty houses and buildings organised around a maze of charming little streets. Not far away is place de l'Abbé-Hénocque, surrounded by quiet streets lined with pastel-coloured workers' cottages built at the beginning of the 20th century.

THE ANTOINIST TEMPLE

The Little House on the Prairie

34, rue Vergniaud
Readings of the Teachings of Father Antoine on Sunday at 10am; other days
(except Saturday) at 7pm
'Operation' (through prayer) in the name of The Father on Sundays and the first
four days of the week at 10am
Metro Corvisart

© Mbzt

This curious little yellow church belongs to the Antoinist movement, which believes in the fundamental healing power of prayer. A sense of great tranquillity reigns in this small interior, worthy of something you might see in an episode of *Little House on the Prairie*: the men wear long black preachers' coats, while the women must wear not only a long black robe but also have their hair done in a style typical of the 19th century. Silence is 'de rigueur' once you are inside; but if you want to, you may go into the 'cabinet' with one of the 'healers', who will pray with you for release from your mental or physical suffering. The struggle against pain is one of the main concerns of Antoinism, as one can see from the title of the principal work by 'The Father' on sale here: *Deliver Us from Evil.*

The Antoinist Faith

Founded in Belgium in 1910, this takes its name from its founder, Antoine, known to the faithful simply as 'The Father'. In 1922 it was recognised as 'A Foundation of Public Service' by the Belgian government. However, a parliamentary report into sects and cults in 1995 classified it as a 'healing movement', describing its beliefs in the following terms: 'The very notion of sickness and disease is denied, as is that of death (belief in reincarnation). It is our intelligence which makes us suffer, and faith alone (not the intervention of doctors) which can suppress suffering.' The Antoinists themselves deny any suggestion that theirs is a sect or cult: worship, they say 'is a moral activity based on faith and self-sacrifice. It is public, and open freely to one and all'. They also point out that 'The Father' 'received patients for over 22 years. When he started this activity, he had savings which enabled him to live without working; when he died, he no longer had any possessions.' Today Antoinism has 64 temples and 90 reading-rooms worldwide, principally in France, Belgium, Australia and Luxembourg. There are around 2,500 believers in France and 200,000 worldwide.

NEARBY

Cité Florale ⑦

36, rue Brillat-Savarin
RER Cité Universitaire or Metro Maison Blanche

This development was built in 1928, on a former meadow that was often flooded by the Bièvre (see following double-page spread) and therefore hardly suitable for large-scale constructions. The Cité Florale is, as a result, made up of small individual houses each with a garden of flowers. Access is by tree-lined, cobbled streets that bear the names of flowers: rue des Glycines, rue des Iris, square des Mimosas, etc.

The Bièvre river

The Bièvre is a river that used to cross Paris and has now been rerouted. However, numerous traces of the Bièvre are still to be found in Parisian topography and toponymy. The river itself flows from some 30 or so small springs located at Guyancourt, 5 km from Versailles. In the past, it ran for a total of 32 km and entered Paris at Poterne des Peupliers, beneath the old 1840 fortifications and the site of the modern-day boulevard Kellerman. It then formed a large 'S' curve around Butte-aux-Cailles, with the dry branch following the route of rue de la Fontaine-Mouchard, rue Brillat-Savarin and rue Wurtz. This stretch fed a number of small ponds that froze in the winter and supplied the ice that was kept in glacières (stone ice-houses) during the summer — hence the name of rue de la Glacière, immediately to the west of the Bièvre. Continuing on its course, the Bièvre then flowed beyond the Fermiers Généraux city walls; its exact location is indicated in boulevard Blanqui by the one pillar of the elevated railway that is higher than the others. At this point, its two branches split around the Île aux Singes. Beyond the Faubourg Saint-Marcel, the Bièvre turned west to flow into the Seine near what is now the departures area of Gare d'Austerlitz. In prehistoric times, the Seine formed a large loop towards the north, between Bercy and l'Alma, passing by the foot of the hills of Belleville and Montmartre, while the Bièvre occupied what is the present-day route of the Seine from Austerlitz station onwards; the two rivers flowed into each other at Alma. In time of flood, the Seine occupied the bed of the Bièvre and abandoned its previous bed to the north; this became an area of marais (marshes), hence the name of the Marais district. The Bièvre was of great importance for the city's Left Bank. In the 12th century, channels were drawn off it to provide irrigation for gardens and waterpower for mills. The Canal des Victorins, for example, supplied water from the river to the Abbaye Saint-Victor; traces of this channel under the abbey walls can still be seen in the underground area of the post office at the corner of rue du Cardinal Lemoine and boulevard Saint-Germain (see page 169). In the 14th century, the purity of the river's water made it particularly appealing to dyers and brewers. In the 16th century, its banks were occupied by the tanneries and taweries which had been forcibly evicted from place de Grève. However, by the 19th century their growing presence had made the entire river both malodorous and unhealthy (a survey of 1860 numbered more than 100 industrial establishments present along its banks). After important rechannelling work carried out between 1824 and 1864, it became necessary to cover over the Bièvre, a project that was completed in 1910. Contrary to expectations, the famous rue de Bièvre is not located along the old course of the river but on that of the channel drawn off it in the 12th century to serve the Abbaye Saint-Victor.

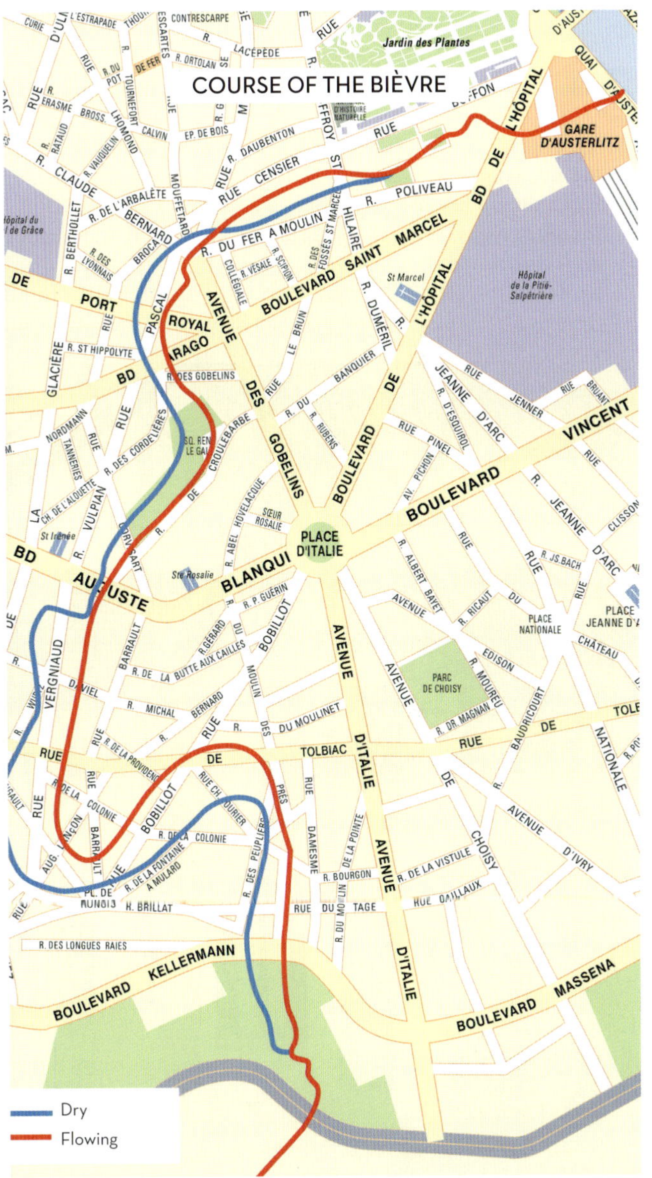

LITTLE ALSACE

The most attractive subsidised housing in Paris?

10, rue Daviel
Metro Corvisart

Built from 1912 onwards by the architect Jean Walter, the Little Alsace (Petite Alsace) complex is probably the most charming scheme of subsidised housing in Paris.

The 40 houses, with pitched roofs in typical Alsatian style, are grouped around a flower-planted courtyard.

The place is just as it was originally designed for the Habitation Familiale Association.

The Paris City Council Housing Department still runs the scheme, so – technically – you could even put yourself down on the waiting list.

LITTLE RUSSIA ⑨

Homes for Russian taxi-drivers

22, rue Barrault
Metro Corvisart

Little Russia (Petite Russie) is an amazing place, made up of two ranks of cottage-style homes designed from 1912 onwards to provide accommodation for Russian émigrés fleeing the Revolution.

Mainly aristocrats, a large number of these newcomers would then take on work as taxi-drivers, using the garage below their homes to park their cars.

Unfortunately it is not easy to gain access here. If a resident does open the door for you, go up the staircase to the esplanade, lined by an amazing collection of cottages with raised ground floors. The view from the terrace is also worth the journey: to the south, it overlooks Little Alsace (see opposite), to the left, the bed of the Bièvre river (see previous double-page spread).

© domllorens

CITÉ FLEURIE

A bouquet of artists

65, boulevard Arago – Metro Glacière

Built in 1880 with materials 'recycled' from the 'Food Pavilion' at the 1878 Universal Exposition, the superb Cité Fleurie is the oldest artist community in Paris.

Access is via a gateway, but you could wait until one of the tenants is leaving and then ask if you might have a look inside. In total there are 29 studios, each with a white façade and all still occupied by artists.

The famous names among past residents include Gauguin (who lived with Daniel de Montfreid), Modigliani (who lived with the Mexican painter, Zanaga) and Jean-Paul Laurens.

Due to the personal intervention of the President of the French Republic Georges Pompidou, the Cité Fleurie became a listed area in the 1970s.

NEARBY

Cité verte ⑪

147, rue Léon-Maurice Nordmann
Metro Glacière

This houses artists in a total of 24 studio homes aligned on either side of a tree-lined street. Built just after the Cité Fleurie, it has the same calm and rural atmosphere; however, it is more difficult to gain access to.

RODIN'S HIGH RELIEFS

Little-known work by Auguste Rodin

73, avenue des Gobelins
Metro Gobelins or Place d'Italie

On the façade of the former Théâtre des Gobelins, an 800-seat Italian theatre built in 1869 by French architect Alphonse Cusin, the high reliefs of the façade are, surprisingly, the work of the famous Rodin, best known for his sculptures, including those in the museum named after him. Auguste Rodin was at the time a young student at the Beaux-Arts and the nearby École des Gobelins. The two high reliefs represent Drama (played by the man) and Comedy (played by the woman). The first film screenings took place as early as 1906, although the venue did not become a proper cinema until 1934. The building now houses the Jérôme Seydoux-Pathé Foundation, a centre for research, documentation and consultation on cinema history. The façade with its high reliefs, classified since 1977, has remained intact.

TEMPLE OF HUMAN RIGHTS 

A mysterious Freemason temple

5, rue Jules Breton
droithumain-france.org
Not open to the public – Metro Saint-Marcel

Set in a discreet street of the 13th arrondissement, the façade of 5, rue Jules Breton is truly astonishing: inspired by Egyptian architecture, it has lotus-flower columns and a balcony balustrade adorned with an ansate cross motif. Above runs the inscription *Le Droit Humain* (Human Rights), which is the name of an Order of Freemasonry founded in 1893 by George Martin (1844–1916). The peculiarity of this Order is that it is a mixed one, and the inscription below the columns summarises the great principle which inspired its founder: 'Within humanity, women have the same duties as men. They must have the same rights both within the family and within society.' Le Droit Humain now has around 12,000 members.

INSTITUTE OF HUMAN PALEONTOLOGY

A unique place dedicated to prehistoric man

1, rue René Panhard
+33 1 43 31 62 91
fondationiph.org
The institute is open to the public only during conferences and various events
(calendar to be consulted on website)
Metro Saint-Marcel

At the corner of rue René Panhard and boulevard Saint-Marcel are the impressive high reliefs that run along the façade of a massive brick and stone building, the seat of the Institut de Paléontologie Humaine (IPH). It is an amazing place unmatched anywhere in the world.

Created in 1910 on an initiative by Albert I of Monaco, its vocation was to offer researchers a perennial structure to develop prehistoric science. The institute – recognised as a public utility on 15 December 1910 by decree of the President of the Republic – became the world's first research centre dedicated to the study of human fossils.

The prince entrusted the construction (1914–20) to Emmanuel Pontremoli (Grand Prix de Rome, future director of the Beaux-Arts), who commissioned sculptor Constant Roux to carve a beautiful horizontal frieze on the exterior façade. It evokes the traditional way of life of hunter-gatherers and prehistoric man: bison hunting, cooking fish or repairing a boat among the Australian aborigines.

Interestingly, Roux had one restriction that was respected to the letter: on the height of the frieze (about 1 metre), he had to represent all his characters at full size, which is why they are seen crouched, sitting or stretched out.

Regular public conferences in the IPH amphitheatre allow visitors to see the beautiful library with its rhinoceros skeleton, surrounded by more than 17,000 books, as well as a fine research laboratory where many skulls and bones are stored.

The access corridor has paintings that reproduce the murals of the cave of Altamira in Spain (according to surveys by Abbé Breuil). The paintings date from 1914.

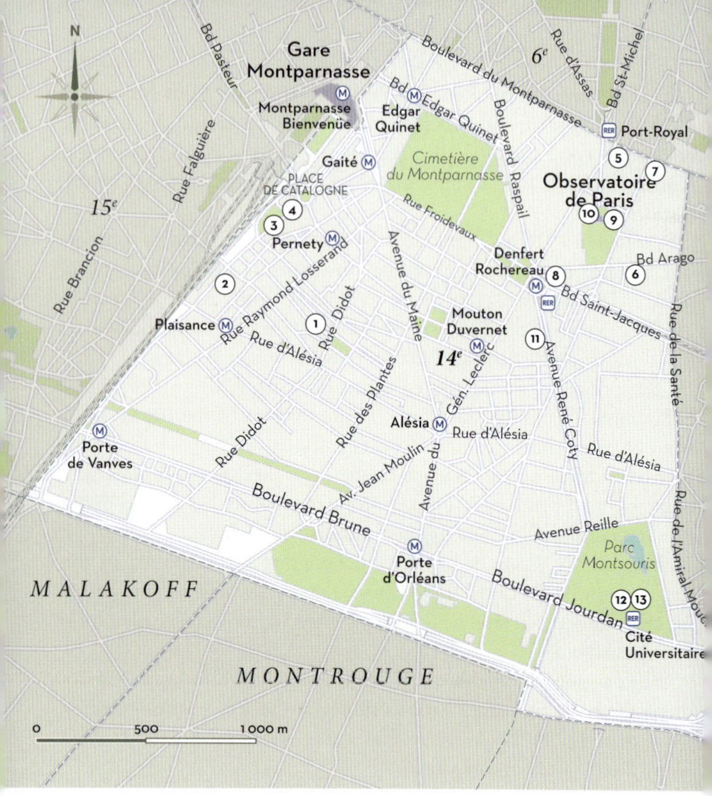

14th arrondissement

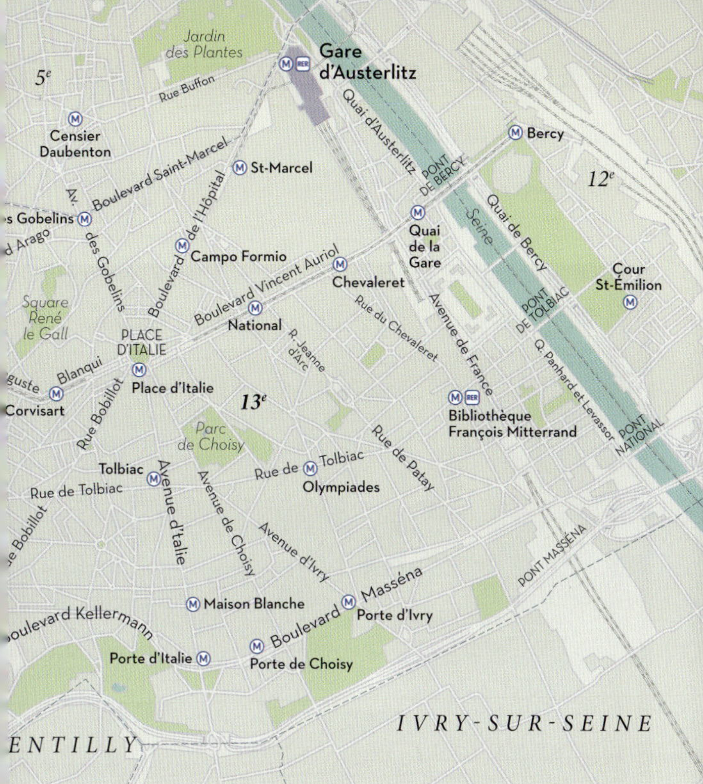

5e
Jardin des Plantes
Gare d'Austerlitz
Rue Buffon
M RER
Censier Daubenton
M
Boulevard Saint-Marcel
St-Marcel
M
Quai d'Austerlitz
PONT DE BERCY
Bercy
M
12e
Av.
es Gobelins
M
d Arago
des Gobelins
Boulevard de l'Hôpital
Campo Formio
M
Boulevard Vincent Auriol
Chevaleret
M
Quai de la Gare
M
Seine
Quai de Bercy
Cour St-Émilion
M
Square René le Gall
PLACE D'ITALIE
National
M
R. Jeanne d'Arc
Rue du Chevaleret
Avenue de France
PONT DE TOLBIAC
Q. Panhard et Levassor
Blanqui
guste
Place d'Italie
M
13e
Corvisart
M
Rue Bobillot
Parc de Choisy
Rue de Patay
Bibliothèque François Mitterrand
M RER
PONT NATIONAL
Tolbiac
M
Rue de Tolbiac
Avenue d'Italie
Avenue de Choisy
Rue de Tolbiac
M
Olympiades
Avenue d'Ivry
e Bobillot
Maison Blanche
M
Masséna
M
Porte d'Ivry
PONT MASSÉNA
Boulevard Kellermann
Boulevard
Porte d'Italie
M
Porte de Choisy
M
PONT MASSÉNA
IVRY-SUR-SEINE
ENTILLY

FAÇADE OF 19, CITÉ BAUER

In the heart of Paris

Metro Plaisance or Pernéty

This magnificent door in the form of a double heart was designed in 1959 by the Hungarian-born artist Alexandre Mezei, who lived here. Clearly inspired by Art Nouveau, it shows a shepherd in the upper right panel playing a flute to an audience of sheep and a sheepdog. This is a fine example of the charming little architectural details that are such a part of the magic of the city.

NEARBY

The menhir at 133, rue Vercingétorix ②

Metro Plaisance

Between a basketball court and a children's playground, the small square opposite No. 133, rue Vercingétorix contains — of all things! — a menhir. The plaque on the ground in front is almost illegible, but you can make out that 'this menhir was presented to the City of Paris by the Chamber of Commerce and Industry of Morbihan. The work of seven Breton granite workers, it was unveiled by Monsieur Alain Poher, President of the Senate, on 18 December 1983'. Until 2017, lovers of Brittany could find another trace of the region on the other side of the railway tracks: an actual Breton lighthouse.

CHURCH OF NOTRE-DAME-DU-TRAVAIL

The first example of an ecclesiastical use of industrial architecture

59, rue Vercingétorix
+33 1 44 10 72 92 – notredamedutravail.net
Monday–Friday 7.30am–7.45pm, Saturday 9am–7.30pm,
Sunday 8.30am–7.30pm
Masses: Saturday at 6.30pm and Sunday at 10.45am; Sunday mass in
Portuguese at 9am and in Latin at 6pm (except July and August)
Metro Gaîté

From the outside this looks like many other churches, but the interior – the work of the architect Jules Astuc – is a remarkable example of the use of industrial architecture. Clearly influenced by the designs of Eiffel and Baltard, the metal structure of the nave is made from 135 tonnes of iron and steel.

Very atypical for a church, this interior was the brainchild of Abbé Soulange-Bodin, who was appointed to the parish of Plaisance in 1896. His ambition was to build a church that would 'unite workers of all classes within the realm of religion.' Designed to make the workers feel at home by reminding them of their factories, the new church was – perhaps inevitably – dedicated to Notre-Dame-du-Travail; however, the statue predates the church.

> The church is also home to a trophy of war. Weighing 552 kg, the bell was presented to the church in 1865 by Napoleon III; it comes from the city of Sebastopol and was seized during the Crimean War.

NEARBY

Place de l'Amphithéâtre and place de Séoul ④

Entrance in rue Vercingétorix
Metro Plaisance

Rebuilt in the 1980s, the place de Catalogne district is the work of the Catalonian architect Ricardo Bofill. While not everyone appreciates place de l'Amphithéâtre and place de Séoul, there is no denying that they are a striking example of a contemporary reading of classical architecture.

The point of access is not obvious, so many Parisians are not even aware of these two city squares, which have pleasantly quiet and peaceful gardens.

CLOISTER OF COCHIN HOSPITAL ⑤

A hidden paradise

123, boulevard de Port-Royal
Officially closed to the public
Access possible by request to the hospital's administrative staff
RER Port-Royal

A little corner of paradise unknown to most Parisians, the cloister of Cochin Hospital is a marvel that should not be missed.

Entering from boulevard du Port-Royal, follow the arrows to the chapel. The cloister was once part of the convent of the nuns of Port-Royal-des-Champs, a Cistercian order founded at the beginning of the 13th century in the Chevreuse valley.

This Parisian convent opened in 1625 under the abbess Angélique Arnauld and would, from 1635 onwards, become famous as a centre of Jansenism; Blaise Pascal, for example, was a regular visitor to this community of the Daughters of the Holy Sacrament.

Suppressed during the Revolution, the convent was converted into a prison, ironically known as 'Port-Libre'. The place was first used as a hospital in 1795.

NEARBY

The last 'vespasienne' in Paris ⑥

Metro Saint-Jacques

In boulevard Arago, just in front of the prison of La Santé, is the last 'vespasienne' in Paris. Dating from the beginning of the 19th century, these distinctive features of Paris owed their existence to the Prefect of the Seine region, Comte Rambuteau, who for obvious public-health reasons ordered the creation of urinals to replace the *'barils d'aisance'* (barrels filled with sawdust in which gentlemen had previously relieved themselves at street corners).

The 'vespasiennes' were not only more sanitary, they offered more privacy, as the clients were shielded from public view by metal sheeting. Progress has led to the introduction of coin-operated public toilets that are self-cleaning and, more importantly, can also be used by women. However, although the city council voted for the removal of 'vespasiennes' on 21 December 1959, it was not until 1980 that the first four coin-operated cabins were installed; note that progress has also put an end to a public service that had been free of charge. No one knows why this particular 19th century 'vespasienne' survived, but now there is talk of having it 'listed'.

The word 'vespasienne' comes from the name Vespasian, emperor of Rome in AD 69. Renowned for his greed, he introduced a tax on urine and had urinals erected that the Romans had to pay to use. Unsurprisingly, he is also credited with the expression: 'money has no odour'.

20 metres underground: one source of the city's building materials

Hôpital Cochin
27, rue du Faubourg-Saint-Jacques
+33 1 43 89 78 03 – seadacc.com – association@seadacc.com
E-mail: jlhr-faure@wanadoo.fr (don't hesitate to write two or three times) or by letter to the Association SEADACC at the Hôpital Cochin (see address above)
Applications by letter are often given priority over those by e-mail
Length of visit: 1–2 hours. Access impossible for persons of restricted mobility, and inadvisable for those suffering from claustrophobia
RER Port-Royal

Perhaps a visit to the Denfert-Rochereau Catacombs is rather too conventional; but finding an illegal point of entry to undertake a do-it-yourself visit to Paris's underground passageways is definitely too risky …

The Capuchin Quarries provide the perfect happy medium. Located some 20 metres underground, they still have an air of adventure about them, not having been too sanitised by the association of enthusiasts who, lamp and spade in hand, have spent years of passionate work restoring these ancient quarries. Now a listed site, this is a unique place, with no equivalent anywhere in the world.

It was here that in the 15th and 16th centuries workers quarried the stone that would be used to build the chapel of the Capuchin monastery. Injuries were frequent and, 20 metres overhead, Jean-Baptiste Cochin had an infirmary built to treat the casualties, creating the institution that became the modern-day Cochin Hospital.

The quarries also provided some 30% of the stone used in building Notre-Dame, and were ultimately used to cultivate underground mushrooms: the manure from the horses drawing the city's carriages was often tipped down here, turning these humid tunnels into the perfect environment for growing tasty mushrooms.

Guided by one of the Association volunteers, the visit begins with the descent of a hundred or so steps, which brings you to tunnels 'wide enough for a man pushing a wheelbarrow.' The sodium lamps (designed to preserve the ecosystem) bathe everything in a strange light, in which the walls of the tunnels gleam with moisture (humidity levels here can be up to 90%).

The climax of the visit is the extraordinary Fontaine des Capucins. Complete with steps that go down to the phreatic water level, this semi-cylindrical well was dug in 1810.

ARAGO'S EMPTY PEDESTAL

A statue melted down to make weapons in Germany

Place de l'Île de Sein
Metro Saint-Jacques or Denfert-Rochereau

On the boulevard Arago, opposite the Observatoire gardens, an empty pedestal is engraved with the name of the French physicist François Arago (1786–1853). Although as you can well imagine the pedestal once carried his statue, it was destroyed during the Second World War, following a law of 11 October 1941. This advocated the removal of statues and monuments in public places to smelt the metal and, officially, sulphate vines and feed industrial production. In reality, the Vichy government was obviously obeying injunctions from Germany which used the metal to make weapons, even if some were also reused by the sculptors of the Third Reich as part of their propaganda. Although a commission could rule on the monuments to be preserved because of their official importance for the country, some could not escape destruction, like this one, probably due to the fact that Arago was a Freemason (as was the scientist Raspail, 1794–1878, see below) – Freemasonry was regarded as degenerate by the Nazis.

On Square Jacques Antoine, a few steps from place Denfert-Rochereau, you'll also find the empty pedestal of Raspail's statue.

NEARBY

A travelling mansion ⑨

RER Port-Royal

Originally built on the corner of the Champs-Élysées and rue de la Boétie by Jean-Baptiste Le Boursier in 1784, the Hôtel de Massa (38, rue du Faubourg-Saint-Jacques) was at the centre of a property development in the early 20th century. Instead of being demolished, it was simply dismantled stone by stone and reassembled at its current location in 1929. Today it houses the Société des gens de lettres, founded in 1838 by Isidore Taylor, who was also responsible for the purchase and transport of the Luxor Obelisk to Paris.

© Siren Comm

The Dibbets Medallions

In 1994, the City of Paris commissioned an original work from the artist Jan Dibbets: 135 bronze medallions (diameter: 11 cm) bearing the name Arago with the letters N (North) above and S (South) below.

Laid out along the line of the Paris Meridian (which was the international meridian of reference before it was supplanted by Greenwich; see page 409), these medallions commemorate François Arago, who pursued his calculations of the meridian as far as the Balearic Islands.

Set into the city's pavements, the medallions run for a total of 17 km. Searching them out is a very good way of stimulating a child's interest in this scientific subject through the form of a game that can be played while walking around the city. Unfortunately, 30 of these medallions have already gone missing.

Méridienne Verte

These medallions of the Green Meridian were a project devised by architect Paul Chemetov (designer of the Ministry of Finance in Bercy) as part of the celebrations for the new millennium.

The idea was to plant trees throughout France to mark out the line of the Paris meridian (from Dunkirk in the north to Prats-de-Mollo in the Eastern Pyrenees).

Within Paris itself, the line of the meridian would be marked by medallions: three to the west of the large water basin in the Jardin du Luxembourg, one to the south-east of Jardin Marco-Polo (avenue de l'Observatoire and the last at the corner of avenue Denfert-Rochereau and avenue de l'Observatoire.

HEADQUARTERS OF THE KING'S HYDRAULIC ENGINEER

Royal water supplies

42, avenue de l'Observatoire
paris-historique.org – contact@paris-historique.org
Programme of events available at +33 1 48 87 74 31; also open during the
'Journées du Patrimoine' (Heritage Days) – Association Paris Historique
Metro Denfert-Rochereau

By telephoning beforehand for the lecture schedule, it is possible to arrange to visit this very curious HQ of the King's hydraulic engineer, built in 1619–1623 by the Gobelin brothers to a design by Salomon de Brosse. There is also a *regard* (peephole – see page 527) through which it was possible to inspect the waters flowing from the Arcueil aqueduct. Today, however, these waters no longer flow underneath the house but go directly to the Montsouris reservoir. The visit gives you some idea of the different methods used over the centuries to supply Paris with water. There are three ancient *bassins* (water tanks): Bassin du Roi, de la Ville and Des Carmelites.

As their names suggest, these served different areas of the city: the Palais du Luxembourg, the Val-de-Grâce and the Carmelite monastery plus a total of thirteen different drinking fountains.

NEARBY

The peephole in avenue René Coty ⑪

Metro Mouton-Duvernet

Behind the fine building of La Rochefoucauld geriatric hospital is a rather remarkable little structure (entrance by avenue du Général Leclerc). It houses an inspection peephole that gave access to the water flowing from Arcueil (see above).

Arcueil aqueduct

Contrary to what you might expect, aqueducts still supply Paris with water (see page 529), and the Arcueil aqueduct is one of them: every day, 145,000 m³ of water flow along it, across the Bièvre valley. The modern-day Arcueil aqueduct actually combines two structures dating from very different periods: the Marie aqueduct and the La Vanne aqueduct.

The former was inspired by a project devised by Sully for using an ancient Gallo-Roman conduit that drew water from the Rungis and Wissous springs. It was built in 1613–1623 at the behest of Marie de Médicis, hence the name.

When in operation, the Marie aqueduct filled a reservoir near Montagne Sainte-Geneviève and supplied the Fontaine Médicis at the Palais du Luxembourg.

Nowadays, it still carries 2,000 m³ of water per day, from the Rungis springs to the water tanks of Parc Montsouris. The La Vanne aqueduct constitutes the upper level of the Arcueil aqueduct. Standing 14 metres above the Marie aqueduct, it was built by the engineer Belgrand as part of Baron Haussmann's urban development scheme.

A surviving trace of the Paris meridian

Parc Montsouris (boulevard Jourdan side)
RER Cité Universitaire

Known as the 'mire du Sud', this 4 metres high stone bears a curious inscription: 'In the reign of ... (Napoleon's name has been erased), a marker stone for the observatory. MDCCCVI.' Originally erected in the garden of the Paris Observatory, this served to align the instruments used in that institution. It was moved to its present site in 1806, though due to work in the park it is now slightly off-line with the Paris meridian.*

The Paris Meridian

Before being replaced by the Greenwich meridian in 1884, the Paris meridian was the meridian of reference for all the world's geographers. Work on plotting it began in 1669, just two years after the foundation of the Paris Observatory, through the centre of which it runs. That charting was completed in 1718 by the Cassinis (father and son) and by Philippe de La Hire. Upon request from the Convention, the meridian was recalculated by Delambre and Méchain in 1792–1798 so that it might serve as the basis for determining the exact length of 'one metre' (see page 204). All of these figures – Cassini, Delambre and Méchain – have streets near the Observatory named after them. Later, Arago and Biot would extrapolate Delambre and Méchain's measurements as far as the Balearic Islands. The meridian line is today charted on Parisian pavements by 135 medallions engraved with Arago's name (see page 402).

Within the capital itself, the northern limit of the meridian is marked by an obelisk (the 'mire du Nord') located at 1, avenue Junot in Montmartre; unfortunately, it is part of a private residence and so cannot be visited, even if listed as a historic monument. The original northern marker was a simple wooden pillar raised in 1675 by Abbé Jean Picard; the stone obelisk was raised in 1736 'by order of the king'.

The 'mire du Sud' is located in Parc Montsouris in the 14th arrondissement (see opposite).

A further trace of the Paris meridian can be seen in the floor of the galeries du Carrousel at the Louvre, under the inverted pyramid.

Another alignment marker can be seen at Villejuif, on the outskirts of Paris. It was raised in the 18th century by the topographer Jacques Cassini, son of Jean-Dominique Cassini who is credited with being the father of French astronomy.

A meridian is an imaginary line running from the North to the South Pole which links all those points where at noon (solar time) the Sun is at its zenith.

STONE AT FONDATION DEUTSCH DE LA MEURTHE ⑬

A vestige of the Thiers enclosure

Parc de Montsouris – Boulevard Jourdan
RER Cité Universitaire

Students at Cité Internationale Universitaire de Paris perhaps don't realise, as they pass the stone on the right of the entrance to 37, boulevard Jourdan, behind the foundation's building on the campus, that this is one of the last vestiges of the Thiers enclosure (see opposite). On the stone you can read '1842 Bon 82': it was part of Bastion No. 82, built in 1842. The enclosure had 94 bastions (pentagon-shaped projections in the wall).

Not far away, the base of the Arcueil gate, at the corner of rue Émile Deutsch de La Meurthe and boulevard Jourdan, is another sign of the Thiers enclosure. For the other remains of the enclosure, see opposite.

The boulevards of Napoleonic marshals

The layout of the Thiers enclosure (more precisely the 'military road' that ran along it) is now quite clearly visible on a map of Paris: it almost perfectly follows the current layout of Boulevards des Maréchaux. These boulevards have all taken the names of generals (rather than marshals) of the Napoleonic army. They are all there, except for Grouchy and Marmont, unforgiven by Bonapartist opinion for their weaknesses and betrayals. Duroc isn't there either. Although killed by the enemy, he'd only been 'Marshal of the Palace' charged with the command of the imperial palaces.

The grounds of Thiers

After the defeats of Napoleon, the invasion of France by the so-called 'allied' forces (Austria, Russia, Prussia) and the entry of foreign troops into Paris in 1814 and 1815, the various governments studied at length how to fortify the capital.

A compromise was finally reached and in 1840 Adolphe Thiers decided to build a 34-km-long wall, enclosing 2,500,000 residents over an area of 7,800 hectares. It had an average width of 140 metres with a paved interior road (the future Boulevards des Maréchaux), the rampart itself, an external ditch and an embankment, to which was added a 250-metre zone where construction was banned.

In front, along 1,500 to 5,000 metres of the enclosure now in the Parisian suburbs, Vauban-type (military architect) fortifications were added. In 1860, Paris annexed the area between the wall of the Fermiers Généraux and the new fortifications, encompassing all or part of many villages (Auteuil, Passy, Batignolles, la Villette, Belleville, Ménilmontant, Bercy, Grenelle). Tax collection was simultaneously moved to the gates of the new fortifications. This imposing modern work failed to prevent the defeat of 1870, but it nevertheless protected the city from heavy degradation.

The area closed to construction was gradually covered with all kinds of barracks. From 1945, the fortifications were destroyed and replaced by HLM, stadiums, university towns, gardens, etc.

Current remains of the Thiers enclosure

– Boulevards des Maréchaux for geographical limit.

– Bastion No. 1 (12th arrondissement).

– Poterne des Peupliers (13th arrondissement), under which the Bièvre flowed into Paris before going underground.

– Some remains in Kellermann park, between boulevard Kellermann and the Périphérique (ring road) (13th arrondissement).

– Base of Porte d'Arcueil, at the corner of rue Émile Deutsch de La Meurthe and boulevard Jourdan (14th arrondissement).

– Section of wall in Hauts de Malesherbes gardens (Bastion No. 44) (17th arrondissement).

– Section of wall at the bend of rue André Suarès (17th arrondissement).

– Stone from Bastion No. 82 at Fondation Deutsch de La Meurthe.

– Section of wall at 28, avenue de la Porte de la Villette (19th arrondissement).

RURAL ARCHITECTURAL WALK ON SOUTH SIDE OF 14TH ARRONDISSEMENT

Artists in the countryside

The south side of the 14th arrondissement is full of little-known countryside corners (some totally hidden from the street), as well as buildings designed by modernist architects such as Auguste Perret or Le Corbusier. Where there's a door code, you can sometimes get in by asking a resident.

– 29, rue Boulard, private (try asking): beautiful passage lined with houses all with gardens. Gauguin, then just a bank clerk, had his first taste of painting here in his friend Émile Schuttneckar's studio.

– Villa Adrienne, 17, avenue du Général Leclerc: established in 1870 to accommodate military and clergy, Villa Adrienne is a small paradise for residents close to the very noisy Place Denfert-Rochereau. Laid out around a private park, this harmonious and serene setting lacks nothing: manicured lawns, beautiful trees, welcoming benches and impassive statues. Around the park the villa extends over three sides of beautiful buildings of white brick and stone, decorated with balconies of carved terracotta bearing the names of famous figures such as Racine and Corneille, while the fourth side is completed by magnificent mansions.

14 bis, rue Mouton-Duvernet: The entrance porch conceals a lovely winding leafy path and bungalows with gardens and elegant porches.

– Villa Hallé, 36, rue Hallé: charming private passage that was used for the filming of *Le Bon Plaisir* with Catherine Deneuve. A few steps away, at the junction of rue Hallé and rue d'Alembert, note the pretty half-moon square.

– Square Montsouris: house in the background designed by Le Corbusier. The square is actually a street, perhaps one of the most beautiful in Paris.

– Rue Georges Braque: at No. 6, Perret built a house where the painter Braque lived.

– Rue du Parc Montsouris, Villa du Parc Montsouris and impasse Nansouty.

– Villa Seurat: No. 7 bis, house built by the famous architect Perret for the sculptor Chana Orloff. Soutine and Henri Miller also stayed on this passage.

– 110, avenue du Général Leclerc: remarkable small private passage

– Villa Alésia: 111, rue d'Alésia and 39 bis, rue des Plantes.

– Villa Jamot, 105 and 107, rue Didot: even if the entrance is protected by a door code, wait a while for someone to come out and ask to see this lovely paved double passage.

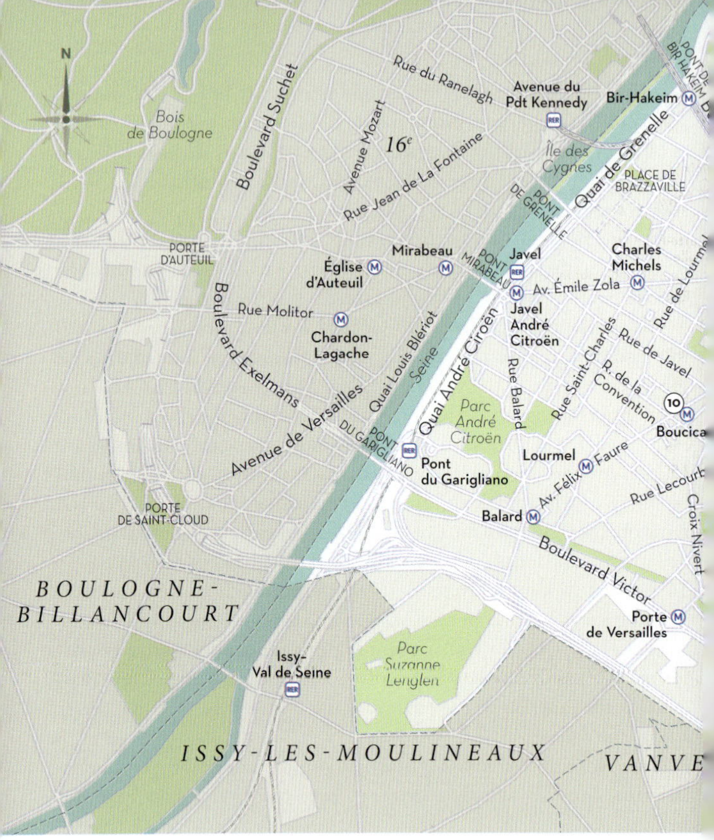

15th arrondissement

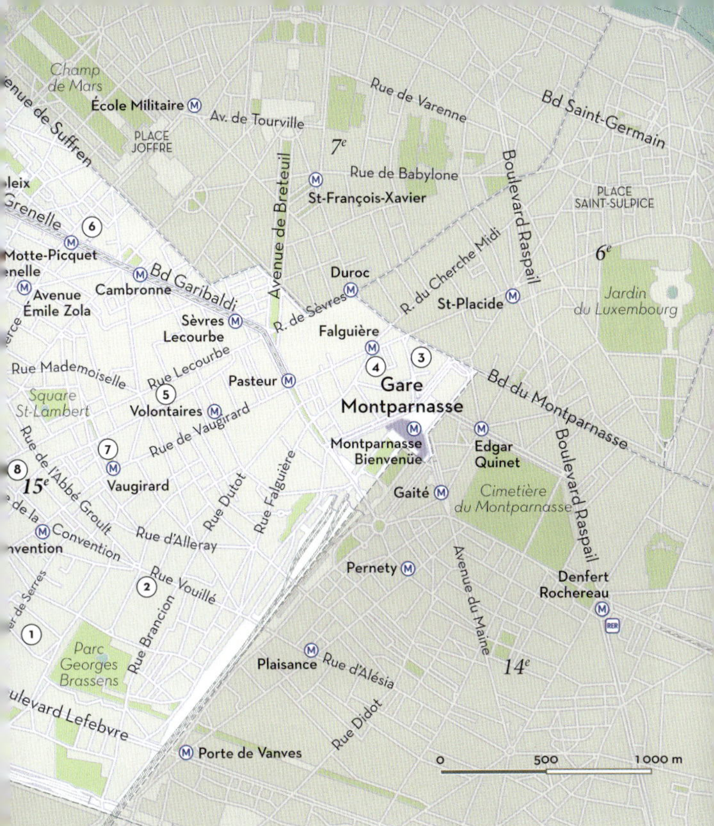

Champ de Mars
École Militaire Ⓜ
Av. de Tourville
Rue de Varenne
Bd Saint-Germain
Avenue de Suffren
PLACE JOFFRE
7ᵉ
Rue de Babylone
St-François-Xavier Ⓜ
Boulevard Raspail
PLACE SAINT-SULPICE
leix
Grenelle
⑥
Ⓜ
Motte-Picquet
enelle
Ⓜ
Avenue
Émile Zola
Ⓜ
Cambronne
Bd Garibaldi
R. de Sèvres
Duroc
Ⓜ
R. du Cherche Midi
St-Placide Ⓜ
6ᵉ
Jardin du Luxembourg
Sèvres Ⓜ
Lecourbe
Falguière
Ⓜ
Rue Mademoiselle
Rue Lecourbe
Pasteur Ⓜ
④
③
Square St-Lambert
⑤
Volontaires Ⓜ
Rue de Vaugirard
Gare Montparnasse
Bd du Montparnasse
⑦
Ⓜ
Rue de l'Abbé Groult
Vaugirard
Rue Dutot
Rue Falguière
Montparnasse Bienvenüe Ⓜ
Edgar Quinet Ⓜ
Boulevard Raspail
⑧
15ᵉ
Ⓜ
Convention
nvention
Rue d'Alleray
Gaité Ⓜ
Cimetière du Montparnasse
r de Serres
②
Rue Vouillé
Rue Brancion
Pernety Ⓜ
Avenue du Maine
Denfert Rochereau
Ⓜ RER
①
Parc Georges Brassens
Plaisance Ⓜ
Rue d'Alésia
Rue Didot
14ᵉ
ulevard Lefebvre
Ⓜ Porte de Vanves
0   500   1 000 m

LA RUCHE

A beehive of artists

2, passage Dantzig
Visits by appointment only and during 'Journées du Patrimoine' (Heritage Days)
Contact Mr Herth at +33 1 48 28 16 38
Metro Porte de Versailles or Porte de Vanves

Nestling discreetly in a magnificent garden of age-old trees at the entrance to the cul-de-sac, La Ruche (literally, The Beehive) owes its existence to Alfred Boucher (1850–1904), a well-known sculptor and generous philanthropist, who in 1902 set up this phalanstery for struggling young artists.

A Prix de Rome winner, Alfred Boucher, stopped in Milan on his way home from Italy and sold several of his works. Returning to the capital, he immediately invested this small nest egg in a plot of land, where La Ruche would be created. The material for the main building was salvaged from the pavilions which had been erected for the 1900 Universal Exposition – most notably, the Kiosque des Vins du Médoc designed by Gustave Eiffel – and the structure owes its name of 'The Beehive' to its polygonal form. At its centre is a wonderfully designed staircase that is flooded with light, with the three floors being occupied by small studios which, over the years, have been used by artists such as Léger, Zadkine, Soutine, Chagall and Modigliani.

Nowadays, La Ruche consists of a total of four buildings, the second of which was also constructed using material salvaged from the Universal Exposition. At one point it was threatened with sale and demolition, but thanks to a campaign of artists – headed by Chagall and Malraux – it survived. In 1971 the place was bought by René and Geneviève Seydoux, who set up a foundation that still manages the property as a community for artists. The buildings are now listed and provide accommodation for around 60 people (originally there were 140 residents). Alongside sculptors, painters and engravers, you will now find film-makers, set designers, cartoonists and graphic artists.

NEARBY
Villa Santos-Dumont ②
Metro Porte de Vanves or Convention
Laid out in the 1920s on a plot that had previously been a vineyard, the beautiful villa Santos-Dumont development was the work of the architect Raphaël Paynot and quickly attracted various artists already resident in the Montparnasse district – for example, Zadkine, Léger and Brauner. Today, the residents are still mainly artists, who have worked to maintain the peace and quiet of this street.

© Ralf.treinen

ESPACE KRAJCBERG

A reminder of the bohemian lifestyle

21, avenue du Maine
+33 1 42 22 90 16
espacekrajcberg.fr
contact@espacekrajcberg.fr
Groups must call
Metro Montparnasse-Bienvenüe

Away from the noise and bustle of the Montparnasse district, No. 21, avenue du Maine leads into a wonderful cobbled cul-de-sac lined with trees; originally this was the courtyard of an inn for the coaches serving the west of France.

At the beginning of the 20th century, the owner of this land had the brilliant idea of buying some of the buildings that were being dismantled after the 1900 Universal Exposition; these were then reassembled here, on either side of the street, to provide some 30 or so studios for penniless artists. From 1912 onwards Marie Vassilieff, who was the driving force behind the Académie du Montparnasse and the Académie Russe, offered accommodation here to the artists who were to form the École de Paris. She also set up a sort of canteen for the poorer among them; those who, in their times of direst need, profited from her hospitality included Picasso, Braque, Modigliani, Léger, Derain, Max Jacob and Fujita. Today, this place is still the haunt of artists (painters, actors, florists, set designers), who struggle valiantly to preserve the vitality of this oasis of greenery. Created in 1998, the Musée du Montparnasse centres on Marie Vassilieff's own studio; mounting temporary exhibitions dedicated to specific themes, it aims to make the illustrious past of this area better known.

Located at the end of the alleyway, the Espace Krajcberg opened its doors in 2003. It houses the works which the Brazilian sculptor donated to the city of Paris, together with a centre documenting his work. A place of encounter between French and Brazilian culture, this space aims, through art, to make visitors aware of environmental problems.

CHURCH OF SAINT SÉRAPHIN DE SAROV

A tree within a church

91, rue Lecourbe
saintseraphindesarov-eglise.fr
Saturday 2pm–8pm and Sunday 9am–1pm or during 'Journées du Patrimoine'
(Heritage Days)
Metro Volontaires

Hidden away in the back courtyard of the building at 91, rue Lecourbe, the Orthodox church of Saint Séraphin de Sarov is a little gem. Totally invisible from the street outside (to reach it, go through the first courtyard into the second, then turn right), the church takes its name from a Russian hermit who had himself immured while still alive. The first parish church here, founded in 1933, was little more than a shack built around a tree; however, the present structure (built in 1974) has real charm. Standing amidst the weeds of this small garden, the church has wooden outer walls surmounted by a blue onion dome decorated with the three-arm Orthodox cross. A place of touching simplicity, the interior is adorned with a multiplicity of icons; at the heart of the chapel you can also see the lower part of the tree around which the original structure was built. Serving the Russian community of the 15th arrondissement, the church of Saint Séraphin de Sarov is well worth a visit for the warm atmosphere generated during religious services. Information is posted at the entrance; and if you are lucky, you might get to be present at one of the Russian banquets which take place during the course of the year.

The Cavalerie Pelota Courts ⑤

Club de Pelote Basque – 8, rue de la Cavalerie
+33 1 45 67 06 34 – trinquetdelacavalerie.fr
Daily (it is better to go after 4pm)
From 2pm to 5pm on Wednesday the courts are given over to beginner children
(even those whose parents are not members)
Metro La Motte-Picquet – Grenelle

Listed in the supplementary register of historic buildings in 1986, the superb pelota courts of La Cavalerie were set up in 1929 by a group of Argentinians; they occupy the seventh floor of the building. Though the sign says 'Private Club', visitors are welcome and can watch from the gallery; only members are allowed to play (applicants require two existing members as sponsors). Membership also gives you access to a small bar and lounge worthy of an English gentleman's club.

NEARBY

15, square de Vergennes ⑥

Entrance by the porch of 279, rue de Vaugirard
fmep.fr/architecture.php
+33 1 56 23 00 22 – info@15squaredevergennes.com
Tuesday–Saturday 12pm–7pm, closed August and public holidays
Guided tours by appointment by phone or by mail
Metro Vaugirard

Built in 1931–1932 by Robert Mallet-Stevens for the master glassmaker Louis Barillet, this former workshop has recently been converted into a centre of contemporary art and design. The work done on the building by the previous owners totally failed to respect its character, but in 1993 the structure was included in the supplementary register of listed buildings and then purchased (in 2001) by an art lover who had it restored to its original condition. Now, the organisation of space within the interior is as it was intended to be, with massive windows extending over different levels and white Art Deco glasswork by Louis Barillet himself. The restoration is, in itself, a phenomenal achievement, given that there are only three extant photographs of that original interior.

Garden of Blomet clinic ⑦

134–136, rue Blomet – Metro Convention
Apply at reception or telephone at +33 1 45 32 89 50 or +33 1 86 86 86 00
contact@clinique-blomet.fr

Rather modern in appearance, the Blomet Clinic has a neo-Gothic chapel. The clinic also features a very pleasant garden, where a polite request will gain you the chance of a relaxing stroll.

Cité Morieux ⑧

56, rue de la Fédération
Metro Bir-Hakeim

Pretty little cul-de-sac lined with country-style houses.

Sculpture 'Le Corbeau ⑨ et le Renard'

40, avenue Félix Faure
Metro Boucicaut

A fine sculpture inspired by La Fontaine's fable of *The Crow and the Fox* adorns the façade of 40, avenue Félix Faure.

FRESCOES IN THE CHURCH OF SAINT-CHRISTOPHE DE JAVEL

St Christopher blessing pilots and racing drivers

28, rue de la Convention
+33 1 45 78 33 70
scjavel.net
secretariat@scjavel.net
Daily 8.30am–7.30pm
Masses: check the timetable on the website
Metro and RER Javel

The façade of the entrance porch is adorned with extraordinary frescoes. Designed in the 1930s by Henri-Marcel Magne, they show St Christopher helping not just travellers but navigators, pilots, train drivers and motorists. This surrealist vision is an invitation to enter the church and admire the choir frescoes, the fine interior and the attractive modern stained glass (again by Magne). Javel is a district closely linked with the transport industries: not only were there the old Citröen works (on the site of the park of the same name), but also factories that produced locomotives, hot-air balloons and aerostats. Naturally enough, the new church was dedicated to St Christopher, the patron saint of travellers.

Built in 1926–1930, Saint-Christophe de Javel was the first church in the world designed to be constructed entirely in prefabricated reinforced concrete, which accounts for its low cost and the speed with which it was completed. The structure was financed by a subscription among motorists. Nowadays it seems quite incredible, but each subscriber to the project simply paid the equivalent of the cost of one can of petrol. The cardinal-archbishop of Paris used to come here to bless the cars of the owners who had gathered for a Mass in front of the church, attracted by the chance of protection this offered; more mundane forms of car insurance did not become obligatory in France until 1958.

Saint Christopher and the Golden Legend

Tradition has it that St Christopher bore Christ on his shoulders across a raging torrent. In fact, the Greek etymology of his name, *Christos phoros*, means: 'He who carries Christ'. The history of the saint is told in *The Golden Legend* by Jacques de Voragine, a 14th century Dominican from Genoa. One of the major works of Christian hagiography, this contains stories from the lives of 180 saints and martyrs, together with some episodes from the Life of Christ, all organised according to the Church's liturgical year.

'Eau de Javel'

At the end of the 18th century, industrialists were granted a licence to set up a plant near the Javelle mill (in the present-day district of Javel) to produce vitriol. It was here that scientists would first produce sodium hypochlorite, which would later become commonly known in France as eau de Javel.

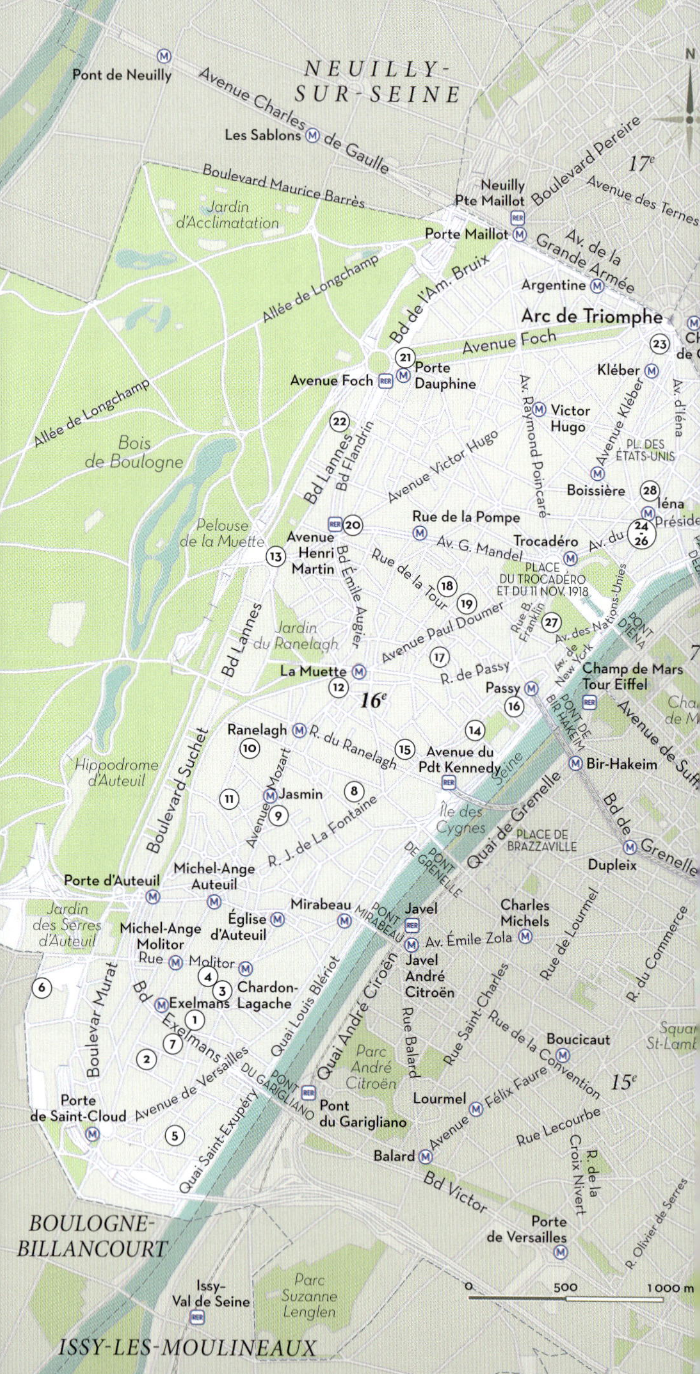

Pont de Neuilly
NEUILLY-SUR-SEINE
Avenue Charles de Gaulle
Les Sablons
Boulevard Maurice Barrès
Jardin d'Acclimatation
Neuilly
Pte Maillot
Boulevard Pereire
17e
Avenue des Ternes
Porte Maillot
Av. de la Grande Armée
Bd de l'Am. Bruix
Argentine
Arc de Triomphe
Ch
de C
23
Avenue Foch
Kléber
21
Porte Dauphine
Av. Raymond Poincaré
Victor Hugo
Avenue Kléber
Av. d'Iéna
Avenue Foch
22
Bd Lannes
Bd Flandrin
PL. DES ÉTATS-UNIS
Avenue Victor Hugo
Boissière
28
Iéna
Préside
24
26
Rue de la Pompe
Trocadéro
Av. du
20
Avenue Henri Martin
Bd Émile Augier
Av. G. Mandel
13
Rue de la Tour
PLACE DU TROCADÉRO
ET DU 11 NOV. 1918
18
Bd Lannes
Jardin du Ranelagh
Avenue Paul Doumer
19
Rue B. Franklin
27
Av. des Nations-Unies
Av. de New York
PONT D'IÉNA
17
Allée de Longchamp
La Muette
12
16e
R. de Passy
Passy
Champ de Mars
Tour Eiffel
Cha
de M
Bois de Boulogne
16
PONT DE BIR-HAKEIM
Ranelagh
R. du Ranelagh
14
Avenue de Suf
Pelouse de la Muette
10
15
Avenue du Pdt Kennedy
Bir-Hakeim
Allée de Longchamp
11
Avenue Mozart
Jasmin
8
Seine
Bd de Grenelle
Grenelle
9
R. J. De La Fontaine
Île des Cygnes
Quai de Grenelle
Dupleix
Hippodrome d'Auteuil
Boulevard Suchet
PLACE DE BRAZZAVILLE
Porte d'Auteuil
Michel-Ange Auteuil
Mirabeau
Javel
Charles Michels
R. du Commerce
Jardin des Serres d'Auteuil
Église d'Auteuil
PONT MIRABEAU
Av. Émile Zola
Rue de Lourmel
Michel-Ange Molitor
Javel André Citroën
Rue Saint-Charles
R. de la
Squa
St-Lamb
Rue Molitor
Boulevard Murat
4
Chardon-Lagache
Quai Louis Blériot
Rue Balard
Rue de la Convention
Boucicaut
3
Quai André Citroën
Rue Lecourbe
6
Bd Exelmans
1
Exelmans
7
Parc André Citroën
15e
2
Avenue de Versailles
Quai Saint-Exupéry
Lourmel
Avenue Félix Faure
Porte de Saint-Cloud
PONT DU GARIGLIANO
Pont du Garigliano
Balard
R. de la Croix Nivert
5
Bd Victor
BOULOGNE-BILLANCOURT
Porte de Versailles
R. Olivier de Serres
Issy-Val de Seine
Parc Suzanne Lenglen
0   500   1 000 m
ISSY-LES-MOULINEAUX
N

16th arrondissement

EIFFEL AERODYNAMICS LABORATORY

Eiffel's wind tunnel

67, rue Boileau
Group visits Friday at 2pm, by appointment: +33 1 42 88 47 40 or
aerodynamiqueeiffel.fr
Group visits by appointment (1 month ahead) or during the 'Journées du
Patrimoine' (Heritage Days)
Metro Exelmans, Michel-Ange – Molitor or Chardon-Lagache
RER Pont du Garigliano

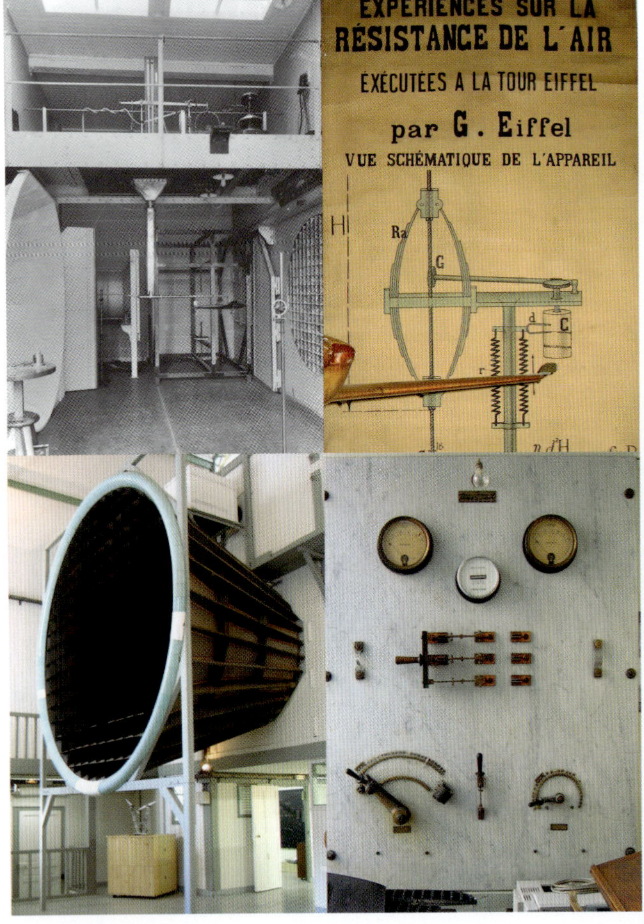

A listed historic monument, this laboratory is a remarkable piece of industrial archaeology that is now open to the public.

It remains intact thanks to the foresight of Gustave Eiffel, who in 1920 stipulated that the laboratory should not be closed down and demolished as long as the wind tunnel was operational; his wishes have been respected by the Société Aérodynamique Eiffel and, in particular, by the current curator, Mr Peter, who joined the company as an engineer in 1959.

World-famous for the tower that bears his name, Gustave Eiffel was also a pioneer in the field of aerodynamic technology. Remarkably well preserved, this laboratory, which opened in 1912, is still operational. Eiffel himself ran it until 1920, using scale models of planes to compile the first scientific data on the nascent technology of aircraft and flight. As well as such aerodynamical experiments, the laboratory was to diversify and open its facilities to the automobile and construction industries. In fact, it was here that tests were carried out on the models of the Citroën ZX for the Paris-Dakar rally, the Amiens football stadium and the CNIT building at La Défense.

Comprising a vast hangar and various workshops, the laboratory constructs models and then measures their performance in various wind tunnel tests. Originally, the laboratory had two wind tunnels, but the smaller (diameter: 1 metre) was dismantled in 1933.

The larger (diameter: 2 metres) has been operational for over 90 years and is still used to test the resistance of industrial models to winds of up to 100 km/h.

If no model is undergoing tests the day you visit, take advantage of the opportunity to ask if you can feel the effects of the wind tunnel yourself; it is a phenomenal experience. Within the hangar there are also attractive displays of models of racing cars, aircraft and of the wind tunnels themselves. Note also the famous freefall apparatus, which is used to measure the air resistance of objects by dropping them from the top of the tower.

VILLA MULHOUSE

Very special housing for workers

Villas Dietz-Monin, Émile Meyer and Cheysson
Located between rue Parent-de-Rossan and rue Claude Lorrain
Entrance at 84 and 86, rue Boileau – Metro Exelmans

While the houses that make up this unusual group of rural-style streets are now far from cheap, this was not always the case. Émile Cheysson (1836–1910) was, in fact, Inspector General with the state's Ponts et Chaussées (civil engineering) Department and published hundreds of articles and leaflets on the problems of social housing. At the beginning of the 20th century, this committed social reformer was the driving force behind the creation of what was originally an area of low-cost housing.

NEARBY

Hameau Boileau, Villa Molitor, Villa de la Réunion ③

38, rue Boileau – 7, rue Molitor – 29, rue Chardon-Lagache
Metro Chardon-Lagache or Michel-Ange – Molitor

This tiny area in the south of the 16th arrondissement contains a number of private roads, culs-de-sac and housing developments which are the stuff of daydreams for idle strollers or eager property investors in search of a haven of peace. The houses and city mansions of the Hameau Boileau, Villa Molitor and Villa de la Réunion nestle within their own private gardens and can only be glimpsed through the railings of gates which close off the approach roads. At each gate are ardent watchmen, keen to preserve the peace and quiet enjoyed by the residents (perhaps a famous singer or an optician who has made a fortune).

Bas-reliefs at 16, rue Chardon-Lagache ④

Metro Chardon-Lagache

The Art Deco building at 16, rue Chardon-Lagache was built by Jean Hillard in 1934. It boasts two sets of attractive bas-reliefs, four storeys in height, that are often overlooked even by locals. Designed by the sculptor Georges Maxime Chiquet, a pupil of Bouchard, whose museum is nearby, the panels depict work in vineyards and on the land.

Villa Sommeiller ⑤

149, boulevard Murat and 45, rue Claude Terrasse
Metro Porte de Saint-Cloud

Not far from the boulevards of Les Maréchaux, the little-known Villa Sommeiller, 75 metres long, is one of the charming rural passages in the south of the 16th arrondissement. Protected by a digicode (but you can see it through the grid), it is named after engineer Germain Sommeiller (1815–71), who was responsible for the Mont Cenis tunnel through the Alps.

LE CORBUSIER'S APARTMENT

In the inner sanctum of the master

24, rue Nungesser et Coli
+33 9 63 52 30 22 – reservation@fondationlecorbusier.fr
fondationlecorbusier.fr/visite/appartement-le-corbusier-paris
By appointment on Monday and Wednesday mornings
Metro Porte de Saint-Cloud or Porte d'Auteuil

Standing among dressed stone buildings, the apartment at 24, rue Nungesser et Coli, made of glass blocks, is likely to surprise the curious walker. The sixth and seventh floors of this building contain the apartment-workshop of Le Corbusier, designed in 1933 by the famous architect with the help of his cousin Pierre Jeanneret.

Le Corbusier lived here from 1934 until his death. Owned by the Fondation Le Corbusier, the apartment can now be visited in small groups exclusively by appointment. The tour is not guided, but the architecture student who welcomes you will be happy to answer your questions. If you are the only visitor, you may even be offered a coffee.

The apartment is a duplex with wonderful dual-aspect views: on one side, the whole of Boulogne-Billancourt as far as Mont-Valérien can be seen, along with a view of the Roland-Garros stadium; on the other, the apartment overlooks the Jean Bouin stadium and Porte Molitor. In this eagle's eyrie, books, successive spaces and light filtered through polished windows encourage meditation and creativity. The visitor is able to see the architect's workshop, office area and bedroom, with its unusual shower made entirely of concrete. As is often the case with Le Corbusier, the windows are installed horizontally. Upstairs there is a guest room, complemented by an original covered terrace.

The apartment is sparsely furnished but it is still worth making a detour to visit the inner sanctum of one of the most innovative architects of the early 20th century. It is a good starting point for a walk through the Boulogne of the 1930s, with its many hotels and buildings designed by great architects.

NEARBY

Church of Tous-Les-Saints-de-la-Terre-Russe ⑦

19, rue Claude Lorrain – +33 1 45 27 24 82 – Mass: Daily 6pm
Metro Exelmans

The only external evidence of the presence of a church tucked away on the ground floor of this brick building is the wooden doorway; it is surmounted by a blind arcade in the form of the kokoshnik head-dress once traditional among Russian peasant women. The church itself does not come under the authority of the patriarchs of either Moscow or Constantinople, but is part of the patriarchate known as 'The Russian Church beyond the Frontiers'. Just a few hundred metres away stands another Russian Orthodox church, the Church of the Apparition of the Virgin (87, boulevard Exelmans). Equally close by, at 39, rue François Gérard, there is a Russian Catholic church that observes the Byzantine rite. Many White Russians were fairly well off and liked this district.

CASTEL BÉRANGER

Also known as Castel Dérangé

14, rue La Fontaine
Metro Ranelagh or Jasmin

The full scope of Hector Guimard's talent was not widely known when he was commissioned to design this building in the heart of the then village of Auteuil. The owner of the site, however, showed great foresight in her decision, because the building (1897–1898) won the City of Paris Façade Competition in 1899 and immediately established the fame of its architect. Containing a total of 36 apartments, the structure makes use of stone, pale-pink brick, wood, cast iron, steel, glazed stoneware and ceramics – and is undoubtedly Guimard's masterpiece. The project embodies all the fundamental principles of Art Nouveau, with the architect even designing such details of the interior as carpets, wallpapers and doorknobs. While the public at large failed to appreciate the building – quickly turning Castel Béranger into Castel Dérangé (deranged) – some important contemporary figures (such as the painter Paul Signac) had no doubts, proclaiming Guimard to be a genius and choosing this building as their home.

For further information on Guimard's other buildings and on Art Nouveau in general, see the following double-page spread.

NEARBY
45, rue Ribera ⑨
Metro Jasmin

A superb bas-relief by the architect Boussard, dating from the end of the 19th century. Not far away are some unusual seated caryatids, at 1, rue de l'Yvette.

Hector Guimard

Born in Lyon in 1867, Hector Guimard is the central figure in French Art Nouveau. His most important artistic legacy is perhaps the metro stations which he designed between the years 1899 and 1904. Today, some 66 of the 380 which once existed still survive, the most famous being the stations of Porte Dauphine and Abbesses (which have splendid glass roofs). The master architect also designed numerous houses and apartment buildings. Most of these are to be found in the 16th arrondissement, where Guimard himself lived.

In the 16th arrondissement:

– Castel Béranger: 14, rue La Fontaine (1897–1898) (see previous double-page spread)

– Group of 17–19 and 21, rue La Fontaine, 8 and 10, rue Agar (1909–1911) and 43, rue Gros

– Hôtel Mezzara: 60, rue La Fontaine (1910)

– Hôtel Roszé: 34, rue Boileau (1891)

– Hôtel Jassedé: 41, rue Chardon-Lagache (1894)

– École du Sacré-Cœur: 1, av. de la Frillière (1895)

– Immeuble Jassedé: 142, av. de Versailles and 1, rue de Lancret (1903)

– Hôtel particulier: 3, square Jasmin (1921)

– 36–38, rue Greuze (1927–1928)

– Villa Flore: 120, av. Mozart (1924–1926)

– Hôtel Guimard: 122, av. Mozart (1909–1913)

– Hôtel Delfau: 1, rue Molitor (1894)

– 18, rue Henri Heine (1930)

– 11, rue François Millet (1909)

– Atelier de Carpeaux: 39, bd Exelmans (1894); this is an early work, unrelated to Art Nouveau

Elsewhere in Paris and in France:

– Synagogue: 10, rue Pavée, Paris, 4th arrondissement, 1913 (see page 134)

– Villa La Hublotière (1896): 72, route de Montesson, 78810 Le Vésinet (Yvelines)

– Maison Coilliot: 14, rue de Fleurus, Lille, 1898–1900

– Castel Val: 4, rue des Meulières, Auvers-sur-Oise, 1903

– Castel Orgeval: 2, av. de la Mare-Tambour, Villemoisson-sur-Orge, 1904

– Chalet Blanc: 2, rue du Lycée, Sceaux, 1904

– Villa Hemsy: 3, rue de Crillon, Saint-Cloud, 1913

Art Nouveau

The term itself comes from the name of the art gallery which the Hamburg dealer Samuel Bing (1838–1905) opened in Paris in 1895; his 'Art Nouveau' would subsequently show work by all the great figures of this artistic movement. The German/Austrian equivalent, 'Jugendstil', was taken from the title of the satirical magazine *Jugend* launched by the German publisher Georg Hirth in Munich in 1896 which published numerous designs that exemplified new artistic trends, even if the term *Jugendstil* is now predominately used to refer to a more geometric type of design. Elsewhere in Europe, Art Nouveau went by different names. In Austria it was the 'Sezessionstil', associated with the Secessionist movement founded by G. Klimt in 1897; in England, it was known as 'Liberty Style' after the department store famous for its modern-design textiles. Later came the 'Modern Style', which combined the two major trends in European Art. As for more popular terms, the flowing forms of Art Nouveau were sometimes referred to in France as examples of the *'nouille style'* (noodle style) or even spaghetti style. More than a simple artistic movement, Art Nouveau embodied a new way of thought and life, breaking with the accepted norms of existing society. Striving for liberation from exploitation, Church domination and the repression of women, it emphasised a level of eroticism and sensuality that would previously have been unthinkable. Look, for example, at the numerous stylised and sensual depictions of women that adorn the façades of Art Nouveau buildings. However, having flourished in the years up to 1914, Art Nouveau was severely affected by the First World War and its aftermath. Given that the buildings designed by Art Nouveau architects were neither cheap nor easy to produce on a large scale, the movement was unable to satisfy the need for mass rebuilding required at the time. In Paris itself, the undisputed leader of Art Nouveau was Hector Guimard; however, other architects – such as Jules Lavirotte (see page 241) – also made their mark in the city.

RUE MALLET-STEVENS

⑩

A modernist manifesto

Metro Ranelagh

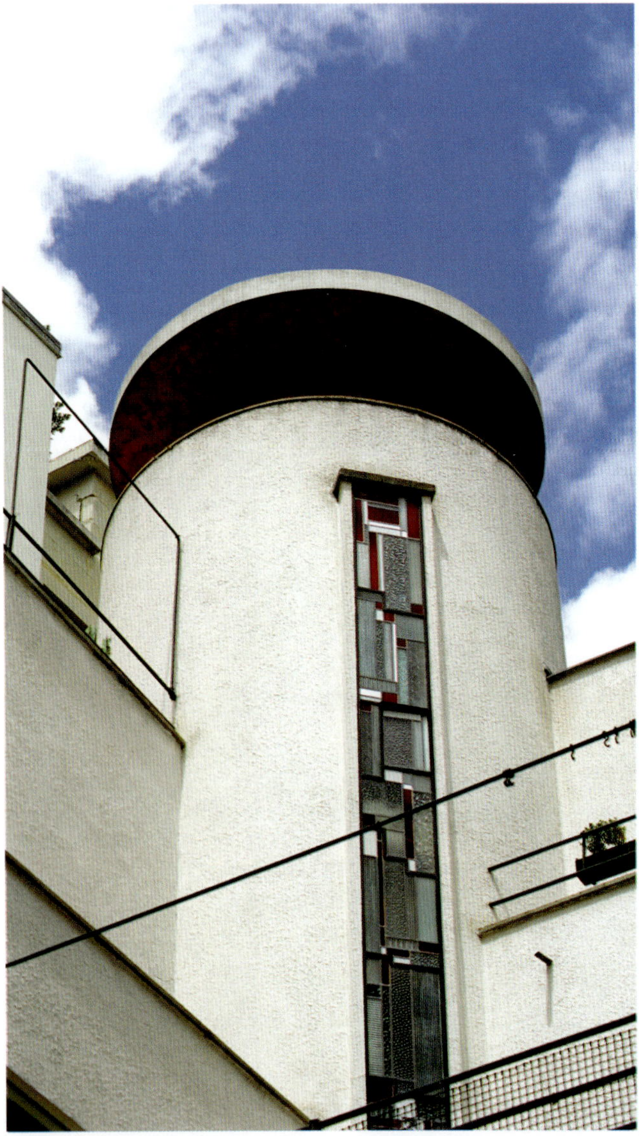

Built from 1926 onwards by Robert Mallet-Stevens, this housing development is a 'manifesto' of modern architecture and comprises a total of five individual buildings. At No. 12 is the home and studio of the architect himself, while No. 10 was the home/studio of the sculptors Joël and Jean Martel, No. 8 was home to the pianist Mme Reifenberg, No. 7 was occupied by Daniel Dreyfus and No. 3/5 by Mme Allatini. At the end of the street, No. 1 is the caretaker's cottage. The design of each of these buildings plays upon the juxtaposition of smooth-sided white cubes in terraces, recesses, towers and jutting roofs; in Robert Mallet-Stevens' words, 'the architect sculpts one single massive block: a house.' Unfortunately, the listing of the buildings in 1975 came too late to save the furnishings and fittings which had been designed by the architect himself.

NEARBY

Maison La Roche 

10, square du Docteur Blanche (entrance at 55, rue du Docteur Blanche)
+33 9 63 52 30 22
info@fondationlecorbusier.fr – reservation@fondationlecorbusier.fr
Tuesday–Saturday 10am–6pm, only by appointment
Metro Jasmin

This is home to the Fondation Le Corbusier, and a visit here is a real aesthetic treat. With its interplay of volumes and partition walls, its raised platforms, walkways and sloping ramps, the space will give you some idea of the work of the architect, enabling you to appreciate the reputation he achieved in spite of the numerous, sometimes justified, criticisms levelled at his designs.

Modern architecture in the 16th arrondissement

Along with the Art Nouveau buildings by Guimard, the 16th arrondissement – and particularly Auteuil district – was a place of experimentation for a number of early 20th century architects. When the villages of Passy and Auteuil were incorporated within the city of Paris, the former was already substantially built-up, while the latter basically comprised just the three streets which linked it to Passy: the present-day rue d'Auteuil, rue Molière and rue La Fontaine. There was therefore space to build on and money to spend, and those who wanted to turn this into a little architectural paradise included not only Guimard, Le Corbusier and Mallet-Stevens, but also Henri Sauvage (the Studio Building at 65, rue La Fontaine), Ginsberg (42, avenue de Versailles) and the Perret brothers (25 bis, rue Franklin and 51–55, rue Raynouard; the latter actually the brothers' home). Luckily for the curious stroller, most of these buildings are concentrated within a rather small area.

VILLA BEAUSÉJOUR

Russia in Paris

7, boulevard de Beauséjour
Grid of the villa closed by an intercom: ask permission to an inhabitant to have a look
Metro La Muette

Despite its very French name, this is really a tiny Russian village of wooden isbas (including a typical coach inn). Originally created for the 1867 Universal Exposition, these characteristic wooden cottages were later reassembled here in the heart of the 16th arrondissement.

Only one of the four came directly from Russia, the others were made in Paris to instructions and designs from the Russian Committee for the Exposition. Still inhabited, all four are now in the supplementary register of listed buildings.

Russia in Paris

Attracted by freedom of expression and culture, the Russians, encouraged by the policy of openness led by Pierre le Grand (1672–1725), began to travel truly in France from the 18th century, although in August 1790 Catherine II pronounced an *oukase* to prevent the spread of French Revolutionary ideas. From 1814 to 1817, Russian soldiers occupied the capital (when the word bistro – 'fast' in Russian – was created: the soldiers asked for a drink they wanted to drink quickly) and exchanges resumed. The Bolshevik Revolution of 1917 caused many Russians (called 'white', in opposition to the 'red' communists) to flee and, in the West, it was France that welcomed most Russians, particularly in the 15th and 16th arrondissements of Paris.

The city hosted about half of all Russian refugees in France. Wishing to preserve their culture and rites, they quickly founded many parishes (mainly Orthodox) that today dot these two districts. Russian places of worship in the capital include:

– Church of the Présentation-de-la-Vierge. 91, rue Olivier de Serres (15th arrondissement). Hidden behind a block of houses, the church has little architectural interest. Services are on Saturday at 6pm and Sunday at 10.30am. Ecumenical Patriarchate of Constantinople.

– Church of the Trois-Saints-Hiérarques. 5, rue Pétel (15th). Moscow Patriarchate.

– Church of Tous-les-Saints-de-la-Terre-Russe. 19, rue Claude Lorrain (16th). Russian Orthodox Church Outside Russia (ROCOR, see page 431).

– Church of the Apparition-de-la-Vierge. 87, boulevard Exelmans (16th). Ecumenical Patriarchate of Constantinople.

– Church of the Sainte-Trinité. 39, rue François Gérard (16th). Roman Catholic Church.

– Church of Saint-Séraphin-de-Sarov. 91, rue Lecourbe (15th) (see page 418). Ecumenical Patriarchate of Constantinople.

– Alexandre Nevski Cathedral. 12, rue Daru (8th) (see page 288). Ecumenical Patriarchate of Constantinople.

– Church Saint-Serge-de-Radonège. 93, rue de Crimée. (19th) (see page 504). Ecumenical Patriarchate of Constantinople.

Also worth mentioning: Zadkine Museum, 100 bis, rue d'Assas (6th). Conservatoire Serge Rachmaninoff de Paris and La Cantine Russe, 26, avenue de New York (16th).

PILÂTRE DE ROZIER'S FLIGHT MARKER

Memories of the first manned flight

Place de Colombie – RER Avenue Henri-Martin or Metro Ranelagh

As the stele in Place de Colombie records, Pilâtre de Rozier (1754–85) and the Marquis d'Arlandes took off on 21 November 1783 in their hot-air balloon east of the park of the old Château de la Muette (see opposite). They landed 26 minutes later at Butte-aux-Cailles, signing off the first manned flight in history. The first ascent in a balloon with animals aboard (a rooster, a duck and a sheep) took place on 19 September in Versailles, in front of the king, followed by the first untethered manned flight on 21 November at Folie Titon (now in the 11th arrondissement), although the balloon was attached to the ground with a rope (captive flight). Pilâtre de Rozier died on 15 June 1785 attempting to cross the Channel in a balloon.

Why does RER line C loop around Jardin du Ranelagh?

A careful look at the Paris Métro map shows that, curiously, RER C (which uses the rails of the former Petite Ceinture) turns a corner when approaching the current location of Jardin du Ranelagh.

This garden is the site of the former park of Château de la Muette (part of the buildings still exist at 2, rue André Pascal, headquarters of the OECD), which was once a royal residence. A former hunting lodge of the kings, the estate was converted by Charles IX into a small castle he offered to Marguerite de Valois (Queen Margot) when she married the future Henri IV. In 1606 she gave it to the future Louis XIII. It was later occupied by Louis XV then Marie Antoinette, who spent her last night there before her marriage to Louis XVI.

Opened by sections between 1852 and 1869, the former railway line of the Petite Ceinture was around Paris (32 km long) inside Boulevards des Maréchaux.

Its route and tracks still exist today but most tracks are disused (only part is now reused for RER C). This is how, when it was built, the line circumnavigated the beautiful estate with its rich royal past.

BALZAC HOUSE

'I have some Belgian lace'

47, rue Raynouard
+33 1 55 74 41 80
Daily 10am–6pm, except Monday and public holidays
Admission free to permanent collections
Metro Passy

Now converted into a museum, this is where Balzac lived from 1840 to 1847. The house was particularly suitable for the novelist as it served as a refuge from his creditors: there are two separate entrances, one on rue Raynouard and one, lower down, giving onto rue Berton. Visitors were not even admitted unless they knew the password, one of the most famous of which was 'I have some Belgian lace'. Nowadays, the charm of the place lies in this anecdote – and the delightful garden.

Inside, the museum has manuscripts, first editions and different depictions of the writer by artists who were his contemporaries; unfortunately, there are few personal objects, as most of these were sold off by Balzac's widow after his death. More than the collections themselves, it is the rather old-fashioned air of the place which makes it attractive. Note the large genealogical table that the novelist drew up to indicate all the family relationships between the various characters of his *La Comédie humaine*.

NEARBY

The Benjamin Franklin Obelisk ⑮

66, rue Raynouard, at the corner of rue Singer
RER Avenue du Président Kennedy

Imposing and yet little noticed locally, this bas-relief in the form of an obelisk is set into the wall of 66, rue Raynouard. It marks the spot where Franklin installed France's first lightning conductor. It was in the

grounds of the (now destroyed) Hôtel de Valentinois, where he stayed during his time in Paris, that Franklin erected the instrument which he had first invented in 1756. The American Congress's ambassador to France, Benjamin Franklin was also one of the authors of the American Declaration of Independence. The neighbourhood pays tribute to him in various ways: nearby is rue Franklin; the Collège Saint-Louis-de-Gonzague is better known simply as 'Franklin'; and on the corner of avenue Paul Doumer stands a statue of the American statesman.

THE UNUSUAL GLASSES AT THE WINE MUSEUM

A Wine Museum in ... rue des Eaux

Musée du Vin
Rue des Eaux and 5, square Charles Dickens
+33 1 45 25 63 26
museeduvinparis.com
info@museeduvinparis.com
Daily 10am–6pm, except Monday
Restaurant: Tuesday–Saturday 12pm–3pm
Metro Passy

Opened in 1984 by the Échansons de France association of wine enthusiasts, this Wine Museum is ironically located in rue des Eaux ('Waters Street'). The place itself occupies a maze of tunnels which, in the 16th and 17th centuries, were used by the Minim friars of Passy, whose monastery produced a light white wine. Driven out during the Revolution, the monks abandoned the tunnels to the neglect they would suffer right up until the place was bought twenty years ago.

Now the various niches house the equipment used in cultivating vineyards and in winemaking and tasting; there are even such comic objects as a left-handed carafe or wine glasses impossible to knock over. The visit ends with a glass of wine (included in the price). And if that leaves you feeling hungry, you can also stay for lunch (except on Mondays).

NEARBY

Hameau de Passy

48, rue de Passy – Metro Passy
A small rural-style passageway running from rue de Passy through to rue Vital.

THE TOWER
OF RUE DE LA TOUR

A hidden remnant that gave its name to the street

88, rue de la Tour – Metro Rue de la Pompe

Unknown even to its inhabitants, the rue de la Tour owes its name to a tower that still exists today; it is located in the courtyard of 88, rue de la Tour and can be seen when standing at the corner of rue Desbordes-Valmore and rue de la Tour.

Some say that the tower formed part of the old Château de la Tour, which was owned in 1305 by the cupbearer of Philippe le Bel (see below). It then served as a prison and was later surmounted by a windmill, from which the street took its first name, rue du Moulin de la Tour. The tower was restored during the First Empire and again in 1897. It currently forms part of an institution for young girls run by the Sisters of Saint Clotilde.

The cupbearer was the officer responsible for serving drinks to a ruler or high-ranking dignitary. Due to the constant fear of being poisoned, the cupbearer had to be completely trustworthy and was sometimes required to taste the wine before serving it.

NEARBY

Cul-de-sac 70, rue de la Tour (19)

Metro Rue de la Pompe or Trocadéro

A charming little paved cul-de-sac surrounded by houses with gardens.

The principle behind artesian wells

Unlike traditional wells, the water in artesian wells does not need to be pumped, but rises freely to the surface. The term artesian originates from the fact that the first to note this phenomenon were the monks of Lillers Abbey in Artois. The principle at work is similar to that exemplified by liquids in communicating vessels. It occurs in particular geological circumstances, when the point of exit of a well is located below what is known technically as the piezometric level (this corresponds to the highest level of the water table that supplies the water in the well).

HOW AN ARTESIAN WELL WORKS

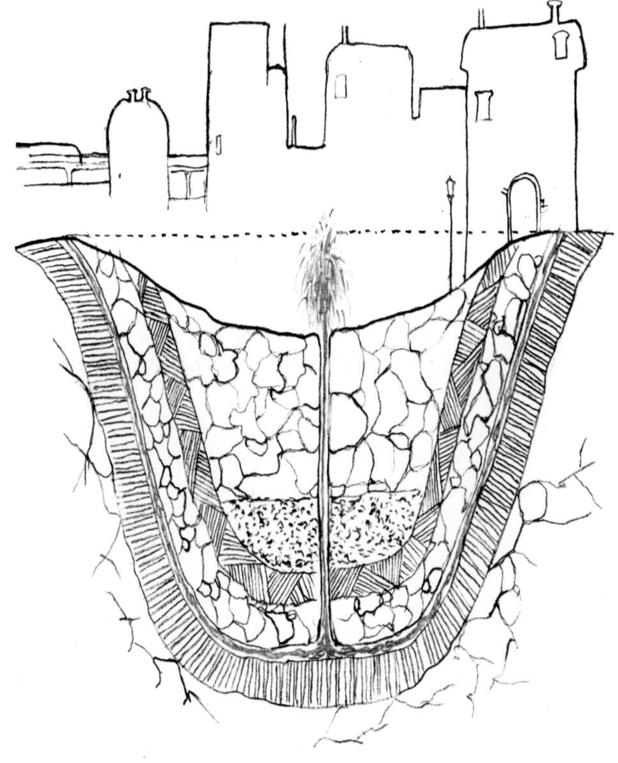

ARTESIAN WELL

A survivor of the epic efforts to supply the city with water

Square Lamartine – Metro Rue de la Pompe or RER Avenue Henri-Martin

Begun in 1855 and opened in 1866, the Passy well is the last functioning artesian well in Paris. Sunk to a depth of 587 metres, its aim was ambitious: to supply water not only for the local residents but also for the complete irrigation of the Bois de Boulogne and for its two lakes. Despite its current ferrous taste, due to the fact that iron pipes were used in the well, the water is still perfectly safe to drink; it is tested regularly. The well's output has declined considerably since the 19th century, however, falling from 25,000 m³ to 350 m³.

Artesian wells in Paris

After the cholera epidemic of 1832, the city looked for uncontaminated sources of water. One solution was the drilling of artesian wells that would draw on water from a water table which was deeper (more than 500 metres underground) and therefore less vulnerable to bacterial infection. Five such wells were sunk. The first was the Grenelle well, which emerged in place Georges Mulot (the square is named after the entrepreneur behind the scheme). Sunk to a depth of 587 metres in 1866, the Passy well stands in what is now square Lamartine in the 16th arrondissement. The Hébert well (place Hébert, in the 18th arrondissement) was sunk in 1863, then redrilled in 1891, but it was covered over in 2004. The Butte-aux-Cailles well (rue Bobillot in the 13th arrondissement) produced hot water and was sunk to a depth of 678 metres in 1863; redrilled in 1904, it was covered over in 2002; contrary to popular belief, it is not the source of the water for the Butte-aux-Cailles swimming pool. Finally, there is the Blomet well in the 15th arrondissement. This was completed — to a depth of 587 metres — in 1929. Other private wells were also sunk within the city: that serving the Say Refinery was sunk in 1869, whereas the Maison de la Radio well dates from 1956. Today only the Passy well is operational; the phreatic level for all the wells being the same; the drilling of any new wells would immediately lower the pressure in the others.

ENTRANCE TO PORTE DAUPHINE METRO STATION ㉑

A dragonfly in Paris

Entrance opposite 90, avenue Foch
Metro Porte Dauphine

Created by the master of Art Nouveau, Hector Guimard (see page 434), this entrance to the Porte Dauphine station on Line 2 of the Paris Métro is a real masterpiece. Opened on 13 December 1900, it has a glass roof ending in an upward fanning canopy, with curved borders resting on branching columns. The panels around the tunnel entrance are in orange-glazed ceramic. The particularly light and airy form of the structure has earned it the nickname *'la libellule'* (dragonfly).

NEARBY

A blockhouse in the Bois de Boulogne ㉒

Metro Porte Dauphine

Just near the Porte Dauphine, at 45, avenue du Maréchal Fayolle, is a blockhouse dating from the Second World War. It now accommodates the local scout troop.

AUTOMOBILE HIGH RELIEFS AT HOTEL MERCEDES

Blowing in the wind

9, rue de Presbourg
Metro Kléber

The imposing building at 9, rue de Presbourg was built in 1905 in a discreet Art Nouveau style by French architect Georges Chedanne, who was awarded the Prix de Rome in 1887.

Entirely made from cut stone, the building features superb high reliefs in which sculptors Boutry, Sicard and Gasq participated. High reliefs dedicated to motor racing, a relatively new sport at the time, gave the building an image of modernity and luxury, well suited to the neighbourhood where it was originally a hotel.

Today we admire the delicious details that are discreetly represented: women with hair flowing in the wind, protective helmets and glasses, a man repairing his car, the determined faces of intrepid drivers. It is a small moment of poetry.

STAIRCASE OF CONSEIL ÉCONOMIQUE ET SOCIAL HEADQUARTERS

A concrete masterpiece

Iéna Palace – Place d'Iéna
+33 1 44 43 63 27 – sed@lecese.fr
Closed for renovation until September 2028
Metro Iéna

Classified as a Historic Monument in 1993, Iéna Palace, which has been home to the Conseil Économique et Social (Economic and Social Council) since 1959, was built by the architect Auguste Perret (1854–1954). The palace was originally designed to house the Musée des Travaux Publics (Museum of Public Works, as part of the 1937 Exhibition) which opened its doors in 1939 in the wing on the place d'Iéna side but closed in 1954 due to lack of visitors.

Unknown to the general public, it nevertheless has a spectacular internal staircase that alone justifies making an appointment to see it. Note that in some cases you can visit Iéna Palace without an appointment to admire the staircase by asking at reception.

Although the staircase is actually massive, its apparent lightness is a great surprise. And thanks to very subtle architectural work, it even seems to float in the void.

The beautiful stair railings is the work of master ironworker Raymond Subes, who also designed the spectacular telescopic street lamps on Carrousel Bridge.

Auguste Perret is responsible for several other important buildings in Paris and the provinces, including the Mobilier National (13th arrondissement) (1934–36), building at 25 bis, rue Benjamin Franklin (16th arrondissement), Théâtre des Champs-Élysées (8th arrondissement), church Notre-Dame in Le Raincy, part of downtown Le Havre and the Perret tower in Amiens.

MOSAICS OF IÉNA PALACE

25

Hidden Masonic symbols

Iéna Palace – Place d'Iéna
Metro Iéna

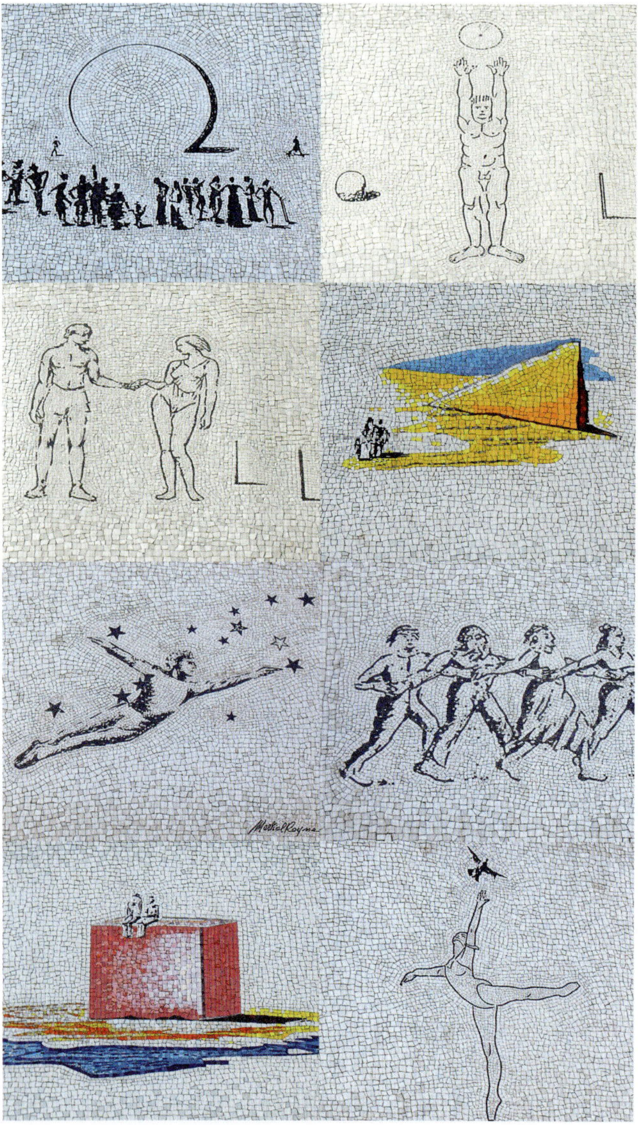

The Second World War having prevented their installation, it wasn't until 1992 that the frieze of Iéna Palace was decorated with 11 mosaics of Masonic inspiration. These were created by Italian painter and mosaic artist Luigi Guardigli following a design by the French artist and actor Martial Raysse. We observe the world (of initiates), the cut stone (of perfection), the pyramid (of initiation), the chain of union (or spiritual link that unites all the masons of the world) and the stages of life (initiatic): Apprentice grade (primary degree), Companion (secondary grade) and Master (ternary grade). Interestingly, in the official brochures none of this is mentioned and the different mosaics are supposed to represent the basic figures (triangle, circle, square), the first three digits (one, two, three), the essential values of the Republic (Liberty, Equality, Fraternity) and the constants of action (hope and work).

The number of mosaics, 11, represents Strength and Determination, also 5.5 + 5.5, the Kabbalistic number of a 5th-grade Perfect Master, whose symbol is the five-pointed star that represents a man, arms and legs apart, receptive to the universal influences of the five elements of nature (ether, air, fire, water, and earth).

NEARBY

Statue by Martial Raysse 

Iéna Palace – Place d'Iéna
Metro Iéna

In front of the mosaics stands a curious double statue named *Sol et Colombe ou la naissance de la pensée* (Sol and Colombe or the birth of thought), also by Raysse. Officially, the work represents 'the symbolic image of one of those young couples who, with each new generation, animate through the various trades the spirit of our country and ensure its sustainability and glory'. Still officially, we see a young man carrying the rod of justice and the sphere of knowledge, and a girl standing who, by showing the benefits of mosaics (see opposite), announces the future. The whole is mounted on a base of white pebbles representing an eight-pointed star. In practice, this sculpture is also eminently Masonic: the two figures are framed by the two columns that symbolise those of the ancient Temple of Solomon in Jerusalem (Joakin and Boaz), the woman symbolises Isis and the man Horus. He also looks at the statue of Washington, a high-ranking Freemason, standing a short distance away in place d'Iéna.

Remains of the old Hôtel de Ville and Tuileries Palace in Trocadéro Gardens ㉗

Metro Trocadéro

In the lower part of Trocadéro Gardens, on the Passy side, are some vestiges from the Hôtel de Ville (built by Domenico da Cortona for François I) and the Tuileries Palace (designed by Philibert Delorme for Catherine de Médicis). These were brought here after the two buildings had been destroyed by fires set at the end of the Commune in 1871.

> For further information on the remains of the Hôtel de Ville and the Tuileries, see page 285 and page 106.

NEARBY

The Garden of the Buddhist Pantheon ㉘

Annex to Guimet Museum
19, avenue d'Iéna
By appointment only
Tea ceremonies quarterly (see guimet.fr/fr/activites-visites)
Metro Iéna

Since 1991 the area behind the Buddhist Pantheon has been made over into a small Japanese garden. The small wooden tea pavilion regularly serves tea ceremonies carried out according to Japanese tradition – an exercise in social refinement that borders on the spiritual.

17th arrondissement

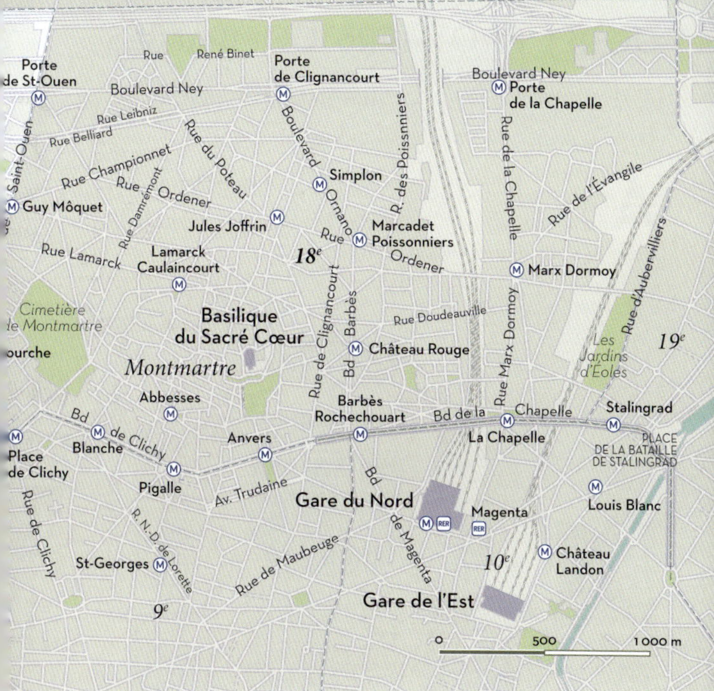

SAINT-OUEN
SAINT-DENIS
Porte
de St-Ouen
Rue René Binet
Porte
de Clignancourt
Boulevard Ney
Boulevard Ney
Porte
de la Chapelle
Rue Leibniz
Rue Belliard
Rue Saint-Ouen
Guy Môquet
Rue Championnet
Rue Damrémont
Rue Ordener
Rue du Poteau
Boulevard Ornano
Simplon
R. des Poissnniers
Rue de la Chapelle
Rue de l'Évangile
Rue d'Aubervilliers
Jules Joffrin
Rue
Marcadet
Poissonniers
18e
Ordener
Marx Dormoy
Rue Lamarck
Lamarck
Caulaincourt
Cimetière
de Montmartre
Basilique
du Sacré Cœur
Rue de Clignancourt
Bd Barbès
Rue Doudeauville
Château Rouge
Rue Marx Dormoy
19e
Les
Jardins
d'Éoles
ourche
Montmartre
Abbesses
Barbès
Rochechouart
Bd de la
Chapelle
Stalingrad
Bd
de Clichy
Blanche
Anvers
La Chapelle
PLACE
DE LA BATAILLE
DE STALINGRAD
Place
de Clichy
Pigalle
Av. Trudaine
Gare du Nord
Louis Blanc
Rue de Clichy
R. N. D. de Lorette
St-Georges
Rue de Maubeuge
Bd de Magenta
Magenta
10e
Château
Landon
9e
Gare de l'Est
0
500
1 000 m

FORMER HEADQUARTERS OF DOREL BROTHERS' COMPANIES

A remarkable little-known art deco façade

45, rue de Tocqueville – Metro Malesherbes

At 45, rue de Tocqueville stands a remarkable art deco façade, entirely covered with small tiles of stoneware enamelled in brown tones. It is decorated with polychrome mosaics of red, green and gold.

Architect Frédéric Bertrand (1869–1956), a student of Julien Guadet at the École Supérieure des Beaux-Arts in Paris, designed the building from 1921–23 for the family business, founded in 1900. Chemical engineers Félix Dorel and his brother developed printing processes that were the ancestors of photocopying.

The trademark procédés Dorel (Dorel processes) was registered and as indicated by the inscriptions that overhang the entrance grilles, the company specialised in the reproduction of drawings, maps, architectural plans, industrial and documentary photography, and in photomechanical impressions.

Offices and workshops occupied the first three floors, very well lit by large glass openings. The fourth and last floor was built in a second phase in 1938 to accommodate the Dorel family. It elegantly finishes the façade with a large bow window (oriel) protruding.

The mosaics are the work of Philippe and Georges Mazzioli, respectively the son and nephew of Giacomo Mazzioli, who participated in the creation of the mosaics of Opéra Garnier. This ornament emphasises with elegance and lightness the geometrical lines of the façade: two multicoloured strips line the second floor horizontally, thin red garlands frame the bays of the first floor, and blue and red spirals adjoin the bow window.

Finally, note in this art deco building the skilful integration of Art Nouveau with the scrolls of the railings placed in front of the bay windows.

The Dorel company ceased operations in the 1970s, and the building was converted into housing in 1998. A last renovation was carried out from 2008–09 without affecting the façade, which is protected.

LIBRARY OF
THE RUE LEGENDRE

A forgotten marvel

20, rue Legendre
Contact the association Concorde Les Amis de la Mission Catholique Polonaise,
on +33 1 55 35 32 26
Metro Malesherbes, Villiers or Monceau

The former restaurant Polonia contains a small gem, which the current managers are happy to show to visitors: on the fourth floor of this old city mansion is a wonderful library which the Polish association Concorde (which now runs the place) had restored in 2003.

The lift is broken and the stairs are steep, but you will not regret making the effort. Originally, the room must have housed an old chapel, which was then taken over by a Masonic lodge.

Nowadays, the books have gone, but what remains is this superb neo-Gothic interior: carved wood, paintings, coffered ceiling and a remarkable fireplace. In a corner sits a piano, waiting to be played.

NEARBY
Villa des Ternes ③

96, avenue des Ternes
39, rue de Guersant
Metro Porte Maillot

This magnificent housing development comprises a number of small avenues leading to wonderful private properties nestling in their own gardens: Avenues de la Chapelle, des Arts, Yves du Manoir, des Pavillons and de Verzy. No.1 bis, avenue de Verzy and No.13, avenue Yves du Manoir are, however, subsidised public housing, built in spite of the strenuous efforts of the other residents. Even these new additions have their own air of luxury, as the architects (B. Bourgade and M. Londinsky) have laid out the steps and pitched roofs in such a way that each apartment appears to be a small detached house. The architect of 10, avenue Yves du Manoir strove to copy the Palace of Darius at Susa. A high relief is all that is left.

SAINT-FERDINAND ROYAL CHAPEL

A travelling chapel

Church of Notre-Dame de la Compassion – 2, boulevard d'Aurelle de Paladines
+33 1 45 74 83 31 – paroissecompassion.fr
Daily 9am–5pm
Metro or RER Porte Maillot

Squashed between the ring road and the Hyatt Regency Paris Étoile Hôtel, the Chapelle Royale Saint-Ferdinand is rather unusually located for a church. So it may come as no surprise to learn that this royal

mausoleum, consecrated in 1843, no longer stands where it was first built (the original site now being occupied by the Palais des Congrès).

The chapel was built as a memorial to the duc d'Orléans, Ferdinand-Philippe, the eldest son of Louis-Philippe, who died in 1842 at the age of 32 when the horses of his carriage bolted and he was thrown violently to the ground. It was moved here in 1968 when work began on the Palais des Congrès complex. The reassembly stone by stone took two years in all, and though the chapel is incongruous here, it has not lost everything in the move: it now has a parish crypt laid out in Greek-cross plan and designed in an attractively eclectic style.

The stained glass in the original chapel was the work of the architects Fontaine and Lefranc, to cartoons by Ingres. One intriguing detail is that the faces of all saints here were clearly inspired by members of the royal family – St Louis, for example, looks remarkably like Louis-Philippe.

When saints take the faces of real characters ...

Juicy detail: the faces of the saints depicted were strongly inspired by members of the royal family. You'll recognise, for example, King Louis-Philippe who took the features of his patron saint ...

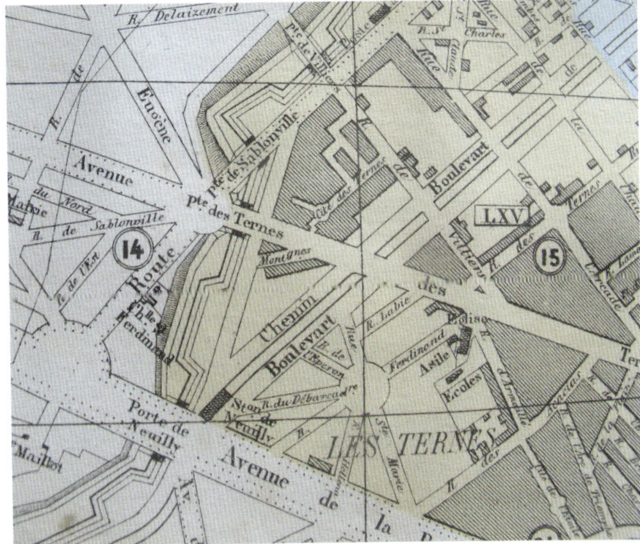

Map from 1860 showing the former site of the chapel

THE FLOWER TOWER IN HAUTS-DE-MALESHERBES GARDENS ⑤

Flower power

8, rue Stéphane Grappelli and 23, rue Albert Roussel
Metro Wagram

Occupying what was wasteland attached to the Gare Saint-Lazare, the Hauts-de-Malesherbes gardens were opened in March 2005. The project coordinator was the famous architect Christian de Portzamparc, and among the various astonishing features of this contemporary addition to Paris perhaps the most surprising is what looks like a building of plants, the Flower Tower.

The work of architect Édouard François and botanist Patrick Blanc, each side of the structure is covered with large white plant holders over-flowing with greenery and shrubs, creating the very real impression of the building being one huge flower.

NEARBY

Vestige of a wall section of the Thiers enclosure   ⑥

Metro Wagram

Facing the Flower Tower building, the garden opens onto a section of wall of the old enclosure of Thiers (see page 411).

Geography of Parisian theatres

A number of Paris theatres – Théâtre des Bouffes-du-Nord, Théâtre de l'Atelier, Théâtre Hébertot, l'Européen, etc. – all lie to the north of the Grands Boulevards. This is due to the fact that this side of the boulevards lay outside the Fermiers Généraux city walls (the outline of which is, roughly, that of lines 2 and 6 of the Paris metro; see page 468).

Beyond that barrier, theatres were classified as 'provincial' and thus they had the right to put on the plays mounted by the 'city' theatres just 40 days after their 'première'. Their location at the very gates of the city meant, however, that these theatres could attract larger audiences, and thus choose among the very best of the provincial actors, who saw such places as a springboard to work on the Paris stage.

To the south of Paris, the same logic explains the location of the Théâtre du Ranelagh and the Gaîté-Montparnasse.

The Paris area

For military or commercial purposes, over the course of its history Paris has been surrounded by seven successive enclosures. Some of these fortifications have left physical traces, others are suggested in the arrangement of the streets, but all have made their mark:
– Gallo-Roman enclosure (4th century) (see page 119)
– 10th century and 11th century enclosure (see map)
– Philip Augustus enclosure (1190–1215) (see map)
– Charles V (1356–1420) enclosure (see page 76)
– Fossés Jaunes (Yellow Ditches) enclosure (1543–1640) (see page 76)
– Mur des Fermiers Généraux (Wall of the Tax Farmers General) enclosure (1785–90) (see map)
– Thiers enclosure (1840). The map below shows their successive locations.

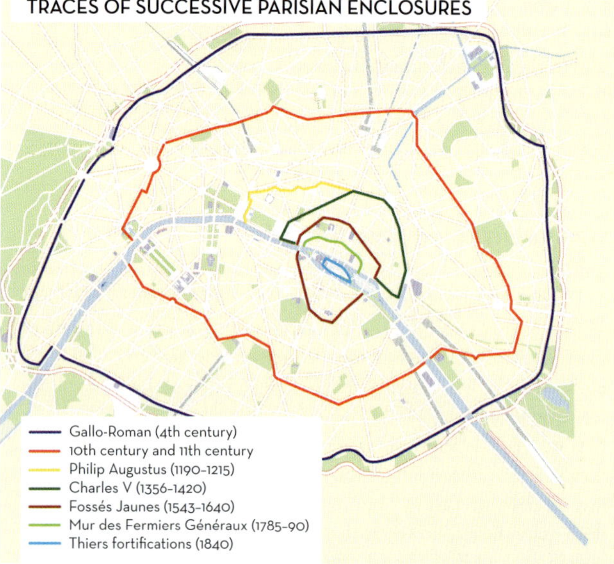

The elevated railways: course of the Fermiers Généraux city walls

The course of the Fermiers Généraux city walls is now followed almost exactly by lines 2 and 6 of the Paris metro. This is particularly clear in the elevated railway sections of these lines: between Barbès and Belleville (line 2) and Pasteur and Passy (line 6).

The Ledoux Rotundas

In the 18th century, the inhabitants of Paris paid an *octroi* (duty) on consumer products entering the city – everything from wine and meat to hay and wood – while in the countryside there was a *taille*, a tax on land itself. With the increased urban development of the city and its faubourgs, the fiscal limits between these two areas of taxation became more difficult to establish, and fraud was common. For this reason, the Fermiers Généraux, farmers who had either paid for or been granted the right to collect taxes, proposed that the city be enclosed within a new wall. In 1785 Louis XVI ordered the construction of this tax barrier and the redefinition of fiscal territories. The architectural aspects of the new plan were entrusted to the royal architect, Nicholas Ledoux. Stretching more than 24 km, the new walls enclosed an area of 3,400 hectares with 600,000 inhabitants. The sixth ring of walls to be built in Parisian history, the new structure was to be 3-metres-high and 1-metre-thick, with an interior ring road 12-metres-wide. The ban on construction outside the walls extended for 100 metres, though there was a 30-metre boulevard planted with trees. Taxes and duties were collected at 55 entrance 'barriers', 24 of which were complete with accommodation for customs officers. For the scheme, Nicholas Ledoux drew his inspiration from classical architecture, producing structures of an opulence that bore little relation to their function. The magnificence of this scheme – plus the high cost of the land expropriated – meant that by 1787 the initial budget had been wildly exceeded. Still, despite the Revolution and the destruction it brought, the wall was completed and was fully operational by 1790. But there was widespread and violent opposition to it. Furthermore, the structure proved incapable of ending the high levels of tax fraud (still around 20%), so on 1 May 1791 the National Assembly voted to abolish the octroi duties and the institution of the Fermiers Généraux. Due to the financial problems faced by the City of Paris, such duties were however reintroduced in 1798. In 1860, the collection points were moved to the entrances of the new fortifications that had been built in 1840. The barriers built by Ledoux were demolished: the barrière de Chartres (now in Parc Monceau), de La Villette, du Trône (at Nation) and d'Enfer (place Denfert-Rochereau). Duties on goods entering the city were not totally abolished until 1943.

La Villette Rotunda

STAR OCTAHEDRON ON ANDRÉ BRETON'S TOMB

An ode to women, source of life and wisdom

Batignolles cemetery
Division 31, row 12, tomb 18, slab in centre of square
8, rue Saint-Just
16 March–5 November, 8am–6pm; 6 November–15 March, 8am–5.30pm;
Saturdays from 8.30am; Sundays and public holidays from 9am
Metro Porte de Clichy

At Batignolles cemetery, the tomb of André Breton (1896–1966), poet and founder of Surrealism, is simply decorated with a curious star octahedron and a short epitaph: *JE CHERCHE L'OR DU TEMPS* (I SEEK THE GOLD OF TIME), taken from his *Introduction au discours sur le peu de réalité* (Introduction to the Discourse on the Paucity of Reality), a text written in 1924.

This octahedron recalls an object that Breton found in August 1966 at Domme in the Dordogne, shortly before the end of his life. He saw a link with the star-filled Hermetic castle in the suburbs of Prague, which he mentioned in *L'Amour fou* (Mad Love): 'On the side of an abyss built from philosopher's stone, the star-filled castle opens up.' The star is a recurring theme in Breton's book Arcane 17 (1944–47), which dealt with the Tarot card of the same name, also called 'star', showing Aquarius with eight stars above, almost all with eight branches, like the star octahedron that Breton found.

Like his other work *Prolegomènes à un troisième manifeste du surréalisme ou non*, Arcane 17 represents, against the background of the Second World War, the search for a new myth, that of the celebration of women that Breton calls on governments to pass on. The figure of Aquarius shows a Virgin pouring the water of universal life, above which shines the star of the philosophers', the compass of 'the gold of time' which Breton seeks on his grave.

While the star octahedron recalls the woman as a source of life and wisdom, it is also one of the five solids of Plato, or perfect solids (hexahedron, icosahedron, tetrahedron, octahedron and dodecahedron). According to this ancient traditional philosophy (see the following double-page spread), the octahedron is in affinity with the air element and the planet Saturn, itself associated with Chronos, the primordial deity of time in the Orphic traditions: the octahedron is therefore very judiciously placed on Breton's grave, the cemetery and tomb being a perfect reminder of time that passes inevitably.

In several works Breton showed his attraction to the Hermetic works of alchemist Fulcanelli, whether in the *Second Manifeste du surréalisme* (Second Manifesto of Surrealism) or in the essays *La lampe dans l'horloge* (The Lamp in the Clock) and *Fronton rouge* (a French red wine).

For more on the origin and meaning of Plato's five solids, see the following double-page spread.

The five basic solids and sacred geometry

Sacred geometry is a worldview according to which the basic criteria for existence are perceived as being sacred.

Through them can be contemplated the *Magnum Mysterium*, the Universal *Grand Project*, by learning its laws, principles and the inter-relationships of shapes.

These universal shapes are systematised in a geometric complex in which each figure has its own mathematical and philosophical interpretation.

They are applied in projects of *sacred architecture* and *sacred art*, which always use the 'divine' proportions in which Man reflects the Universe, and vice versa. It is a common belief that *sacred geometry* and its mathematical relationships, which are harmonic and proportional, are also found in Music, Light and Cosmology.

Man first discovered this system of values in prehistoric times, in the megalithic and Neolithic cultures, for example, and some consider it to be a universal facet of the human condition.

Sacred geometry is fundamental to the construction of sacred structures, such as synagogues, churches and mosques, and also plays a role in creating the interior sacred space of temples, through the altars and tabernacles.

Passed down from Greco-Egyptian culture and exported to ancient Rome, *sacred geometry* in the European Middle Ages inspired the creation of Roman and Gothic architecture of Europe's medieval cathedrals, which incorporate this geometry of sacred symbolism.

It is said that Pythagoras (Samos, c. 570 BCE – Metapontum, c. 497 BCE) was the one who founded the system of *sacred geometry* in his school in Croton, Greece.

This Greek philosopher and mathematician is believed to have brought the knowledge he acquired in Egypt and India back to Greece.

Using the golden ratio (1.618) and applying it to the geometric forms of the five basic solids, Pythagoras created the mathematical method universally known as *Pythagorean geometry*.

To create the five solids (the tetrahedron or pyramid, the hexahedron or cube, the octahedron, the dodecahedron and the icosahedron), about which Plato would later philosophise (to such a point that they would become known as the *five Platonic solids*), Pythagoras was inspired by the Greek myth about the child-god Dionysus' toys: a basket, dice, top, ball and mirror.

On a cosmic level, the basket represents the Universe; the *dice*, the *five Platonic solids* symbolising the natural elements (ether, air, fire, water, earth); the *top* is the atom of matter; the *ball*, the Earth's globe; and, finally, the *mirror* reflects the work of the Supreme Geometrist (*Dionysus*), which itself is the universal manifestation of Life and Consciousness, of God towards Man and vice versa. Each of the five Platonic solids also represents a planetary energy that is connected by its form to a natural element.

Thus, the *dodecahedron* is traditionally linked to Venus and ether, the natural quintessence, expressed by a temple's dome.

The *octahedron*, linked to Saturn and the air, represents the transept's cross.

The *tetrahedron*, linked to Mars and fire, is symbolised by the openings in the temple through which light gushes forth.

The *icosahedron*, linked to the Moon and water, establishes the harmony of forms in the temple design, defining the connecting lines between the altars and columns.

Finally, the *hexahedron* (cube), fixes the Sun to its element, the Earth, by determining the shape of the temple's foundation or floor.

The main purpose of *sacred geometry* is thus to create Universal Perfection through perfect mathematical forms and calculations, and, by using *sacred architecture*, to connect the Multiple to the Single in a space that is geometrically dedicated to this end.

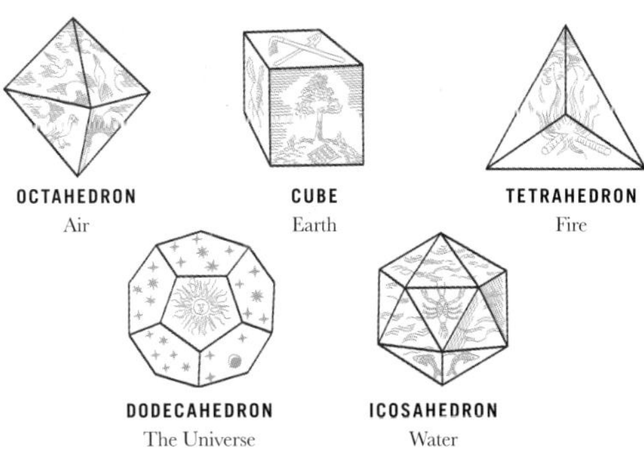

OCTAHEDRON
Air

CUBE
Earth

TETRAHEDRON
Fire

DODECAHEDRON
The Universe

ICOSAHEDRON
Water

CITÉ DES FLEURS

Each of the original owners was required to plant three flowering trees

Start 154, avenue de Clichy / 1, rue Guy Môquet
End 59, rue de La Jonquière / 8, rue Saint-Just
Metro Brochant or RER Porte de Clichy

The Cité des Fleurs (City of Flowers) is a particularly pastoral, 320-metre-long private street accessible to the public 7am–7pm Monday to Saturday and 7am–1pm Sunday and public holidays. Laid out in 1847 by Jean-Edmé Lhenry and Adolphe Bacqueville de La Vasserie, two property owners who combined their land, the Cité des Fleurs is one of the finest examples of a rural atmosphere within the capital. As the development was near the Goüin factory manufacturers of locomotives and spinning machines, well-off engineers from these factories were soon building homes there.

The contracts that led to its creation between 1847 and 1850 were particularly detailed and still serve as a reference for present-day owners, who undertake to follow a number of obligations relating to various factors such as the alignment of façades, how many floors could be built, the height of connecting walls, the layout of courtyards and gardens, the trees growing there (originally three different fruit trees had to be planted, now well developed) or the presence of supporting walls for fencing, flanked by pilasters topped with a unique model of a Medici vase …

NEARBY

Cour Saint-Pierre and Cité Lemercier ⑨
47, avenue de Clichy and 28, rue Lemercier – Metro La Fourche

Two private streets, but open to the casual stroller. Both of them share

a pleasantly provincial atmosphere that seems to date from another era. Cour Saint-Pierre is made up of two-storey buildings perfectly aligned on either side of the cobbled street, each one lovingly adorned with flowers and plants by the residents. Cité Lemercier is made up of detached houses, each standing in its own garden. Jacques Brel himself succumbed to the charm of the place, living for a time at Hôtel du Chalet.

Square Nicolay ⑩
77 bis, rue Legendre
Metro Pont Cardinet

A private square with a very attractive interior garden, visible through the railings. The other side of the square gives onto rue des Moines.

Museum of the Grande Loge de France ⑪
8, rue de Puteaux
gldf.org
Guided visits: Wednesday 11am–12.30pm and 2pm–3.30pm,
Friday 2pm–3.30pm, by appointment
Admission free
Metro Rome

For an introduction to Freemasonry: two temples and a library that houses some 100,000 works on the subject of Freemasonry, the esoteric and the paranormal.

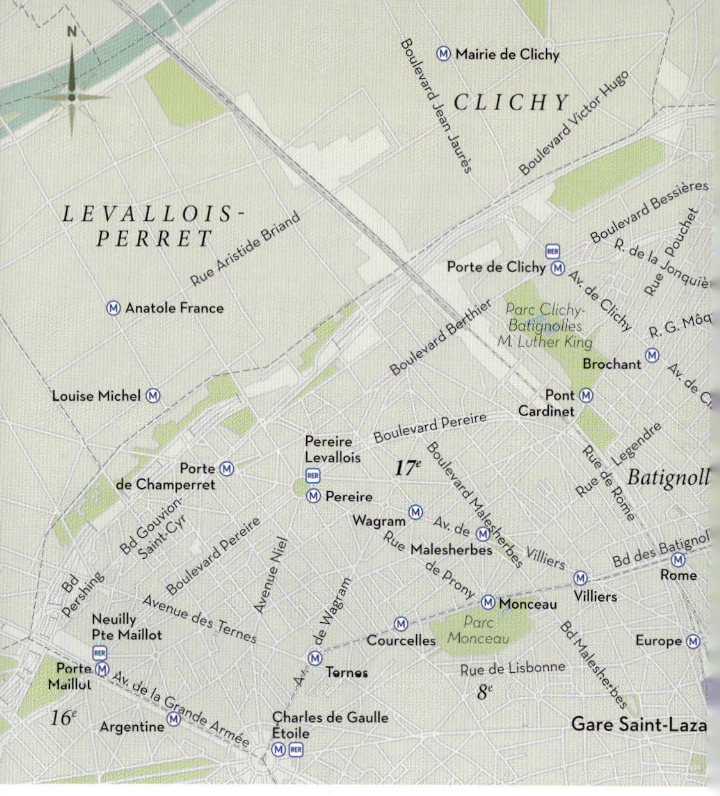

18th arrondissement

SAINT-OUEN
SAINT-DENIS
Porte de St-Ouen
Rue René Binet
Porte de Clignancourt
Boulevard Ney
Porte de la Chapelle
Boulevard Ney
Rue Leibniz
Rue Belliard
Rue Championnet
Rue du Poteau
Guy Môquet
Rue Damrémont
Rue Ordener
Simplon
Marcadet Poissonniers
Rue de la Chapelle
Rue de l'Évangile
Rue d'Aubervilliers
Jules Joffrin
Rue Ornano
Rue Ordener
Lamarck Caulaincourt
Rue Lamarck
18e
R. des Poissonniers
Marx Dormoy
Cimetière de Montmartre
Fourche
Montmartre
Basilique du Sacré Cœur
Rue de Clignancourt
Bd Barbès
Rue Doudeauville
Château Rouge
Rue Marx Dormoy
Les Jardins d'Éoles
19e
Stalingrad
Abbesses
Anvers
Bd de la Chapelle
La Chapelle
PLACE DE LA BATAILLE DE STALINGRAD
Blanche
Bd de Clichy
Place de Clichy
Pigalle
Barbès Rochechouart
Louis Blanc
Av. Trudaine
Gare du Nord
Magenta
Château Landon
Rue de Clichy
R. N.-D. de Lorette
St-Georges
Rue de Maubeuge
Bd de Magenta
10e
Gare de l'Est
9e
0   500   1 000 m

SRI MANIKA VINAYAKAR ALAYAM HINDU TEMPLE ①

Hinduism in the heart of Paris

17, rue Pajol
+33 1 40 34 21 89
templeganesh.fr
srimanicka@yahoo.fr
Admission free 8.30am–8pm – three poojas a day
Metro Marx Dormoy, La Chapelle or Gare du Nord

No need to take a plane to travel to exotic places: in Paris, a simple metro ticket gives the chance to experience the extraordinary and complex rituals of the Hindu religion.

Dedicated to the god Ganesh, the elephant-headed son of Shiva, this is the only Hindu temple in the city. It was founded in 1985 thanks to the determination of one man, Mr Sanderasekaram, who on his arrival here noticed that within the uprooted and scattered Hindu community of France (which numbers more than 100,000) religious worship was limited to small domestic altars within individual households.

Like other members of his family (see below) Mr Sanderasekaram founded a temple – Sri Manika Vinayakar Alayam – which quickly became a central gathering point for the Sri Lankan Tamil community.

Though now too small to house the whole congregation, the temple still offers a remarkable welcome to outsiders. A vegetarian meal is generously served to all of those present at the ceremonies on Saturday and Sunday.

Temple-building seems to run in the Sanderasekaram family. The father had a temple and statue to Ganesh raised in Jaffna (northern Sri Lanka), while his brother did the same in London and his niece in Australia.

The *pooja* is a ritual that each Hindu performs in the morning after having washed and dressed but before eating. Though there are individual variations, the ritual basically involves the chanting of a special mantra and the offering of food and drink to specific deities. The rite of *abhishekam* is basically a bathing ceremony. The statue of the deity is undressed, sprinkled with water, then with milk, honey, rose water and curdled milk in order to purify it. Once its robes have been replaced, a garland of flowers is placed on the statue, while priests (*pujaris*) chant mantras.

Villa Poissonnière ②

41, rue Polonceau and 42, rue de la Goutte-d'Or
Metro Château Rouge or Barbès-Rochechouart

In the middle of the Goutte-d'Or district stands the Villa Poissonnière development. Built in 1840, this pretty cobbled street is lined by small houses standing in their own gardens. Entrance is by an almost hidden *porte cochère* (carriage entrance) that gives onto rue de la Goutte-d'Or; the rue Polonceau entrance is often closed.

SHOP KATA

A shoe store in an old cinema

34, boulevard Barbès and 9, rue des Poissonniers
Monday–Saturday 10.30am–7pm
Metro Barbès-Rochechouart or Château Rouge

From outside, nothing suggests the Kata shoe store at 34, boulevard Barbès has been housed since 1988 in an amazing old theatre-like cinema.

Built in 1914, the former *Barbès Palace* is not so pretty as the nearby *Louxor* in Barbès-Rochechouart, but its Louis XVI-style decoration has been preserved. The room has kept its fluted columns crowned with Ionic capitals and masks and the old stage is still closed by a red curtain, which dominates a head covered with a lyre. A unique but major difference with its beginnings (in January 1922, it was screened *L'Assommoir*) today is the low-end shoes sold there, in an improbable clash of cultures and times.

An advantage of the location is that it can be used as a shortcut to reach boulevard Barbès from rue des Poissonniers (or vice versa); the store has two separate entrances, which is ideal to avoid undesirables.

VILLA DES PLATANES

In the shade of flowering plane trees

58, boulevard de Clichy
Metro Blanche or Pigalle

Boulevard de Clichy is not only sex shops; there are also some pleasant surprises here. Unfortunately, Villa des Platanes (at No. 58) is shut away behind a wrought-iron gate. Still, if one of the residents is leaving, you might be lucky enough to see more than can be glimpsed through the railings. Built in 1896 by the architect Deloeuvre, the development is laid out around two courtyards, which are entered by passing through a passageway with a coffered roof. A fine spiral staircase in the first courtyard leads up to the second, where the buildings are distributed around a wonderfully quiet garden.

NEARBY
Cité du Midi

48, boulevard de Clichy – Metro Blanche or Pigalle
A few yards away from the Villa des Platanes is another oasis of quiet that can make you forget all about the bustling boulevard and its shops. One can still see the white ceramic façade of the old Pigalle public baths.

7, impasse Marie Blanche

Metro Blanche
Tucked between 19, rue Cauchois and 9, rue Constance, this charming cul-de-sac contains a very surprising house. Built in 1835, the house at 7, impasse Marie Blanche has a pink, medieval-style façade, complete with a machicolated tower and half-timbering.

Foundation of the Jesuits in Montmartre

On 15 August 1534, Ignatius of Loyola – together with Francis Xavier and five other companions – went to the Chapel of the Martyrium, located on what was supposed to have been the site of St Denis's martyrdom. During a mass celebrated in the crypt, at the moment of Holy Communion they pronounced vows of poverty and chastity, dedicating themselves to the welfare of souls. This was the beginning of the Society of Jesus, which would become more famous under the name of the Jesuits. The chapel was destroyed during the Revolution, but then rebuilt on what was supposed to have been its original site at 11, rue Yvonne le Tac.

Cocteau Light Fittings

The Cinema Studio 28, which opened at 10, rue Tholozé in 1928, is the oldest cinema in Paris that is still in operation. The light fittings in the main cinema were designed by Jean Cocteau.

CERAMIC DECORATION AT 43 BIS, RUE DAMRÉMONT

Wonderful panels in Montmartre

Building accessible Monday–Friday 9am–6.30pm
Keypad-operated gate closed at weekends and public holidays
Metro Lamarck-Caulaincourt

Built in 1910 by Coinchon, these former public baths have an entrance adorned with twelve wonderful faïence panels separated by marble columns; these depict various children's games (with so many details that precise streets of Montmartre can be identified) along with a beautiful aquatic scene. Mainly the work of Francisque Poulbot, whose name was given to the 'poulbots', as poor children in Montmartre were called, these mosaics date from 1910 and are now listed as historic monuments.

© Pauline Le Goff

NEARBY

Les Fusains ⑧
22, rue de Tourlaque – Metro Lamarck-Caulaincourt

Unfortunately – because of the theft of some statues from the interior garden – this has for some years been shut. Undoubtedly the most attractive of all the city's various housing/studio developments for artists, Les Fusains was constructed using material salvaged from the 1889 Universal Exposition. Residents have included artists such as Renoir and Derain.

© Pauline Le Goff

Ceramic decoration at 59, rue Caulaincourt ⑨
Metro Lamarck-Caulaincourt

The entrance to this private building is decorated with fine ceramics of young female figures: one is shown at the seaside, another among vines, and yet others holding a watering can or an umbrella. Beyond the entrance is an attractive little garden.

AMIRAUX SWIMMING POOL

A pyramid of subsidised housing, containing a swimming pool

6, rue Hermann-Lachapelle and 13, rue des Amiraux
Horaires consultables sur internet :
paris.fr/equipements/piscine-des-amiraux-2944
Metro Simplon or Marcadet-Poissonniers

The Amiraux swimming pool is a perfect example of the "hygienist" notions behind subsidised public housing at the beginning of the 20th century. Built as part of a public-housing scheme commissioned by the City Council's HBM (Office of Affordable Housing), the structure was designed by the architect Henri Sauvage. Seven storeys high, the building itself is a pyramid of stepped terraces, which means that each apartment enjoys natural light and has a garden balcony.

The architect had initially intended that the centre of the pyramid be occupied by a cinema, but the city council opted instead for a swimming pool.

Work began in 1922, and the first tenants began to move in 1925; the swimming pool itself opened in 1930. The facility has been renovated several times and is now a listed building.

The pool measures 33 by 10 metres and has two levels of walkways leading to the individual changing-rooms. Inside and outside, the walls are faced with the same white ceramic tiles as used in the Metro, which adds to the "Old Paris" feel of the place; the slightly retro atmosphere here was exploited by the filmmaker Jean-Pierre Jeunet when he chose Amiraux swimming pool as the setting for a scene in his film *Le Fabuleux destin d'Amélie Poulain*.

In the 6th arrondissement (rue Vavin) is another building by Henri Sauvage which uses the same principle of tiered terraces.

A mass in Aramaic, the language Christ spoke

Every Sunday at 11am, the Chaldean Mission (13–15, rue Pajol) celebrates a mass in Aramaic, the language Christ spoke. The Chaldean Catholic rite dates back to 16th century Turkey.

For information: +33 1 42 09 55 07.

NEARBY

Montmartre aux Artistes ⑯

187–189, rue Ordener

Metro Guy Môquet

With its 184 studios, Montmartre aux Artistes is the largest community of artists in Europe. It dates back to the first half of the 20th century and was the idea of Louis Lejeune (1884–1969), winner of the Prix de Rome for sculpture in 1911. The first residents began to move in in 1933, when the project was far from completed. Access to the area is relatively easy, and you can stroll among the various structures. The studios themselves, however, are not open to the public.

NEARBY

Mosaics in the rue Ramey fishmonger's ⑫
Metro Château Rouge

The fishmonger at the corner of rue Ramey and rue du Baigneur is decorated with fine mosaics which, appropriately enough, depict a fishing scene.

An uncultivated garden at Saint-Vincent ⑬
17, rue Saint-Vincent – RER or Metro Gare du Nord
Guided visits during spring and summer – visitesnature@paris.fr

For a long time this site of 1,500 m² was just wasteland, gradually becoming overgrown with weeds and shrubs that then attracted various kinds of wildlife. The landscape architects of Paris City Council saw this as a perfect opportunity to maintain rare examples of flora and fauna within the very heart of Montmartre. To preserve the biodiversity here, they simply consolidated the sloping terrain, created a small pond and laid out a path for strollers to visit the garden without causing any damage. The result is wonderful.

Courtyard at 11 bis, rue du Mont-Cenis ⑭
Metro Lamarck-Caulaincourt

The presence of an estate agent's office at the end of the passage explains why the gate to this charming courtyard is open on weekdays during office hours. At the far end stands a delightful well. The gate to the passage bears the coat of arms of the Lécuyer family, one of the oldest families on Montmartre Hill.

The real origin of the word 'bistro'

The plaque on the façade of the restaurant La Mère Catherine in place du Tertre, Montmartre, gives an often-repeated explanation of the origin of the word 'bistro': "On 30 March 1814 the Cossacks shouted their famous 'bistro', and thus on the hill of Montmartre was created a worthy ancestor to our own bistros. 180th Anniversary. The Old Montmartre Association." True, 'bistro' does mean "quick, fast" in Russian, but the story of impatient Cossacks ordering their drinks appears to be nothing other than a pleasant anecdote; the real origin of the word seems to be local slang.

Saint Denis and street names in Montmartre

Halfway along rue Girardon a plaque recalls the legend that, after being decapitated upon the hill that would subsequently be known as Mont des Martyres (Hill of Martyrs), St Denis picked up his head and then walked to the spot where he would actually be buried, some 8 kilometres away (the site of the basilica that bears his name). A little further up, not far from place du Tertre, rue Rustique and rue Saint-Éleuthère are named after the two deacons who preached Christianity alongside St Denis.

A cemetery that opens one day a year

2, rue Mont-Cenis
Open on the parish feast day in June
Metro Abbesses

Built in 1833 at the behest of the parish priest, Abbé Ottin, the Montmartre Calvary is a Via Crucis that commemorates Christ's Passion. It is one of the most unusual – and secret – places in the city and has a total of nine Stations of the Cross together with an artificial grotto that serves as the Holy Sepulchre (the tomb from which Christ emerged at his resurrection). Despite the indulgences granted by the pope, the Calvary did not attract many pilgrims and the abbé had to abandon religious services here. The construction of the Church of Sacré-Coeur later ate into the site, and two of the Stations of the Cross had to be moved.

NEARBY

Calvaire cemetery 
2, rue Mont-Cenis – Metro Abbesses
Open on All Saints' Day (1 November) and during 'Journées du Patrimoine'
(Heritage Days) and Gardens Days (please contact the Montmartre Cemetery
Management Office on +33 1 53 42 36 30)
Located alongside the Montmartre church of Saint-Pierre, this is the most unusual cemetery in Paris; it is only open on All Saints' Day. The cemetery owes its name to the fact that it stands alongside a 'Calvary' erected in 1833 around the church of Saint-Pierre which it served (see below). It was laid out in 1801 to replace an earlier cemetery that had been destroyed during the Revolution (taking the date of the creation of a cemetery to be that of the first individual tombs and not of unmarked graves on the site, that first cemetery dated from 1688). Though opened three years before Père-Lachaise, this is not – as many believe – the oldest cemetery in Paris; the cemetery of the Portuguese Jewish community in the 19th arrondissement dates from 1780 (see page 496).
Following the creation of the Saint-Vincent cemetery, the Calvaire cemetery was closed temporarily in 1823, then finally in 1831 (there were some burials here in 1828, 1830 and 1831). Now it contains a total of 85 very simple tombs, death apparently erasing all differences between the aristocrats of Bas-Montmartre (the present 11th arrondissement) and the humble families of Haut-Montmartre. One of the famous figures buried here is the navigator Bougainville. Contrary to legend, d'Artagnan is not buried here; Pigalle, the sculptor, was buried here but his tomb was another victim of the Revolution.

Columns of the Temple of Mars 
Metro Abbesses
In the church Saint-Pierre de Montmartre (2, rue du Mont-Cenis), four marble columns are thought to come from the Temple of Mars that stood here almost 2,000 years ago.

Far from the Madding Crowd: Strolling in Montmartre

While the summit itself can be unbearable when swarming with tourists, there is a more picturesque part of the hill which is still spared invasion by the crowds. Let us start at the charming metro station of Lamarck-Caulaincourt, from which steps lead up to avenue Junot, one of the finest in Paris.

At No. 15 is the house that the Austrian architect Adolf Loos (1870–1933) built in 1926 for the Dadaist poet Tristan Tzara; it is a perfect expression of the architect's abhorrence of all forms of ornamental decoration.

At No. 23, Villa Léandre is named after the local humorist, Charles Léandre; the low, Anglo-Norman-style brick houses are covered in climbing vines and the whole place is wonderfully charming.

Note the door of No. 4 at the end, which is inspired by the sails of a windmill, once a common feature on the hill of Montmartre.

At 21, avenue Junot, passage Lepic-Junot (sometimes referred to as passage de la Sorcière) cuts right through the heart of the 'maquis de Montmartre' (the scrubland that once occupied this site). A large stone still juts out right in the middle of the road; there is also a 'pétanque' court. This is reserved for members, but a polite request will get you something to drink at the bar, which you can then sip while enjoying the spectacle of a game of 'boules'. From the passage, turn left into rue Lepic. Almost immediately on your left you will catch sight of La Galette windmill, which is one of the last two in Paris.

Walking up the avenue on your left, you are back in avenue Junot, where No. 1 is one of the finest private residences in Paris. Until a few years ago, the presence here of the 'mire du Nord', a listed monument (see page 409), meant that you could gain access to this fantastic place of climbing vines, where rabbits scurry around at the foot of La Galette windmill. The small theatre in front of the entrance to the house has two-seater sofas for couples ...

A little further on, at 11, avenue Junot, you can peek into the Hameau des Artistes that links the avenue to rue Lepic (No. 75); the keypad-operated gate is generally closed. Retracing your steps to the beginning of avenue Junot, you come to place Marcel Aymé, which has an amusing statue of a man walking through a wall; this was placed here in homage to Marcel Aymé's novel *Le passe-muraille*, about a man who could do just that. Going down rue de l'Abreuvoir, on the right is a large uncultivated garden that serves as the setting for a few houses and artists' studios. This is a sort of Villa Medici within Paris itself: for very modest rents, foreign artists can have the use of studios of 60 m² to 100 m² for an entire year.

The place is not open to the public. Slightly further down is place Dalida, with superb views towards Sacré-Cœur – probably the most picturesque view in Paris. If you want the statue of the famous singer to acquire the smooth patina of Juliet's statue in Verona, then you are advised to briefly fondle her shapely breasts before turning right, up towards the vines. The metro station is close by.

The doors of 45, rue Lepic open unexpectedly onto an inner street with the workshops of artists and craft workers.

Mitterrand's lamp posts

Until May 1987, the date of the artist's death, François Mitterrand and Dalida cultivated a relationship whose setting was the Parisian villa of the singer, La Chaussette, rue d'Orchampt. They say that Mitterrand sometimes went there alone at night, so the security services insisted that streetlights be installed. This is how rue d'Orchampt got its first public lighting.

© Andrea Garcia

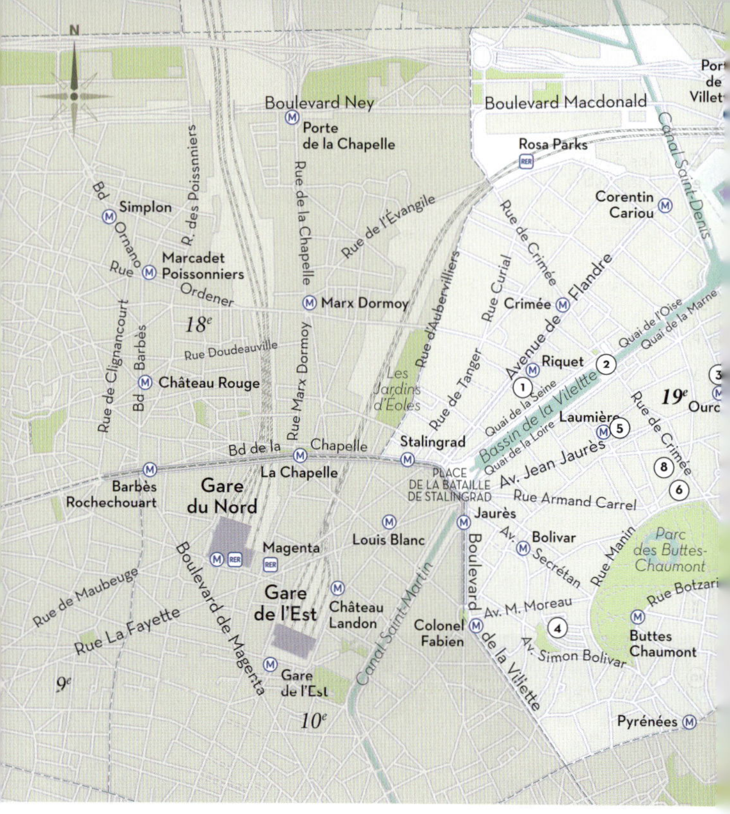

19th arrondissement

BOBIGNY
PANTIN
Pantin
RER
Canal de l'Ourcq
Cité des Sciences
et de l'Industrie
Bobigny – Pantin
Raymond Queneau
M
Parc
de la Villette
Église de Pantin
Philarmonie
de Paris
Avenue Jean Lolive
M
Porte
de Pantin
Hoche
M
Bd Sérurier
Av. Jean Jaurès
M
Rue Jules Auffret
Rue Manin
Bd Sérurier
Bd d'Algérie
LE PRÉ-
ST-GERVAIS
LES LILAS
ue David
7
M
Danube
d'Angers
Serge
Gainsbourg
M
Rue de Mouzaïa
M
Pré-St-Gervais
Mairie des Lilas
M
Botzaris
Bd Sérurier
R. de Paris
Crimée
PLACE
DES FÊTES
9
M
Place des Fêtes
11
Porte des Lilas
M
Avenue Pasteur
10
Rue de Belleville
M
Télégraphe
Bd Mortier
M
Jourdain
20e
0
500
1 000 m

PORTUGUESE JEWISH CEMETERY ①

A cemetery among the low-income housing blocks

44, avenue de Flandre
Consistoire Israélite de France: 17, rue Saint-Georges
Metro Notre-Dame de Lorette
Jacques B'Chiri: +33 1 40 82 26 90 – +33 6 09 21 15 04
Metro Stalingrad or Riquet

I f it was not for the discreet historical information sign, nothing would indicate that behind the imposing building at No. 44, avenue de Flandre is a cemetery measuring 35 by 10 metres. Surrounded by apartment buildings, this plot of land is home to a dozen tombstones and two sarcophagi, bearing some inscriptions that are still legible despite the ravages of time. The history of this cemetery bears witness to the ostracism suffered by the Jewish community under the Ancien Régime: along with Protestants, actors, and suicides, Jews were not allowed to be buried in cemeteries. But a certain Carnot, owner of the Étoile inn, located at the spot where No. 46, avenue de Flandre now stands, gave permission in 1691 for Jews to bury their dead here, on condition that they did so in secret and in return for payment: 50 francs for an adult, 20 francs for a child.

In 1780, the Sephardic Jewish community originating in Portugal bought two adjoining gardens and opened the Portuguese Jewish cemetery. This initiative was led by Jacob Rodriguez Pereire, agent for the Portuguese Jewish émigrés living in Paris, who had obtained a stipend from Louis XV for organising the education of the deaf and dumb. The burials were then allowed by the king, as long as they took place "nocturnally, without fuss or ceremony". The cemetery was finally abandoned in 1810, Napoleon having opened all the cemeteries to the Jewish community. Today listed as a historic monument, the cemetery is looked after by the Consistoire Israélite de France. To visit, arrange an appointment at the Consistoire, where the Hévra Kadicha (final duty) service will lend you the keys to the cemetery, to be returned afterwards.

La Villette rotunda, built in 1790, is one of four Parisian pavilions belonging to the city's former *barrière d'octroi* (tax barrier) that still remain standing. You can also see the barriers of Chartres (in parc Monceau), Le Trône (at Nation), and Enfer (place Denfert-Rochereau) (see page 469).

NEARBY

Crimée bridge: the last drawbridge in Paris ②
End of La Villette basin, beginning of the Ourcq canal
Operates 24 hours per day, seven days per week
Metro Crimée

Built in 1885 by the same company that installed the lifts in the Eiffel Tower, the Crimée bridge (pont de Crimée), also called the "pont de Flandre", is the last drawbridge in Paris: when boats are passing through, its articulated wheels mounted on Greek columns acting as racks literally lift up the roadbed. To view this spectacle of industrial history, pedestrians can use the nearby walkway.

COMPAGNONS CHARPENTIERS DES DEVOIRS DU TOUR DE FRANCE MUSEUM

③

The journeymen's masterpieces

Entry through Aux Arts et Sciences Réunis *restaurant*
161, avenue Jean Jaurès – +33 1 42 40 53 18
Visit only by appointment
Metro Ourcq

Located in the oldest journeymen's guild building in Europe, at the rear of *Aux Arts et Sciences Réunis* restaurant, the Compagnons Charpentiers des Devoirs du Tour de France Museum notably possesses the collection of journeymen's masterpieces that were put on display at the 1900 Universal Exhibition held in Paris. Journeymen who undertake the Tour de France are still provided lodgings today on the premises of the restaurant, which was originally their guild canteen.

Compagnonnage: advancement through work

Oral tradition traces *Compagnonnage* (Companionship), a French network of craftsmen and artisans, to the construction of the Temple of Solomon in Jerusalem (10th century BC). The existence of trade guilds in the Middle Ages similar to today's versions is specifically recorded. Despite what you might think, *Compagnons* still exist today and only workers carefully selected for their professional and moral qualities are admitted. The trainee, sponsored by a *Compagnon*, first completes his apprenticeship (approximately three years). He then completes the Tour de France serving apprenticeships with masters and staying in Cayennes (community meeting places and boarding houses) over a period of five to seven years.

Training continues until the worker presents his masterpiece, basically a work that proves his achievements and marks his skill. This long journey, which is one of the seven fundamentals of *Compagnonnage* (welcome, work, travel, community, transmission, initiation, masterpiece), has only one objective. This is to train, in a spirit of fraternity, tradesmen whose ideal is to advance through a craft. As a guarantee of the quality of their work, many *Compagnons* are called upon to restore the most beautiful buildings of French heritage, receive the *Meilleur Ouvrier de France* (Best Craftsman of France) award, or work in the most illustrious houses.

The organisation has no connection with Freemasonry, despite the similarity of some symbols (especially the square and compass) – Freemasons just took over some of these pre-existing symbols from the *Compagnons*.

In Paris, four branches coexist: the Union des Compagnons du Tour de France des Devoirs Unis (1st arrondissement), the Compagnons Charpentiers des Devoirs du Tour de France (see opposite), the Association des Compagnons du Devoir (4th arrondissement) and the Compagnons du Tour de France (6th arrondissement).

Compagnonnage and Freemasonry

The Compagnons du Devoir is an organisation of master craftsmen with origins going back beyond the Middle Ages to the time of Emperor Numa Pompilius (715–673 BC) and the artisans of Ancient Rome. Numa's contribution to the development and expansion of the Roman Empire was the creation of the first 31 *collegia fabrorum*. These early crafts bodies were formed of architects and craftsmen imbued with the wisdom of ancient religions and philosophies.

From the 6th to the 8th centuries the *collegia fabrorum* influenced European monastic orders and Byzantine institutions with their knowledge of Hermeticism and of Neopythagoreanism. At this time many Compagnons adopted the Christian faith (especially the Benedictine tradition) to avoid the Inquisition. However, many of them ultimately abandoned the religious habit. These monks, who were behind the creation of the greatest European masterpieces (cathedrals, palaces, castles), disappeared over time, only to reappear in the 15th century to oversee projects, but without religious affiliations. They survived until the middle of the 17th century, then disappeared once again. There was a further resurgence in the 18th century (1717), although only symbolically, based on speculative Freemasonry claims that it is the traditional heir of the operative masonry of ancient times. Hence the symbols and rituals of Compagnonnage and Freemasonry share many common elements, despite their fundamental difference.

Legends surrounding compagnonnage refer to three mythical founders of the Compagnons du Devoir: King Solomon, Maître Jacques and Père Soubise.

The Solomon legend is particularly important amongst the myths of the compagnons on the matter of the *devoir de liberté* (duty of freedom). But it has a later origin than the others and seems to have been introduced into the compagnons' workshops around the turn of the 19th century. It is based on the Masonic allegory about the Phoenician architect Hiram Abiff in the service of King Solomon and spread into the rituals of the various societies of compagnons. For them, the men that God can use to carry out his work are those referred to in the Old Testament as the sons from the quiver (Psalms 127:5).

According to the main legend, Maître Jacques learned to cut stone as a child, before setting off on a journey at the age of 15 years. At the age of 36 he arrived at the construction site of the Temple of Solomon in Jerusalem. There he became the overseer of masons and joiners. He shared the charge of joiners and masons with his travelling companion, Soubise, who would later become known in France as Père Soubise.

Biblical references to the construction in Jerusalem of the Temple of King Solomon make no mention of Jacques or of Soubise. On the other hand, legends surrounding the construction of Orléans Cathedral, arising from historical medieval sources, describe the presence there of two overseers, Jacques Moler and the Benedictine Soubise. They were faced with a strike of workers that degenerated into a dreadful battle followed by a split into factions. It seems that this legend may be based on later historic facts; that is to say, the split between the Catholic and Protestant compagnons, and on the destruction by the latter of the spire of Orléans Cathedral in 1568.

COMMUNAL GARDEN OF LA BUTTE BERGEYRE

An island in the city centre

80, rue Georges Lardennois
jardinbergeyre@gmail.com
Wednesday 2pm–5pm and Sunday 11am–5pm
Metro Colonel Fabien

Built around 1927 on the site of an old amusement park (Les Folles Buttes), Bergeyre hill is like an island in the middle of the city.

Almost invisible from the streets below, it is located in a pocket of land on a hill between Rues Simon Bolivar, Manin and Mathurin Moreau. Crossed by the streets Georges Lardennois, Rémy de Gourmont, Edgar Poe, Philippe Hecht and Barrelet de Ricou, the hill is artificial and was built in the late 19th century with the rubble of the construction of the nearby Buttes-Chaumont park.

In 1918, the Bergeyre stadium was built there and named after a rugby player who died in the First World War.

The stadium, which had a capacity of 15,000 seats, housed the Olympique de Paris football club, which was itself absorbed by the Red Star in 1926. It was here that CAP (Cercle Athlétique de Paris) and Le Havre played in the Coupe de France final of 1920 (won 2–1 by the Parisians).

In 1924, the Bergeyre stadium even hosted football matches for the Olympic Games that took place in Paris that year. The stadium was demolished in 1926 and housing was built on the hill.

The instability of the soil prevented dense urbanisation (as local residents concerned about the cracks in their houses know well).

There are attractive houses, some vines and a garden shared by residents aware of their luck and anxious to preserve their tranquillity, 90 metres above the chaos.

The garden is open to the public twice a week, so you can appreciate the hives and the different fruit trees. This is perhaps one of the most charming of all communal gardens in the city.

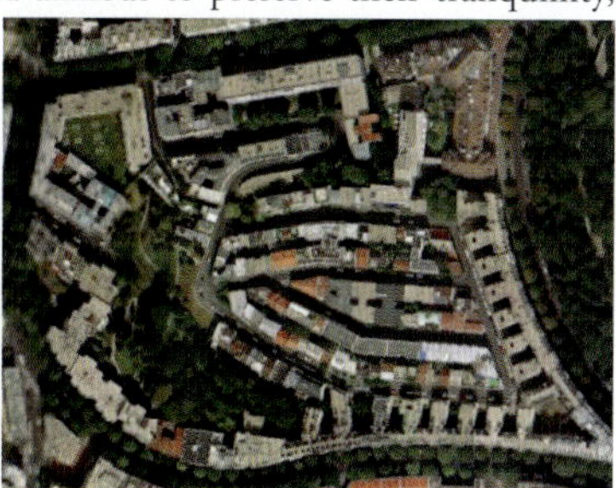

NEARBY

Jean Jaurès Gymnasium ⑤

87, avenue Jean Jaurès – +33 1 42 08 57 11
Daily 7am–11pm (reserved to clubs and associations)
Metro Laumière

Take the time to ask at the reception for permission (readily granted) to have a look at this very beautiful gymnasium. This was built reusing a metal framework from the Galerie des Machines at the Universal Exhibition of 1878, like the famous Y hangar at Meudon. It was enlarged in 1913 by the architect Gautier and took the name of Gymnase Allemagne (German gymnasium), which it lost after the First World War, as did rue d'Allemagne, which became avenue Jean Jaurès.

CHURCH OF SAINT-SERGE-DE-RADOGÈNE

An extraordinary Orthodox church hidden at the top of a mound

93, rue de Crimée
+33 6 32 68 41 92
Mass Sunday 10am–12.30pm
Metro Laumière or Ourcq

Concealed behind the gate at 93, rue de Crimée, perched at the top of a mound and screened by a row of trees at the end of a lane, the church of Saint-Serge-de-Radogène is perhaps one of the most charming churches in Paris.

Strange and exotic, the church has been through two histories under two different religions. Built in 1861 in the southern neighbourhood of Buttes-Chaumont at the initiative of the Lutheran pastor serving the émigré community of German workers in France, it was devoted to Protestantism until the declaration of war in 1914 forced German workers to return to their country.

Confiscated by the French government, it remained abandoned until 1924, when it was bought by the Russian

Orthodox Church and the Russian community that had fled the Bolshevik Revolution. This change of use required some architectural modifications, as the Protestants did not indulge in much decoration or religious representations ...

A wooden stairway was added in order to allow direct access from the exterior to the storey in which the church is situated. It was decorated with frescoes created by Dimitri Stelletsky portraying the holy fathers of the Orthodox faith. The doors on the ground floor as well as the upper storey were also painted with magnificent religious scenes, and the north side of the building received a carillon with a traditional Russian arcading.

The biggest surprise, however, occurs when you discover the interior of the church: submerged in the inevitable scent of wax and incense, you will behold, among the shadows of the walls entirely covered with more frescoes, a most remarkable iconostasis including more than a hundred icons, and a set of royal doors, authentic works made by the Moscow School from the 16th century. Magical.

LA MOUZAÏA

The American quarries

Neighbourhood within the loop on the 7 bis Metro line
Metro Danube

If people in love with La Mouzaïa don't all share the same exact definition of the perimeter occupied by this very peculiar neighbourhood in the 19th arrondissement, they do agree on its extraordinary charms. More or less delimited by the Botzaris, Danube, Pré Saint-Gervais, and place des Fêtes Metro stations, the neighbourhood has an exotic name that recalls Algeria, but its sights and scents are those of a provincial French village.

This very appealing belvedere was annexed by the city of Paris in 1860. The ground is as full of holes as Gruyère cheese, due to the presence of gypsum quarries that were mined until 1872. Some say that both the White House in Washington, D.C. and the Statue of Liberty were built with gypsum extracted here (which would explain why the neighbourhood was for a time called 'Les carrières d'Amérique', as one of the streets still reminds us). But it seems that this romantic story has no basis in fact.

On the other hand, the quarry does account for the fragility of the terrain that prevents any large-scale property development schemes from being carried out here: following an attempt to set up a horse-trading market, the area was finally given over to the building of detached individual dwellings with simple architectural plans (a ground floor topped by a single storey). Usually possessing both a front garden and a backyard, these dwellings are spread out on both sides of some twenty different lanes. The gradual completion of this project (which took nearly four decades) allowed a certain diversity of architectural styles to emerge in these houses. Originally intended for working-class families, today they are enjoyed by the privileged few.

NEARBY

Masons at 97 bis, rue de Crimée   ⑧

Metro Laumière

An astonishing façade at No. 97 bis, rue de Crimée, where the usual classical atlantes have been replaced by masons depicted at work on the building itself.

NEARBY

◀ *13, rue des Fêtes* 

Access usually restricted by a digital code panel – Metro Place des Fêtes

Nearby the concrete expanse of the place des Fêtes, rue des Fêtes conceals, at No. 13, a heavenly little garden-city built at the beginning of the 20th century on the grounds of a private townhouse that still stands at No. 11. Access is by a narrow passage that leads to a series of delightful detached dwellings surrounded by greenery. To be able to enjoy the arbour, the flower-filled terraces, the trees and the village-like atmosphere, it is probably best to visit during one of the "open workshop" days held in the Belleville neighbourhood: this place is now home to many artists. Otherwise, the gate is usually kept locked by a code panel.

Cité du Palais-Royal-de-Belleville 

151, rue de Belleville – Metro Jourdain

Hidden behind two successive courtyards, the cité du Palais-Royal-de-Belleville is a superb group of pretty low-rise houses standing on either side of a quiet tree-lined lane, once typical of the highly dispersed dwellings occupied by the working classes in Belleville. According to residents, the pompous name of this settlement comes from the fact that the sets for the Palais-Royal theatre used to be stored here. Not far from here, at No. 13, rue de la Villette, the Villa de l'Adour, opened in 1817 under the name of Villa Barthélemy, is in another charming cul-de-sac.

Rues Émile Desvaux and Paul de Kock 

Metro Télégraphe

Rue Paul de Kock is closely connected to rue Émile Desvaux as it starts at No. 4 of the latter and ends in a cul-de-sac at a flight of steps located at No. 30 on the same street ... Together, they form a disparate grouping of houses dating from the 1920s by no means lacking in charm.

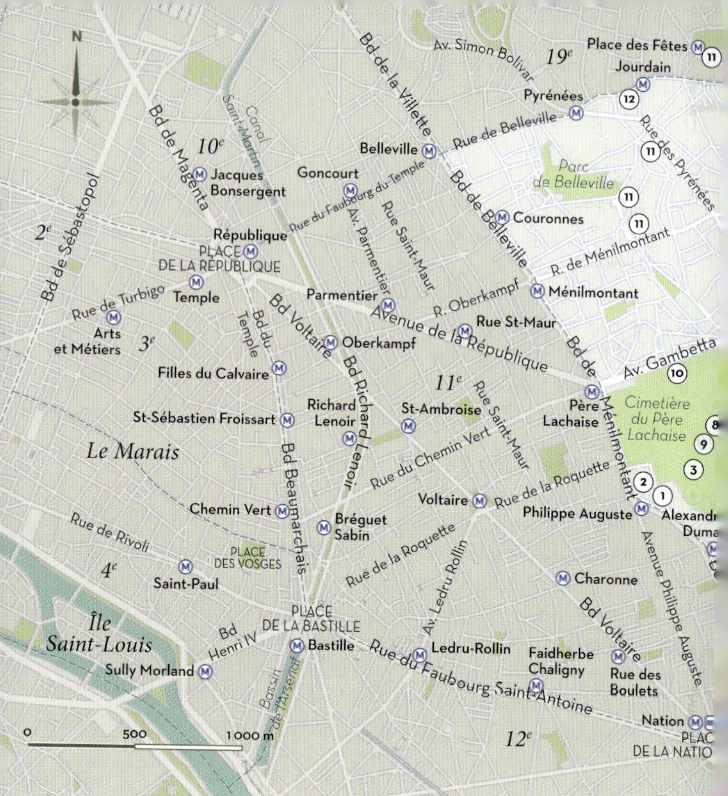

20th arrondissement

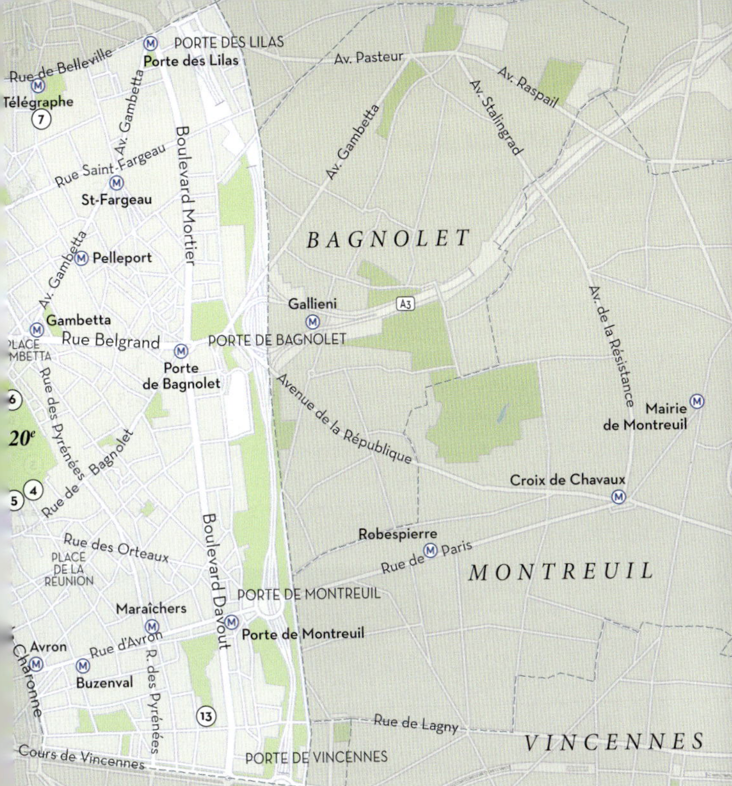

Rue de Belleville
PORTE DES LILAS
Porte des Lilas
Télégraphe
7
Av. Pasteur
Av. Raspail
Av. Stalingrad
Av. Gambetta
Rue Saint-Fargeau
Av. Gambetta
St-Fargeau
Boulevard Mortier
BAGNOLET
Av. Gambetta
Pelleport
Gallieni
A3
Av. de la Résistance
Gambetta
Rue Belgrand
PORTE DE BAGNOLET
PLACE GAMBETTA
Porte de Bagnolet
Mairie de Montreuil
6
Rue des Pyrénées
20e
Avenue de la République
Rue de Bagnolet
Croix de Chavaux
5
4
Rue des Orteaux
Robespierre
Boulevard Davout
PLACE DE LA REUNION
Rue de Paris
MONTREUIL
Maraîchers
PORTE DE MONTREUIL
Rue d'Avron
Porte de Montreuil
Avron
Charonne
R. des Pyrénées
Buzenval
13
Rue de Lagny
VINCENNES
Cours de Vincennes
PORTE DE VINCENNES

KITCHEN GARDENS ①

A restful kitchen garden

8, rue du Repos
Metro Philippe Auguste

The residents at No. 8, rue du Repos have the incredible luck of possessing one of the most surprising green spaces in Paris. After crossing a first inner courtyard, a second opens onto a hallway that leads to an extraordinary kitchen garden lying at the foot of the wall of Père-Lachaise cemetery, which contains a dozen private plots. Everything needed is here, buckets for watering the plants, rakes, and even a scarecrow to ward off the crows from the cemetery on the other side of the wall.

Be tactful: this place is private and off-limits to the general public. The only means of entering is to ask permission from one of the building's residents, as an exceptional favour.

NEARBY
Other marks from the 1724 censuses ②
Metro Philippe Auguste

At the corner of rue du Repos and rue Pierre Bayle, letters are discreetly engraved on the façade of the building. They read: Cte FF and Cte GG. These letters are further remnants (see page 343) of the census of Parisian houses commissioned by Louis XV in 1724 from Jean Bausire, the city's master builder, and his son Jean-Baptiste, with the aim of preventing private individuals from building without authorisation. Cte stands for Comité, and the letters GG and FF are markers used for these two streets during the census.

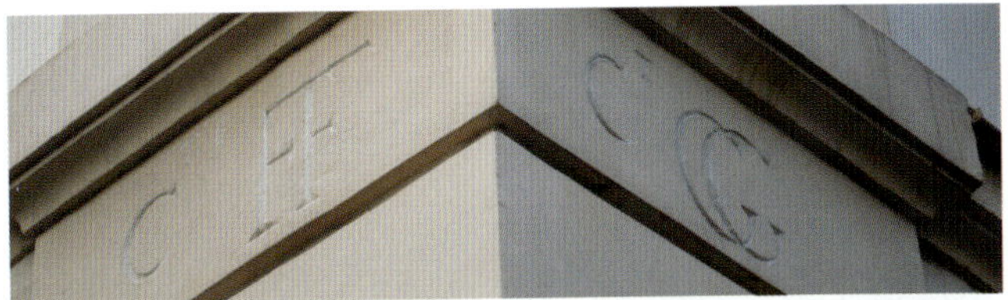

Grapevines in Paris

The Paris region has an ancient wine-making tradition, which gradually declined due to the population increase, urban development, the phylloxera blight, and competition from other regions. There are nevertheless traces of this past in street names: rue du Pressoir (winepress), rue des Vignes (grape-vines), rue des Vignoles, rue Vineuse ... The Goutte-d'Or (golden drop) neighbourhood also owes its name to a wine produced there during the Middle Ages. In addition to the famous clos Montmartre, today grapevines still grow in other parts of the French capital: Square Félix Desruelles, 168 bis, boulevard Saint-Germain (Saint-Germain-des-Près church) – 12 vine stocks planted in 1993; Garden of the presbytery of Saint François Xavier church (see page 249); In rue Blanche fire station (9th arrondissement, see page 302); In the cellar of Jacques Mélac wine bar (9th arrondissement); At parc de Bercy (12th arrondissement); At parc Georges Brassens (15th arrondissement); In the town hall of the 16th arrondissement; Jardin du Trocadéro, beneath the Musée de l'Homme (16th arrondissement); At parc de Bagatelle (16th arrondissement); Rue Georges Lardennois (19th arrondissement) – 200 vine stocks planted; At jardin de Belleville (200 vine stocks).

TOMB OF THE CAILLAT FAMILY ③

A rare Art Nouveau tomb designed by Hector Guimard

Père-Lachaise cemetery
Main entrance at 28 ter, boulevard de Ménilmontant
Division 2 – section 2 – Avenue du Conservateur
Metro Philippe Auguste

During the 19th century many sculptors and architects turned Père-Lachaise cemetery into a true museum of funerary art. The architect Hector Guimard, a leading figure in the Art Nouveau movement in France (see page 434), contributed to this, and left behind a burial site that is very little known, even if easy to find.

Enter through the main entrance, turn right and then follow the bend of avenue du Conservateur to the left. The tomb of the Ernest Caillat family is on the right, along the enclosing wall. Granite and bronze, the tomb designed in 1899 is distinguished by its almost cylindrical volume and its organic 'whiplash' lines. Guimard had adopted these Art Nouveau sinuous, dynamic lines mimicking the curves found in nature from 1895, after a stay in Brussels where he discovered Victor Horta's Hôtel Tassel (see *Secret Brussels*, by the same publisher). The play of lines of the tomb is very similar to the ironwork at the entrance to Castel Béranger in the 16th arrondissement (see page 432) and is found in the porticoes with candelabras of the entrances to the brand-new Paris Métro that he produced between 1900 and 1903. The inscription on the tomb is remarkable and also very representative of art nouveau curves. But how did Hector Guimard, who was then occupied with different construction sites in the capital, get in touch with the Caillat family before designing the tomb of Ernest Caillat, who died on 24 March 1899? Guimard conceived architecture as a total art, which included the interior ornamentation of his buildings and furniture. So why not make a sepulchre? As indicated in Ernest's death certificate, the Caillat family address was 34, rue Chardon-Lagache in Auteuil district (16th arrondissement), where Hector Guimard lived and worked – and where most of his Parisian works are found. So Guimard and the Caillat family probably met around their neighbourhood.

THE NATURAL GARDEN

Wild weeds in the heart of Paris

120, rue de la Réunion
+33 1 43 28 47 63
Monday–Friday 8am–sunset, Saturday, Sunday and holidays 9am–sunset
Metro Alexandre Dumas

At the very end of rue de la Réunion, at the foot of the Père-Lachaise cemetery, there is a small public garden unlike any other. Here, one does not find expert floral compositions or carefully mowed lawns: this natural garden (like the jardin Saint-Vincent in Montmartre) is a free space where plants take root spontaneously, where both flora and fauna express themselves without human interference, and where both watering and mowing are banned. Since the garden was created, the people responsible for its upkeep have tended to observe the evolution of life therein rather than maintain it artificially. The garden pond is full of newts and tadpoles that swim peacefully among the irises and water mint. Information panels scattered through undergrowth, trellises and lawns offer details about the animal and plant species.

NEARBY
Villa Riberolle, Villa Godin and Cité Aubry ⑤
Metro Alexandre Dumas

Just a few steps away from the natural garden there are other spaces to inspire souls in search of rural surroundings: Cité Aubry is a charming little passage following a curved path leading to an alternative cultural venue, the Goumen Bis. A little further on, at No. 35, rue de Bagnolet, Villa Riberolle is one of the most appealing sights in the neighbourhood (easy access on weekdays, but the gate is closed at weekends). It is also worth making a slight detour to see rue de Lesseps in order to take in its charms, without forgetting, nearby, the very pleasant Villa Godin with its maisonettes and gardens on either side of the paved lane.

Parisian heights

Montmartre: 130 metres. The highest point in Paris
Belleville: 128.5 metres. Highest point in east Paris at No. 40, rue du Télégraphe
Ménilmontant: 108 metres
Buttes-Chaumont: 80 metres
Passy: 71 metres
Chaillot: 67 metres
Montparnasse: 66 metres
Buttes-aux-Cailles: 62 metres
Montagne Sainte-Geneviève: 61 metres

An amazing memorial of the invention of the telegraph

Père-Lachaise cemetery – Division 29, row 2 (T, 30)
Metro Père-Lachaise

Located in the 2nd row of division 29, the tomb of Claude Chappe is one of the most amazing in Père-Lachaise cemetery. Shaped like a rock, it is surmounted by a mobile telegraph that Chappe invented. A Chappe tower can still be seen in Paris at 103, rue de Grenelle, as well as Chappe's original tombstone (see page 256).

How did the Chappe telegraph work?

With the French Revolution the transfer of information still followed the rhythm of the horses. Claude Chappe (1763–1805), a physicist from Brûlon in the Sarthe region, invented a means of communication using optical semaphore that allows the rapid transmission of a message at great distances. Thanks to his brother Ignace, a member of the Legislative Assembly, he succeeded in imposing his invention on the men of the Convention, and was commissioned to build a first line linking Paris and Lille. The invention was first called a tachograph, then "telegraph", from the Greek *tele graphein*, *TELE (far)*, and *GRAPHEIN (write)*. Chappe towers could be round, pyramidal or square, and were placed on an already existing monument (for example, a castle, Magne tower in Nîmes, a bell tower, etc.).

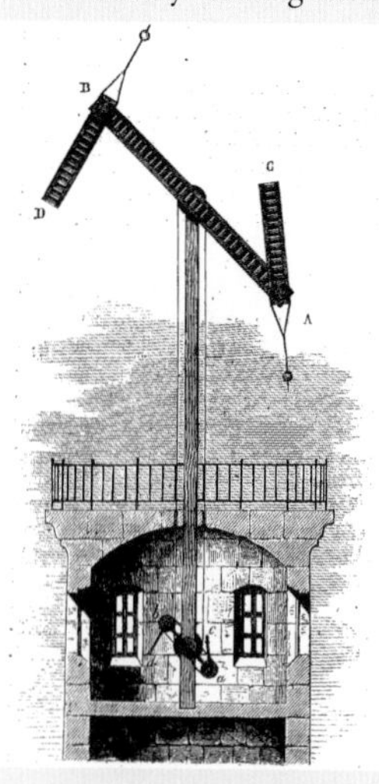

Entirely manual, they operated for hundreds of kilometres and consisted of a signal and a working room on the floor where the operator observed the neighbouring towers via two specially designed telescopes, then actuated the signal handling system and recorded the transmitted signals in a register. In 1844, 534 towers criss-crossed the territory connecting the most important French towns. In 1845, the first electric telegraph line was installed in France between Paris and Rouen: the Chappe towers quickly became obsolete.

NEARBY
Plaque at 40, rue du Télégraphe ⑦
Metro Télégraphe

Taking advantage of the height of Belleville hill, Claude Chappe experimented with his telegraphic system in 1792–93 (see page 256). (At the level of the present-day 40, rue du Télégraphe – former parc Saint-Fargeau – at 128.5 metres altitude, Belleville is the second-highest point of eastern Paris on municipal land after Montmartre, see page 67). In 1793, the telegraph was used to announce the victory of Republican troops. In his first experiments, local residents believed that he was actually sending clandestine messages to Louis XVI who was incarcerated in the Prison du Temple. Chappe's salvation only came by a quick escape after destroying all his installations in a rage. The names of the nearby streets and métro stations also recall these experiences. Note that six months earlier, with his brothers, he'd already had the same experience on one of the pavilions of the Étoile barrier: wood thieves had then destroyed their machine.

A Chappe tower can still be seen in Paris at 103, rue de Grenelle, as well as Claude Chappe's original gravestone (see page 256).

8

TOMB
OF GEORGES RODENBACH

When the rose represents the soul that flies away …

Père-Lachaise cemetery
Division 29, row 2 (T, 30)
Metro Père-Lachaise

Don't ask for the whereabouts of Georges Rodenbach's tomb at reception – the staff will be strangely unable to answer and might make you feel they have something better to do than to answer visitors' absurd questions …

Instead go to division 15 (shown on any standard map). Totally unknown, the tomb of this Symbolist poet and novelist is particularly surprising: a man with his eyes closed is holding a rose and taking it out of his coffin.

On the front of the tomb, a cross in non-traditional form is engraved next to the name of the deceased.

Born into a wealthy family in Tournai, Belgium, Georges Rodenbach (1855–98) was one of the greatest Belgian writers of the 19th century. He came to live in Paris, met Mallarmé, Proust and Daudet, and became a member of the esoteric movement of the Rose-Croix. In 1892 he published what remains his masterpiece, *Bruges-la-Morte*, which evokes the town as a living being.

His last book was *Le Carillonneur* (*The Bells of Bruges*), published in 1897.

His membership of the Rosicrucian movement explains the symbolism of his tomb: for this movement, which believes in reincarnation, the rose is the symbol of the evolving soul that survives physical death and so escapes from the body after death.

The Rosicrucians

Although the origins of the Order are in ancient Egypt, it was with the publication of three manifestos, *Fama Fraternitatis* (1614), *Confessio Fraternitatis* (1615) and *The Chemical Wedding of Christian Rosenkreuz* (1616), that the Rosicrucians became known to the public. Celebrities such as Descartes, Érik Satie or Claude Debussy are thought to have belonged to the movement. The Order, spiritual rather than religious, has as its goal the pursuit of wisdom and refers in particular to the inscription on the Temple of Apollo at Delphi in Greece: 'Know thyself and thou shalt know the universe and the gods.'

MASONIC TOMBS AT PÈRE-LACHAISE

Symbols that are sometimes well hidden

Père-Lachaise cemetery
Metro Père-Lachaise

Although Père-Lachaise cemetery is home to the tombs of notable Freemasons (Raspail, Arago, Cambacérès, Monge, Bartholdi, Oscar Wilde, etc.), they don't all necessarily have such symbols.

Raspail's, for example, includes a veiled Isis, but this reference is not obvious: it is first taken for a woman in tears, hiding her face behind her widow's veil.

The vast quantity of pyramids and obelisks on the graves of other Masons comes from the Egyptian fashion that was prevalent in Paris in the first half of the 19th century.

The pyramidal monument dedicated to the memory of the mathematician and Mason Gaspard Monge (1762–1818) evokes his participation in the campaign of Egypt, under the orders of Napoleon Bonaparte. Visitors can also look for the burial of famous sculptor and Freemason Bartholdi, or that of architect Pierre-François Fontaine (1762–1853), another so-called Freemason.

The monument dedicated to him is octagonal in shape and at each angle are engraved an open compass, a delta and a level interlaced. Marshal Ney, shot in 1815, is buried in the district of the great servants of the Empire. His grave is the work of sculptor and mason David d'Angers.

The legend says that the field-marshal's urn was empty (see opposite).

Rue Gasnier-Guy is the steepest street in Paris: the height difference is 17.4%.

Why is Marshal Ney's grave empty?

Officially shot on 16 September 1815, Marshal Ney, who fought valiantly under Napoleon, was thought to be buried in division 29 until 1903, when restoration work on the mausoleum revealed that the tomb was empty. The investigation led quite quickly to a certain Peter Stuart Ney, in the United States, who just before his death in 1846 had confessed to being Marshal Ney, allegedly shot a few years earlier! Like General Wellington, Ney was a Rose-Cross knight of the Black Eagle: it is purported that he was saved by the general who respected the oath of loyalty that bound the members of the brotherhood. It is claimed that after the death of Napoleon, Wellington personally intervened with Louis XVIII and, thanks to his complicity, Marshal Ney was able to discreetly board the *City of Philadelphia* headed for the United States. Ney eventually died in South Carolina, North America, in 1846.

Records at Père-Lachaise

– Most photographed tomb: Chopin
– Most flowery tomb: Allan Kardec (the founder of Spiritism)
– Most visited tomb: Jim Morrison (singer of The Doors)
– Most touched tomb: Victor Noir (journalist who died at 22, now a kind of symbol of fertility)
– Largest tomb: Adolphe Thiers
– Highest tomb: Félix de Beaujour (in the shape of a chimney and over 20 metres high, this is the work of the so-called Cendrier (Ashtray)
– Oldest tomb: Parmentier (the man who introduced the potato to France)

Raymond Roussel: chess enthusiast at Père-Lachaise

Writer Raymond Roussel, a chess enthusiast, had an original idea for his death in 1933. In order to respect his passion until the end, he asked to be buried alone in a vault of 32 boxes – half the total number of squares on a chessboard.

U-shaped streets, T-shaped streets

Rue Ligner is one of the only streets in Paris in a U-shape: it therefore has the distinctiveness of two intersections with the same street, rue de Bagnolet. In the 16th arrondissement, rue Agar is one of the few T-shaped streets.

LE MUR DES FÉDÉRÉS: GHOSTS OF THE PARIS COMMUNE

A ghostly wall

Square Samuel Champlain
Metro Gambetta

Alongside Père-Lachaise cemetery, square Samuel Champlain has a wall that is both strange and striking in its realism: sculpted in the rock, ghostly faces struggle to emerge. One sees a worker, a priest, a *fédéré* (a member of the Communard militia) and a mother holding her child. Bullet holes surround these silhouettes.

Built in 1909 by Paul Moreau-Vautier (1871–1936), the wall is a monument dedicated to the victims of revolutions and was constructed using stones from the wall where the last Communards were shot.

That original wall is located within the grounds of the cemetery itself. A plaque recalls this bloody episode during which almost 2,000 Communards were massacred.

The Paris Commune defines a revolutionary period in the French capital which lasted 72 days between March and May 1871. As was the case in many other cities in France (Marseille, Lyon, Saint-Étienne, Toulouse, Narbonne, Grenoble and Limoges), following the nation's defeat in the war against Prussia, insurgents rebelled against the government set up by Thiers at Versailles. They attempted to found workers' communes and proletarian rule.

Water, source of many street names

The history of water in the east of Paris has left numerous traces in the city's toponymy: the rues des Cascades, des Rigoles (brooks), de la Mare (pond), de la Duée (an ancient word for spring), des Savies (another word for spring) all derive their names directly from water usage.

Why does tap water taste different in different neighbourhoods?

Today, spring water still supplies half of the city's drinking water. These springs have differing mineral contents according to their geographical origin, so tap water inevitably varies in quality and taste depending on the neighbourhood.

What is a regard?

In order to preserve the purity of spring water until it reached its final destination, several dry-stone structures were built, extending underground to the water reservoirs. These were located in buildings that were soon nicknamed *regards* (peepholes), because they permitted one to keep an eye on the state of the conduits carrying the city's water.

Belleville: an almost unique geographical feature

While presiding over a great burst of urban development in the 19th century, the prefect of Paris, Baron Haussmann, cut Belleville in two. It is for this reason that the borders of the 10th, 11th, 19th and 20th arrondissements all come together at a single point, just like the American states of New Mexico, Arizona, Colorado and Utah, or the French departments of Alpes-de-Haute-Provence, Vaucluse, Bouches-du-Rhône and Var (see *Secret Provence* by the same publisher).

'REGARDS' IN EAST PARIS

Anachronistic regards

17, rue des Cascades (Regard des Messiers)
42, rue des Cascades (Regard Saint-Martin)
36–38, rue de la Mare (Regard de la Roquette)
213, rue de Belleville (Regard de la Lanterne – 16th century)

From the 12th century, in order to keep Paris supplied with drinking water, springs on the Belleville plateau were tapped. Although today these have dried up, four Parisian *regards* (peepholes – see opposite page), anachronistic vestiges of a bygone era, still stand before time and the curiosity of Parisians. Some of them bear the names of the religious congregations that built them: the Regard Saint-Martin helped to supply water to the Saint-Martin-des-Champs abbey, while the Regard de la Roquette performed a similar role for both La Roquette convent and Saint-Antoine-des-Champs. The Regard de la Lanterne owes its name to the lantern turret that decorates its top and the Regard des Messiers is derived from the names of the guards who watched over the crops before harvest (see map). Another *regard* of the same type exists at Pré-Saint-Gervais.

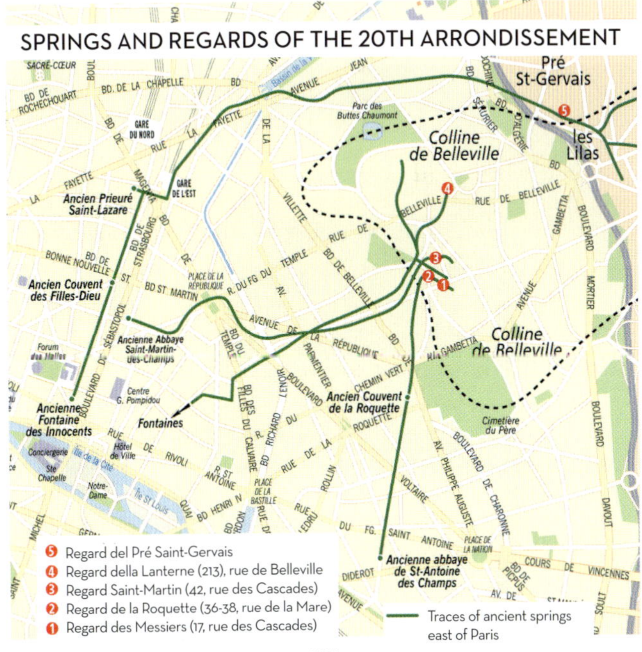

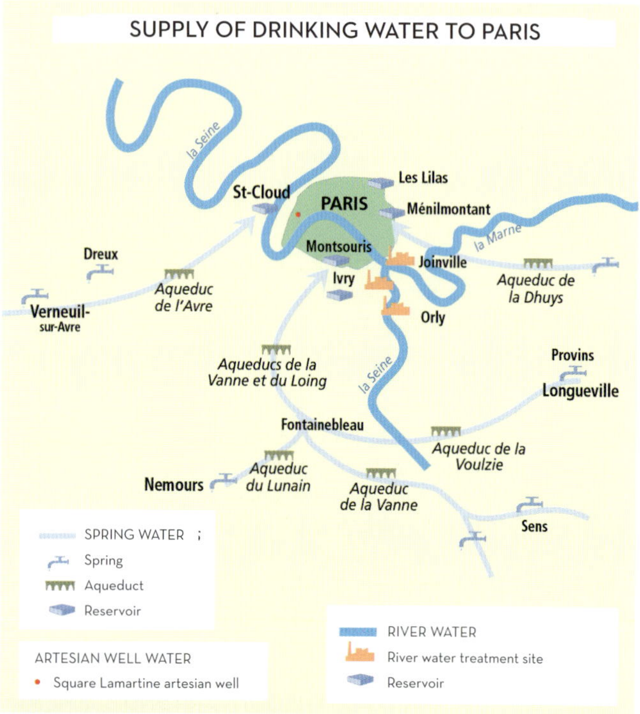
SUPPLY OF DRINKING WATER TO PARIS
la Seine
St-Cloud
PARIS
Les Lilas
Ménilmontant
la Marne
Montsouris
Joinville
Ivry
Orly
Dreux
Verneuil-
sur-Avre
Aqueduc
de l'Avre
Aqueduc de
la Dhuys
Aqueducs de la
Vanne et du Loing
la Seine
Provins
Longueville
Fontainebleau
Aqueduc de la
Voulzie
Nemours
Aqueduc
du Lunain
Aqueduc
de la Vanne
Sens
SPRING WATER
Spring
Aqueduct
Reservoir
ARTESIAN WELL WATER
Square Lamartine artesian well
RIVER WATER
River water treatment site
Reservoir

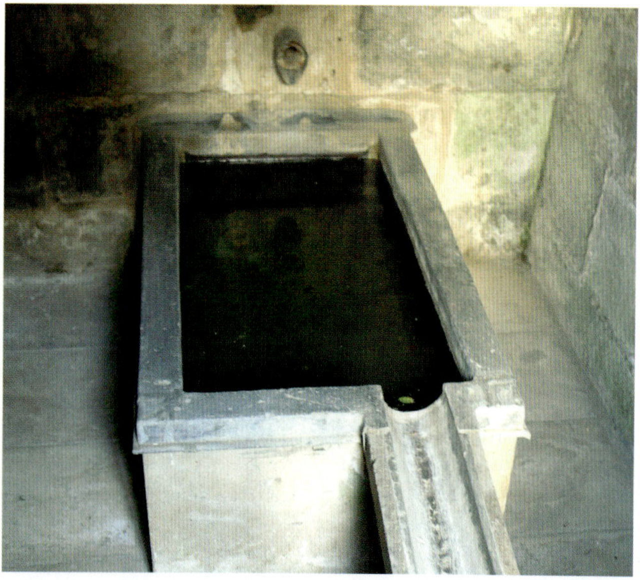

Supplying Paris with water

The city of Paris is today supplied with drinking water in three different ways: from rivers and streams, groundwater (artesian wells, see page 447), and spring water.

– Rivers and streams (Seine and Marne). This water is today treated by three plants located at Orly, Ivry, and Joinville. Before modern filtering methods were invented, river water was the simplest means for Parisians to find drinking water. This water, polluted by tanners, butchers and dyers, among others, was in fact not really suitable for human consumption. Under Napoleon I, the construction of the Ourcq canal and La Villette basin provided a new source of water for the northern part of the city. The water was then carried to the west by means of an aqueduct encircling Paris from La Villette to Monceau.

– Wells extracting groundwater provide water of better quality. At the beginning, these wells were not very deep (4 to 5 metres), but since the streets were not always paved, pollution easily seeped in and also rendered this water unfit for consumption. In the 19th century, artesian wells tapped water at depths reaching 600 metres, thus resolving the problem of surface pollution. But due to problems of flow, only the Lamartine well still operates today.

– The third solution was to tap spring water and carry it to Paris by means of spectacular aqueducts. The first were the Gallo-Roman aqueducts: one of these collected water from Rungis (see page 405) and another from Belleville. Between the 12th and 14th centuries, the religious orders on the Right Bank tapped water from springs in eastern Paris (see map) and constructed underground aqueducts as well as the regards that can still be seen today (see page 527). A little later, Marie de Médicis ordered the building of the famous Médicis aqueduct (see page 405) in the south of Paris. As anachronistic as it must seem, these aqueducts are still being used in the 21st century. Today, five main aqueducts carry spring water towards Paris: La Vanne aqueduct (built on the same route as the former Médicis aqueduct that passes by Arcueil), Le Loing, Le Lunain and La Voulzie aqueducts which also run to the south, and L'Avre aqueduct to the west. To the northeast, a sixth aqueduct, La Dhuis, carries 20,000 m³ of water per day (about 5% of the total supply) over 131 km. The principle of the aqueduct is quite simple: by means of the difference in levels between the point of origin and the point of arrival, to carry water wherever it is needed.

Today, almost half of Parisian water comes from springs. The city's drinking water, whether it comes from rivers and streams, or from springs, is held in five reservoirs: Les Lilas, Ménilmontant, Montsouris, Ivry and Saint-Cloud.

Country walks through the courtyards in the north of the 20th arrondissement

The northern part of the 20th arrondissement has managed to preserve a good part of its traditional habitat and is full of little-known linked courtyards, most of which are invisible from the street.

– 18, rue de Belleville: after a courtyard and a hallway, you come across a row of workshops drowning in greenery.

– 23, rue Ramponeau (Forge de Belleville): A former key factory that was once illegally squatted by an artists' association (Arclefs) before being renovated by La Bellevilleuse association for use by artists.

– 38, rue de Belleville: a surprising series of four inner courtyards. Try following one of the residents inside.

– Villa Castel, 16, rue du Transvaal: the provincial atmosphere of this site served as the setting for several scenes in the legendary film, *Jules et Jim*, directed by François Truffaut.

– Cité Leroy, villa de l'Ermitage and cité de l'Ermitage: charming little streets bordered by pretty houses.

– 17, rue du Retrait: leave cité de l'Ermitage by the vaulted passage that comes out at No. 116, rue de Ménilmontant and go up this street to the crossing with rue de Retrait.

– Cité du Palais-Royal-de-Belleville (photo opposite): 151, rue de Belleville. Officially, located in the 19th arrondissement (see page 509), but not to be missed.

– Villa Olivier Métra: 28, rue Olivier Métra. A pretty private cul-de-sac accessible to discreet walkers, but closed at the far end by a mysterious iron gate.

– Villa Georgina (from the name of an owner's daughter): a charming group of old detached houses and small gardens.

– Villa du Borrégo: 33, rue du Borrégo. Pretty crooked houses surrounded by greenery alongside the Belleville reservoir.

NEARBY

African plants at No. 10, rue du Jourdain ⑫

Metro Pyrénées

Dating from 1885, several buildings look out over a stretch of greenery which is in fact composed of African plants and grasses brought to Belleville by Senegalese riflemen who settled here after the end of the First World War.

The only level crossing in Paris ⑬

Metro Porte de Vincennes

In a somewhat gloomy street in the 20th arrondissement, rue de Lagny, is the only level crossing in Paris, which lets trains from line 2 of the metro pass through on their way to be repaired or parked nearby.

It was September 1995 and Thomas Jonglez was in Peshawar, the northern Pakistani city 20 kilometres from the tribal zone that he was to visit a few days later. It occurred to him that he should record the hidden aspects of his native city Paris, which he knew so well. During his seven-month trip back home from Beijing, the areas he crossed took in Iran and Kurdistan. He never took a plane but travelled by boat, train or bus, hitchhiking, cycling, on horseback or on foot, reaching Paris just in time to celebrate Christmas with the family. On his return, he spent two fantastic years wandering the streets of the capital to gather material for his first 'secret guide', written with a friend. For the next seven years he worked in the steel industry until the passion for discovery overcame him.

He launched Jonglez Publishing in 2003 and moved to Venice three years later. In 2013, in search of new adventures, the family left Venice and spent six months travelling to Brazil, via North Korea, Micronesia, the Solomon Islands, Easter Island, Peru and Bolivia. After seven years in Rio de Janeiro, he now lives in Berlin with his wife and three children.

Jonglez Publishing produces a range of titles in nine languages, published in 40 countries.

ACKNOWLEDGEMENTS

Florence Amiel, Dan Assayag, Mathilde Bargibant, Émilie de Beaumont, Kees and Aude van Beek, Emmanuel Bérard, Florent Billioud, Antoine Blachez, Philippe Bonfils, Christine Bonneton, Ludovic Bonneton, Ghislaine Bouchet, Jean-Claude Boulliard, Louis-Marie Bourgeois, Jean-Baptiste Bourgeois, Marie and Brandino Brandolini, Geneviève Brasc-Bautier, Roger Wemyss Brooks, Jane Brooks, Elodie Buch, Catherine Buyse, Claude Carrau, Jean-Laurent Cassely, Dominique Charneau, Marie-Christine Chenet, Christian Chevalier, Jeannine Christophe, Marie-Véronique Clin, Céline Colombani, Philippe Darmayan, Jacques Dumay, Françoise Durand, Charles Eon, Agnès and Mikael Eon, Anne Esambert, Baptiste Essevaz-Roulet, Guillaume Fonkenell, Marguerite-Marie Formery, Vincent Formery, Servane and Giovanni Giol, Philippe Gloaguen, Amaël Gohier, Azmina Goulamaly, Romaine Guérin, Patrick Haas, Elvire Haberman, Eric Henry, Fabrice Hertel, Jean-Marc Héry, Aliette Jalenques, Antoine Jonglez, Aurélie Jonglez, Stéphanie and Guillaume Jonglez, Timothée Jonglez, Yann Josse, Stéphanie Kergall, Suzanne de Lacotte, Ghislain de La Hitte, Gilles Lajotte, Benoît de Larouzière, Hervé du Laurent, Julien Le Bigot, Jean-Michel Le Cléac'h, Olivier Lefranc, Xavier Lefranc, Odile Le Fur, Professeur Henry de Lumley, Bruno Marguerite, Jean-René Martin, Claire Merveilleux du Vignaux, Sophie Mestchersky, Karine Mourot, JG Nizet, Francis Oger, Adriana Panepinto, Pascal Payen-Appenzeller, Georges Peberel, Marianne and Fabrice Perreau-Saussine, Francois and Sally Picard, Régine Pierre-Chollet, Patricia de Pimodan, Nicole Priollaud, Michel Ravassard, Clarabelle Rebelle, Valérie Renaud, Stéphanie Rivoal, Dominique Roger, Béatrice and Pierre Rosenberg, Stéphane Samuel Rubin, Ewa Rutkowski, Bertrand Saint Guilhem, Dimitri Salmon, Guido Salsili, Pierre Santoul, Bernard Sevestre, Damien Seyrieix, André Silba-Loebnitz, Vadim Smith, Corinne Stampfli, Micheline Terquem, Ambroise Tézenas, Marie-Christine Valla, Delphine Valluet, Chantal Vanderavert, Amelie Vialet, Henri Villeroy, Raphaëlle and Matthieu Vincent, Karine Zacharias, l'association Paris historique, M. le responsable du manège Dodo du jardin des Plantes, Lieselotte Buehler, Jacques-Franck Degioanni, Don and Linda Levison, Noé Gaillard, Sybille Wermelskirchen, Philippe Delasalle and everyone who opened their doors to us for this mammoth task

ADDITIONAL CONTRIBUTIONS

Maud Ratton.

Cartography: Cyrille Suss — **Layout:** Emmanuelle Willard Toulemonde — **English translation:** Thomas Clegg, Caroline Lawrence and Jeremy Scott — **Copy-editing/proofreading (English text):** Dikshit Akbari — **Publishing:** Clémence Mathé

© JONGLEZ 2026
Edition: 10th
ISBN: 978-2-36195-846-6
Printed in Bulgaria by Dedrax - June 2026